Step Up to

Fifth Grade Mathematics

Practice Materials

Written by
Kathleen Newman
Gayle Fuller

Edited by
Gayle Fuller
Wynell Harper
Kris Fuller

Graphics by
Kim Fuller

Cover Design by
Cassie Fuller

May 2005
Fourth Printing

Table of Contents

Introduction

<u>**Step Up to the TAKS**</u> meets the specifications published by the Texas Education Agency for the Texas Assessment of Knowledge and Skills and includes the Texas Essential Knowledge and Skills.

Each TAKS objective has been addressed under general mathematics categories represented in different sections in this book. At the beginning of each section there is an informational page with three components.

Component One provides the TAKS objective and instructional target along with any additional specifications provided by TEA.

Component Two divides the instructional targets into steps from simple to complex levels of difficulty. After the steps there is an **Assessment** that includes a problem to assess mastery of each of the steps. An answer key is located at the end of each section.

Component Three lists the vocabulary words for each concept. The identification and knowledge of these terms add to the on-going mathematics vocabulary needed in higher level math.

The activities are TAKS formatted and reach the level of difficulty found on the test. There is a page for each type of format that has been presented in the specifications and released tests. **"Sample for Analysis"** pages precede problem solving level pages to use with an overhead projector to model strategies. (Suggestion: Send the "Sample for Analysis" home with the student in order for the parents to understand the strategies and reinforce them at home.)

Note from the editor: The organization of this book encourages you to integrate these worksheets into your curriculum so instruction flows evenly without interruption to "teach to the test." I strive to provide "on target" practice materials for the test in order for instruction to be focused and intentional. After each released test I will update the books to meet any new formatted questions. Look at the cover page to determine the date of printing for each book.

TAKS Objectives and Related TEKS

Objective 1: The student will demonstrate an understanding of numbers, operations, and quantitative reasoning.
Number, operation, and quantitative reasoning. The student uses place value to represent whole numbers and decimals. The student is expected:
(5.1A) use place value to read, write, compare, and order whole numbers through the billions place; and
(5.1B) use place value to read, write, compare, and order decimals through the thousandths place.

Number, operation, and quantitative reasoning. The student uses fractions in problem-solving situations. The student is expected to:
(5.2A) generate equivalent fractions;
(5.2B) compare two fractional quantities in problem-solving situations using a variety of methods, including common denominators; and
(5.2C) use models to relate decimals to fractions that name tenths, hundredths, and thousandths.

Number, operation, and quantitative reasoning. The student adds, subtracts, multiplies, and divides to solve meaningful problems. The student is expected to:
(5.3A) use addition and subtraction to solve problems involving whole numbers and decimals;
(5.3B) use multiplication to solve problems involving whole numbers (no more than three digits times two digits without technology);
(5.3C) use division to solve problems involving whole numbers (no more than two-digit divisors and three-digit dividends without technology);
(5.3D) identify prime factors of a whole number and common factors of a set of whole numbers: and
(5.3E) model and record addition and subtraction of fractions with like denominators in problem-solving situations.
Number, operation, and quantitative reasoning. The student is expected to:
(5.4A) round whole numbers and decimals through tenths to approximate reasonable results in problem situations; and
(5.4B) estimate to solve problems where exact answers are not required.

Objective 2: The student will demonstrate an understanding of patterns, relationships, and algebraic reasoning.

Patterns, relationships, and algebraic thinking. The student makes generalizations based on observed patterns and relationships. The student is expected to:
(5.5A) use pictures to make generalizations about determining all possible combinations;
(5.5B) use lists, tables, charts, and diagrams to find patterns and make generalizations such as a procedure for determining equivalent fractions; and
(5.5C) identify prime and composite numbers using models and patterns in factor pairs.

Patterns, relationships, and algebraic thinking. The student describes relationships mathematically. The student is expected to:
(5.6A) select from and use diagrams and number sentences to represent real-life situations.

Objective 3: The student will demonstrate an understanding of geometry and spatial reasoning.
Geometry and spatial reasoning. The student generates geometric definitions using critical attributes. The student is expected to:
(5.7A) identify critical attributes including parallel, perpendicular, and congruent parts of geometric shapes and solids; and
(5.7B) use critical attributes to define geometric shapes or solids.

Geometry and spatial reasoning. The student models transformations. The student is expected to:

(5.8A) sketch the results of translations, rotations, and reflections; and

(5.8B) describe the transformation that generates one figure from the other when given two congruent figures.

Geometry and spatial reasoning. The student recognizes the connection between ordered pairs of numbers and locations of points on a plane. The student is expected to:

(5.9A) locate and name points on a coordinate grid using ordered pairs of whole numbers

Objective 4: The student will demonstrate an understanding of the concepts and uses of measurement.

Measurement. The student selects and uses appropriate units and procedures to measure volume. The student is expected to:

(5.10A) measure volume using models of cubic units.

Measurement. The student applies measurement concepts. The student is expected to:

(5.11A) measure to solve problems involving length (including perimeter), weight, capacity, time, temperature, and area; and

(5.11B) describe numerical relationships between units of measure within the same measurement system such as an inch is one-twelfth of a foot.

Objective 5: The student will demonstrate an understanding of probability and statistics.

Probability and statistics. The student describes and predicts the results of a probability experiment. The student is expected to:

(5.12A) use fractions to describe the results of an experiment; and

(5.12B) use experimental results to make predictions.

Probability and statistics. The student solves problems by collecting, organizing, displaying, and interpreting sets of data. The student is expected to:

(5.13A) use tables of related number pairs to make line graphs;

(5.13B) describe characteristics of data presented in tables and graphs including the shape and spread of the data and the middle number; and

(5.13C) graph a given set of data using an appropriate graphical representation such as a picture or line.

Objective 6: The student will demonstrate an understanding of the mathematical processes and tools used in problem solving.

Underlying processes and mathematical tools. The student applies Grade 5 mathematics to solve problems connected to everyday experiences and activities in and outside of school. The student is expected to:

(5.14A) identify the mathematics in everyday situations;

(5.14B) use a problem-solving model that incorporates understanding the problem, making a plan, carrying out the plan, and evaluating the solution for reasonableness; and

(5.14C) select or develop an appropriate problem-solving strategy, including drawing a picture, looking for a pattern, systematic guessing and checking, acting it out, making a table, working a simpler problem, or working backwards to solve a problem.

Underlying processes and mathematical tools. The student communicates about Grade 5 mathematics using informal language. The student is expected to:

(5.15B) relate informal language to mathematical language and symbols.

Underlying processes and mathematical tools. The student uses logical reasoning to make sense of his or her world. The student is expected to:

(5.16A) make generalizations from patterns or sets of examples and nonexamples.

Sample Grid

Ronnie's family is planning a vacation. They will drive 1,283 miles the first day and 1,475 miles the next day. How many more miles will they drive the first day than the second day? Record your answer and fill in the bubbles on your answer document. Be sure to use the correct place value.

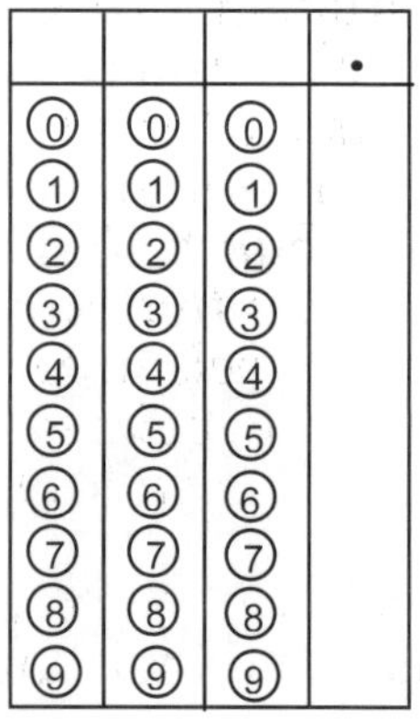

Strategy:

1. To solve the problem you would subtract 1,283 from 1,475. The answer would be 192 miles.
2. Now write a 1 in the box on the left which is the hundreds column. Write the 9 in the box in the tens column and a 2 in the ones column.
3. Now go down the column under the 1 and find the bubble with the 1 in it. Color in that bubble with your pencil.
4. Do the same for the 9 and the 2.
5. You should have 1 in the far left box, a 9 in the middle box and a 2 in the box on the right.
6. The decimal point is in place to the right of the ones column. Nothing should be done under the decimal point.
7. Now that wasn't so hard was it???

Cassie babysat for 6 hours. She made $3 an hour. How much money did she make?

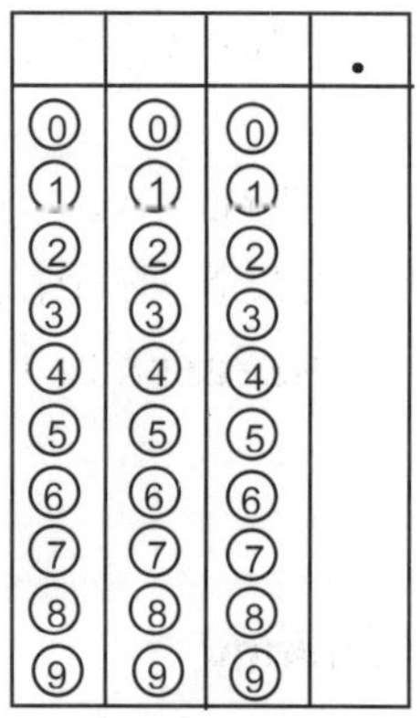

Strategy:

1. 6 hours at $3 an hour would be $18.
2. There are no hundreds in 18 so you can leave it blank or you can place a zero.
3. Place a 1 in the tens column and an 8 in the ones column.
4. Now that was easy.

At fifth grade, griddable test items will be limited to a three-column grid. Answers will range from 0 to 999. (TEA Specs)

Number Concepts

The student is expected to use place value to read, write, compare, and order whole numbers through the billions place. **(TEKS 5.1A) (TAKS 1)** *For place value items, students will match a digit in a number with its place value, or match a number with its name written in words. In comparison items, students will identify a number that is greater than or less than a given number. In ordering items, students will identify the list of numbers that are in least to greatest order or greatest to least order, or will identify the order of labels associated with the numbers. Students should be able to sequence numbers or words associated with numbers when ordering a list of numbers (for example, listing the names of the states in order from least to greatest based on population).*

The student is expected to use place value to read, write, compare, and order decimals through the thousandths place. **(TEKS 5.1B) (TAKS 1)**

The student is expected to round whole numbers and decimals through tenths to approximate reasonable results in problem situations. **(TEKS 5.4A) (TAKS 1)** *The student should be able to round numbers before performing any computations when estimating. The use of compatible numbers may be necessary.*

The student is expected to estimate to solve problems where exact answers are not required. **(TEKS 5.4B) (TAKS 1***)* *The student should be able to use information given in the form of numbers or ranges of numbers when working problems.*

Suggested Sequence
Simple to Complex

Step One ....Place Value/Compare and Order Whole Numbers and Decimals (TAKS 1:5.1A, 1:5.1B)
Step Two ....Round and Estimate Whole Number and Decimals (TAKS 1:5.4A)
Step Three.............Estimate Range Whole Numbers/Decimals (TAKS 1:5.4B)
Assessment

Vocabulary

- 🕮 Greatest to Least
- 🕮 Least to Greatest
- 🕮 Tenths
- 🕮 Hundredths
- 🕮 Thousandths
- 🕮 Best Estimate

Number Concepts: Step One A

The student is expected to use place value to read, write, compare, and order whole numbers through the billions place. (TAKS 1:5.1A)

Use the information in the chart to answer the following questions.

US Population	
American Indian	1,959,234
Asian	7,276,662
African American	29,986,060
Hispanic	22,354,059
Caucasian	199,686,070
Other Races	9,804,847

1. Which of the following lists the races in order from least number of people to greatest number of people?

   A American Indian, Asian, Hispanic, Other Races

   B American Indian, Asian, Other Races, Hispanic

   C Caucasian, African American, Hispanic, Other Races

   D Asian, Other Races, Caucasian, Hispanic

2. Which conclusion can be drawn from this chart?

   A The Hispanic population has increased in the last year.

   B The Asian population could be rounded to 7,000.

   C The population of African Americans is four times greater than Asians.

   D The Other Races includes Australians.

Use the information in the chart to answer the following questions.

State Population and Land Area		
State	**Population**	**Land Area (square miles)**
Alabama	4,252,982	52,423
Alaska	603,617	1,700,139
Arizona	4,217,940	114,006
Georgia	7,200,882	59,441
Hawaii	1,186,815	10,932

3. What is the order from smallest land area to largest land area of four of the above listed states?

   A Hawaii, Alabama, Georgia, Arizona

   B Alabama, Georgia, Arizona, Hawaii

   C Hawaii, Georgia, Alabama, Arizona

   D Alaska, Arizona, Georgia, Alabama

4. Which conclusion can be drawn from this chart?

   A Alaska is the only state listed on the chart that has a population that exceeds its land area.

   B Arizona's population is greater than Alabama's population.

   C Alabama's land area is two times larger than the land area of Arizona.

   D Georgia has over 45,000 more square miles of land than Hawaii.

Number Concepts: Step One B

The student is expected to use place value to read, write, compare, and order whole numbers through the billions place. (TAKS 1:5.1A)

Use the information in the chart to answer the following questions.

Populations in 1990	
World	5,288,000,000
Africa	643,000,000
Asia	3,172,000,000
Australia	16,000,000
Europe	693,000,000
North America	427,000,000
South America	297,000,000

1. How would the population of the World be written?

   A Five hundred billion, two hundred eighty-eight million
   B Five billion, two hundred eighty-eight million
   C Five million, two hundred eighty-eight million
   D Five billion, two hundred eighty-eight thousand

---

2. How would the population of Asia be written?

   A Three million, one hundred seventy-two thousand
   B Three hundred billion, one hundred seventy-two million
   C Three thousand billion, one hundred seventy-two million
   D Three billion, one hundred seventy-two million

---

3. Which of the following continents has a population under five hundred million?

   A Africa
   B Europe
   C North America
   D Asia

---

4. Which of the following continents' populations has a 2 in the ten millions place?

   A North America
   B South America
   C Asia
   D Europe

5. Which conclusion can be drawn from this chart?

   A The population of Europe makes up over half of the population of the World.
   B The population of North and South America combined is greater than the population of Europe.
   C The population of Asia is a little less than half the population of the World.
   D Australia has a population of less than ten million.

Number Concepts: Sample for Analysis

The student is expected to use place value to read, write, compare, and order decimals through the thousandths place. (TAKS 1:5.1B)

Decimal Compare and Order

Mrs. Villapando is calculating the average number of students that attended school each month during the fall semester. On her report, Mrs. Villapando lists these averages in order from greatest to least. Which shows the average student attendance listed in the correct order?

A 754.23, 754.8, 763.27, 763.4
B 763.27, 763.4, 754.23, 754.8
C 763.4, 763.27, 754.8, 754.23
D 763.4, 763.27, 754.23, 754.8

Strategy:

1. Look at the first four numbers for choice A.
2. Arrange these numbers from greatest to least beside the answer choices. Don't forget to line up the decimals to see the true place value of each number.
3. Find your answer in the answer choices. It is answer choice C.

Hint:
763.4 is also equal to 763.40. You may want to place the 0 in the hundredths place to help you remember that 763.40 is greater than 763.27.

Tip:
When asked to find "greatest to least", "least to greatest" could be one of the answer choices, as in answer choice A. Read the problem carefully and circle "least to greatest" or "greatest to least" in the problem. Check your answer against the stated problem.

Number Concepts: Step One C

The student is expected to use place value to read, write, compare, and order decimals through the thousandths place. (TAKS 1:5.1B)

1. Martin measured 4 plants for a science lab. He wanted to write down their heights by size from largest to smallest. If the heights are written from left to right, how should the heights be written for plants with heights of 30.94 centimeters, 32.5 centimeters, 31.98 centimeters, and 28.75 centimeters?

A 30.94 cm, 32.5 cm, 31.98 cm, 28.75 cm
B 28.75 cm, 30.94 cm, 31.98 cm, 32.5 cm
C 32.5 cm, 28.75 cm, 30.94 cm, 31.98 cm
D 32.5 cm, 31.98 cm, 30.94 cm, 28.75 cm

2. Scott and his friends were out fishing. The fish they caught all appeared to be the same size. The lengths of their fish are listed on the table below.

Fisherman	Fish Length (Inches)
Scott	24.375
Ronnie	24.357
Eddie	24.307
Ruiz	24.37

According to this table, who caught the longest fish?

A Scott　**C** Eddie
B Ronnie　**D** Ruiz

3. How is six billion, four hundred one thousand, six and three thousandths written as a number?

A 641,600,000.003
B 6,401,006. 003
C 6,000,401,006.003
D 6,000,401,006.03

4. Martin weighed his plants. The tomato plant weighed 1.52 kilograms. The ivy plant weighed 1.19 kilograms. The corn plant weighed 1.41 kilograms, and the bean plant's weight was 1.7 kilograms. If Martin wrote the weight of his plants from lightest to heaviest, which of the following ways would he write the weights?

A Ivy, tomato, corn, bean
B Tomato, ivy, corn, bean
C Bean, ivy, tomato, corn
D Ivy, corn, tomato, bean

5. The average rainfall for the past four years in Ellis County is listed in the table below.

Year	Rainfall (Inches)
1999	40.23
2000	40.32
2001	40.032
2002	40.203

According to this table, in which year was the greatest amount of rainfall?

A 1999　**C** 2001
B 2000　**D** 2002

6. How is five hundred twenty-three thousand, two and three hundredths written as a number?

A 532,002.03
B 523,020.03
C 323,002.03
D 523,002.03

Number Concepts: Step One D

The student is expected to use place value to read, write, compare, and order decimals through the thousandths place. (TAKS 1:5.1B)

1. On Tuesday, Martin gave each plant 43.5 milliliters of water. On Wednesday he gave them 4.35 milliliters of water. On Friday, Martin poured 44.254 milliliters of water on each plant, and on Monday each plant received 44.9 milliliters of water. If Martin wrote down the days from when he gave the plants the least water to when he gave them the most water, which of the following would show the proper order of days?

A Monday, Friday, Tuesday, Wednesday
B Wednesday, Tuesday, Friday, Monday
C Tuesday, Wednesday, Friday, Monday
D Wednesday, Tuesday, Monday, Friday

---

2. Each day Martin exposed his plants to different amounts of sunlight. The plants received 5.501 hours of light on Monday and 5.25 hours of light on Tuesday. On Wednesday, the plants were given 4.0 hours of light and 4.75 hours on Thursday. Which of the following shows the hours of sunlight written from greatest to least?

A 4.0, 4.75, 5.25, 5.501
B 5.501, 5.25, 4.75, 4.0
C 4.0, 4.75, 5.501, 5.25
D 5.25, 5.501, 4.75, 4.0

---

3. According to the owner of GF Educators Inc., there are a total of 9,457,023 pencils in inventory at their three locations. What does the 4 in this number represent?

A Four hundred
B Forty thousand
C Four hundred thousand
D Four hundred million

4. Erin and her friends play softball. Erin lives 0.8 of a mile west of the ball field. Tara lives 0.71 of a mile east of the field, while Nicole lives 0.67 of a mile north of the softball field, and Laurel lives 0.7 of a mile north of the softball field. Which of the following lists the players from greatest to least distances from the field?

A Nicole, Laurel, Tara, Erin
B Erin, Laurel, Tara, Nicole
C Erin, Tara, Laurel, Nicole
D Nicole, Erin, Laurel, Tara

---

5. Coach Maness calculated the average number of points scored per game by 4 softball teams. He listed them in order from highest average score to lowest average score. Which of the following shows the averages in the order that Coach Maness wrote them?

A 10.4, 10.32, 9.39, 9.701
B 10.4, 10.32, 9.701, 9.39
C 10.32, 10.4, 9.39, 9.701
D 9.39, 9.701, 10.32, 10.4

---

6. How is fifty-seven thousand and seven hundredths written as a number?

A 57.07
B 57,000.07
C 57,007
D 57,000.007

Number Concepts: Step Two A

The student is expected to round whole numbers and decimals through tenths to approximate reasonable results in problem situations. (TAKS 1:5.4A)

1. Jerry earns an average of $28 per yard for mowing yards. Which is the best estimate of how much he would earn mowing 5 yards?

   A $30 **B** $60 **C** $120 **D** $150

2. The 4-H Club had an exhibit at the county fair. They had a total of 198 visitors on Thursday and Friday night, 267 visitors on Saturday, and 153 visitors on Sunday. Which is the best estimate of the total number of visitors to the 4-H booth during these 4 days?

   A 600 **B** 700 **C** 900 **D** 1,000

3. Mr. Hillman is an author. He traveled 2,460 miles to Guatemala to learn about the people there. He wrote 587 pages of notes about the Guatemalan people. If he were to publish his writings in 6 books, what is the best estimate of the number of pages in each book?

   A 150 **B** 100 **C** 50 **D** 10

4. Andrea's 2 highest scores on her favorite video game are 989 and 708. What is the best estimate for the difference between these 2 scores?

   A 300 **B** 400 **C** 1,600 **D** 1,700

5. A cruise ship is getting ready to set sail for the Hawaiian Islands. The cruise line has sold 642 tickets for this trip. Island Tours Travel Agency sold 304 tickets, and Fun in the Sun Travel Agency sold 298 tickets. What is the best estimate of the number of tickets the 2 travel agencies have sold?

   A 500 **B** 600 **C** 700 **D** 800

6. When all the runways at the airport are being used, 39 planes can take off each hour. Which is the best estimate of how many planes can take off in a 20-hour period?

   A 400 **B** 600 **C** 800 **D** 1,000

7. Kelly earned $24 on each of two babysitting jobs and $17 for one babysitting job. She earned $12 when she helped her grandmother. She earned $16 when she washed her dad's car. Which is the best estimate of how much she has earned?

   A $100 **B** $90 **C** $70 **D** $60

8. A new movie opened at the theater Friday night. There were 204 moviegoers on Friday night, 308 moviegoers on Saturday, and 397 moviegoers on Sunday. Which is the best estimate of the total number of moviegoers at the theater during these 3 days?

   A 600 **B** 700 **C** 800 **D** 900

9. Heather ordered sports erasers for her store. There are 144 erasers in a package. She ordered one package of basketball erasers and two packages of football erasers. She also ordered 54 soccer ball erasers and 73 baseball erasers. Which is the best estimate of the total number of erasers Heather ordered?

   A 400 **B** 540 **C** 560 **D** 600

Number Concepts: Sample for Analysis

The student is expected to round whole numbers and decimals through tenths to approximate reasonable results in problem situations. (TAKS 1:5.4A)

Round Decimals

Miriam bought a pair of sandals for $49.13, a skirt for $21.72, and a dress for $59.62. Which is the best estimate of the amount Miriam spent for her sandals and skirt before tax to the nearest ten cents?

A $70.80
B $70.90
C $108.70
D $130.40

Strategy:

1. Read carefully to find out what you need to solve the problem.
2. You need to know the best estimate of the price Miriam paid for her sandals and skirt, not all 3 items.
3. Price of sandals $49.13 rounds to $49.10
   Price of skirt $21.72 rounds to $21.70
4. Add $49.10 and $21.70. The total is $70.80.
5. Choice A is the correct answer.

Hint:
Watch out for extraneous information!
You must round and then do the operation.

Tip:
Choice B is the answer if you round after doing the operation.
Choice C is an estimate of the price of the sandals and the dress.
Choice D is an estimate of the price of the sandals, the dress, and the skirt.

Carefully read the entire problem and determine what it is asking.

Number Concepts: Step Two B

The student is expected to round whole numbers and decimals through tenths to approximate reasonable results in problem situations. (TAKS 1:5.4A)

1. Nathan and Jacob went to the store to buy Mother's Day gifts. Together the 2 boys spent $6.95. Of this total, Jacob spent $3.02. What is the best estimate of the amount of money Nathan spent before tax to the nearest dollar?

   A $3.00 **C** $4.50
   B $4.00 **D** $5.00

2. Josiah bought shoes for $39.98, a shirt for $31.95, and a pair of pants for $40.90. Which is the best estimate of the amount Josiah spent before tax to the nearest dollar?

   A $75 **C** $113
   B $95 **D** $125

3. Kris bought a shirt for $12.25 and 2 ties for $8.36 each. What is the best estimate of the amount Kris paid before tax to the nearest ten cents?

   A $20.70 **C** $32.90
   B $29.10 **D** $33.00

4. Ralph ate lunch at Burgerland. He ordered 2 small cheeseburgers for $1.75 each, an order of fries for $0.95 and a strawberry shake for $1.95. All prices included tax. Which is the best estimate of the amount Ralph paid for his lunch to the nearest dollar?

   A $4.50 **C** $6.00
   B $5.00 **D** $7.00

5. Connie rode her bicycle 5.24 miles on her newspaper delivery route on Sunday. If she rides her bike the same distance on her route for the rest of the week, which is the best estimate of how far Connie rode her bike during the week to the nearest tenth of a mile?

   A 40 **C** 36.4
   B 36.7 **D** 26.2

6. The table shows the number of boxes of cookies sold by the 4 teams of Girl Scouts during the first month of the sale.

Teams	Boxes of Cookies
Red	437
Blue	276
Green	389
Yellow	286

   About how many boxes of cookies were sold during this month?

   A 1,200 **C** 1,400
   B 1,300 **D** 1,500

7. Kenny's dad filled the car with 15.25 gallons of gas on Monday. On Thursday his dad filled the car with 13.63 gallons of gas. What is the best estimate of the amount of gas his dad bought in those two days to the nearest tenth of a gallon?

   A 30 **C** 28.9
   B 29 **D** 28.8

8. Rosa needs 14.2 yards of fabric to make curtains for her room. She also plans to use 9.7 yards of the same fabric for a bedspread. What is the best estimate of the amount of fabric she needs to the nearest yard?

   A 23.9 **C** 24.9
   B 24 **D** 30

Number Concepts: Sample for Analysis

The student is expected to estimate to solve problems where exact answers are not required. (TAKS 1:5.4B)

Estimation Where Exact Answers Are Not Required

A passenger train leaves the train station with 438 passengers. It stops to pick up 774 more passengers. Which is the best estimate of how many people are on the train now?

A Less than 150 people
B Between 800 and 1,000 people
C Between 1,000 and 1,500 people
D Over 1,500 people

Strategy:

1. Read the problem to determine what operations your will use. (Addition)
2. Round each number to the nearest hundred.

Add		Nearest Hundred
438	→	400
+ 774	→	+ 800
		1,200

3. There are about 1,200 passengers on the train.
4. Find the answer choice which would be 1,200.
5. Since 1,200 is between 1,000 and 1,500, choose answer C.

Number Concepts: Step Three A

The student is expected to estimate to solve problems where exact answers are not required. (TAKS 1:5.4B)

1. Syd was able to average 9 miles per hour on a 14-hour canoe trip. Which is the best estimate of the number of miles Syd traveled during the 14 hours?

   A Less than 50 miles
   B Between 75 and 90 miles
   C Between 100 and 150 miles
   D More than 160 miles

---

2. Mary Beth and 3 of her friends went shopping for birthday cards. They bought 4 cards costing \$1.75, \$2.95, \$2.09, and \$2.75. What is the best estimate of the total cost of these cards?

   A Less than \$4
   B Between \$4 and \$6
   C Between \$6 and \$8
   D More than \$8

---

3. The average depth of the Inca Lake is 298 meters. The average depth of the Tao Lake is 735 meters. The Lano Lake has an average depth of 528 meters. What is the best estimate of the difference in the average depths of the Lano and Inca Lakes?

   A Less than 100 m
   B Between 150 and 250 m
   C Between 250 and 300 m
   D More than 300 m

---

4. Ray earns \$13 per hour building oil field machinery. Last week, Ray worked 49 hours. Which is the best estimate of the amount of money Ray earned last week?

   A Less than \$100
   B Between \$100 and \$250
   C Between \$250 and \$400
   D More than \$400

5. Last year, there were 942 people in Dallas County employed in the printing and publishing industry. During the same year, there were 762 people working in the chemical industry. Which is the best estimate of the total number of people who worked in the printing and publishing plus the chemical industry last year in Dallas County?

   A Less than 500
   B Between 500 and 800
   C Between 800 and 1,100
   D More than 1,100

---

6. Kendra's sister is on the cross-country team. She ran 3.5 miles on Monday and 4.2 miles on Tuesday. She ran 2.5 miles on Wednesday. Which is the best estimate of the total distance she ran?

   A Less than 5 miles
   B Between 5 and 10 miles
   C Between 10 and 20 miles
   D More than 20 miles

---

7. William bought a package of strawberry stick candy and a package of grape stick candy. There were 86 pieces of candy in each package. He also bought 9 lemon sticks and 18 orange sticks. Which is the best estimate of the number of pieces of candy he bought?

   A Less than 100
   B Between 100 and 150
   C Between 150 and 200
   D More than 200

Number Concepts: Step Three B

The student is expected to estimate to solve problems where exact answers are not required. (TAKS 1:5.4B)

1. Rachel was able to average 69 miles per hour on a 9-hour car trip. Which is the best estimate of the number of miles Rachel traveled during the 9 hours?

   A Less than 700 miles
   B Between 700 and 750 miles
   C Between 750 and 800 miles
   D More than 800

2. Courtney went shopping for books at the used bookstore. She bought books costing \$9.75, \$14.95, \$8.09, and \$7.75. What is the best estimate of the total cost of these books?

   A Less than \$20
   B Between \$20 and \$25
   C Between \$25 and \$35
   D More than \$35

3. Anna earns \$19 per hour as a chemist for an oil company. Last week, Anna worked 41 hours. Which is the best estimate of the amount of money Anna earned last week?

   A Less than \$600
   B Between \$500 and \$600
   C Between \$600 and \$700
   D More than \$700

4. Louis was checking the prices of a plane ticket from Dallas to San Francisco. An economy class ticket costs \$768 round trip. If Louis upgraded to first class, the ticket for the same trip costs \$1,303. Which is the best estimate of the savings if Louis flies economy class instead of first class?

   A Less than \$200
   B Between \$200 and \$400
   C Between \$400 and \$600
   D More than \$600

5. Carol used 7.3 yards of fabric to make a tablecloth. The material cost \$2.64 a yard, but was on sale for \$1.77 a yard. Which is the best estimate of the amount of money she saved?

   A Less than \$1.00
   B Between \$2.00 and \$5.00
   C Between \$5.00 and \$8.00
   D More than \$9.00

6. Tina bought 5 lemons for \$2.56. She also bought 2 pineapples for \$2.26 each. What is the best estimate of the total cost of these items?

   A Less than \$5
   B Between \$5 and \$10
   C Between \$10 and \$15
   D More than \$15

Number Concepts: Assessment

TAKS Objectives: 1:5.1A, 1:5.1B, 1:5.4A, 1:5.4B

Use the information in the chart to answer the following questions.

US Tax Collections		
Year	**Income Tax**	**Estate Tax**
1995	$4,124,164,000	$443,947,000
1998	$4,808,703,000	$493,405,000
2000	$5,637,148,000	$528,106,000
2002	$4,750,079,000	$494,431,000

1. Which of the following lists the years in order from least amount of estate taxes collected to greatest amount of estate taxes collected?

   A 1995, 1998, 2002, 2000
   B 1998, 1995, 2002, 2000
   C 2000, 2002, 1995, 1998
   D 2000, 2002, 1998, 1995

2. Which conclusion can be drawn from this chart?

   A The increase in the price of gasoline created the payment of more taxes in the year 2000.
   B In the year 2000 there were more estate taxes paid than income taxes paid.
   C In the year 2000 almost 1 billion dollars more income tax was collected than in 2002.
   D There were more estate taxes collected in 1995 than income taxes.

3. What does the 9 represent in the number for the estate taxes in 1998?

   A Nine hundred
   B Nine hundred thousand
   C Nine million
   D Ninety million

Use the information in the chart to answer the following questions.

Texas Population by County	
Dallas	1,853,624
Dawson	15,295
Delta	4,857
Limestone	25,216
Lipscomb	3,502
Travis	98,587

4. Which of the following lists the order of the greatest populated areas from greatest number of people to least number of people of the above listed counties?

   A Dawson, Limestone, Travis, Dallas
   B Dallas, Travis, Limestone, Dawson
   C Dallas, Travis, Dawson, Limestone
   D Lipscomb, Delta, Dawson, Limestone

5. Which conclusion can be drawn from this chart?

   A The population of Dallas County exceeds the combined population of the remaining counties on the chart.
   B Travis County has half as many people than Dallas County.
   C Lipscomb is the least populated county in Texas.
   D Limestone has 10 times more people than Dawson.

6. What does the 5 represent in the number for Dallas County's population?

   A Five thousand
   B Fifty thousand
   C Five million
   D Fifty million

7. Dad hired Robert to clean out the garage. He worked on it 2.4 hours on Monday and 2.45 hours on Tuesday. On Wednesday he worked 2.54 hours and 2.53 hours on Thursday. Which is the best estimate of the length of time he worked to the nearest tenth of an hour?

A 10 hours
B 9.9 hours
C 9.8 hours
D 9.7 hours

---

8. Carmen bought a package of zoo animal stickers and two packages of farm animal stickers. There were 258 stickers in each package. She also bought a package of bear stickers and a package of star stickers. There were 147 stickers in each package. Which is the best estimate of the total stickers Carmen bought?

A 1,100
B 1,000
C 900
D 800

---

9. Hal made 26 key chains in one hour. Which is the best estimate of the number of key chains he could make in 8 hours?

A Less than 100
B Between 110 and 130
C Between 140 and 160
D More than 170

---

10. When all the runways at the airport are being used, 74 planes can take off each hour. Which is the best estimate of how many planes can take off in a 12-hour period?

A 100
B 500
C 700
D 1,000

11. There were 4 sprinters choosing new shoes for racing. Each girl wanted the lightest pair of shoes possible. Which of the following shows the weights of the shoes listed in order from lightest to heaviest?

A 2.6 lb, 2.71 lb, 3.8 lb, 3.08 lb
B 3.8 lb, 3.08 lb, 2.71 lb, 2.6 lb
C 2.71 lb, 2.6 lb, 3.8 lb, 3.08 lb
D 2.6 lb, 2.71 lb, 3.08 lb, 3.8 lb

---

12. The earth's crust is 0.08 aluminum, 0.28 silicon, 0.47 oxygen, and 0.17 other elements. Mr. Hajda wrote these amounts on the board from greatest portion of the earth's crust to least portion. Which of the following shows the components of the earth's crust as Mr. Hajda listed them?

A Oxygen, silicon, other elements, aluminum

B Other elements, aluminum, silicon, oxygen

C Aluminum, other elements, silicon, oxygen

D Oxygen, silicon, aluminum, other elements

---

13. If Cassie runs 6 miles a day for 10 days in a two week period, which is the best estimate of the number of miles she runs?

A Less than 10

B Between 20 and 40

C Between 50 and 70

D More than 80

Number Concepts: Answer Key

Step One A
1. B
2. C
3. A
4. D

Step One B
1. B
2. D
3. C
4. A
5. B

Step One C
1. D
2. A
3. C
4. D
5. B
6. D

Step One D
1. B
2. B
3. C
4. C
5. B
6. B

Step Two A
1. D
2. B
3. B
4. A
5. B
6. C
7. B
8. D
9. B

Step Two B
1. B
2. C
3. B
4. D
5. C
6. C
7. C
8. B

Step Three A
1. C
2. D
3. B
4. D
5. D
6. C
7. D

Step Three B
1. A
2. D
3. D
4. C
5. C
6. B

Assessment
1. A
2. C
3. D
4. B
5. A
6. B
7. B
8. A
9. D
10. C
11. D
12. A
13. C

Prime and Composite

The student is expected to identify prime factors of a whole number and common factors of a set of whole numbers. **(TEKS 5.3D) (TAKS 1)** *Students will match a whole number with its prime factors. All factors used at this level will be whole-number factors. The factors may be given in list form (e.g., 2, 3, 5) or in product form (e.g., 2 x 2 x 3 x 5). Common factors of two or more whole numbers will be given in list form.*

The student is expected to identify prime and composite numbers using concrete models and patterns in factor pairs. **(TEKS 5.5C) (TAKS 2)** *All factors used at this level will be whole-number factors. Students will match a list of factors with a given prime number or composite number, or will identify the list that contains all the factors of a prime or a composite number that is not given. Students will identify a prime number or a composite number from a set of given numbers, or identify the number that is NOT a prime number or is NOT a composite number. Students are expected to generate their own list of factor pairs from the information given.*

Suggested Sequence
Simple to Complex

Step One .... Prime and Composite Numbers (TAKS 2:5.5C)
Step Two .... Prime Factorization (TAKS 1:5.3D)
Step Three .... Factors of Composite Numbers (TAKS 1:5.3D)
Step Four .... Common Factors (TAKS 1:5.3D)
Assessment

Vocabulary

- 🕮 Equivalent
- 🕮 Equal
- 🕮 Factors
- 🕮 Common Factors
- 🕮 Prime Number
- 🕮 Prime Factors
- 🕮 Composite Numbers
- 🕮 Prime Factorization

Prime and Composite: Sample for Analysis

The student is expected to identify prime and composite numbers using models and patterns in factor pairs. (TAKS 2:5.5C)

Prime and Composite

Which number is a prime number?

A 35 **B** 33 **C** 27 **D** 17

Strategy:

1. A prime number is the number which has no factors other than 1.
2. 35's factors are 5 x 7.
3. 33's factors are 3 x 11.
4. 27's factors are 3 x 9.
5. 17's factors are 17 x 1 and that is all. 17 cannot be broken down into two factors other than itself and one; therefore, it is a prime number.

Which number is a composite number?

A 7 **B** 17 **C** 23 **D** 25

Strategy:

1. A composite number is a number which is the product of two numbers. One of the numbers cannot be 1.
2. 7 is a prime number. It cannot be broken down.
3. 17 is a prime number. It cannot be broken down.
4. 23 is a prime number. It cannot be broken down.
5. 25 is a composite number. The two factors are 5 x 5.

Hint: All even numbers except 2 can be broken down. All numbers ending in 5 are composite except the single number 5; it is prime. There are very few two-digit numbers with a 7 in the ones place that are composite numbers.

7 - prime
17 - prime
27 - composite (9 x 3)
37 - prime
47 - prime
57 - prime
67 - prime
77 - composite (7 x 11)
87 - composite (3 x 29)
97 - prime

Try 9:

9 - composite
19 - prime
29 - prime
39 - composite
49 - composite
59 - prime
69 - composite
79 - prime
89 - prime
99 - composite

Prime and Composite: Sample for Analysis

The student is expected to identify prime and composite numbers using models and patterns in factor pairs. (TAKS 2:5.5C)

"Not Prime" is Composite
"Not Composite" is Prime

Which number is ***not*** a prime number?

A 3
B 13
C 17
D 26

Strategy:

1. According to their definitions, prime and composite could be considered opposites.

2. When it asks for "is ***not*** a prime," it really means "is a composite," so substitute: "Which number is a composite number?" Do not be confused by ***not***. Think opposite and look for its opposite.

3. The correct answer is D 26 because it can still be broken down to (2 x 13).

Prime and Composite: Step One A

The student is expected to identify prime and composite numbers using models and patterns in factor pairs. (TAKS 2:5.5C)

1. Which number is ***not*** a prime number?

A 3 **C** 5
B 7 **D** 9

---

2. Which number is ***not*** a composite number?

A 7 **C** 6
B 8 **D** 4

---

3. Which number is a prime number?

A 12 **C** 14
B 13 **D** 15

---

4. Which number is a composite number?

A 23 **C** 27
B 29 **D** 13

---

5. Which number is ***not*** a prime number?

A 13 **C** 33
B 23 **D** 43

---

6. Which number is ***not*** a composite number?

A 9 **C** 27
B 19 **D** 30

---

7. Which number is a prime number?

A 6 **C** 8
B 7 **D** 9

8. Which number is a composite number?

A 7 **C** 27
B 17 **D** 37

---

9. Which number is ***not*** a prime number?

A 31 **C** 37
B 47 **D** 36

---

10. Which number is ***not*** a composite number?

A 54 **C** 27
B 63 **D** 13

---

11. Which number is ***not*** a prime number?

A 3 **C** 17
B 9 **D** 23

---

12. Which number is ***not*** a composite number?

A 27 **C** 11
B 49 **D** 33

---

13. Which number is ***not*** a prime number?

A 99 **C** 19
B 17 **D** 29

---

14. Which number is a prime number?

A 53 **C** 81
B 33 **D** 39

Prime and Composite: Step One B

The student is expected to identify prime and composite numbers using models and patterns in factor pairs. (TAKS 2:5.5C)

1. Which is a prime factor of the composite number 16?

   A 3   C 4
   B 2   D 8

2. Which is a prime factor of the composite number 24?

   A 9   C 4
   B 8   D 3

3. Which is a prime factor of the composite number 36?

   A 23   C 9
   B 13   D 3

4. Which is a prime factor of the composite number 45?

   A 15   C 5
   B 9   D 2

5. Which is a prime factor of the composite number 20?

   A 10   C 4
   B 5   D 3

6. Which is a prime factor of the composite number 39?

   A 13   C 9
   B 11   D 6

7. Which is a prime factor of the composite number 254?

   A 133   C 117
   B 127   D 103

8. Which is a prime factor of the composite number 291?

   A 73   C 97
   B 87   D 117

9. Which is a prime factor of the composite number 66?

   A 11   C 6
   B 7   D 5

10. Which is a prime factor of the composite number 78?

    A 39   C 34
    B 37   D 13

11. Which is a prime factor of the composite number 147?

    A 49   C 7
    B 9   D 5

12. Which is a prime factor of the composite number 57?

    A 39   C 19
    B 29   D 9

Prime and Composite: Sample for Analysis

The student is expected to identify prime factors of a whole number and common factors of a set of whole numbers. (TAKS 1:5.3D)

Prime Factorization

Which group shows the prime factorization of the number 36?

A 2 x 2 x 2 x 2 x 3
B 2 x 3 x 5
C 2 x 2 x 3 x 3
D 2 x 2 x 2 x 3

Strategy:

1. Look at each answer choice.

2. Multiply the numbers to determine the product:

A 2 x 2 x 2 x 2 x 3 = 48
B 2 x 3 x 5 = 30
C 2 x 2 x 3 x 3 = 36
D 2 x 2 x 2 x 3 = 24

3. The product of answer choice *C* = 36.

4. Mark choice *C* on your answer sheet.

Hint:
Use parentheses to help you keep the numbers from confusing you:

2 x 2 x 3 x 3 =
(2 x 2) x (3 x 3) =
4 x 9 =
36

Prime and Composite: Step Two

The student is expected to identify prime factors of a whole number and common factors of a set of whole numbers. (TAKS 1:5.3D)

1. Which group shows the prime factorization of the number 66?

   A 2 x 3 x 11
   B 6 x 11
   C 2 x 2 x 3 x 3 x 3
   D 3 x 3 x 11

2. Which group shows the prime factorization of the number 54?

   A 2 x 2 x 3 x 3
   B 2 x 3 x 3
   C 2 x 3 x 3 x 3
   D 2 x 3 x 9

3. Which group shows the prime factorization of the number 81?

   A 3 x 3 x 3 x 3
   B 9 x 9
   C 2 x 2 x 2 x 3 x 3
   D 2 x 2 x 2 x 2 x 2 x 3

4. Which group shows the prime factorization of the number 150?

   A 2 x 2 x 5 x 5
   B 2 x 3 x 5 x 5
   C 2 x 5 x 7
   D 2 x 2 x 2 x 3 x 5

5. Which group shows the prime factorization of the number 88?

   A 2 x 2 x 3 x 11
   B 2 x 3 x 3 x 11
   C 2 x 2 x 2 x 11
   D 2 x 2 x 2 x 2 x 3

6. Which group shows the prime factorization of the number 78?

   A 2 x 2 x 17
   B 2 x 3 x 13
   C 2 x 2 x 2 x 3
   D 2 x 2 x 3 x 3 x 7

7. Which group shows the prime factorization of the number 120?

   A 2 x 2 x 3 x 5
   B 2 x 2 x 2 x 3 x 5
   C 2 x 2 x 2 x 2 x 5
   D 2 x 2 x 2 x 3 x 3 x 5

8. Which group shows the prime factorization of the number 24?

   A 8 x 3
   B 2 x 2 x 2 x 2 x 3
   C 2 x 2 x 3 x 3
   D 2 x 2 x 2 x 3

9. Which group shows the prime factorization of the number 45?

   A 2 x 2 x 5
   B 9 x 5
   C 3 x 3 x 5
   D 2 x 2 x 2 x 3

10. Which group shows the prime factorization of the number 64?

    A 2 x 2 x 2 x 2 x 2 x 2
    B 2 x 2 x 2 x 2 x 3
    C 8 x 8
    D 2 x 2 x 2 x 2 x 2

11. Which group shows the prime factorization of the number 96?

    A 2 x 2 x 2 x 2 x 3 x 3
    B 2 x 2 x 3 x 3 x 3
    C 2 x 7 x 7
    D 2 x 2 x 2 x 2 x 2 x 3

12. Which group shows the prime factorization of the number 18?

    A 2 x 3 x 3
    B 2 x 9
    C 2 x 2 x 2 x 2 x 5
    D 2 x 2 x 3

Prime and Composite: Sample for Analysis

The student is expected to identify prime factors of a whole number and common factors of a set of whole numbers. (TAKS 1:5.3D)

Whole Number Factors

Which group names all the whole number factors of a composite number?

A 1, 3, 6, 18

B 1, 17

C 1, 4, 8, 16

D 1, 2, 4, 7, 14, 28

Strategy:

1. The last number of each answer will be your composite number.

2. In answer A the last number is 18. What is all the factors of 18? They are 1, 2, 3, 6, and 9 (1 x 18, 2 x 9, 3 x 6) and these are all the factors (1, 2, 3, 6, 9, 18) In answer A the 2 and 9 were left out.

3. In answer B the last number is 17 and 17 is not a composite number and the question asked for the factors of the composite number.

4. In answer C the last number is 16. (1 x 16, 2 x 8, 4 x 4) The factors are 1, 2, 4, 8, 16. The 2 was left out.

5. In answer D the last number is 28. (1 x 28, 2 x 14, 4 x 7) The factors are 1, 2, 4, 7, 14, 28. They are all there in answer D.

Prime and Composite: Step Three

The student is expected to identify prime factors of a whole number and common factors of a set of whole numbers. (TAKS 1:5.3D)

1. Which group names all the whole number factors of a composite number?

   A 1, 2, 3, 4, 6, 12 C 1, 2, 9, 18
   B 1, 2, 5, 15 D 1, 3, 8, 24

2. Which group names all the whole number factors of a composite number?

   A 1, 4, 9, 36 C 1, 3, 5, 15
   B 1, 4, 6, 24 D 1, 3, 4, 12

3. Which group names all the whole number factors of a composite number?

   A 1, 19 C 1, 3, 6, 9, 18
   B 1, 2, 5, 10 D 1, 13

4. Which group names all the whole number factors of a composite number?

   A 1, 23 C 1, 2, 16
   B 1, 7, 49 D 1, 4, 6, 24

5. Which group names all the whole number factors of a composite number?

   A 1, 2, 13, 26 C 1, 2, 4, 16
   B 1, 5, 6, 30 D 1, 2, 8, 16

6. Which group names all the whole number factors of a composite number?

   A 1, 3, 9, 27 C 1, 6, 9, 54
   B 1, 4, 7, 28 D 1, 7, 8, 56

7. Which group names all the whole number factors of a composite number?

   A 1, 3, 5, 10 C 1, 23
   B 1, 4, 7, 28 D 1, 2, 4, 5, 10, 20

8. Which group names all the whole number factors of a composite number?

   A 1, 3, 39 C 1, 3, 7, 21
   B 1, 2, 16 D 1, 10, 20

9. Which group names all the whole number factors of a composite number?

   A 1, 2, 19, 38 C 1, 7, 9, 63
   B 1, 3, 39 D 1, 19, 57

10. Which group names all the whole number factors of a composite number?

    A 1, 11, 33
    B 1, 9, 81
    C 1, 2, 3, 6, 13, 26, 39, 78
    D 1, 7, 14

11. Which group names all the whole number factors of a composite number?

    A 1, 2, 22, 44 C 1, 3, 4, 12
    B 1, 3, 7, 21 D 1, 7, 9, 63

Prime and Composite: Sample for Analysis

The student is expected to identify prime factors of a whole number and common factors of a set of whole numbers. (TAKS 1:5.3D)

Common Factors

What are the common factors of 24 and 40?

A 2, 4, 8
B 1, 2, 3, 4, 6, 8, 12, 24
C 1, 2, 4, 8
D 1, 2, 4, 5, 8, 10, 20, 40

Strategy: Create a Table with the factors listed. Objective 6 5.14C

1. The factors of a number are all the whole numbers that can be used in multiplication to make that number. You can also think of them as all of the numbers that will divide evenly into a number.
2. When you are looking for common factors, you are looking for the numbers that are factors of **both** numbers.
3. Find the factors of 24: (1, 24) (2, 12) (4, 6) (3, 8)
   (1,) (2,) 3, (4,) (8,) 12, 24
   Find the factors of 40: (1, 40) (2, 20) (4, 10) (8, 5)
   (1,) (2,) (4,) 5, (8,) 10, 20, 40
4. Circle the numbers that are factors of **both** numbers. The circled numbers are the common factors of 24 and 40.
5. Choice C is the correct answer.

Tip: Choice A is a list of some, but not **ALL** of the common factors of 24 and 40.
Choice B is a list of the factors of 24.
Choice D is a list of the factors of 40.

Hint: "1" will **always** be a common factor of any pair of numbers. If you don't see a "1" in the answer choice, you can automatically eliminate that choice.

Prime and Composite: Step Four A

The student is expected to identify prime factors of a whole number and common factors of a set of whole numbers. (TAKS 1:5.3D)

1. What are the common factors of 15 and 18?

   A 1, 3
   B 1, 2, 3, 6, 9, 18
   C 1, 3, 5, 15
   D 1, 2, 3, 5, 6, 9, 15, 18

2. What are the common factors of 8 and 12?

   A 1, 2, 4
   B 1, 6
   C 1, 2, 3, 4, 6
   D 1, 2, 4, 8

3. What are the common factors of 10 and 25?

   A 1, 5, 10
   B 1, 5
   C 1, 2, 5, 10, 25
   D 1, 5, 25

4. What are the common factors of 45 and 15?

   A 1, 3, 5, 15
   B 1, 3, 5
   C 1, 3, 5, 9, 15, 45
   D 1, 3, 5, 9

5. What are the common factors of 28 and 56?

   A 1, 2, 28
   B 1, 2, 3, 4, 7, 28
   C 1, 2, 4, 7, 14, 28
   D 1, 3, 7, 28

6. What are the common factors of 20 and 25?

   A 1, 2, 4, 5, 10, 20
   B 1, 2, 4
   C 1, 2, 4, 3, 6, 12
   D 1, 5

7. What are the common factors of 6 and 24?

   A 1, 2, 3
   B 2, 4, 6, 8
   C 1, 6, 24
   D 1, 2, 3, 6

8. What are the common factors of 25 and 30?

   A 5
   B 1, 5, 25
   C 1, 5
   D 1, 2, 3, 5, 6

9. What are the common factors of 36 and 27?

   A 1, 6, 9
   B 1, 3, 9, 27
   C 1, 2, 3, 4, 6, 9
   D 1, 3, 9

10. What are the common factors of 14 and 24?

    A 1, 2, 4, 6
    B 1, 2
    C 1, 2, 4, 7, 14
    D 1, 2, 4, 6, 14, 24

Prime and Composite: Step Four B

The student is expected to identify prime factors of a whole number and common factors of a set of whole numbers. (TAKS 1:5.3D)

1. What are the common factors of 28 and 42?

   A 1, 2, 7, 14
   B 1, 2, 4, 7, 14
   C 1, 7, 14, 21, 28
   D 1, 2, 3, 4, 6, 7

---

2. What are the common factors of 32 and 48?

   A 1, 2, 4, 8, 16
   B 1, 2, 4, 8, 16, 32
   C 1, 2, 4, 6, 8
   D 1, 2, 4, 8

---

3. What are the common factors of 12 and 18?

   A 1, 2, 3, 4, 6
   B 1, 2, 3, 6
   C 1, 2, 3, 9
   D 1, 3, 6, 12

---

4. What are the common factors of 9 and 21?

   A 1, 3
   B 1, 3, 9
   C 1, 3, 7
   D 1, 3, 7, 9, 21

---

5. What are the common factors of 16 and 40?

   A 1, 2, 4, 16
   B 1, 2, 4, 8
   C 1, 2, 4, 8, 16
   D 1, 2, 4, 16, 20

6. What are the common factors of 32 and 45?

   A 1, 2, 4, 8, 16, 32
   B 1
   C 1, 2, 5
   D 1, 3, 5, 9, 15, 45

---

7. What are the common factors of 40 and 42?

   A 1, 2, 4
   B 1, 2, 4, 6, 8,
   C 1, 2, 21, 40, 42
   D 1, 2

---

8. What are the common factors of 14 and 56?

   A 1, 2, 7
   B 1, 2, 4, 7, 8, 14, 28
   C 1, 2, 7, 14
   D 1, 2, 4, 7, 8

---

9. What are the common factors of 60 and 70?

   A 1, 2, 10
   B 1, 2, 5, 7, 10
   C 1, 2, 6, 7, 10
   D 1, 2, 5, 10

---

10. What are the common factors of 8 and 28?

   A 1, 2, 4, 8
   B 1, 2, 4, 7, 8
   C 1, 4, 7
   D 1, 2, 4

Prime and Composite: Assessment

TAKS Objectives: 1:5.3D, 2:5.5C

1. Which group shows the prime factorization of the number 72?

   A 2 x 3 x 3 x 3
   B 2 x 2 x 3 x 3
   C 2 x 2 x 2 x 3
   D 2 x 2 x 2 x 3 x 3

2. Which group shows the prime factorization of the number 60?

   A 5 x 5 x 5
   B 1 x 2 x 5
   C 2 x 2 x 3 x 5
   D 2 x 5 x 5

3. What are the common factors of 18 and 24?

   A 1, 2, 3, 6, 9, 18
   B 1, 2, 3, 4, 6, 8, 12, 24
   C 1, 2, 3, 4, 6, 8, 9, 12, 18, 24
   D 1, 2, 3, 6

4. What are the common factors of 66 and 21?

   A 1, 3
   B 1, 2, 3, 4, 7, 8, 16, 21, 32, 66
   C 1, 2, 4, 8, 16, 32, 66
   D 1, 3, 7, 21

5. Which number is a prime number?

   A 6
   B 7
   C 8
   D 9

6. Which number is ***not*** a prime number?

   A 13
   B 23
   C 33
   D 43

7. Which number is ***not*** a composite number?

   A 54
   B 63
   C 27
   D 13

8. Which group names all the whole number factors of a composite number?

   A 1, 3, 9, 27
   B 1, 4, 7, 28
   C 1, 6, 9, 54
   D 1, 7, 8, 56

9. Which group names all the whole number factors of a composite number?

   A 1, 3, 5, 10
   B 1, 4, 7, 28
   C 1, 23
   D 1, 2, 4, 5, 10, 20

10. Which number is a composite number?

    A 7
    B 17
    C 27
    D 37

Prime and Composite: Answer Key

Step One A
1. D
2. A
3. B
4. C
5. C
6. B
7. B
8. C
9. D
10. D
11. B
12. C
13. A
14. A

Step One B
1. B
2. D
3. D
4. C
5. B
6. A
7. B
8. C
9. A
10. D
11. C
12. C

Step Two
1. A
2. C
3. A
4. B
5. C
6. B
7. B
8. D
9. C
10. A
11. D
12. A

Step Three
1. A
2. C
3. B
4. B
5. A
6. A
7. D
8. C
9. A
10. C
11. B

Step Four A
1. A
2. A
3. B
4. A
5. C
6. D
7. D
8. C
9. D
10. B

Step Four B
1. A
2. A
3. B
4. A
5. B
6. B
7. D
8. C
9. D
10. D

Assessment
1. D
2. C
3. D
4. A
5. B
6. C
7. D
8. A
9. D
10. C

Fractions/Decimals

The student is expected to generate equivalent fractions. **(TEKS 5.2A) (TAKS 1)** *Students will match a fraction to an equivalent fraction or to a fraction that is NOT equivalent.*

The student is expected to use fractions to describe the results of an experiment. **(TEKS 5.12A) (TAKS 5)**

The student is expected to compare two fractional quantities in problem-solving situations using a variety of methods, including common denominators. **(TEKS 5.2B) (TAKS 1)** *When comparing two fractional quantities, students will identify a fraction that is less than, greater than, or equal to a fraction given in an application context.*

The student is expected to use models to relate decimals to fractions that name tenths, hundredths, and thousandths. **(TEKS 5.2C) (TAKS 1)** *Students will match the decimal number represented by the shaded portion or the missing portion of a given pictorial model to a fraction. The student will match the decimal model to a given fraction, or the fraction model to a given decimal. Fractions and decimals may represent numbers greater than 1.*

The student is expected to model and record addition and subtraction of fractions with like denominators in problem-solving situations. **(TEKS 5.3E) (TAKS 1)** *The students should be able to solve problems with fractions or decimals representing whole numbers, numbers greater than one, or numbers less than one.*

The student is expected to use lists, tables, charts, and diagrams to find patterns and make generalizations, such as a procedure for determining equivalent fractions. **(TEKS 5.5B) (TAKS 2)**

Suggested Sequence
Simple to Complex

Step One....... Relating Fractions to Decimals (TAKS 1:5.2C)
Step Two ...... Generate Equivalent Fractions (TAKS 2:5.5B, 1:5.2A)
Step Three... Compare Two Fractions in a Problem Solving Situation (TAKS 1:5.2B)
Step Four ..... Using Fractions to Describe Results in an Experiment (TAKS 5:5.12A)
Step Five ...... Adding and Subtracting Fractions with Like Denominators (TAKS 1:5.3E)
Assessment

Vocabulary:

- Numerator
- Denominator
- Common Denominator
- Reduce Fraction
- Equivalent Fractions
- Tenths
- Hundredths
- Thousandths

Fractions/Decimals: Sample for Analysis

The student is expected to use models to relate decimals to fractions that name tenths, hundredths, and thousandths. (TAKS 1:5.2C)

Relate Decimals to Fractions

Tony inspects toys at a toy factory. $\frac{6}{10}$ of the toys were assembled properly. Which of the numbers shows this as a decimal?

A 6.10 B 6.0 C 0.6 D 0.06

Strategy:

1. The first place to the left of the decimal point is the ones column. The first place to the right of the decimal point is the tenths column. The second place to the right of the decimal point is the hundredths column.

2. Now look carefully at $\frac{6}{10}$. This represents 6 tenths without any whole numbers so choice A and B are incorrect because they contain whole numbers.

3. The 6 in choice C is in the tenths place and the 6 in choice D is in the hundredths place. The fraction is $\frac{6}{10}$. Choice C is read 6 tenths.

Tip: Read $\frac{6}{10}$ as a fraction. Listen to what you are saying. (Six Tenths)
Compare it to the answers by reading the numbers as decimals.

Answer A:	Six and One Tenth
Answer B:	Six
Answer C:	Six Tenths
Answer D:	Six Hundredths

Fractions/Decimals: Step One A

The student is expected to use models to relate decimals to fractions that name tenths, hundredths, and thousandths. (TAKS 1:5.2C)

1. David surveyed 1,000 students to find how many participated in a sport after school hours. There were 0.065 of the total number of students who participated in a sport after school. Which answer choice shows this as a fraction?

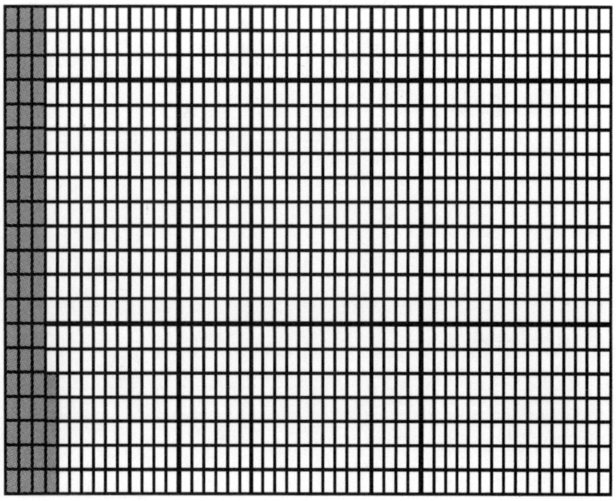

A $\frac{6}{5}$ B $\frac{5}{6}$ C $\frac{65}{100}$ D $\frac{65}{1000}$

---

2. Mike did a survey of 100 students. He found that $\frac{45}{100}$ of the students had brown hair. Which of the answer choices shows this as a decimal?

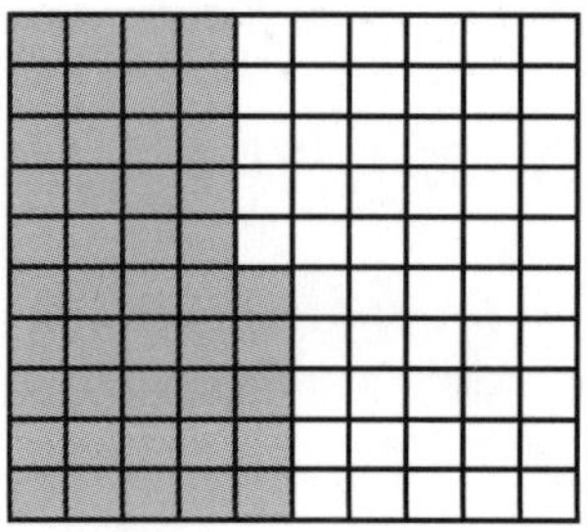

A 100.45 C 1.45

B 4.5 D 0.45

3. Mike's survey showed that 0.35 of the students had blonde hair. It also showed that 0.65 of the students were not blonde. Which of the answer choices shows the number that wasn't blonde as a fraction?

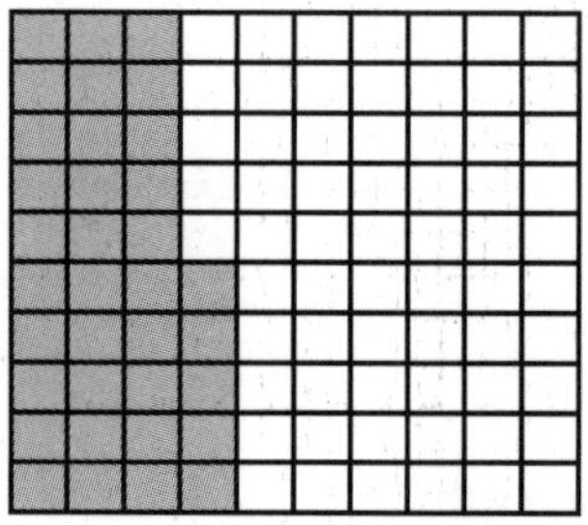

A $\frac{5}{6}$ C $\frac{10}{65}$

B $6\frac{5}{10}$ D $\frac{65}{100}$

---

4. Randy runs a mile everyday. Today he ran $1\frac{7}{10}$ miles. Which of the answer choices shows this as a decimal?

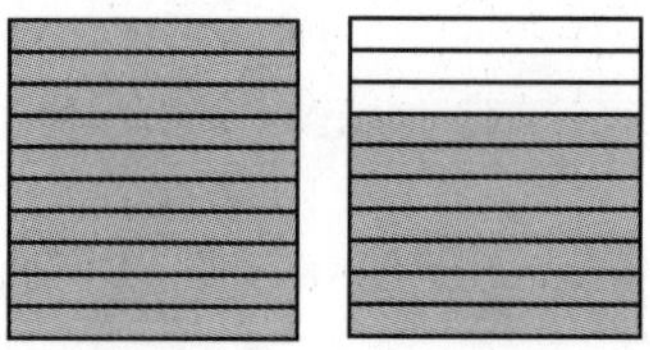

A 1.7 C 1.07

B 7.10 D 1.007

Fractions/Decimals: Step One B

The student is expected to use models to relate decimals to fractions that name tenths, hundredths, and thousandths. (TAKS 1:5.2C)

1. While riding to California to go to Disney Land, Dennis counted cars. There were $\frac{7}{1000}$ of the cars that were purple. Which of the answer choices shows this as a decimal?

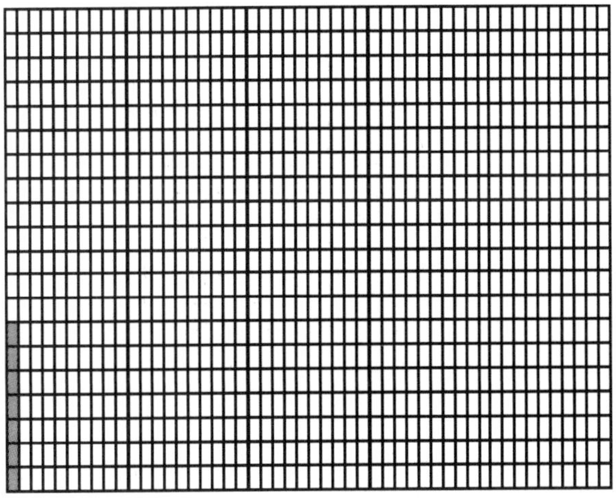

A 7,000 C 0.07

B 7.000 D 0.007

2. The model shaded shows $1\frac{2}{10}$.

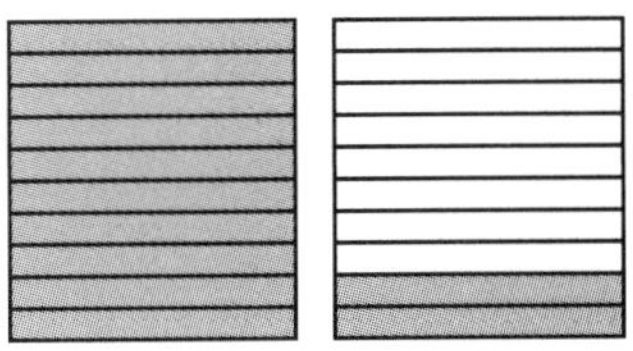

Which one of the answers below is equal to $1\frac{2}{10}$?

A 2.0 C 1.02

B 1.2 D 0.12

3. Out of the first 10 cars that Dennis counted, 8 of the cars were green. Which of the answer choices shows the cars not green?

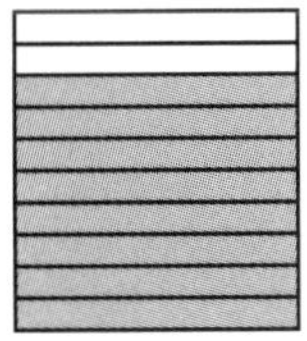

A $\frac{2}{10}$ C $10\frac{1}{2}$

B $\frac{8}{10}$ D $2\frac{1}{10}$

4. The model shaded shows $\frac{47}{100}$.

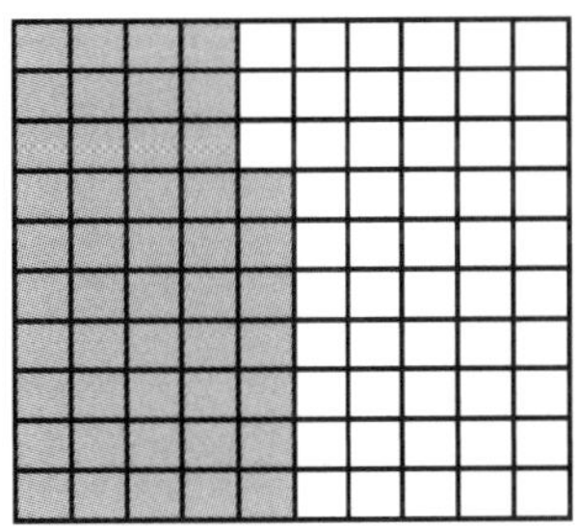

Which one of the answers below is equal to $\frac{47}{100}$?

A 47.00 C 0.47

B 4.7 D 0.047

Fractions/Decimals: Step Two A

The student is expected to use lists, tables, charts, and diagrams to find patterns and make generalizations, such as a procedure for determining equivalent fractions. (TAKS 2:5.5B)

1. If the fraction is $\frac{1}{8}$, what is the numerator in an equivalent fraction with a denominator of 72?

Equivalent Fractions

Numerator	1	2	3	4					
Denominator	8	16	24	32					

A 6 **B** 7 **C** 8 **D** 9

2. If the fraction is $\frac{1}{6}$, what is the numerator in an equivalent fraction with a denominator of 48?

Equivalent Fractions

Numerator	1	2	3	4					
Denominator	6	12	18	24					

A 36 **B** 30 **C** 8 **D** 7

3. If the fraction is $\frac{1}{3}$, what is the numerator in an equivalent fraction with a denominator of 21?

Equivalent Fractions

Numerator	1	2	3	4					
Denominator	3	6	9	12					

A 21 **B** 16 **C** 14 **D** 7

4. If the fraction is $\frac{1}{9}$, what is the numerator in an equivalent fraction with a denominator of 63?

Equivalent Fractions

Numerator	1	2	3						
Denominator	9	18	27						

A 64 **B** 36 **C** 9 **D** 7

Fractions/Decimals: Your Turn

The student is expected to use lists, tables, charts, and diagrams to find patterns and make generalizations, such as a procedure for determining equivalent fractions. (TAKS 2:5.5B)

Create your own equivalent fractions for practice.

Equivalent Fractions

Numerator	1	2	3	4	5	6	7	8	9
Denominator									

Equivalent Fractions

Numerator	1	2	3	4	5	6	7	8	9
Denominator									

Equivalent Fractions

Numerator	1	2	3	4	5	6	7	8	9
Denominator									

Equivalent Fractions

Numerator	1	2	3	4	5	6	7	8	9
Denominator									

Equivalent Fractions

Numerator	1	2	3	4	5	6	7	8	9
Denominator									

Equivalent Fractions

Numerator	1	2	3	4	5	6	7	8	9
Denominator									

Equivalent Fractions

Numerator	1	2	3	4	5	6	7	8	9
Denominator									

Equivalent Fractions

Numerator	1	2	3	4	5	6	7	8	9
Denominator									

Equivalent Fractions

Numerator	1	2	3	4	5	6	7	8	9
Denominator									

Fractions/Decimals: Sample for Analysis

The student is expected to generate equivalent fractions. (TAKS 1:5.2A)

Equivalent Fractions

Which of the following fractions is **not** equivalent to $\frac{1}{2}$?

A $\frac{2}{8}$

B $\frac{3}{6}$

C $\frac{4}{8}$

D $\frac{5}{10}$

Strategy:

1. Generate all the fractions with denominators of 8, 6, and 10 that equal $\frac{1}{2}$. (Denominators of 8, 6, and 10 because these are the denominators in the answer choices.)

2. $\frac{1}{2} \times \frac{4}{4} = \frac{4}{8}$ $\frac{1}{2} \times \frac{3}{3} = \frac{3}{6}$ $\frac{1}{2} \times \frac{5}{5} = \frac{5}{10}$

3. Now look in the answer choices to see which one does not equal $\frac{1}{2}$.

4. Answer choice A is $\frac{2}{8}$ and the simplest form is $\frac{1}{4}$ not $\frac{1}{2}$.

Fractions/Decimals: Step Two B

The student is expected to generate equivalent fractions. (TAKS 1:5.2A)

1. Which of the following fractions is equivalent to $\frac{1}{3}$?

A $\frac{2}{8}$ B $\frac{2}{6}$ C $\frac{4}{6}$ D $\frac{4}{8}$

2. Which of the following fractions is ***not*** equivalent to $\frac{1}{4}$?

A $\frac{9}{36}$ B $\frac{7}{28}$ C $\frac{6}{8}$ D $\frac{3}{12}$

3. Which of the following fractions is equivalent to $\frac{4}{5}$?

A $\frac{12}{18}$ B $\frac{8}{10}$ C $\frac{3}{8}$ D $\frac{3}{7}$

4. Which of the following fractions is equivalent to $\frac{3}{7}$?

A $\frac{9}{28}$ B $\frac{6}{14}$ C $\frac{5}{9}$ D $\frac{12}{14}$

5. Which of the following fractions is equivalent to $\frac{5}{9}$?

A $\frac{10}{27}$ B $\frac{20}{36}$ C $\frac{15}{18}$ D $\frac{1}{3}$

6. Which of the following fractions is equivalent to $\frac{6}{12}$?

A $\frac{3}{4}$ B $\frac{1}{2}$ C $\frac{5}{6}$ D $\frac{4}{6}$

7. Which of the following fractions is equivalent to $\frac{2}{3}$?

A $\frac{7}{9}$ B $\frac{5}{6}$ C $\frac{6}{8}$ D $\frac{8}{12}$

8. Which of the following fractions is ***not*** equivalent to $\frac{1}{9}$?

A $\frac{2}{18}$ B $\frac{3}{27}$ C $\frac{4}{36}$ D $\frac{12}{18}$

9. Which of the following fractions is ***not*** equivalent to $\frac{1}{8}$?

A $\frac{2}{16}$ B $\frac{4}{32}$ C $\frac{6}{18}$ D $\frac{3}{24}$

10. Which of the following fractions is ***not*** equivalent to $\frac{1}{5}$?

A $\frac{2}{10}$ B $\frac{4}{25}$ C $\frac{5}{25}$ D $\frac{3}{15}$

Fractions/Decimals: Step Two C

The student is expected to generate equivalent fractions. (TAKS 1:5.2A)

1. Kendall was using a measuring cup that was only divided into $\frac{1}{8}$. Her recipe for cookies called for $\frac{1}{2}$ cup. Which amount is equivalent to $\frac{1}{2}$?

A $\frac{2}{8}$ **B** $\frac{3}{8}$ **C** $\frac{6}{8}$ **D** $\frac{4}{8}$

2. Kendall's recipe for a cake called for $\frac{3}{4}$ of a cup. The cup is only marked in $\frac{1}{8}$. Which amount is equivalent to $\frac{3}{4}$?

A $\frac{5}{8}$ **B** $\frac{3}{8}$ **C** $\frac{6}{8}$ **D** $\frac{2}{8}$

3. Kendall's recipe for an omelet called for $\frac{1}{4}$ of a cup. The cup is only marked in $\frac{1}{8}$. Which amount is equivalent to $\frac{1}{4}$?

A $\frac{2}{8}$ **B** $\frac{7}{8}$ **C** $\frac{6}{8}$ **D** $\frac{4}{8}$

4. Sammy needed a piece of wire that is $\frac{3}{4}$ inch long. He did not have a ruler that was marked in $\frac{1}{4}$. Which amount is equivalent to $\frac{3}{4}$?

A $\frac{12}{8}$ **B** $\frac{9}{15}$ **C** $\frac{6}{12}$ **D** $\frac{6}{8}$

5. Manuel needed to draw a line that is $\frac{2}{3}$ inch long. He did not have a ruler that was marked in $\frac{1}{3}$. Which amount is equivalent to $\frac{2}{3}$?

A $\frac{4}{6}$ **B** $\frac{4}{5}$ **C** $\frac{7}{12}$ **D** $\frac{3}{5}$

6. Henry needed to measure a piece of tile to $\frac{1}{5}$ of an inch. He did not have a ruler that was marked in $\frac{1}{5}$. Which amount is equivalent to $\frac{1}{5}$?

A $\frac{4}{7}$ **B** $\frac{4}{15}$ **C** $\frac{8}{15}$ **D** $\frac{2}{10}$

Fractions/Decimals: Sample for Analysis

The student is expected to compare two fractional quantities in problem-solving situations using a variety of methods, including common denominators. (TAKS 1:5.2B)

Comparing Two Fractional Quantities

Which fraction is larger than $\frac{5}{6}$?

A $\frac{1}{2}$ B $\frac{3}{4}$ C $\frac{7}{8}$ D $\frac{2}{3}$

Strategy:

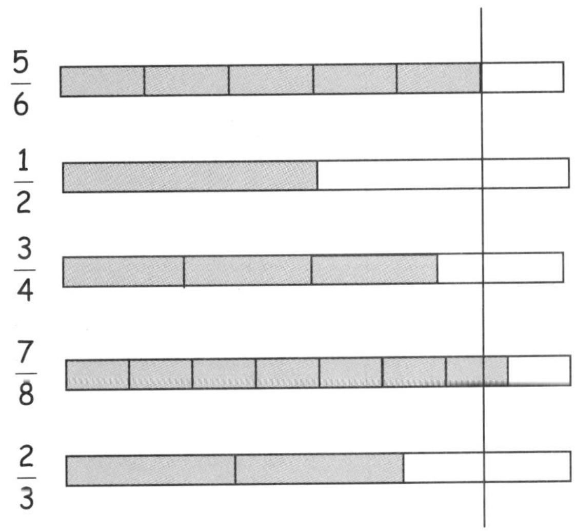

1. If you are having trouble deciding then draw a picture.

2. Just make sure the wholes are the same size. The parts need to be divided equally into the number in the denominator. You shade the number of parts in the numerator.

Fractions/Decimals: Step Three A

The student is expected to compare two fractional quantities in problem-solving situations using a variety of methods, including common denominators. (TAKS 1:5.2B)

1. Betty tried using $\frac{3}{4}$ inch tile on her mosaic table, but they were too large. Which size tile is smaller than $\frac{3}{4}$ inch?

A $\frac{6}{7}$ in. **C** $\frac{5}{6}$ in.

B $\frac{8}{9}$ in. **D** $\frac{2}{5}$ in.

2. Which fraction is greater than $\frac{1}{2}$?

A $\frac{1}{4}$ **C** $\frac{5}{8}$

B $\frac{4}{9}$ **D** $\frac{2}{6}$

3. Charles ran $\frac{2}{3}$ of a mile yesterday. He wants to run further today. Which distance is further than $\frac{2}{3}$ of a mile?

A $\frac{5}{6}$ **C** $\frac{2}{9}$

B $\frac{1}{2}$ **D** $\frac{3}{8}$

4. Which fraction is less than $\frac{5}{8}$?

A $\frac{7}{8}$ **C** $\frac{5}{6}$

B $\frac{8}{9}$ **D** $\frac{1}{3}$

5. Dad needs a nail that is longer than $\frac{7}{8}$ of an inch. Which size is longer then $\frac{7}{8}$ of an inch?

A $\frac{7}{9}$ **C** $\frac{3}{4}$

B $\frac{5}{6}$ **D** $\frac{8}{9}$

6. Which fraction is greater than $\frac{2}{5}$?

A $\frac{1}{2}$ **C** $\frac{2}{8}$

B $\frac{1}{6}$ **D** $\frac{2}{7}$

7. Daniel's eraser is $\frac{6}{7}$ inch long. Ken's eraser is smaller. Which size could Ken's eraser possibly be?

A $\frac{8}{9}$ **C** $\frac{1}{2}$

B $\frac{7}{8}$ **D** $\frac{9}{10}$

8. Which fraction is greater than $\frac{5}{8}$?

A $\frac{3}{4}$ **C** $\frac{7}{16}$

B $\frac{1}{2}$ **D** $\frac{1}{4}$

Fractions/Decimals: Sample for Analysis

The student is expected to compare two fractional quantities in problem-solving situations using a variety of methods, including common denominators. (TAKS 1:5.2B)

Comparing Two Fractional Quantities

Carrie brought a chocolate pie for the school picnic. Karen brought a lemon pie. There was $\frac{3}{4}$ of Carrie's pie eaten and $\frac{4}{8}$ of Karen's pie was eaten. Which pair of fractions compares these two fractions correctly?

A $\frac{3}{4} > \frac{4}{8}$

B $\frac{4}{8} > \frac{3}{4}$

C $\frac{3}{4} = \frac{4}{8}$

D $\frac{4}{8} = \frac{2}{4}$

Strategy:

1. These two fractions need to have the same denominator to compare them. $\frac{4}{8}$ can be changed to fourths. To change the denominator 8 to 4 you need to divide by $\frac{2}{2}$.

$$\frac{4}{8} \text{ divided by } \frac{2}{2} = \frac{2}{4}$$

2. Now compare $\frac{2}{4}$ to $\frac{3}{4}$. $\frac{3}{4}$ is greater than $\frac{2}{4}$ which is also $\frac{4}{8}$.

$$\frac{3}{4} > \frac{4}{8}$$

Answer choice A is $\frac{3}{4} > \frac{4}{8}$.

If the fractions were $\frac{1}{4}$ and $\frac{1}{8}$ would you need to get a common denominator? No, because they both have the same numerator. The smallest number in the denominator is the larger fractional part when both numerators are the same. $\frac{1}{4} > \frac{1}{8}$

Tip: Be very careful of the > and < signs. (The arrow points to the smallest number.)

Fractions/Decimals: Step Three B

The student is expected to compare two fractional quantities in problem-solving situations using a variety of methods, including common denominators. (TAKS 1:5.2B)

1. Maria sold $\frac{1}{6}$ of her tickets for the Thanksgiving supper. Amanda sold $\frac{1}{10}$ of her tickets. Which pair of fractions compares these two fractions correctly?

   A $\frac{1}{6} > \frac{1}{10}$ **C** $\frac{1}{6} < \frac{1}{10}$

   B $\frac{1}{6} = \frac{1}{10}$ **D** $\frac{6}{10} = \frac{1}{1}$

2. Jamie ate $\frac{4}{6}$ of his pizza. Andy ate $\frac{2}{3}$ of his pizza. Which pair of fractions compares these two fractions correctly?

   A $\frac{4}{6} > \frac{2}{3}$ **C** $\frac{4}{6} < \frac{2}{3}$

   B $\frac{4}{6} = \frac{2}{3}$ **D** $\frac{6}{4} > \frac{3}{2}$

3. Everyone seems to be coming down with the flu. $\frac{3}{5}$ of Mr. Rodriquez's class is absent and $\frac{4}{5}$ of Mrs. Sanchez's class is absent. Which pair of fractions compares these two fractions correctly?

   A $\frac{3}{5} > \frac{4}{5}$ **C** $\frac{3}{5} < \frac{4}{5}$

   B $\frac{3}{5} = \frac{4}{5}$ **D** $\frac{5}{4} = \frac{3}{5}$

4. Mike made $\frac{1}{8}$ of the runs during the baseball game. Tony made $\frac{3}{8}$ of the runs. Which pair of fractions compares these two fractions correctly?

   A $\frac{1}{8} > \frac{3}{8}$ **C** $\frac{6}{8} = \frac{3}{8}$

   B $\frac{1}{8} = \frac{3}{8}$ **D** $\frac{1}{8} < \frac{3}{8}$

5. Sara ran $\frac{1}{5}$ of a mile. Kim ran $\frac{1}{8}$ of a mile. Which pair of fractions compares these two fractions correctly?

   A $\frac{1}{8} > \frac{1}{5}$ **C** $\frac{1}{8} < \frac{1}{5}$

   B $\frac{1}{5} = \frac{1}{8}$ **D** $\frac{1}{5} > \frac{8}{1}$

6. In Ms. Ramey's class, there are $\frac{1}{4}$ of the students who have perfect attendance. Mr. Jaren's class has $\frac{2}{8}$ of his class with perfect attendance. Which pair of fractions compares these two fractions correctly?

   A $\frac{1}{4} > \frac{2}{8}$ **C** $\frac{1}{4} < \frac{2}{8}$

   B $\frac{2}{8} = \frac{1}{4}$ **D** $\frac{2}{8} < \frac{1}{4}$

Fractions/Decimals: Sample for Analysis

The student is expected to use fractions to describe the results of an experiment. (TAKS 5:5.12A)

Results of an Experiment

John conducted an experiment on 10 brands of jogging shoes runners use. The joggers kept track of the miles they ran each day. After each jogger had run 100 miles, John carefully examined their shoes. He found that 4 out of 10 pairs of shoes had started to show a break down of the shoe. Which fraction shows how many of the shoes started to show a break down of the shoe?

A $\frac{2}{3}$ B $\frac{1}{2}$ C $\frac{2}{5}$ D $\frac{1}{4}$

Strategy:

1. These problems are really easy if you'll think about what you are doing.
2. Remember- a fraction tells you the relationship of a part to a whole.
3. You're looking for the number of pairs of shoes starting to break down in relation to the number of pairs of shoes in the experiment.

$$\frac{\text{Number of pairs of shoes breaking down}}{\text{Number of pairs of shoes in experiment}} = \frac{\text{part}}{\text{whole}}$$

4. Plug in the numbers from the problem.

$$\frac{\text{4 shoes breaking down}}{\text{10 shoes in experiment}} = \frac{4}{10}$$

5. Now reduce the fraction. $\frac{4}{10} = \frac{2}{5}$
6. Find $\frac{2}{5}$ in the answer choices. Mark choice C

Tip:

Be sure to reduce fractions to their lowest form.

Fractions/Decimals: Step Four A

The student is expected to use fractions to describe the results of an experiment. (TAKS 5:5.12A)

1. Jennie surveyed 10 students to find how many students ate breakfast before school. She found that 6 out of 10 students ate breakfast before school. Which fraction shows how many students ate breakfast before school?

   A $\frac{1}{6}$ C $\frac{1}{2}$

   B $\frac{1}{3}$ D $\frac{3}{5}$

2. Randy surveyed 8 students to find how many students like chocolate. He found that 6 of these students like chocolate. Which fraction shows how many of the students did ***not*** like chocolate?

   A $\frac{3}{4}$ C $\frac{1}{6}$

   B $\frac{1}{4}$ D $\frac{1}{8}$

3. Jacob conducted an experiment on the most popular brands of peanut butter. He found that 9 out of 12 students preferred Biffy Peanut Butter. Which fraction shows how many of the students preferred Biffy Peanut Butter?

   A $\frac{1}{8}$ C $\frac{2}{3}$

   B $\frac{1}{6}$ D $\frac{3}{4}$

4. Margaret surveyed 6 students to find how many liked math. She found that 4 of the students liked math. Which fraction shows how many students did ***not*** like math?

   A $\frac{1}{4}$ C $\frac{1}{2}$

   B $\frac{1}{3}$ D $\frac{2}{3}$

5. Amy asked 10 students if they had pets. There were 4 students who had a pet. Which fraction shows how many of the students did ***not*** have a pet?

   A $\frac{3}{5}$ C $\frac{2}{5}$

   B $\frac{1}{2}$ D $\frac{1}{4}$

6. Nathan asked 6 students if they had ever ridden a horse. There were 4 of these students who had never ridden a horse. Which fraction shows the number of student who had never ridden a horse?

   A $\frac{1}{6}$ C $\frac{3}{5}$

   B $\frac{2}{5}$ D $\frac{2}{3}$

Fractions/Decimals: Step Four B

The student is expected to use fractions to describe the results of an experiment. (TAKS 5:5.12A)

1. Ramona asked 10 students if they have had the chicken pox. There were 8 students that have had the chicken pox. Which fraction shows how many of the students have had the chicken pox?

   A $\frac{4}{5}$ **C** $\frac{2}{5}$

   B $\frac{1}{2}$ **D** $\frac{1}{4}$

2. Lisa picked 10 peaches from the tree in her backyard. 6 of the peaches had worms in them. Which fraction shows how many of the peaches had worms?

   A $\frac{1}{6}$ **C** $\frac{3}{5}$

   B $\frac{2}{5}$ **D** $\frac{2}{3}$

3. Mr. Lynn's class conducted an experiment with plants during a month. 6 out of the 8 plants were healthy at the end of the month. The others were turning brown. Which fraction shows what part of the plants started to turn brown?

   A $\frac{1}{4}$ **C** $\frac{2}{3}$

   B $\frac{1}{3}$ **D** $\frac{3}{4}$

4. Mom was teaching Monica to cook. She was learning how to break eggs to place in a recipe. She was able to break 4 out of 12 eggs without breaking the yolk. Which fraction shows how many of the yolks did not break?

   A $\frac{1}{8}$ **C** $\frac{1}{3}$

   B $\frac{1}{4}$ **D** $\frac{3}{4}$

5. Micah conducted an experiment on different brands of popcorn. She popped 6 different brands of popcorn and 3 of the brands popped all of the kernels. Which fraction shows how many brands had kernels that did ***not*** pop?

   A $\frac{1}{6}$ **C** $\frac{1}{2}$

   B $\frac{1}{3}$ **D** $\frac{5}{6}$

6. Mr. Hernandez had 10 of his students run a timed mile. He told each one to get 8 hours of sleep and a good breakfast of eggs, toast and milk, and then they ran a mile the next day. 6 out of the 10 ran faster. What fraction of the students did ***not*** run faster?

   A $\frac{1}{10}$ **C** $\frac{1}{4}$

   B $\frac{1}{6}$ **D** $\frac{2}{5}$

Fractions/Decimals: Sample for Analysis

The student is expected to model and record addition and subtraction of fractions with like denominators in problem-solving situations. (TAKS 1:5.3E)

Addition and Subtraction of Fractions

Tory ate $\frac{1}{4}$ of the pizza. Tonya ate $\frac{3}{4}$ of the pizza. How much of the pizza was eaten?

A $\frac{2}{4}$ B $\frac{3}{4}$ C 1 D $1\frac{1}{2}$

Strategy:

1. Before you add fractions, you must look carefully at the denominator. If they are the same number, meaning that you will be adding parts that are equal in size, then you can add the numerators. The denominators in this problem both contain a 4 so that gives the green light to adding the numerators.
2. Now you may add the numerators: 1 + 3 = 4. The answer would be $\frac{4}{4}$.
3. Why didn't we add denominators? The denominators only tell us how many pieces it is divided into, but the numerator tells us how many we need to work with.
4. If $\frac{4}{4}$ of the pizza was eaten that means the pizza was cut into 4 pieces and all 4 pieces were eaten. So how much of the pizza was eaten? $\frac{4}{4}$ which is equal to 1 so the whole pizza was eaten. If the answer can be simplified, it must be simplified because the answer will always be in simplest form.

Note: The specifications state: "model and record addition and subtraction of fractions." Instead of saying, "use models," as in the specification relating to fractions to decimals, it says "model and record." There is not a sample to verify the correct format that will be used. The student will need to learn how to create their own model to see the addition or subtraction of the two fractions in case there is not one provided.

Fractions/Decimals: Step Five A

The student is expected to model and record addition and subtraction of fractions with like denominators in problem-solving situations. (TAKS 1:5.3E)

1. Kim is preparing for a swim meet. She swam $\frac{2}{9}$ of a mile at the first practice. She swam $\frac{2}{9}$ of a mile at the second practice. How far did Kim swim during these two practices?

A $\frac{2}{3}$ B $\frac{4}{9}$ C $\frac{1}{2}$ D $\frac{5}{18}$

2. Millie is a helper in the library. The librarian asked her to dust all the books in the nonfiction section of the library. She dusted $\frac{7}{12}$ of the section the first day. On the second day she was only able to dust $\frac{1}{12}$ of the shelf. How much more of the shelf does she still have to dust?

A $\frac{1}{2}$ B $\frac{8}{9}$ C $\frac{1}{3}$ D $\frac{2}{3}$

3. Lillie had 12 eggs. She used $\frac{5}{12}$ of the eggs for breakfast and $\frac{7}{12}$ of the eggs in a cake. How much of the eggs are left?

A $\frac{2}{12}$ B $\frac{4}{5}$ C $\frac{5}{8}$ D 0

4. Pam spent $\frac{3}{8}$ of her allowance on candy. She spent another $\frac{3}{8}$ of her allowance on ribbons for her hair. How much of her allowance does she have left?

A $\frac{6}{7}$ B $\frac{2}{6}$ C $\frac{1}{2}$ D $\frac{1}{4}$

5. Callie ran $\frac{5}{8}$ of a mile during her early morning practice and $\frac{3}{8}$ of a mile during her afternoon practice. How far has she run so far?

A $\frac{3}{8}$ mile C 1 mile

B $\frac{7}{8}$ milc D $\frac{1}{3}$ mile

6. Shelly bought $\frac{3}{10}$ of a yard of red ribbon. She also bought $\frac{1}{10}$ of a yard of blue ribbon. How much ribbon did she buy?

A $\frac{6}{20}$ B $\frac{3}{10}$ C $\frac{2}{5}$ D $\frac{4}{5}$

Fractions/Decimals: Step Five B

The student is expected to model and record addition and subtraction of fractions with like denominators in problem-solving situations. (TAKS 1:5.3E)

1. Andy's dad asked him to paint the picket fence in the front yard. He painted $\frac{1}{6}$ of the fence on Monday and $\frac{1}{6}$ on Tuesday. How much more of the fence does he have to paint?

A $\frac{2}{3}$ **B** $\frac{2}{6}$ **C** $\frac{1}{6}$ **D** $\frac{1}{3}$

2. Juan checked out a book from the library. He had to finish it by Friday which is tomorrow. He read $\frac{2}{5}$ of the book while in the library. He read $\frac{1}{5}$ of the book during lunch. How much more of the book does he have to read before tomorrow?

A $\frac{2}{5}$ **B** $\frac{3}{5}$ **C** $\frac{3}{10}$ **D** $\frac{2}{3}$

3. Mother told Jennie that she had to clean her room before the end of the day. She cleaned $\frac{3}{8}$ of her room before lunch. How much more of the room does she need to clean before the end of the day?

A $\frac{6}{8}$ **B** $\frac{3}{8}$ **C** $\frac{5}{8}$ **D** $\frac{2}{3}$

4. Tyson's mom made him a cake. He ate $\frac{3}{8}$ of the cake right after his mom finished placing the icing on it. His sister ate $\frac{1}{8}$ of the cake. How much of the cake was eaten?

A $\frac{2}{5}$ **B** $\frac{4}{16}$ **C** $\frac{1}{2}$ **D** $\frac{3}{8}$

5. Shirley and Shane shared a bag of jellybeans. They ate $\frac{1}{7}$ of the bag after recess and $\frac{3}{7}$ of the bag after school. How much of the bag is left?

A $\frac{2}{9}$ **B** $\frac{3}{7}$ **C** $\frac{4}{7}$ **D** $\frac{1}{3}$

6. Cassie called all her friends to wish them luck on the tryouts tomorrow. She was on the telephone for $\frac{2}{9}$ of an hour before her mom had her do an errand. She got back on the telephone for another $\frac{4}{9}$ of an hour. How long was Cassie on the telephone?

A $\frac{1}{3}$ hr **B** $\frac{2}{3}$ hr **C** $\frac{6}{7}$ hr **D** $\frac{4}{5}$ hr

Fractions/Decimals: Step Five C

The student is expected to model and record addition and subtraction of fractions with like denominators in problem-solving situations. (TAKS 1:5.3E)

1. Ruiz bought a package of baseball cards that contained 12 cards.

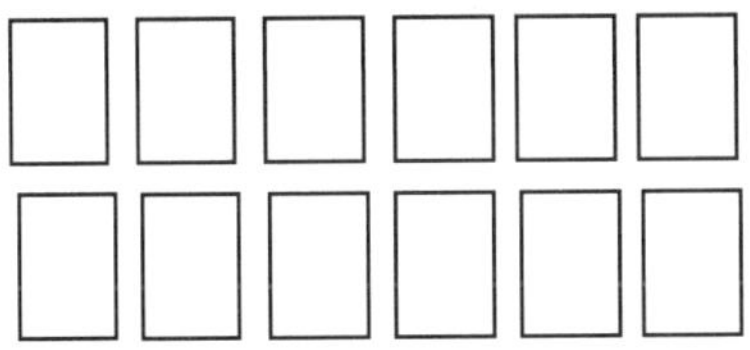

He only kept 8 for his collection and gave the rest to his little brother. What fraction of the cards did he give to his brother?

A $\frac{2}{3}$ **B** $\frac{2}{6}$ **C** $\frac{1}{6}$ **D** $\frac{1}{3}$

2. Aaron rode his bike 8 miles. He rode 3 miles on a dirt road and the rest was on pavement. What fraction of the total distance did he ride on pavement?

A $\frac{5}{8}$ **B** $\frac{3}{8}$ **C** $\frac{1}{2}$ **D** $\frac{2}{3}$

3. Mrs. Garcia bought 9 pencils to give to her students that had perfect attendance for the six weeks. At the end of the first six weeks she gave out 3 pencils and the second six weeks she gave out 5 pencils. What fraction of the pencils does she have left for the third six weeks?

A $\frac{2}{9}$ **B** $\frac{5}{9}$ **C** $\frac{1}{9}$ **D** $\frac{8}{9}$

4. Normally Ben works 6 hours each day at his job at a local fast food restaurant. He went home sick after working for 2 hours. What fraction of the 6 hour shift did he not work?

A $\frac{2}{6}$ **B** $\frac{4}{5}$ **C** $\frac{6}{4}$ **D** $\frac{2}{3}$

5. Connie needs to sell 10 boxes of cookies before Friday. She sold 3 boxes on Monday and 3 boxes on Wednesday. What fraction of the boxes of cookies does she still need to sell?

A $\frac{3}{10}$ **B** $\frac{9}{10}$ **C** $\frac{7}{10}$ **D** $\frac{2}{5}$

6. Gracie had 8 quarters. She spent 4 quarters for a hamburger and 2 quarters for an order of fries. What fraction of the quarters does she have left?

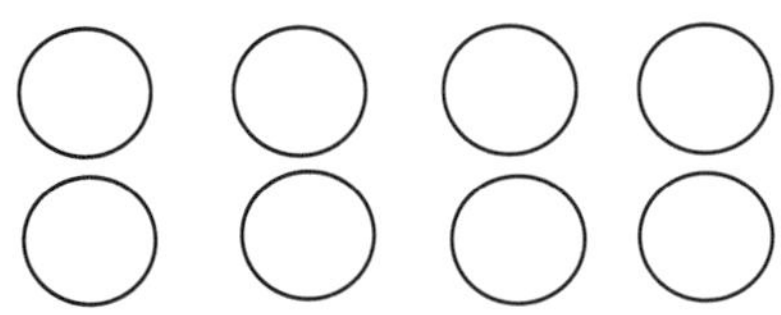

A $\frac{1}{4}$ **B** $\frac{3}{4}$ **C** $\frac{1}{2}$ **D** $\frac{1}{3}$

Fractions/Decimals: Assessment

TAKS Objectives: 1:5.2A, 1:5.2B, 1:5.2C, 1:5.3E, 2:5.5B, 5:5.12A

1. Which of the following fractions is equivalent to $\frac{3}{7}$?

   A $\frac{9}{28}$ **B** $\frac{6}{14}$ **C** $\frac{5}{9}$ **D** $\frac{12}{14}$

2. Which of the following fractions is ***not*** equivalent to $\frac{1}{9}$?

   A $\frac{2}{18}$ **B** $\frac{3}{27}$ **C** $\frac{4}{36}$ **D** $\frac{12}{18}$

3. Mary surveyed 12 students to find how many liked chocolate milk. She found that 5 fourth graders and 4 fifth graders liked chocolate milk. Which fraction shows how many students did not like chocolate milk?

   A $\frac{1}{4}$ **B** $\frac{1}{3}$ **C** $\frac{1}{2}$ **D** $\frac{2}{3}$

4. Jose' runs at least a mile everyday. On Tuesday he ran 1.3 miles. Which of the answer choices shows this as a fraction?

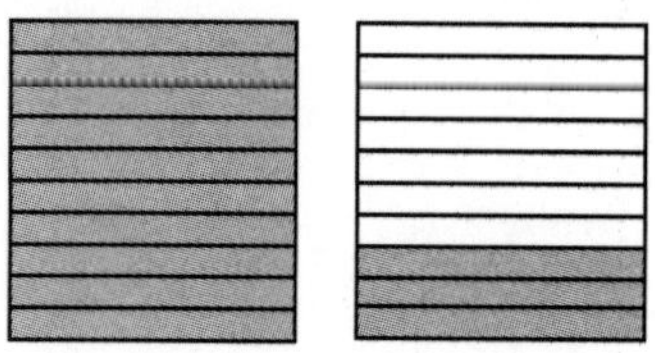

   A $1\frac{1}{3}$ **B** $1\frac{3}{9}$ **C** $\frac{10}{3}$ **D** $1\frac{3}{10}$

5. Which fraction is less than $\frac{3}{4}$?

   A $\frac{1}{2}$ **B** $\frac{4}{5}$ **C** $\frac{6}{7}$ **D** $\frac{7}{8}$

6. Annie asked 8 students if they had a bicycle. There were 4 students who had a bicycle. Which fraction shows how many of the students had a bicycle?

   A $\frac{2}{3}$ **B** $\frac{1}{2}$ **C** $\frac{2}{5}$ **D** $\frac{1}{4}$

7. Melanie made $\frac{1}{6}$ of the runs scored during the baseball game. Terry scored $\frac{3}{6}$ of the runs. Which pair of fractions compares these two fractions correctly?

   A $\frac{1}{6} > \frac{3}{6}$ **C** $\frac{6}{3} = \frac{3}{6}$

   B $\frac{1}{6} = \frac{3}{6}$ **D** $\frac{1}{6} < \frac{3}{6}$

8. Mr. Lee's Labrador Retriever had 9 puppies. He kept 3 and sold the rest. What fraction of the puppies did he sell?

   A $\frac{2}{9}$ **B** $\frac{5}{9}$ **C** $\frac{2}{3}$ **D** $\frac{8}{9}$

9. The Yell Club is having a bake sell. Patsy said she would make $\frac{3}{8}$ of the cupcakes for the sale. What fractional part of the cupcakes will others bake?

   A $\frac{6}{8}$ **B** $\frac{3}{8}$ **C** $\frac{5}{8}$ **D** $\frac{2}{3}$

Fractions/Decimals: Answer Key

Step One A
1. D
2. D
3. D
4. A

Step One B
1. D
2. B
3. A
4. C

Step Two A
1. D
2. C
3. D
4. D

Step Two B
1. B
2. C
3. B
4. B
5. B
6. B
7. D
8. D
9. C
10. B

Step Two C
1. D
2. C
3. A
4. D
5. A
6. D

Step Three A
1. D
2. C
3. A
4. D
5. D
6. A
7. C
8. A

Step Three B
1. A
2. B
3. C
4. D
5. C
6. B

Step Four A
1. D
2. B
3. D
4. B
5. A
6. D

Step Four B
1. A
2. C
3. A
4. C
5. C
6. D

Step Five A
1. B
2. C
3. D
4. D
5. C
6. C

Step Five B
1. A
2. A
3. C
4. C
5. B
6. B

Step Five C
1. D
2. A
3. C
4. D
5. D
6. A

Assessment
1. B
2. D
3. A
4. D
5. A
6. B
7. D
8. C
9. C

Word Problems

The student is expected to use addition and subtraction to solve problems involving whole numbers and decimals. **(TEKS 5.3 A) (TAKS 1)**

The student is expected to use multiplication to solve problems involving whole numbers (no more than three digits times two digits without technology). **(TEKS 5.3B) (TAKS 1)**

The student is expected to use division to solve problems involving whole numbers (no more than two-digit divisors and three-digit dividends without technology). **(TEKS 5.3C) (TAKS 1)** *Extraneous information may be given in the problem. Students will identify the strategy for finding a solution or will find a numerical solution. Students will perform multiple steps to solve the problem. The steps may include one or more arithmetic operations and/or gathering and interpreting information from a graphic source in the item, such as a drawing or a table. Students may need to convert among measurement units in the same system. Measurement units or their abbreviations will be included with the numerical answers. Students will match a problem situation with a number sentence or a diagram. Number sentences may represent missing numbers with a box or with one or more variables, and may represent more than one arithmetic operation.*

The student is expected to identify the mathematics in everyday situations. **(TEKS 5.14A) (TAKS 6)**

Suggested Sequence
Simple to Complex

Step One .... Word Problems (TAKS 1:5.3A, 1:5.3B, 1:5.3C, 6:5.14A)
Assessment

Note: Most of the word problems are two-step problems. The one-step problems have extraneous information in order for the students to exercise their ability to understand when a problem is one-step and when a problem is a two-step problem. There are additional two-step problems in the Measurement, Probability and Statistics, and Problem Solving Sections. "Show Your Work" has been provided space beside the word problems in order for the students to show you where they are having difficulty finding the correct answer.

Look for the Whole

Important Tip: The part is never bigger than the whole.

Addition and Subtraction

Mr. Harper had 48 chickens. The fox crept up last night and stole 5. How many did Mr. Harper have left?

What is the *whole* amount he had? 48
What *part* did the fox steal? 5
What *part* is left? C (unknown)
Whole – Part = Part
48 – 5 = 43

Mr. Harper had 48 chickens, the fox stole 5 and he had 43 left.
43 (Part) is not bigger than 48 (whole)
Reasonable? Yes

Sirena is selling Girl Scout Cookies. She sold 5 boxes on Monday, 4 on Tuesday and 8 on Wednesday. How many boxes has she sold in 3 days?

What is the *whole* amount she sold? (unknown)
What are the *parts*? 5, 4, 8
Part + Part + Part = Whole
5 + 4 + 8 = 17

3 days of selling 5, 4, and 8 boxes of cookies makes 17 boxes sold.
5, 4, 8 (Each Part) is not bigger than 17 (whole)
Reasonable? Yes

Look for the Whole

Important Tip: The part is never bigger than the whole.

Multiplication and Division

Mother baked 56 cookies. She divided them equally among her five children, herself and her husband. How many did each receive?

What is the *whole* amount she baked? 56
Divided among *each*? 7
What *part* each receives? (unknown)
Whole ÷ Each = Part
56 ÷ 7 = 8

56 cookies shared among 7 people will give each person 8 cookies.
8 (Each Part) is not bigger than 56 (whole)
Reasonable? Yes

Heather is going to run 3 miles everyday for two solid weeks to condition for her cross-country meet. How many miles will she have run at the end of two weeks?

What is the *whole* distance? (unknown)
How many is *each*? 3
How many days is she running? 14 days
Time x Each = Whole
14 x 3 = 42

She ran 3 miles a day for 14 days is 42 miles.
3 (Each Part) is not bigger than 42 (whole)
Reasonable? Yes

Watch Out For Those *Tricky Wrong Answers*

1. If you choose the wrong operation, that answer will be among the answer choices.

9 x 36 = **324** is the correct answer

Wrong answers could possibly be:

36 + 9 = **45** 36 ÷ 9 = **4** 36 – 9 = **27**

Just because you get an answer listed does not guarantee it is the right answer.

2. If it is a two-step problem, the answer to the first step will probably be listed as an answer choice.

45 + 35 + 25 = 105 105 ÷ 3 = **35** is the correct answer

Wrong answers could possibly be:

45 + 35 + 25 = **105** 45 + 35 = **80** 80 – 25 = **55**

Just because you get an answer listed does not guarantee it is the right answer.

3. The wrong answers are also errors in adding, subtracting, multiplying or dividing.

247 + 159 = **406** is the correct answer

A wrong answer could be **396**.
7 + 9 = 16 If you forget to carry the 1 you get 396.
A wrong answer could be **306**.
4 + 5 + 1 = 10 If you forget to carry the 1 you get 306.

Why does the test try to trick us?

The test is making sure you are reading the problem and truly finding the reasonable correct answer to the question and not just trying to get an answer that is listed. Most of the time the tricky wrong answers are not reasonable.

Watch Out For Those
Tricky Key Words

Total, altogether, each, in all, left, many more, and *much more* are all key words we look for to tell us what operation to use. In real life no one is there to write the problem and insert the key words in the problem to give us the key to the correct operation. The test problems are real life problems. The test uses *total* and *each* quite often and they aren't necessarily telling you to add or multiply. Sometimes the **wrong answer** will be an addition or multiplication answer when *total* and *each* are used to see if you are just reading the key word and not reading the problem.

Example:

> Mr. Ruiz has 365 popsicle sticks. He needs a **total** of 425 sticks **altogether** so **each** of his students can make an art project. How **many more** sticks will Mr. Ruiz need to buy?

425 + 365 = 790
425 x 365 = 155,125
425 - 365 = 60

Reword the question as a statement that gives the correct answer.
If Mr. Ruiz has 365 popsicle sticks and he needs 425 sticks, then he would need _____ more sticks.

60 makes more sense in the blank than 790 or 155,125, now doesn't it?

Now You Write The *Tricky Wrong Answers*
Watch Out For The *Tricky Wrong Answers*

Tim's dad gave him and his brother *each* $50 for new school shoes. They found a sale: **2 pair for $75** on "no tax day". What is the *total* amount that *each* boy will have *left* after purchasing the shoes at this sale price?

A **B** **C** **D**

Show Your Work

Right Answer A:

Wrong Answer B:

Wrong Answer C:

Wrong Answer D:

Now You Write The *Tricky Wrong Answers*
Watch Out For The *Tricky Wrong Answers*

For lunch Maria ordered a sandwich for $2.75, her sister ordered a hamburger for $1.85 and her dad ordered a hot dog for $1.25. They *each* had a $1.25 drink. Her dad paid for it with a $20 bill. How much *total* change will he receive?

A **B** **C** **D**

Show Your Work

Wrong Answer A:

Wrong Answer B:

Right Answer C:

Wrong Answer D:

Word Problems: Step One A

The student is expected to use addition and subtraction to solve problems involving whole numbers and decimals. (TAKS 1:5.3A)
The student is expected to use multiplication and division to solve problems involving whole numbers. (TAKS 1:5.3B, 5.3C)
The student is expected to identify the mathematics in everyday situations. (TAKS 6:5.14A)

1. Ben is harvesting pumpkins. Albertson has ordered 320 pumpkins to be distributed in their stores in Texas. His machine is able to gather 80 pumpkins in 2 hours. If the machine continuously runs, how long will it take him to harvest a total of 320 pumpkins?

   A 4 hours **C** 16 hours
   B 8 hours **D** 40 hours

   Show Your Work

2. Rachel is a gymnast. Every other gym day Rachel spends 45 minutes working on her routine. Rachel works out at the gym a total of 12 days each month. How much time does Rachel work on her routine in a two-month time period?

   A 4.5 hours **C** 18 hours
   B 9 hours **D** 540 hours

   Show Your Work

3. Callie practiced running the mile-run 3 times yesterday. Her times were 8.25 minutes, 7.64 minutes, and 6.86 minutes. What was the difference in her shortest time and her longest time?

   A 0.61 min. **C** 1.39 min.
   B 0.78 min. **D** 5.11 min.

   Show Your Work

4. 865 people attended the first football game of the season. 712 people attended the second game of the season. 923 people attended the third game of the season and 517 people attended the fourth game. How many fewer people attended the second game than the third game?

   A 221 **C** 153
   B 211 **D** Not Here

   Show Your Work

5. The lowest priced airplane ticket to El Paso is $125. There were 93 tickets sold for the air flight that left Tuesday morning. What was the least amount collected for the tickets?

   A $11,625 **C** $10,625
   B $11,525 **D** Not Here

   Show Your Work

Word Problems: Step One B

The student is expected to use addition and subtraction to solve problems involving whole numbers and decimals. (TAKS 1:5.3A)
The student is expected to use multiplication and division to solve problems involving whole numbers. (TAKS 1:5.3B, 5.3C)
The student is expected to identify the mathematics in everyday situations. (TAKS 6:5.14A)

1. The seating capacity for the new football stadium is 3,000 people on the home side. If there are 250 band members, 36 drill team members, and 14 flag core members that take up part of the seating, how much total seating is left for the remaining fans in the home section?

   A 3,300 **C** 300
   B 2,700 **D** 100

Show Your Work

2. Amanda wanted to go to the ice-skating show for her birthday. Amanda's parents bought 2 adult tickets and 17 student tickets for the show. The adult tickets were \$7 and the student tickets were \$5. How much did Amanda's parents spend on tickets for the ice-skating show?

   A \$99 **C** \$31
   B \$95 **D** \$12

Show Your Work

3. There were 4 girls selling lemonade at 2 lemonade stands. They each sold the same number of glasses at each stand and made a total of \$32. If they split the money evenly, how much will each girl receive?

			.
0	0	0	
1	1	1	
2	2	2	
3	3	3	
4	4	4	
5	5	5	
6	6	6	
7	7	7	
8	8	8	
9	9	9	

Show Your Work

4. Last year Cheryl played in 8 games. She scored 2 goals in the first, third, fifth, and sixth games. She scored 1 point in the second and eighth games. She scored 3 goals in the fourth and seventh games. What was her average goal scored for the eight games?

   A 16 goals **C** 2 goals
   B 14 goals **D** Not Here

Show Your Work

Word Problems: Step One C

The student is expected to use addition and subtraction to solve problems involving whole numbers and decimals. (TAKS 1:5.3A)
The student is expected to use multiplication and division to solve problems involving whole numbers. (TAKS 1:5.3B, 5.3C)
The student is expected to identify the mathematics in everyday situations. (TAKS 6:5.14A)

1. Kristin bought 4 jumbo size packages of stickers. Each package contained 32 sheets of stickers. There were 28 stickers on each sheet. How many stickers did Kristin buy?

   A 3,584 **C** 224
   B 896 **D** Not Here

Show Your Work

2. Tyrone had a jar of pennies. To count the pennies, he stacked them in groups of 5. He counted a total of 870 pennies. How many stacks of pennies did Tyrone make?

			.
0	0	0	
1	1	1	
2	2	2	
3	3	3	
4	4	4	
5	5	5	
6	6	6	
7	7	7	
8	8	8	
9	9	9	

Show Your Work

3. Seneca turned in her time sheet to her employer. She clocked in 6.75 hours on Monday, 7.25 hours on Tuesday, 8.15 hours on Wednesday, 6.25 hours on Thursday, and 8.25 hours on Friday. How many total hours did she turn in for the week?

   A 36.65 **C** 22.17
   B 28.4 **D** 14

Show Your Work

4. Casey bought 2 pounds of avocados at $0.69 a pound. She bought 3 pounds of kiwi fruit at $1.39 a pound. What was the total cost of these two items?

   A $2.08 **C** $5.55
   B $2.77 **D** Not Here

Show Your Work

Word Problems: Step One D

The student is expected to use addition and subtraction to solve problems involving whole numbers and decimals. (TAKS 1:5.3A)
The student is expected to use multiplication and division to solve problems involving whole numbers. (TAKS 1:5.3B, 5.3C)
The student is expected to identify the mathematics in everyday situations. (TAKS 6:5.14A)

1. Lynette plans to drive on the interstate highway to Austin which is 260 miles away. She is going to place the cruise control on 65 miles an hour and is leaving at 2:45. If she does not plan to stop, what time will she arrive in Austin?

   A 4:00 **C** 5:45
   B 4:45 **D** 6:45

Show Your Work

2. David bought a model car during the Christmas holidays. The price tag on the model said, "$8.95 + tax." When the clerk rang up David's purchase, the total cost was $9.83. How much sales tax did David pay on his model car?

   A $0.88 **C** $1.88
   B $0.98 **D** Not Here

Show Your Work

3. Jill measured the size of 4 rental spaces in her building. They had measurements of 365 square feet, 536 square feet, 782 square feet, and 243 square feet. What was the total number of square feet in these 4 spaces?

   A 1,926 sq ft **C** 1,762 sq ft
   B 1,826 sq ft **D** Not Here

Show Your Work

4. Carrie woke up at 8:00 and arrived at work at 10:15 am and left work at 3:45 pm. How long did she work?

   A 7 hours 30 minutes
   B 5 hours 30 minutes
   C 6 hours 30 minutes
   D 5 hours 15 minutes

Show Your Work

Word Problems: Step One E

The student is expected to use addition and subtraction to solve problems involving whole numbers and decimals. (TAKS 1:5.3A)
The student is expected to use multiplication and division to solve problems involving whole numbers. (TAKS 1:5.3B, 1:5.3C)
The student is expected to identify the mathematics in everyday situations. (TAKS 6:5.14A)

1. Thomas is pumping water from a pond to clean it out. The pump is pumping 720 gallons every hour. He stayed to watch it pump the first 1,000 gallons. How many gallons of water will it pump in a 24-hour day?

   A 30 gallons **C** 17,280 gallons
   B 16,280 gallons **D** Not Here

Show Your Work

2. Morgan went to the feed store to buy supplies for her rabbit. Her dad gave her $20. She bought a water bottle for $2.19, a bag of feed for $5.47, and a tube of medicine for $4.29. How much money did Morgan bring back to her dad?

   A $8.05 **C** $11.95
   B $11.95 **D** $31.95

Show Your Work

3. Yvonne had $5.12 in her bank. She wanted a barrette that cost $1.39 and a new hairbrush that cost $1.75. If Yvonne bought the hairbrush, how much money would she have left?

   A $2.14 **C** $7.26
   B $2.89 **D** Not Here

Show Your Work

4. Heather bought 2 blouses at the store. Including tax, she paid $18.73 for 1 and $16.72 for the other. She had $50 to spend. What was the total amount she had left after purchasing the two blouses?

   A $45.35 **C** $34.34
   B $35.45 **D** $14.55

Show Your Work

Word Problems: Step One F

The student is expected to use addition and subtraction to solve problems involving whole numbers and decimals. (TAKS 1:5.3A)
The student is expected to use multiplication and division to solve problems involving whole numbers. (TAKS 1:5.3B, 1:5.3C)
The student is expected to identify the mathematics in everyday situations. (TAKS 6:5.14A)

1. Scott uses his bicycle when he delivers newspapers 5 days a week. Scott's newspaper route is 9 blocks long. He delivers the same number of papers on each block. If Scott delivers 99 papers each day, how many papers does he throw a week on each block?

Show Your Work

2. Scott, Jacob, and their two parents flew from Washington, D.C. to Dallas, Texas. The adult tickets were $419 each and the spouse flies free. The children tickets were $225 each. How much money did the family spend on plane tickets?

Show Your Work

A $644 **C** $1,288
B $869 **D** Not Here

3. On Monday, 4 students bought their teacher some flowers. They spent $40 on the flower arrangement and $12 for a single rose. The students shared the cost equally. How much did each student pay?

Show Your Work

A $10.00 **C** $208
B $52 **D** Not Here

4. Each case of soft drinks contains 24 cans. Syd bought 4 cases of drinks and Vangie bought 12 cases of drinks. How many total cans of soft drinks do they have?

Show Your Work

Word Problems: Step One G

The student is expected to use addition and subtraction to solve problems involving whole numbers and decimals. (TAKS 1:5.3A)
The student is expected to use multiplication and division to solve problems involving whole numbers. (TAKS 1:5.3B, 1:5.3C)
The student is expected to identify the mathematics in everyday situations. (TAKS 6:5.14A)

1. The Pirates are seeing great crowds at their baseball games. Last week a total of 1,460 fans came to 3 of their games. This week there were 521 at Monday's game, 623 at Thursday's game and 726 at Friday's game. Which is the total number of fans that attended the Pirates' games during this two-week period?

A 4,380 **C** 1,870
B 3,330 **D** Not Here

Show Your Work

2. The fifth, sixth, seventh, and eighth graders are going to the State Fair of Texas. There are 126 fifth graders, 139 sixth graders, 113 seventh graders, and 98 eighth graders. Their buses will transport a maximum of 56 students. How many buses will they need?

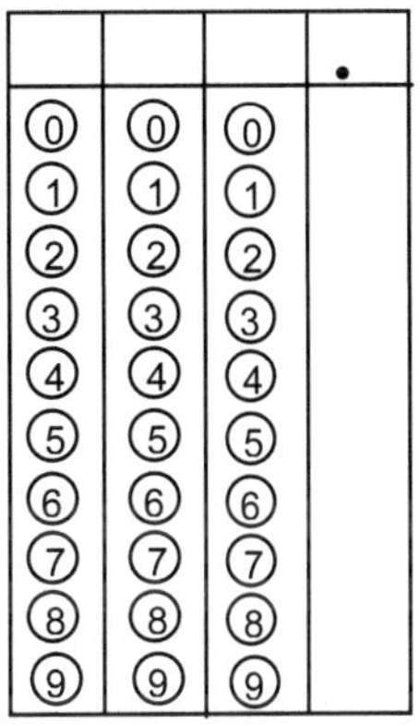

Show Your Work

3. Joey bought a jacket for $42.95. He also found a cap that was marked $12.35 that was on sale for $4.00 off the marked price. He bought the jacket and cap. How much did he spend for these 2 items before tax?

A $46.95 **C** $55.30
B $51.30 **D** Not Here

Show Your Work

4. Karen loves marigolds. She wants to plant 10 plants in the front flowerbed, 13 plants along the driveway, 10 plants under her bedroom window, 14 plants in her backyard, and 13 plants outside her kitchen window. There are 20 plants in a flat. How many flats does she need to buy?

A 60 **C** 30
B 55 **D** Not Here

Show Your Work

Word Problems: Step One H

The student is expected to use addition and subtraction to solve problems involving whole numbers and decimals. (TAKS 1:5.3A)
The student is expected to use multiplication and division to solve problems involving whole numbers. (TAKS 1:5.3B, 1:5.3C)
The student is expected to identify the mathematics in everyday situations. (TAKS 6:5.14A)

1. Heather is shopping for school clothes. She has $75 to spend. She wants to buy a blouse for $16.46, pants for $14.93, a pair of shoes for $25.75, and a belt for $7.94. All prices include tax. How much money will she have left after paying for these 4 items?

Show Your Work

A $72.08 **C** $9.92
B $65.08 **D** Not Here

2. The Wylie Pirates had a stadium full of people at their football game. They sold 824 general admission tickets at $2 and 554 reserved tickets at $5 each. How much money was collected at the ticket booth?

Show Your Work

A $1,648 **C** $4,418
B $2,770 **D** Not Here

3. The student council is collecting canned food donations to send overseas to starving children. Sarah collected 324 cans in her neighborhood and Pam collected 254 cans in her neighborhood. The rest of the members collected 726 cans. How many cans did the student council collect?

Show Your Work

A 1,304 **C** 578
B 1,050 **D** Not Here

4. Ralph mowed 15 lawns and received $17 for each lawn. He spent $75 on a new bicycle. How much money does he have left?

Show Your Work

A $255 **C** $107
B $180 **D** Not Here

Word Problems: Assessment

TAKS Objectives: 1:5.3A, 1:5.3B, 1:5.3C, 6:5.14A

1. Myoshi has $47.54 in her savings account and $7.75 in her piggy bank. She spent $8.24 on a new purse. How much money does Myoshi have now?

   A $63.53 **C** $47.05
   B $55.29 **D** Not Here

2. David is reading a book which contains 394 pages. He read 76 pages the first day and 112 pages the next day. How many more pages must David have to read in order to finish the book?

   A 188 **C** 214
   B 206 **D** Not Here

3. Cramer bought 8 pieces of bubblegum for $0.12 a piece and 9 suckers for $0.15 a piece. He gave the clerk a $5 bill. How much change did he get back?

   A $0.96 **C** $2.31
   B $1.35 **D** $2.69

4. Jamie is going to buy a package of bubble gum. There are 10 pieces in each package. He wants to give himself and each of his 6 friends 4 pieces. How many packages does he need to buy?

   A 1 **C** 3
   B 2 **D** Not Here

5. Natalie received $66 for her birthday. She spent $12.93 on a doll and $16.87 on a game. She also bought fingernail polish and jewelry for $24.36. All prices include tax. How much of her birthday money did she have left?

   A $54.16 **C** $10.84
   B $11.84 **D** Not Here

6. On Saturday 517 people went to the movie theater. That same night, 923 went out to dinner, 865 watched a home video, and 712 went to a concert. How many fewer people went to a concert than went out to dinner?

   A 58 **C** 211
   B 153 **D** Not Here

7. Henry's family is leaving for a vacation to California. His dad is planning to drive an average of 60 miles an hour. They want to cover 420 miles on the first day. How many hours will they drive on the first day?

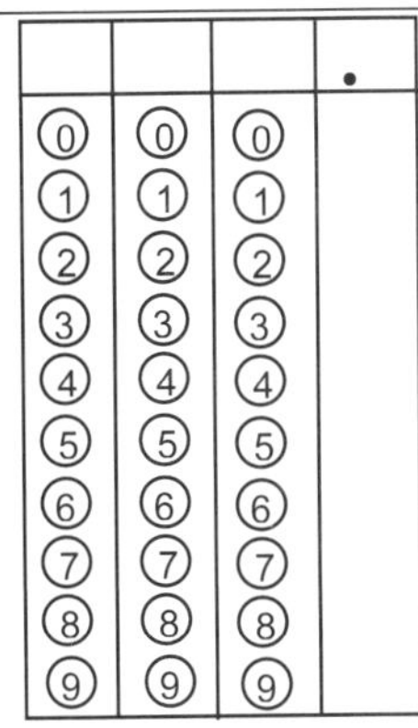

8. Nathan rode his bike at a rate of 6 miles an hour for 2 hours each day. How many miles did Nathan ride his bike during a two-week period?

   A 12 miles **C** 168 miles
   B 84 miles **D** Not Here

9. Nathan cut off 4.8 meters of red twine from a roll of twine containing 10 meters. How many meters were left on the roll?

   A 14.8 meters **C** 4.7 meters
   B 10.48 meters **D** 5.2 meters

10. There were 4 children who raked 16 bags of leaves for Mr. Neighbors. He paid them $5 a bag. If the children divided the money evenly, how much did each child receive?

   A $1.25 **C** $80
   B $20 **D** Not Here

Word Problems: Answer Key

Step One A
1. B
2. B
3. C
4. B
5. A

Step One B
1. B
2. A
3. 8
4. C

Step One C
1. A
2. 174
3. A
4. C

Step One D
1. D
2. A
3. A
4. B

Step One E
1. C
2. A
3. D
4. D

Step One F
1. 55
2. B
3. D
4. 384

Step One G
1. B
2. 9
3. B
4. D

Step One H
1. C
2. C
3. A
4. B

Assessment
1. C
2. B
3. D
4. C
5. B
6. C
7. 7
8. C
9. D
10. B

Geometry

The student is expected to use critical attributes to define geometric shapes or solids. **(TEKS 5.7B) (TAKS 3)** *Geometric shapes and solids, or familiar objects representing shapes or solids, will be represented in pictorial form and may be identified by name. Students will match the figure with its attribute. Attributes may describe characteristics of lines, line segments, angles, faces, or vertices that are contained in the figure.*

The student is expected to identify critical attributes, including parallel, perpendicular, and congruent parts of geometric shapes and solids. **(TEKS 5.7A) (TAKS 3)** *Students will match the name of a geometric shape or solid with one or more of its attributes, or with a pictorial model of the shape or solid. Students will match the shape or solid with a characteristic that does NOT fit among its attributes.*

The student is expected to sketch the results of translations, rotations, and reflections. **(TEKS 5.8A) (TAKS 3)**

The student is expected to describe the transformation that generates one figure from the other when given two congruent figures. **(TEK 5.8B) (TAKS 3)** *Students will match a pictorial representation of a transformation with its name.*

The student is expected to locate and name points on a coordinate grid using ordered pairs of whole numbers. **(TEKS 5.9A) (TAKS 3)** *Students will match a point in the first quadrant of a coordinate grid with its ordered pair.*

The student is expected to use tables of related number pairs to make line graphs. **(TEKS 5.13A) (TAKS 5)**

The student is expected to graph a given set of data using an appropriate graphical representation such as picture or line. **(TEKS 5.13C) (TAKS 5)**

Suggested Sequence
Simple to Complex

Step One............Critical Attributes to Define Geometric Terms, Shapes and Solids (TAKS 3:5.7A, 3:5.7B)
Step Two ....Congruent (TAKS 3:5.7A)
Step Three........Translation, Reflection, Rotation (TAKS 3:5.8A, 3:5.8B)
Step Four ....Points on a Coordinate Grid using Ordered Pairs (TAKS 3:5.9A, 5:5.13A, 5:5.13C)
Assessment

Vocabulary

Two-Dimensional

- Line
- Angle
- Right Angle
- Parallel Lines
- Perpendicular
- Intersect
- Side
- Vertex (Vertices)
- Circle
- Polygon
- Regular Polygon
- Triangle (3 sides)
- Quadrilateral (4 sides)
- Square (4 sides)
- Rectangle (4 sides)
- Trapezoid (4 sides)
- Rhombus (4 sides)
- Parallelogram (4 sides)
- Pentagon (5 sides)
- Hexagon (6 sides)
- Octagon (8 sides)

Three-Dimensional

- Face
- Edge
- Cone
- Sphere
- Cylinder
- Cube
- Triangular Prism
- Square Prism
- Rectangular Prism
- Triangular Pyramid
- Square Pyramid
- Rectangular Pyramid

Both Dimensions

- Line of Symmetry
- Symmetry
- Congruent
- Reflection
- Rotation
- Translation
- Arrangement
- Inscribed

Geometry: Two Dimensional Figures

The student is expected to identify critical attributes including parallel, perpendicular, and congruent parts of geometric shapes and solids. (TAKS 3:5.7A)
The student is expected to use critical attributes to define geometric shapes or solids. (TAKS 3:5.7B)

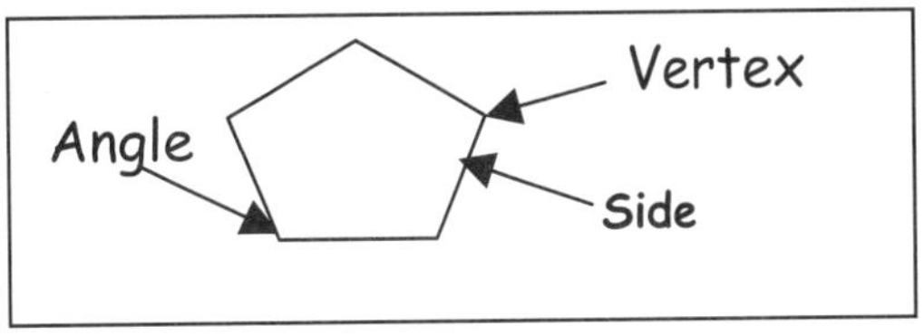

Circle 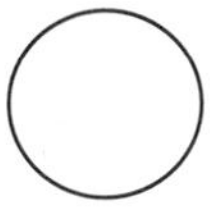

Polygon 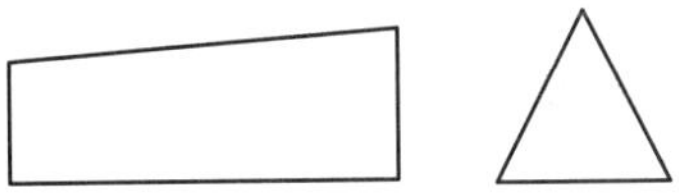 Many Sided Figure

Regular Polygon 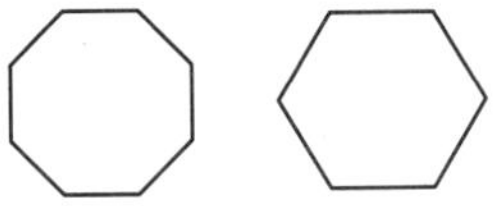 Equal Sides—Equal Angles

Triangle 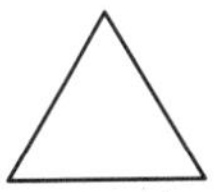 3 Sides

Square  4 Sides

Rectangle 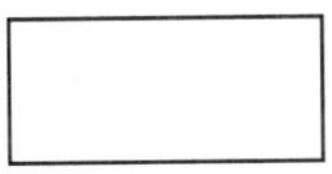 4 Sides

Quadrilateral 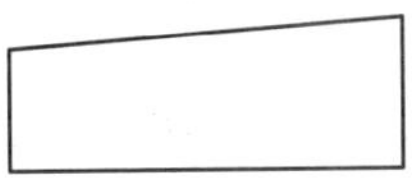 4 Sided Figure—4 Sides

Rhombus 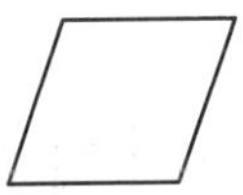 Equal Sides—4 Sides

Parallelogram 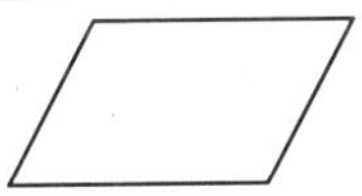 4 Sides

Trapezoid 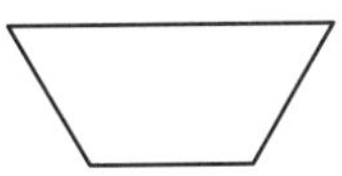 4 Sides

Pentagon 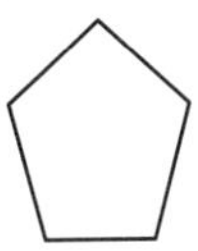 5 Sides

Hexagon 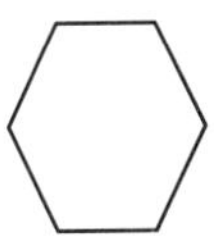 6 Sides

Octagon 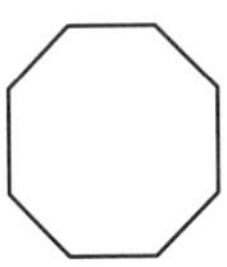 8 Sides

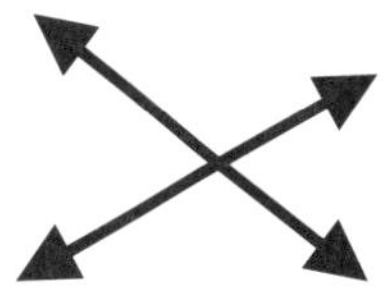

Intersecting Lines

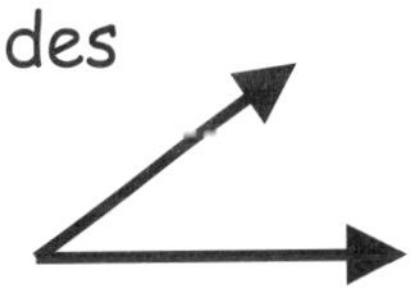

Acute Angle

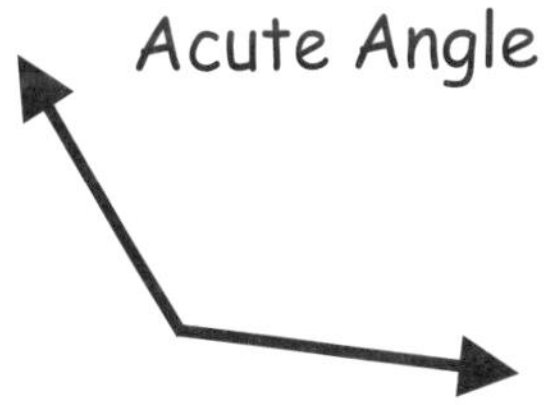

Obtuse Angle

Parallel Lines

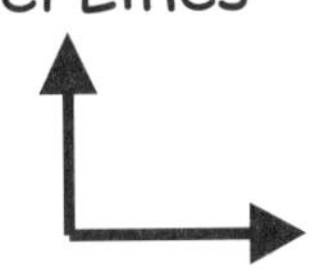

Perpendicular Lines

Geometry: Three Dimensional Figures

The student is expected to identify critical attributes including parallel, perpendicular, and congruent parts of geometric shapes and solids. (TAKS 3:5.7A)
The student is expected to use critical attributes to define geometric shapes or solids. (TAKS 3:5.7B)

Sphere 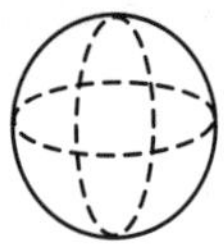

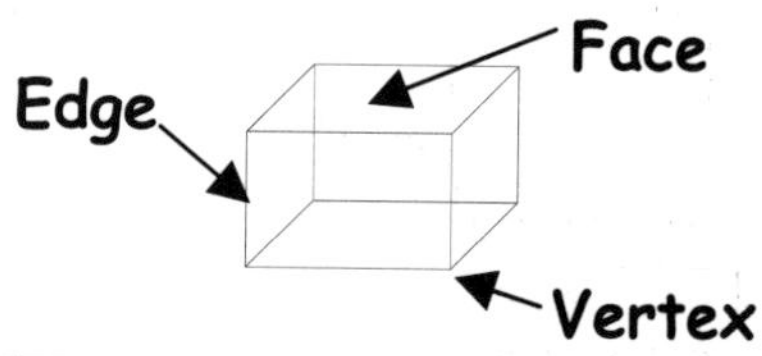

Cube 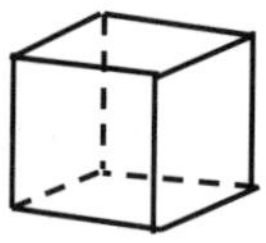 6 Faces—12 Edges

Square Prism 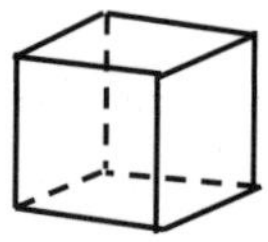 6 Faces—12 Edges

Rectangular Prism 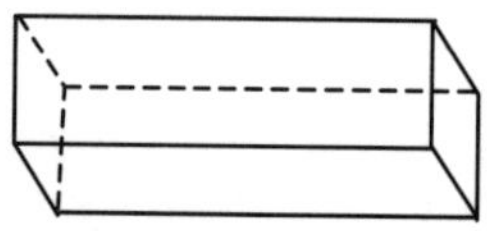 6 Faces—12 Edges

Triangular Prism 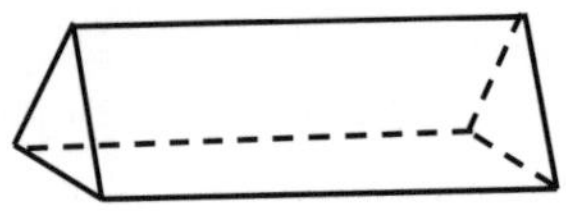 5 Faces—9 Edges

Cone  1 Base—1 Vertex

Cylinder  2 Bases

Square Pyramid 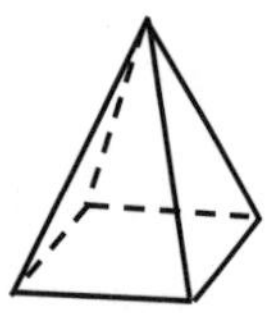 5 Faces--8 Edges (Square Base)

Rectangular Pyramid 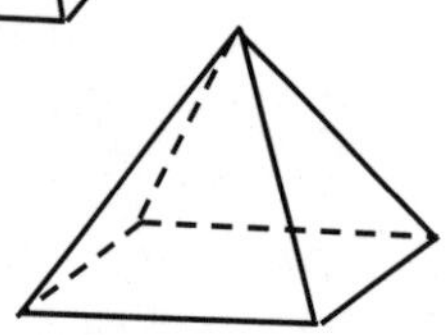 5 Faces—8 Edges (Rectangular Base)

Triangular Pyramid 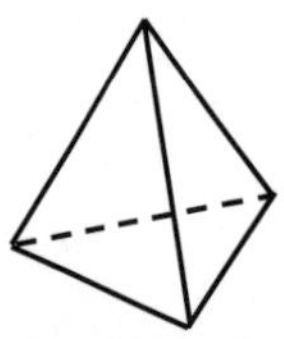 4 Faces—6 Edges (Triangular Base)

Geometry: Step One A

The student is expected to identify critical attributes including parallel, perpendicular, and congruent parts of geometric shapes and solids. (TAKS 3:5.7A)
The student is expected to use critical attributes to define geometric shapes or solids. (TAKS 3:5.7B)

1. Which object best represents a figure with all right angles?

A 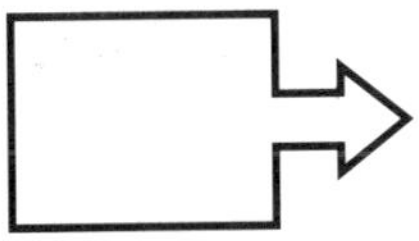

B 

C 

D 

2. Look at the 4 houses pictured below. Which roof has a right angle at the top?

A 

B 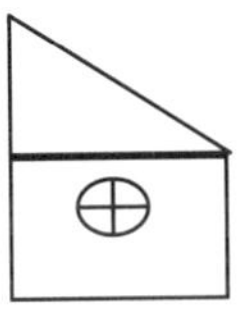

C 

D 

3. Which figure has 2 acute and 2 obtuse angles?

A 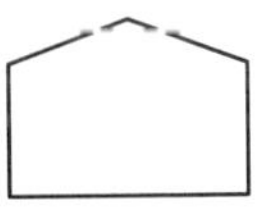

B 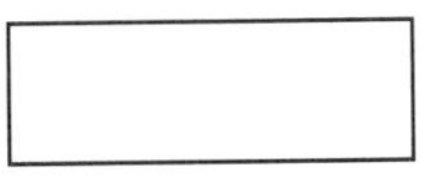

C 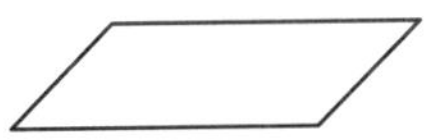

D 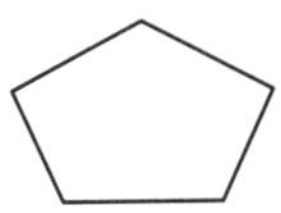

4. Which could ***not*** be used to describe this prism?

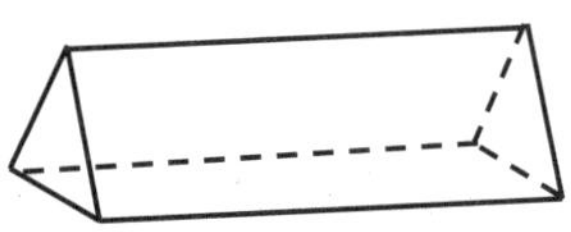

A 9 edges
B 5 faces
C two-dimensional
D rectangular base

5. Which term could ***not*** be used to describe this figure?

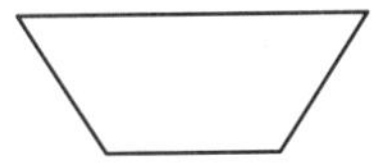

A regular polygon
B quadrilateral
C polygon
D trapezoid

6. Which term could ***not*** be used to describe this figure?

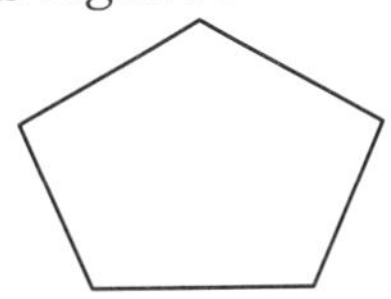

A two-dimensional figure
B quadrilateral
C polygon
D pentagon

7. Which term could ***not*** be used to describe this figure?

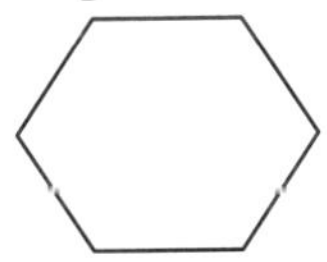

A regular polygon
B hexagon
C polygon
D octagon

8. Which term could ***not*** be used to describe this figure?

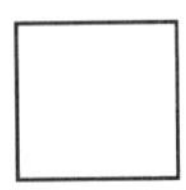

A regular polygon
B quadrilateral
C square
D prism

9. Which figure contains perpendicular lines and parallel lines?

A rhombus
B hexagon
C trapezoid
D rectangle

Geometry: Step One B

The student is expected to identify critical attributes including parallel, perpendicular, and congruent parts of geometric shapes and solids. (TAKS 3:5.7A)
The student is expected to use critical attributes to define geometric shapes or solids. (TAKS 3:5.7B)

1. A square pyramid is shown below.

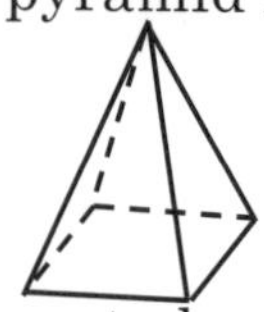

Which statement about the square pyramid is true?

A The square pyramid is also a triangular prism.
B The square pyramid has four faces.
C The square pyramid has three triangular faces.
D The square pyramid has five vertices.

2. A rectangular prism is shown below.

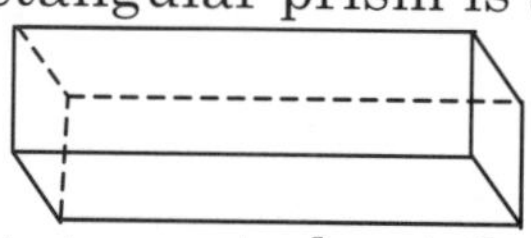

Which statement about the rectangular prism is true?

A The rectangular prism has 6 edges.
B The rectangular prism has 6 rectangular faces.
C The rectangular prism is a square prism.
D The rectangular prism has 6 vertices.

3. Look at the drawing below.

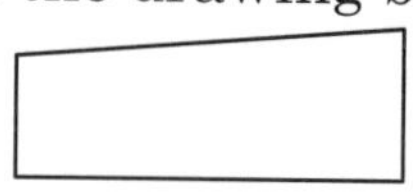

Which statement about this figure is true?

A The figure has 2 sets of parallel lines.
B The figure has 4 perpendicular angles.
C The figure is a quadrilateral.
D The figure is a regular polygon.

4. A pentagon is shown below.

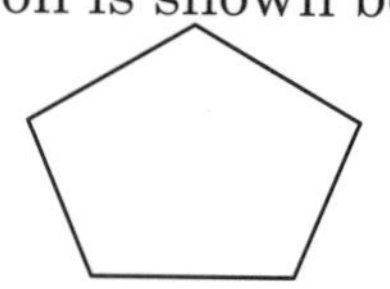

Which statement about the pentagon is true?

A The pentagon has 5 vertices.
B The pentagon has 5 perpendicular lines.
C The pentagon has 2 sets of parallel lines.
D The pentagon is a hexagon.

5. A triangular pyramid is shown below.

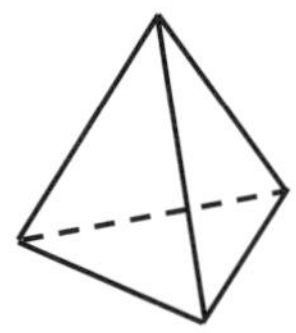

Which statement about the triangular pyramid is true?

A The triangular pyramid has 3 faces.
B The triangular pyramid has 6 edges.
C The triangular pyramid is also triangular prism.
D The triangular pyramid has no vertices.

6. A parallelogram is shown below.

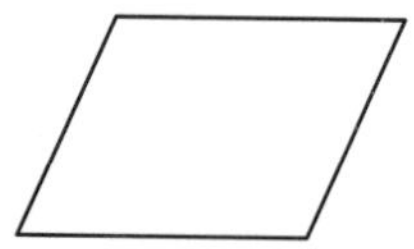

Which statement about the parallelogram is ***not*** true?

A The parallelogram has 2 sets of parallel lines.
B The parallelogram has 2 obtuse and 2 acute angles.
C The parallelogram has 4 perpendicular angles.
D The parallelogram is a quadrilateral.

7. A cylinder is shown below.

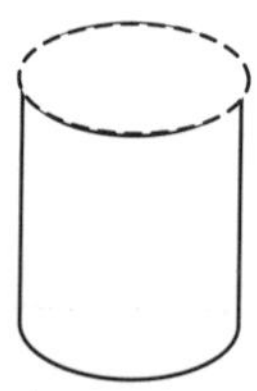

Which statement about the cylinder is true?

A The cylinder has 4 faces.
B The cylinder has 2 parallel bases.
C The cylinder has 6 edges.
D The cylinder has 8 vertices.

Geometry: Step One C

The student is expected to identify critical attributes including parallel, perpendicular, and congruent parts of geometric shapes and solids. (TAKS 3:5.7A)
The student is expected to use critical attributes to define geometric shapes or solids. (TAKS 3:5.7B)

1. Which of these shapes could never have parallel lines?

   A Square
   B Pentagon
   C Octagon
   D Triangle

2. Which of these shapes could never have perpendicular lines?

   A Circle
   B Rectangle
   C Pentagon
   D Square

3. Which of these statements are true about an equilateral triangle?

   A All sides are equal and all angles are equal.
   B Only two of the three sides are equal.
   C The angles are equal to a right angle.
   D The lateral portion of the triangle is equal to the angular portion of the triangle.

4. Which of these figures has 4 more edges than faces?

   A 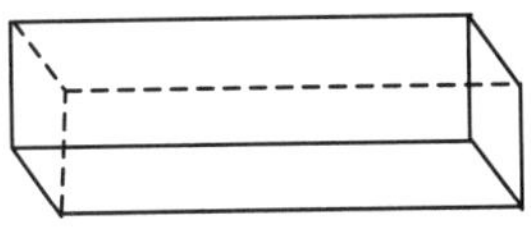
   B 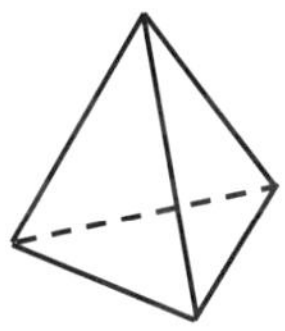
   C 
   D 

5. Which of these figures has 3 more edges than faces?

   A 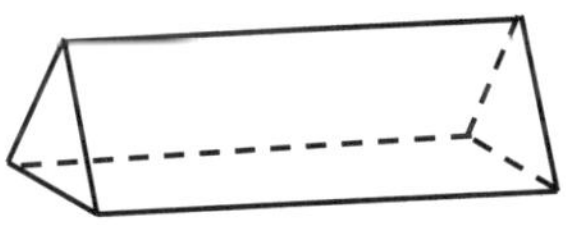
   B 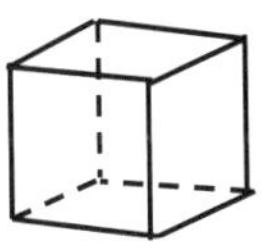
   C 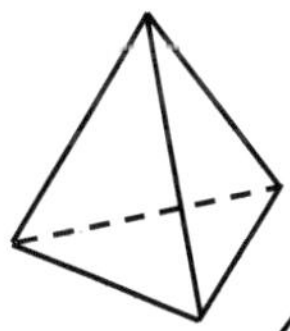
   D 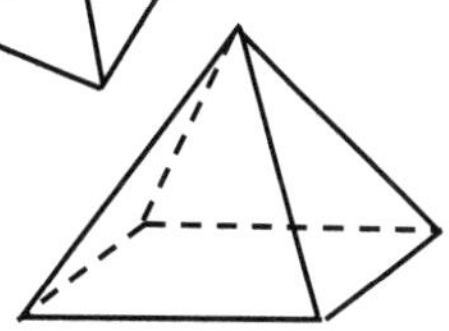

6. Which of these figures has 2 more edges than faces?

   A 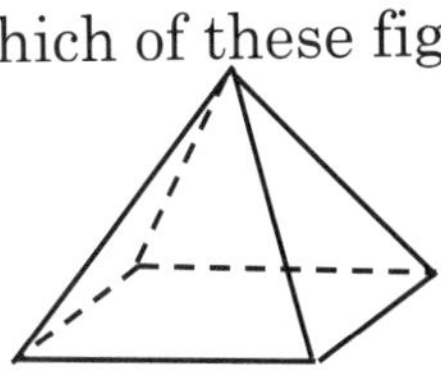
   B 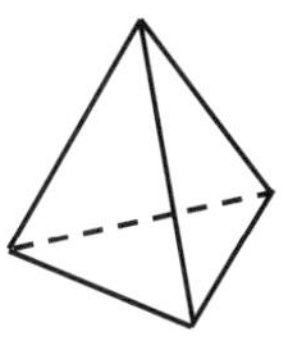
   C 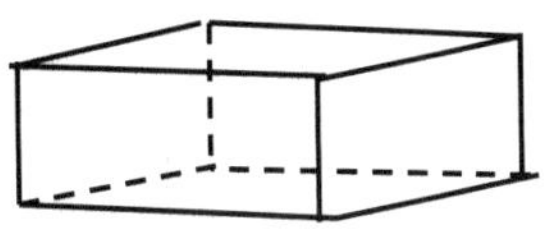
   D 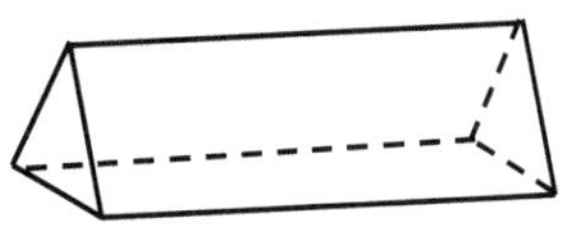

Geometry: Sample for Analysis

The student is expected to identify critical attributes including parallel, perpendicular, and congruent parts of geometric shapes and solids. (TAKS 3:5.7A)

Congruent Figures

Which figures appear to be congruent?

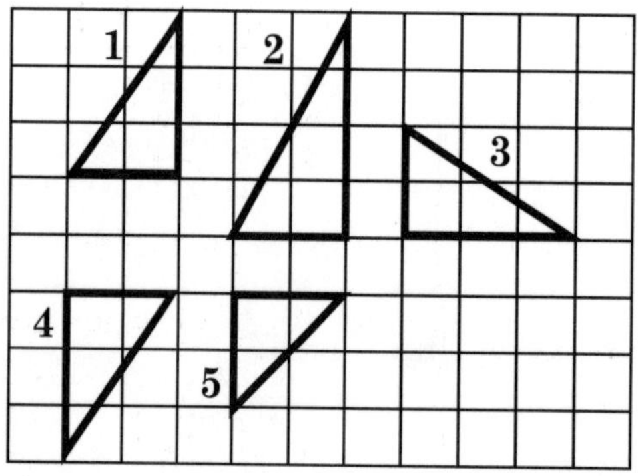

A 1 and 2 **B** 3 and 4 **C** 2 and 4 **D** 1, 3 and 4

Strategy:

1. Think about the definition of congruent. It means figures that are the same size and the same shape.
2. Look at the figures on the graph. At least two of them should be the same size and shape. Find them.
3. Look to see if any other figures match the first pair of congruent figures. Did you find the third congruent shape?
4. Figures **1**, **3** and **4** are all congruent. Find this answer among the answer choices.
5. Mark choice **D** on your answer sheet.

Tip: Read the question carefully. Don't assume that you are only looking for two figures that are congruent. There might be more than two congruent figures.

Geometry: Step Two A

The student is expected to identify critical attributes including parallel, perpendicular, and congruent parts of geometric shapes and solids. (TAKS 3:5.7A)

1. Which figures appear to be congruent?

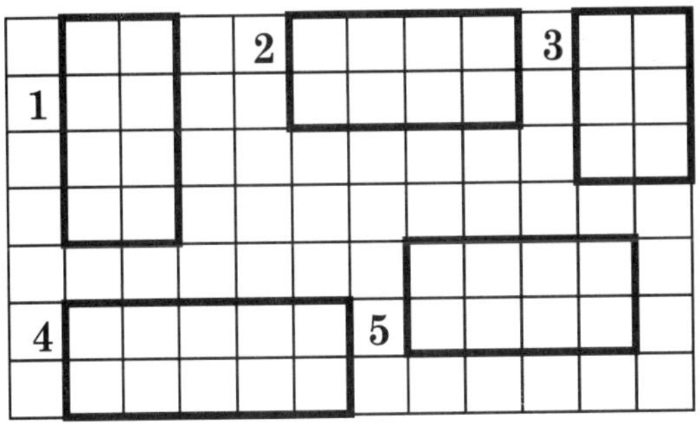

A 1 and 4
B 3 and 4
C 1, 2, and 5
D 2 and 3

2. Which figures appear to be congruent?

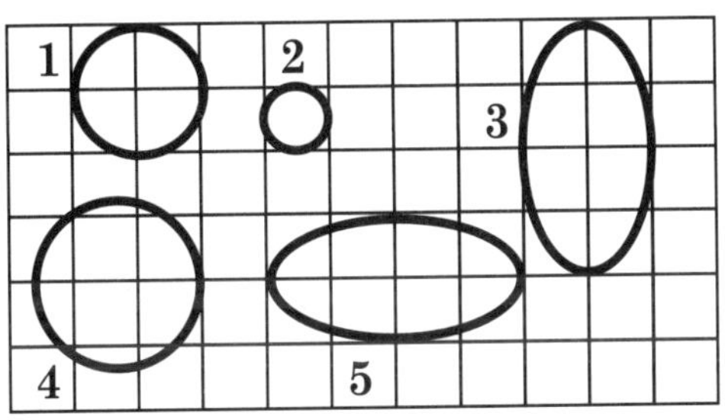

A 1 and 2
B 1,2, and 4
C 3 and 5
D 2 and 4

3. Which figures appear to be congruent?

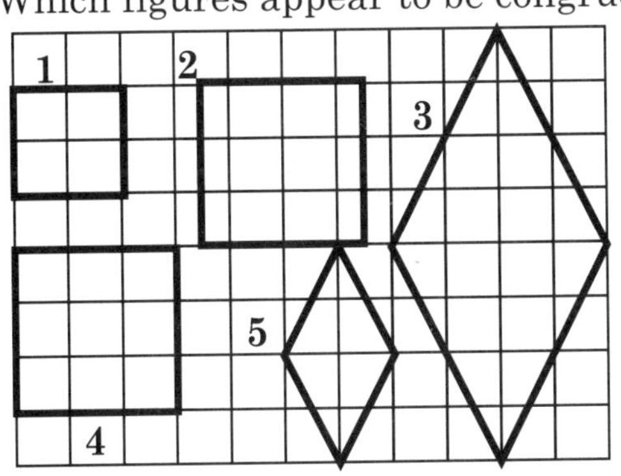

A 1 and 4
B 2 and 4
C 1, 2, and 4
D 2, 3, and 5

4. Which figures appear to be congruent?

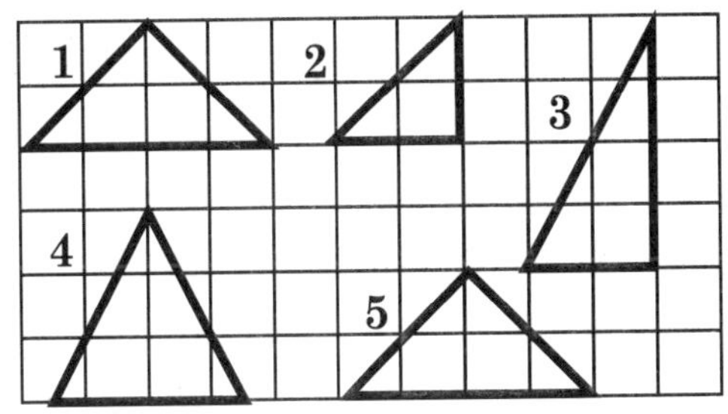

A 1 and 3
B 2 and 3
C 1 and 5
D 1, 3, and 5

5. Which figures appear to be congruent?

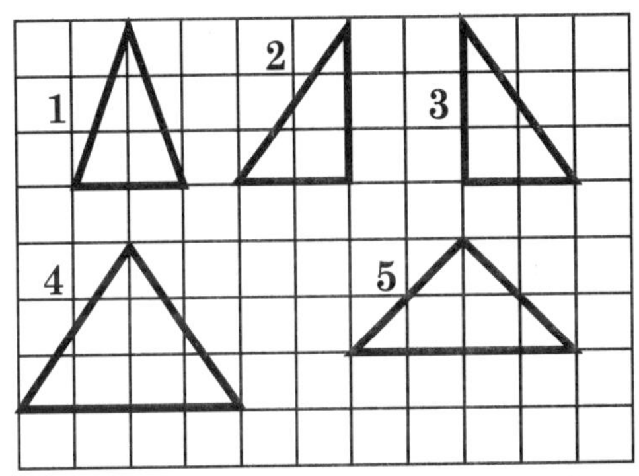

A 1 and 4
B 2 and 3
C 1, 4, and 5
D 2, 3, and 5

6. Which figures appear to be congruent?

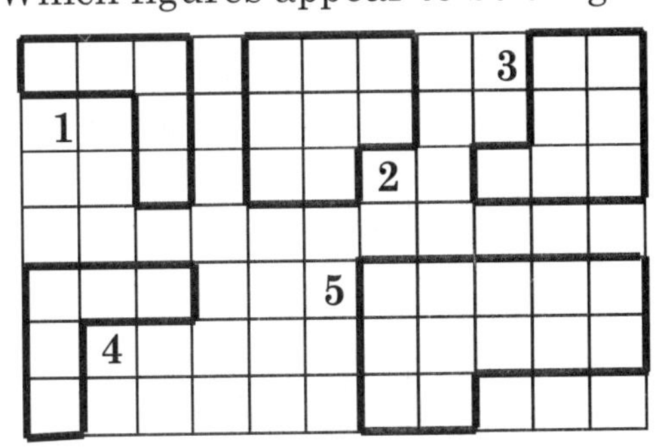

A 1, 4, and 5
B 1 and 3
C 1 and 4
D 1 and 5

Geometry: Sample for Analysis

The student is expected to identify critical attributes including parallel, perpendicular, and congruent parts of geometric shapes and solids. (TAKS 3:5.7A)

Critical Attributes

If ABCDE is congruent to JKLMN, then -

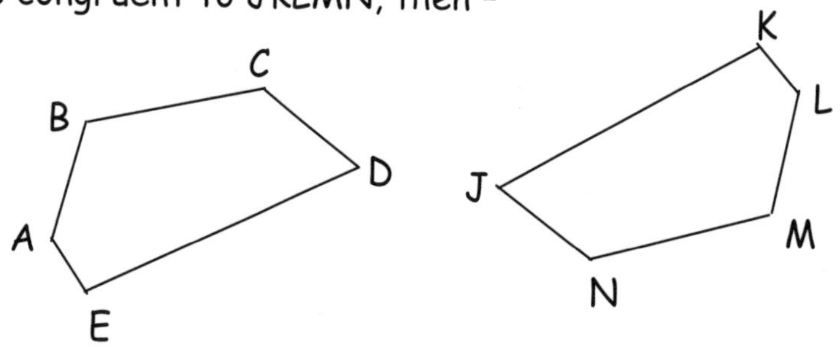

A AB = JN **B** CD = KL **C** BC = JK **D** BC = MN

Strategy:

1. Remember, congruent means same size, same shape.
2. Find the shortest side on each figure. Since the figures are congruent, these sides are the same length.
3. Use the short sides as a point of reference.
4. Now, look at the answer choices and eliminate wrong choices.
   - **A** No, JN is longer than AB
   - **B** No, CD is longer than KL
   - **C** No, JK is longer than BC
   - **D** Yes, because BC and MN are the same length, and are in the same positions on both figures.
5. Mark choice **D** on your answer sheet.

Geometry: Step Two B

The student is expected to identify critical attributes including parallel, perpendicular, and congruent parts of geometric shapes and solids. (TAKS 3:5.7A)

1. If **JKLM** is congruent to **SRQT**, then line segment ______

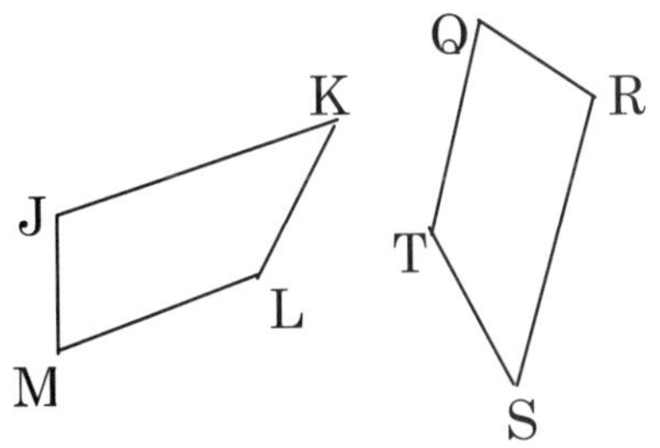

A JM is congruent to QT
B JK is congruent to QT
C ML is congruent to RS
D JM is congruent to QR

2. If **MNOP** is congruent to **QRST**, then line segment ______

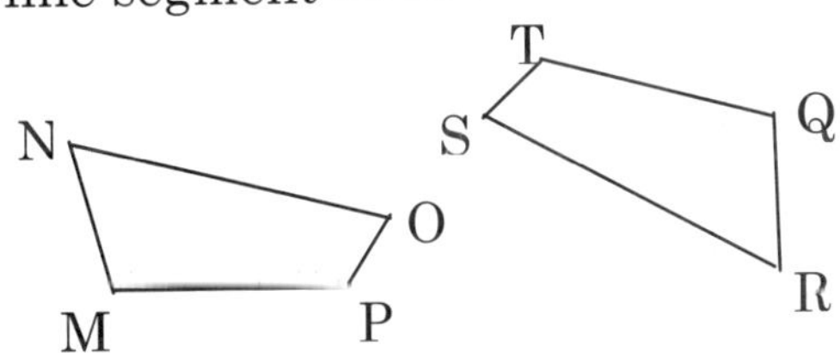

A MN is congruent to ST
B NO is congruent to TQ
C MP is congruent to TQ
D OP is congruent to QR

3. If figure **VWXYZ** is divided along a line of symmetry, then ______

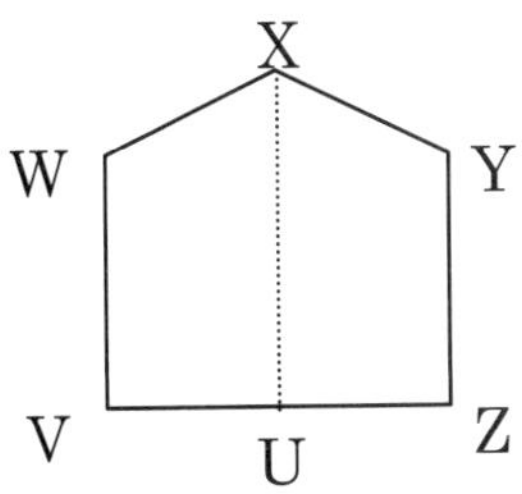

A $\angle VWX = \angle YZU$ **C** $\angle WXU = \angle XYZ$
B $\angle WXU = \angle YXU$ **D** $\angle XUV = \angle XYZ$

4. If the triangle below is divided along a line of symmetry, then line segment ______

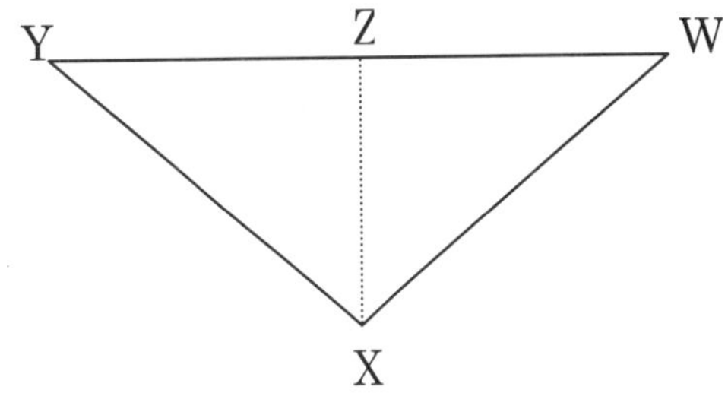

A ZX is congruent to WX
B YZ is congruent to YX
C WX is congruent to WZ
D YX is congruent to WX

5. **ABCD** is a rectangle.

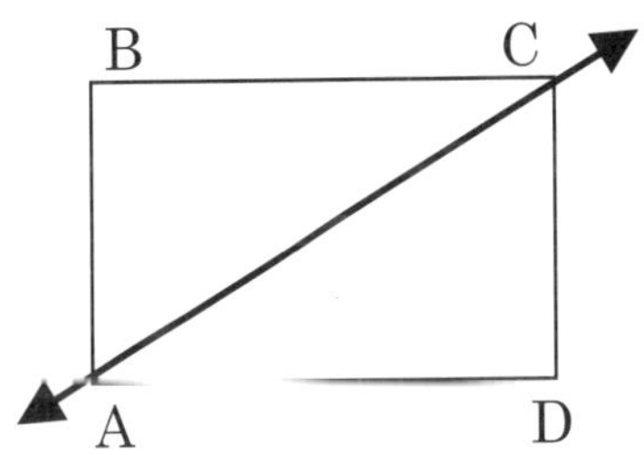

Which statement is true?

A AB = BC **C** AB < DA
B AB > CD **D** CD > BA

6. **GHIJKL** is divided along a line of symmetry.

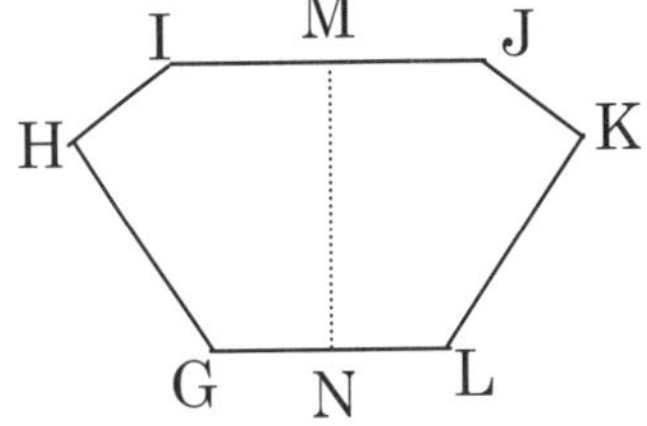

Which statement is true?

A HI > JK **C** JK = GH
B GN = NL **D** HG < KL

Geometry: Step Two C

The student is expected to identify critical attributes including parallel, perpendicular, and congruent parts of geometric shapes and solids. (TAKS 3:5.7A)

1. The figure has a line of symmetry as shown below.

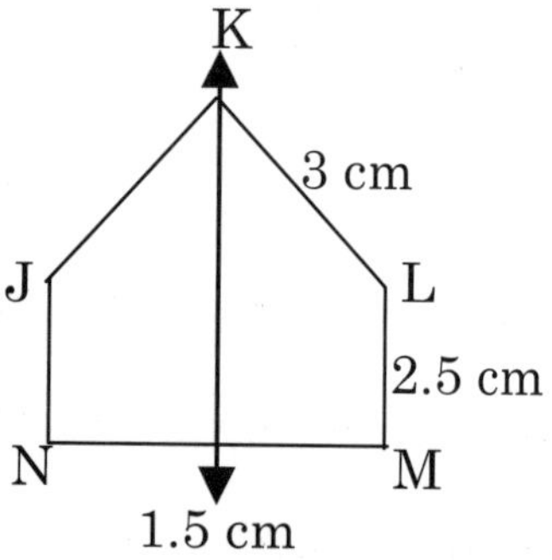

What is the length of line segment JN?

A 0.5 cm
B 1.5 cm
C 2.5 cm
D 3 cm

2. Triangle **XYZ** is congruent to triangle **GHI**.

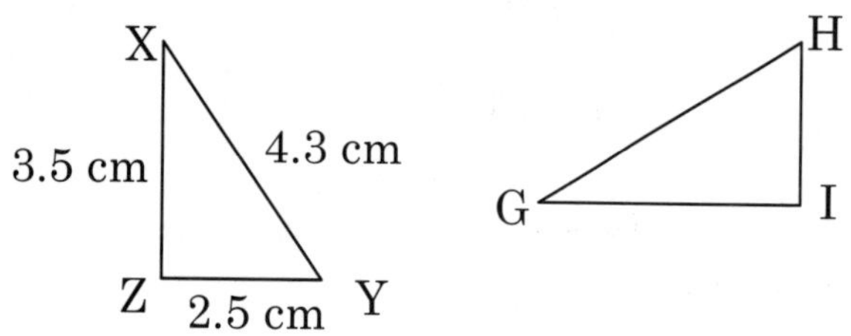

What is the length of segment GH?

A 6 cm
B 4.3 cm
C 3.5 cm
D 2.5 cm

3. The triangle below is divided along a line of symmetry.

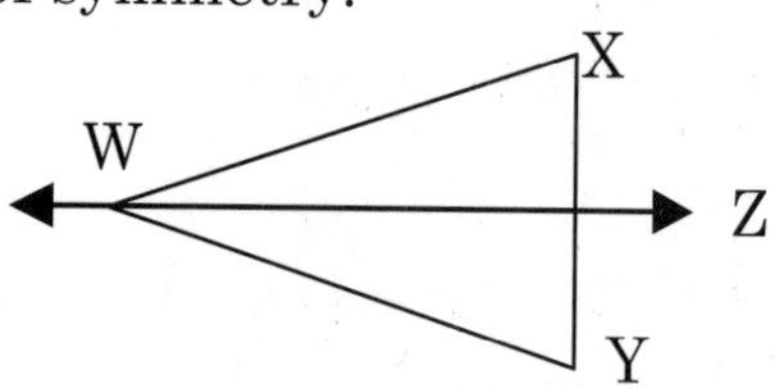

If triangle **WXY** is symmetrical, then—

A XZ is congruent to YZ
B WX is congruent to WZ
C WY is congruent to XY
D WY is congruent to WZ

4. A wire is fastened from each side of a post to stakes in the ground so that the post will stay straight. A line of symmetry can be drawn through the post.

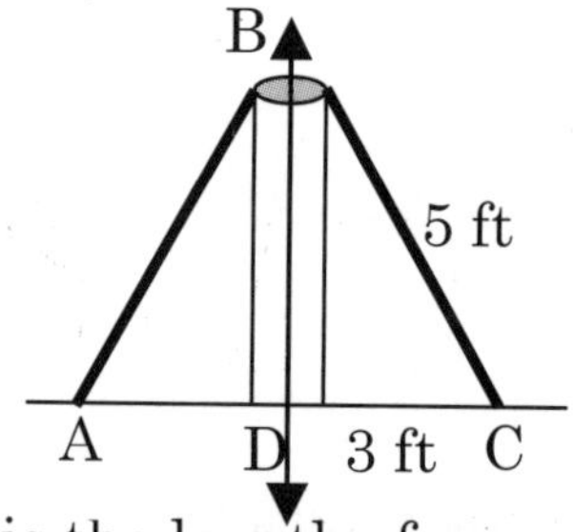

What is the length of wire AB

A 2 ft
B 3 ft
C 5 ft
D 8 ft

5. The figure has a line of symmetry as shown below.

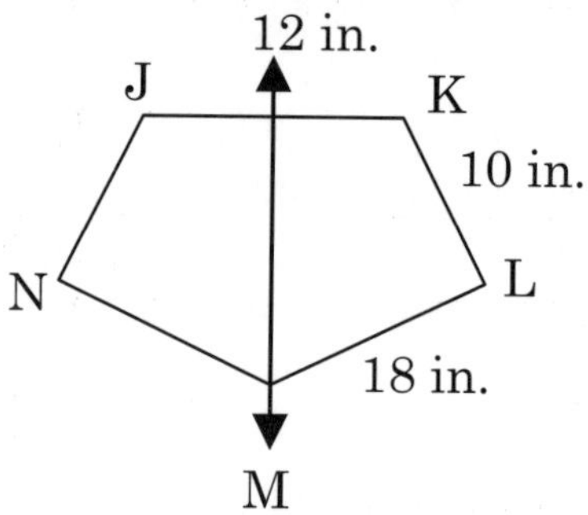

What is the length of line segment MN?

A 7 in.
B 18 in.
C 20 in.
D 25 in.

6. If **JKLMN** is congruent to **PQRST**, then—

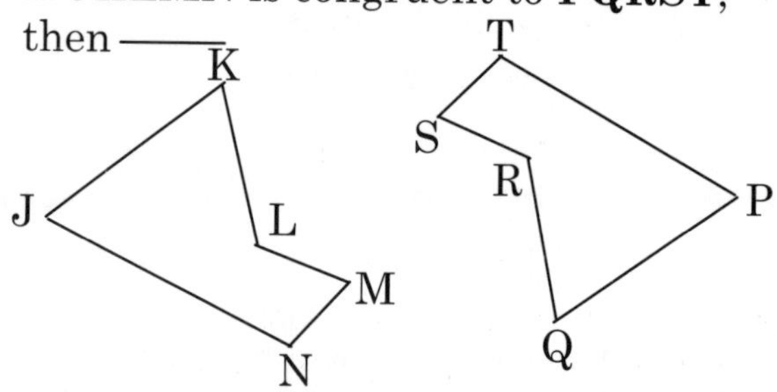

A JK is congruent to TP
B JN is congruent to TP
C MN is congruent to QR
D MN is congruent to SR

Geometry: Step Two D

The student is expected to identify critical attributes including parallel, perpendicular, and congruent parts of geometric shapes and solids. (TAKS 3:5.7A)

1. The figure below is a rectangular pyramid.

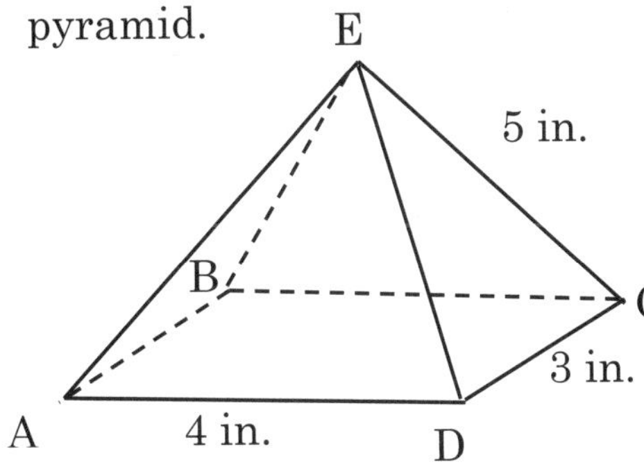

Which statement is true?
A Face ADE is congruent to ABCD.
B Edge ED is 5 inches long.
C Edge BC is 5 inches long.
D Edge AB is 4 inches long.

2. The figure below is a rectangular prism.

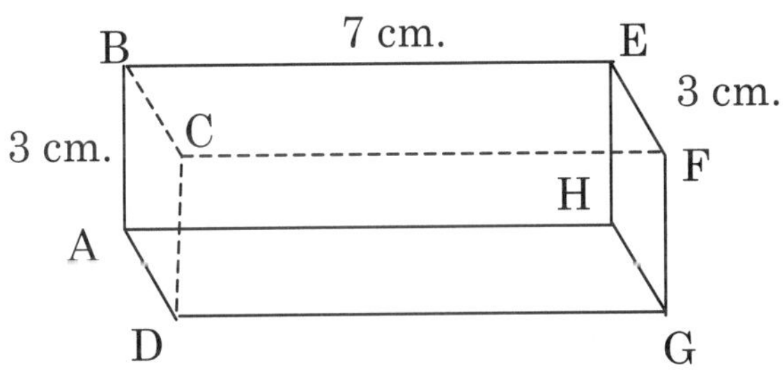

Which statement is true?
A Edge AB is 7 centimeters.
B Face ABCD is congruent to face CBEF.
C Edge DC is 3 centimeters.
D Edge BE is congruent to edge AD.

3. The figure below is a cylinder.

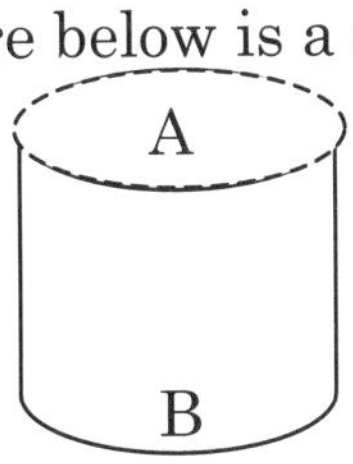

Which statement is ***not*** true?
A Base A is congruent to base B.
B Base A is parallel to base B.
C Base A is perpendicular to base B.
D A cylinder is a three-dimensional figure.

4. The figure below is a triangular prism.

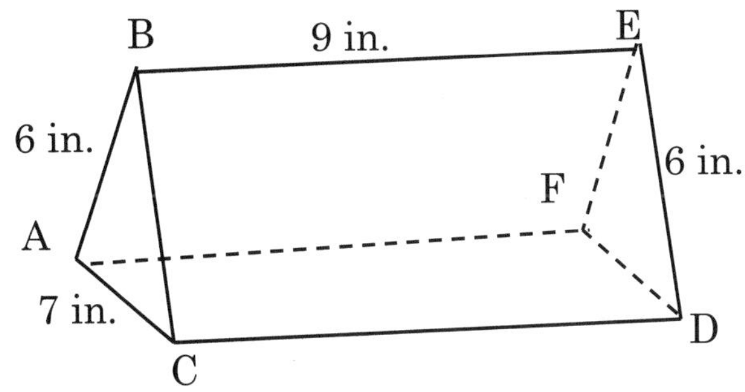

Which statement is ***not*** true?
A Angle ACB is congruent to angle FDE
B Face ABEF is congruent to BCDE
C Line segment FD is 7 inches.
D Line segment CD is 6 inches.

5. The figure below is a square pyramid.

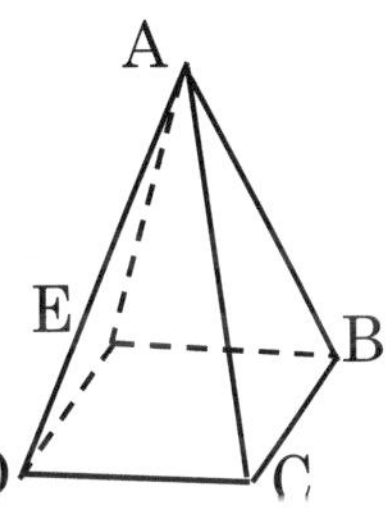

Which statement is true?

A Face DAE is congruent to face DEBC
B Face AEB is congruent to face EDCB.
C Face EDA is congruent to face AEB.
D Line segment AD is congruent to line segment DC.

6. The figure below is a square prism.

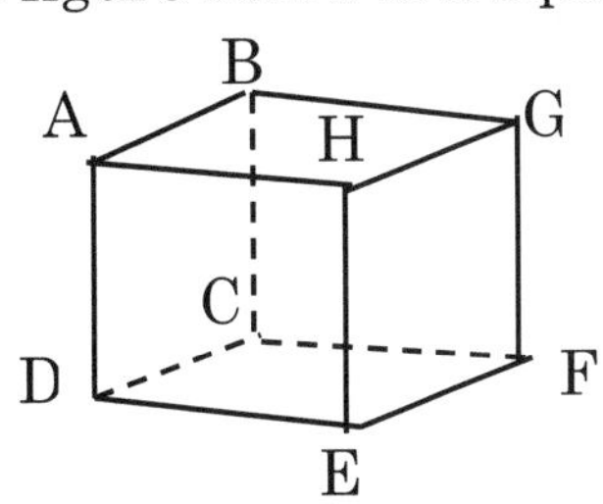

Which statement is ***not*** true?
A Face ABCD is congruent to CDEF.
B Face EFGH is congruent to AHGB.
C Line segment AD is congruent to line segment HE.
D All angles are acute angles.

Geometry: Sample for Analysis

The student is expected to sketch the results of translations, rotations, and reflections. (TAKS 3:5.8A)
The student is expected to describe the transformation that generates one figure from the other when given two congruent figures. (TAKS 3:5.8B)

Which of the following shows an example of a reflection?

A

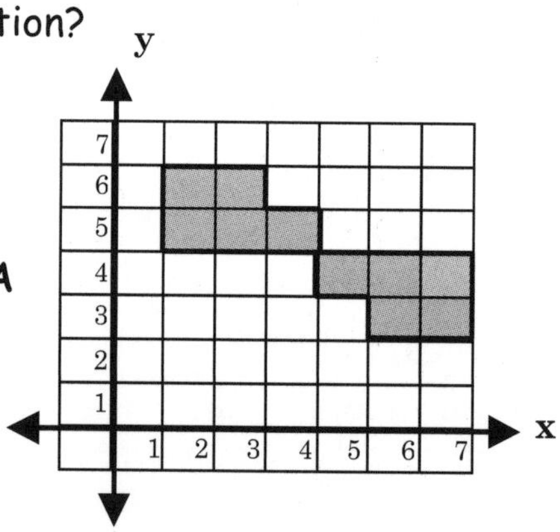

B

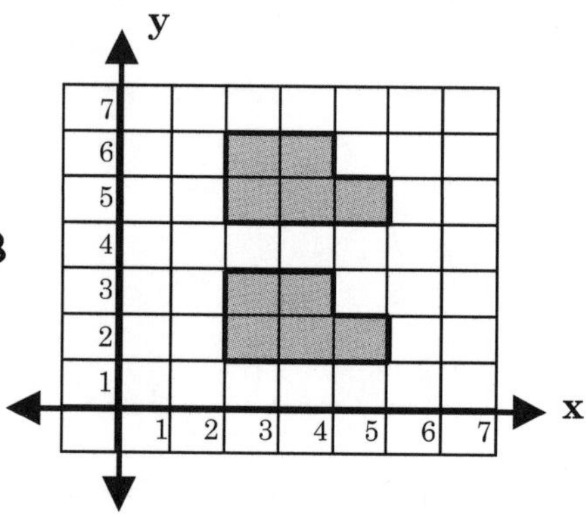

C

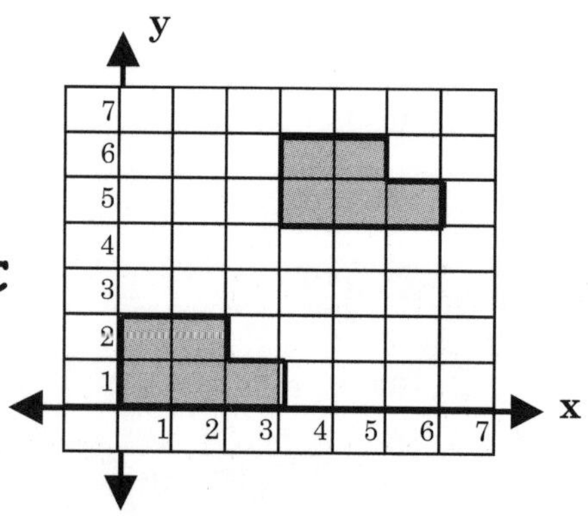

D

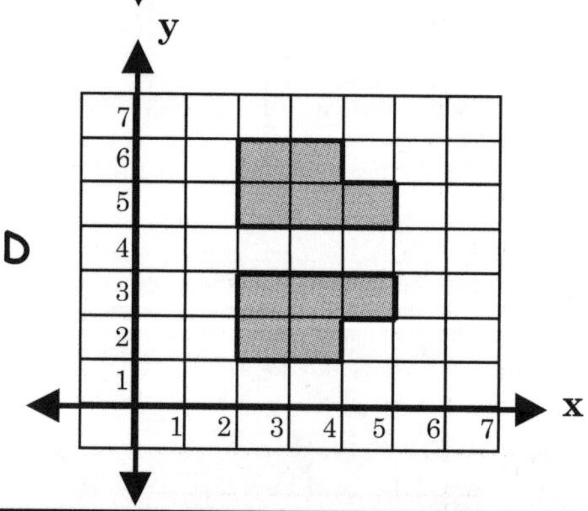

Strategy:

Example A:
The figures in choice A show an example of a rotation. A rotation would be as the hand on a clock moves around the dial. It rotates about a point.

Example B:
The figures in choice B show an example of a translation. A translation is when a figure slides from one point to another.

Example C:
The figures in choice C show another example of a translation. They are just further apart.

Example D:
The figures in choice D show a reflection. A reflection would be as though the figure is in front of a mirror. The second figure is a reflection of the other.

The question asked for a reflection and choice **D** is a reflection.

Geometry: Step Three A

The student is expected to sketch the results of translations, rotations, and reflections. (TAKS 3:5.8A)
The student is expected to describe the transformation that generates one figure from the other when given two congruent figures. (TAKS 3:5.8B)

1. In which diagram is the shaded figure a translation of the unshaded figure?

A

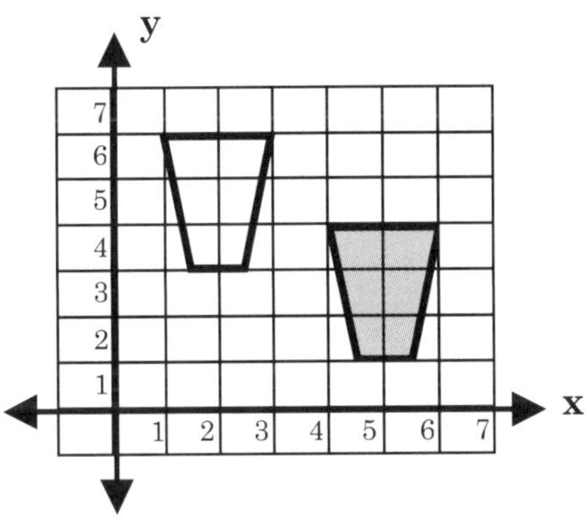

B

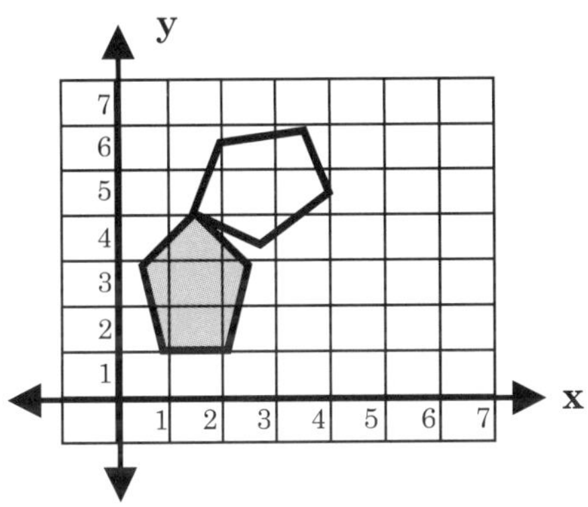

C

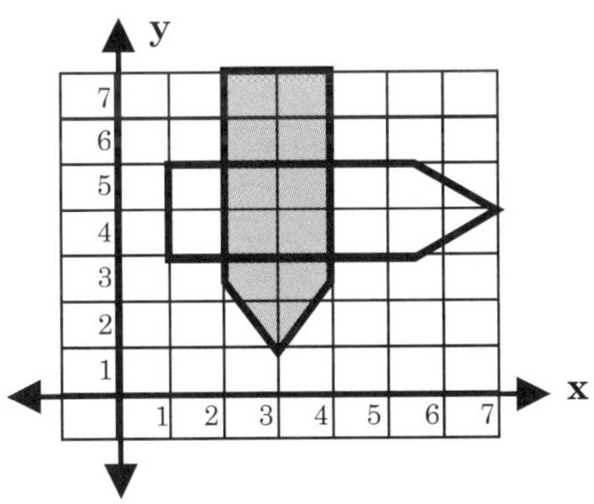

D

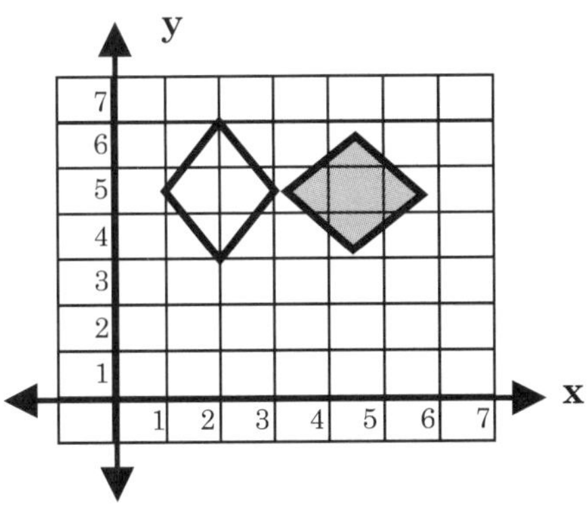

2. In which diagram is the shaded figure a rotation of the unshaded figure?

A

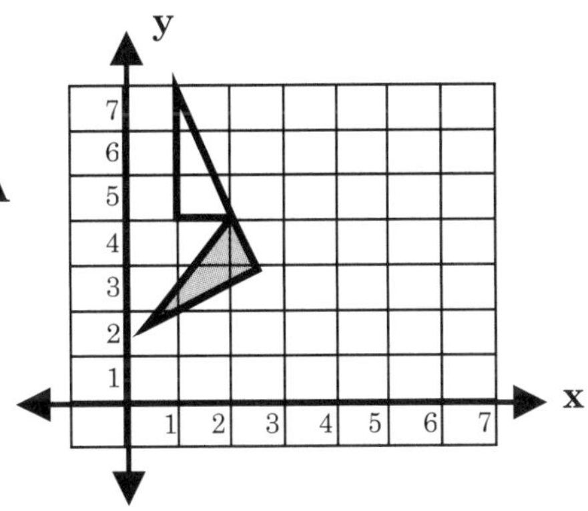

B

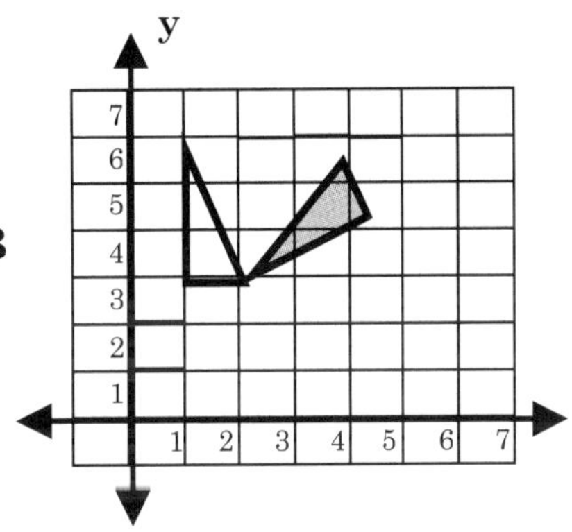

C

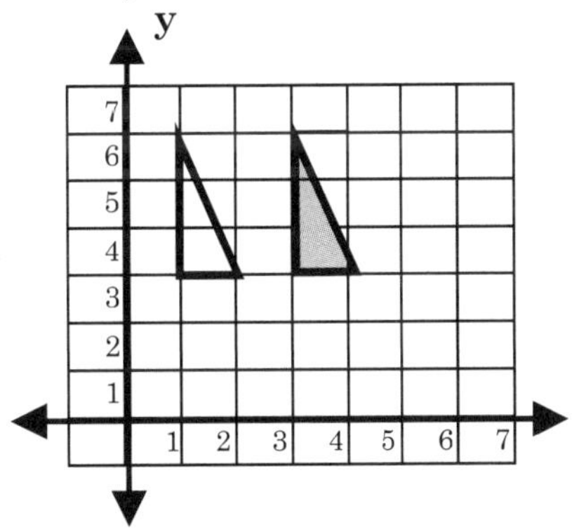

D

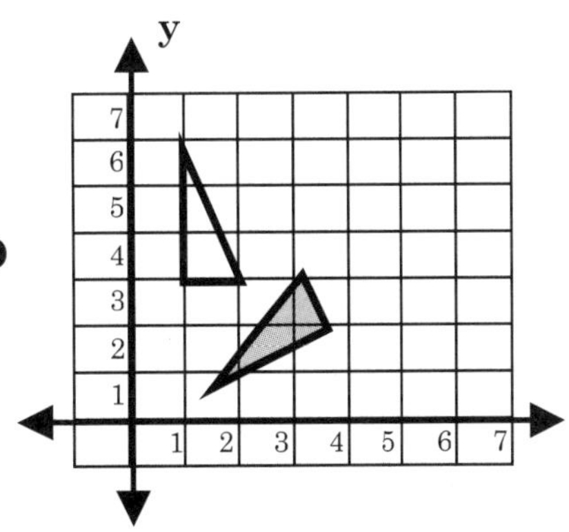

Geometry: Step Three B

The student is expected to sketch the results of translations, rotations, and reflections. (TAKS 3:5.8A)
The student is expected to describe the transformation that generates one figure from the other when given two congruent figures. (TAKS 3:5.8B)

1. In which diagram is the shaded figure a reflection of the unshaded figure?

A 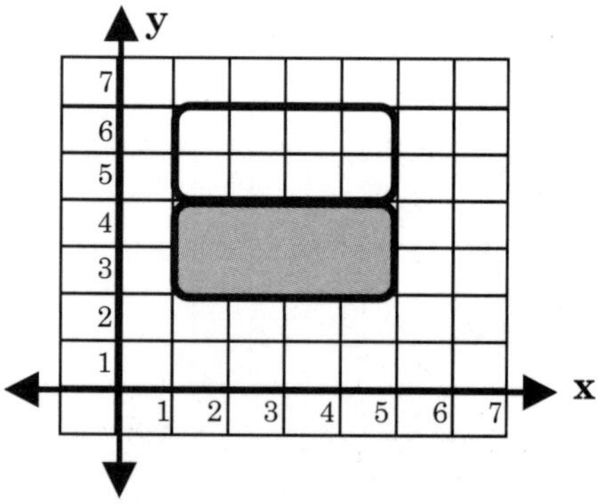

B 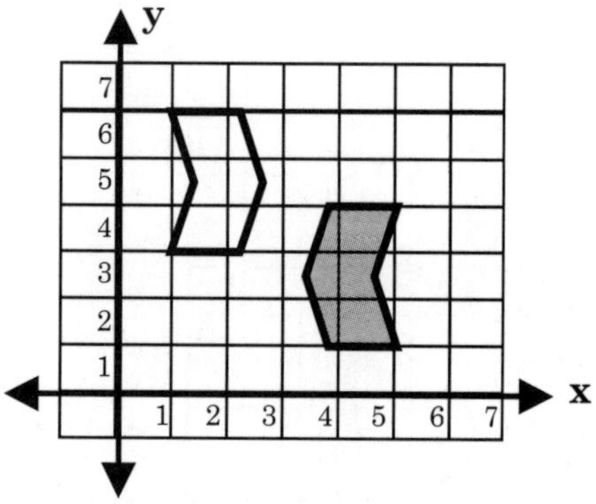

C 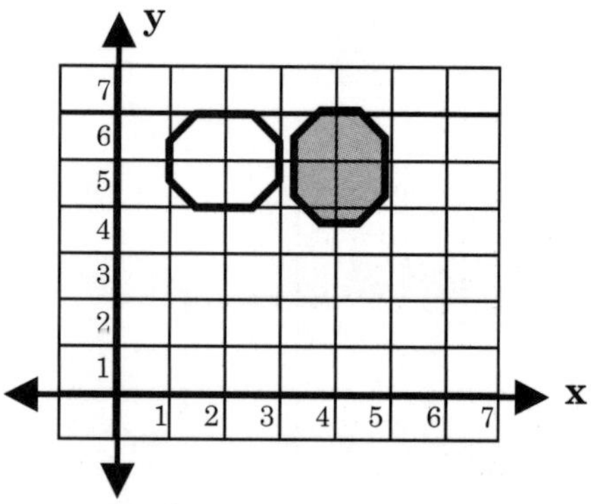

D 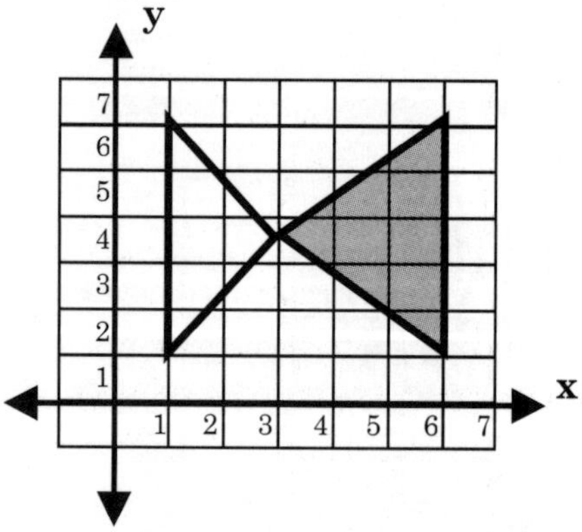

2. In which diagram is the shaded figure a rotation of the unshaded figure?

A 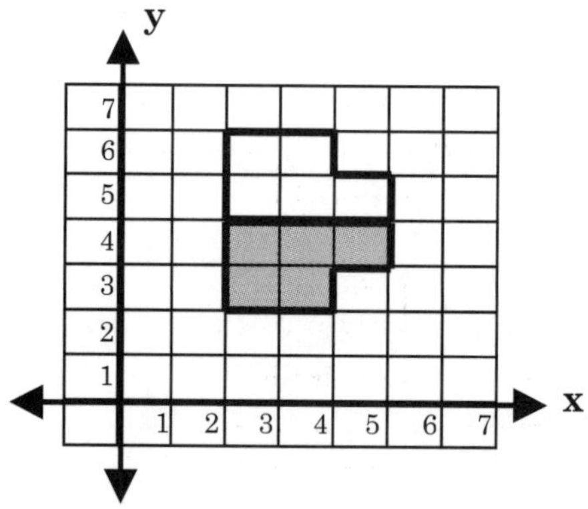

B 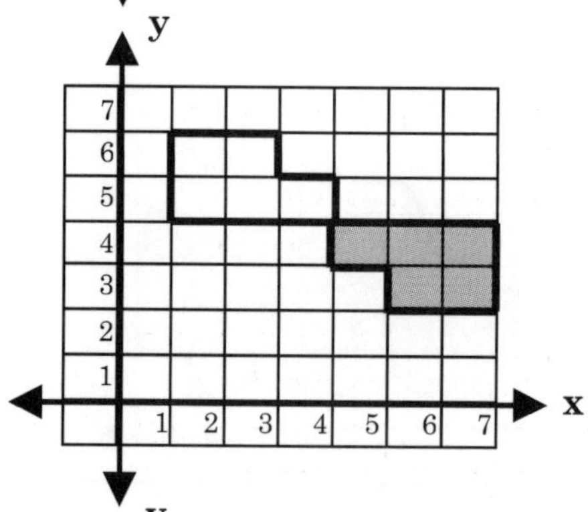

C 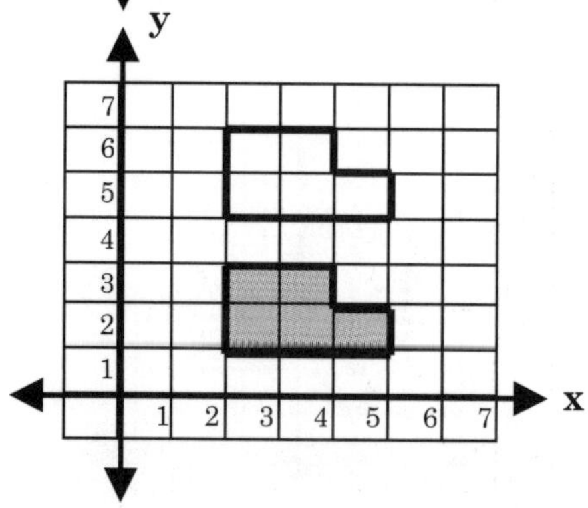

D 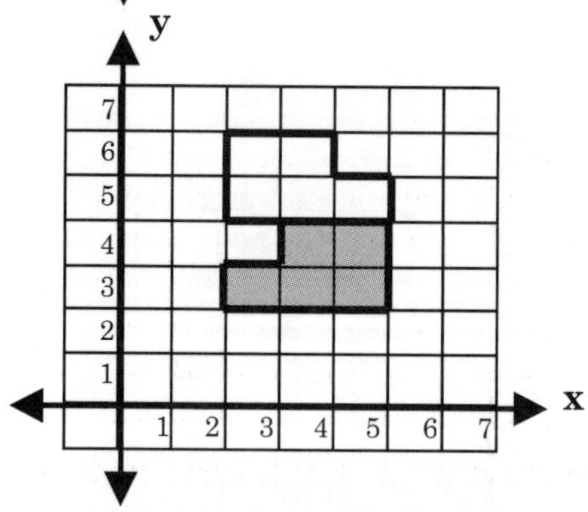

Geometry: Step Three C

The student is expected to sketch the results of translations, rotations, and reflections. (TAKS 3:5.8A)
The student is expected to describe the transformation that generates one figure from the other when given two congruent figures. (TAKS 3:5.8B)

1. In which diagram is the shaded figure a translation of the unshaded figure?

A

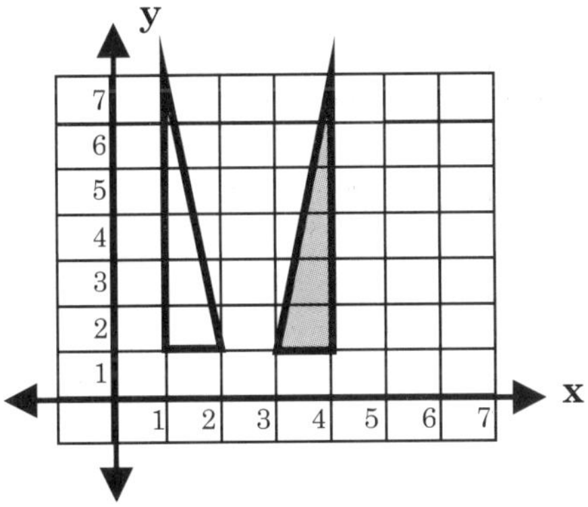

B

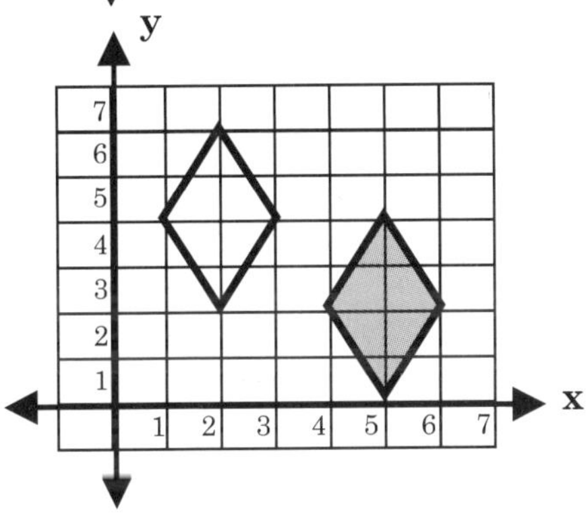

C

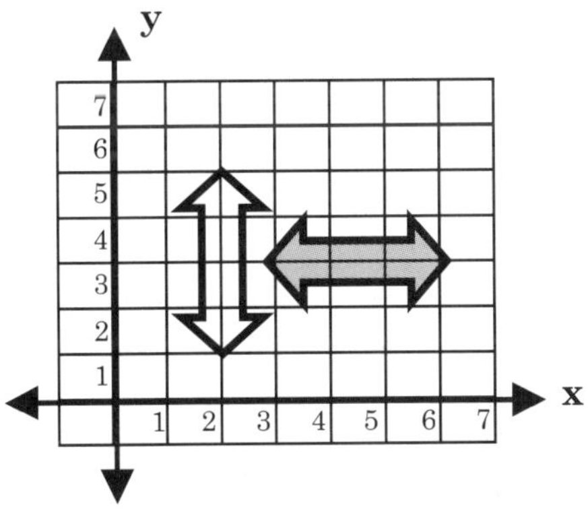

D

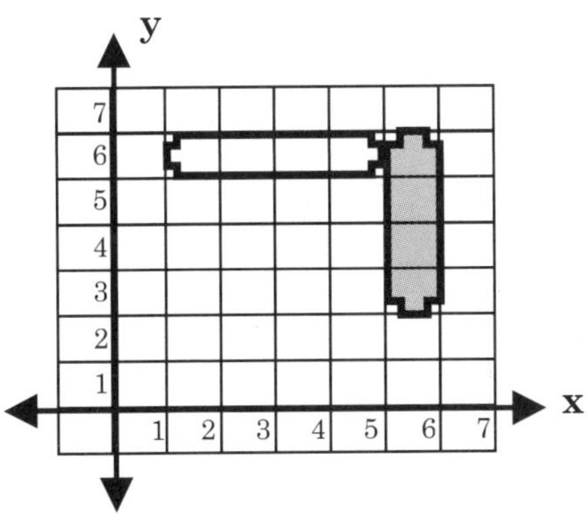

2. In which diagram is the shaded figure a reflection of the unshaded figure?

A

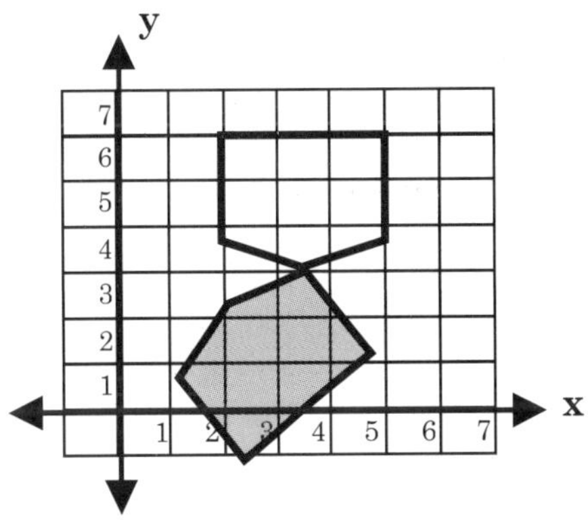

B

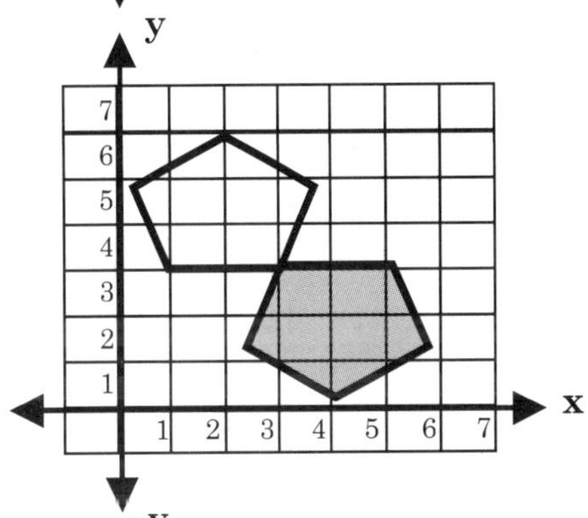

C

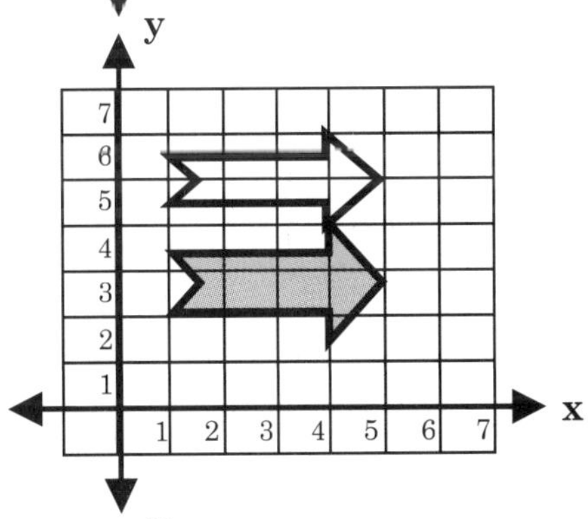

D

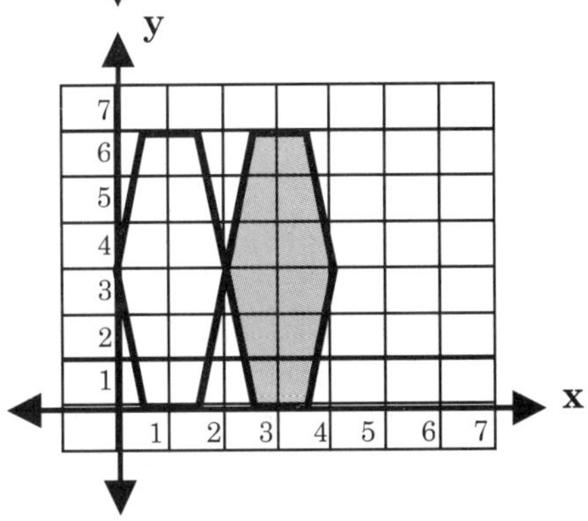

Geometry: Step Three D

The student is expected to sketch the results of translations, rotations, and reflections. (TAKS 3:5.8A)
The student is expected to describe the transformation that generates one figure from the other when given two congruent figures. (TAKS 3:5.8B)

1. Which transformation of the shaded figure is represented in the diagram?

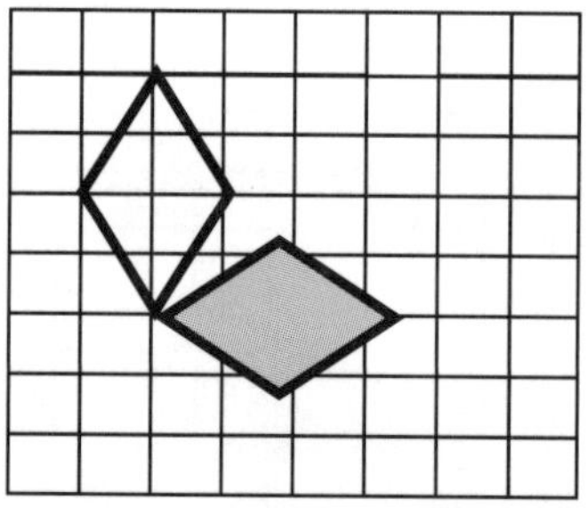

A Reflection
B Rotation
C Translation
D Not Here

2. Which transformation of the shaded figure is represented in the diagram?

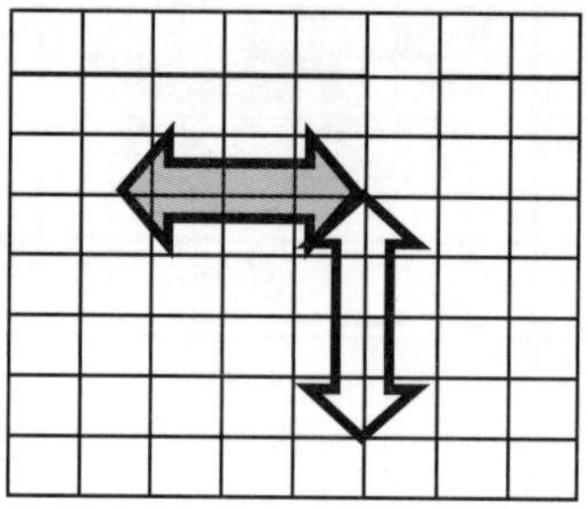

A Reflection
B Rotation
C Translation
D Not Here

3. Which transformation of the shaded figure is represented in the diagram?

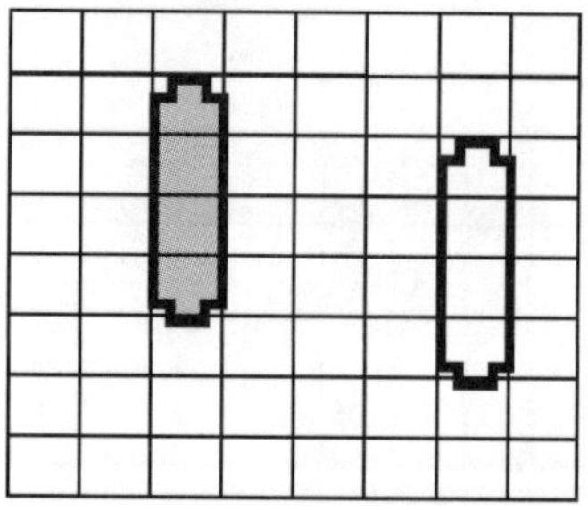

A Reflection
B Rotation
C Translation
D Not Here

4. Which transformation of the shaded figure is represented in the diagram?

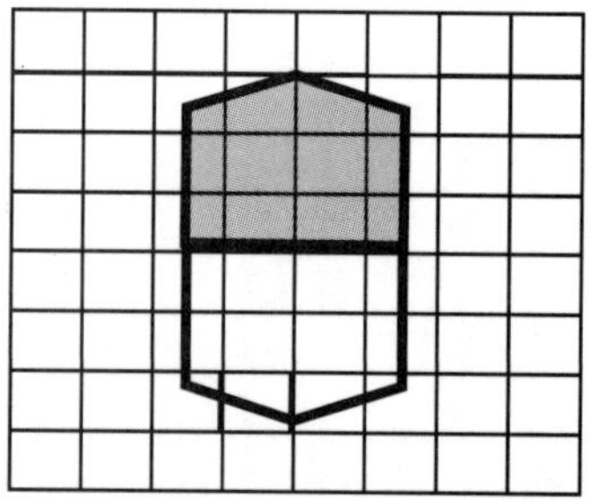

A Reflection
B Rotation
C Translation
D Not Here

5. Which transformation of the shaded figure is represented in the diagram?

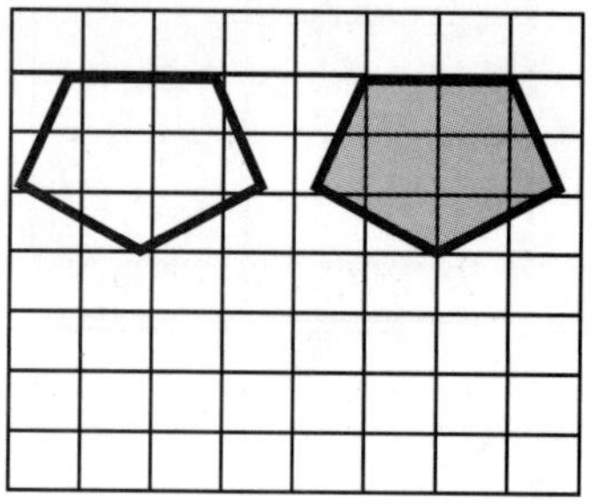

A Reflection
B Rotation
C Translation
D Not Here

6. Which transformation of the shaded figure is represented in the diagram?

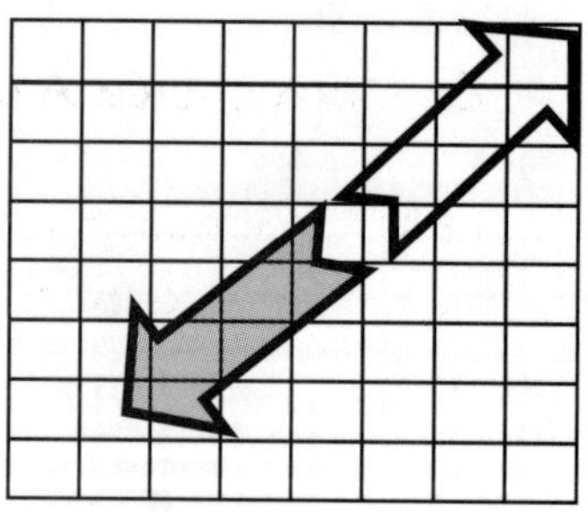

A Reflection
B Rotation
C Translation
D Not Here

Geometry: Sample for Analysis

The student is expected to locate and name points on a coordinate grid using ordered pairs of whole numbers. (TAKS 3:5.9A)

Which point best represents the ordered pair (1,4)?

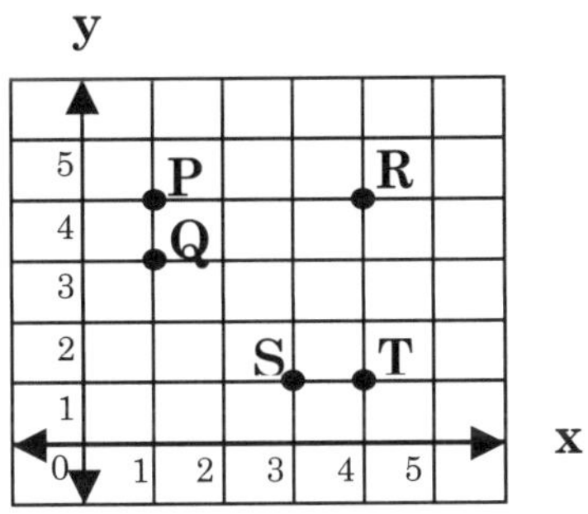

A P **B** Q **C** S **D** T

Strategy:

1. Look at the graph.
2. Notice that the x-axis and the y-axis are marked for you.
3. Find the line that is marked 1 on the x-axis.
4. Find the line that is marked 4 on the y-axis.
5. Look where these two lines meet or intersect. This point is (1,4).
6. (1,4) is marked with the letter P
7. Find P among the answer choices. It is choice **A**.
8. Mark choice **A** on your answer sheet.

Hint: Remember, the first number of an ordered pair is always found on the x-axis.

Geometry: Step Four A

The student is expected to locate and name points on a coordinate grid using ordered pairs of whole numbers. (TAKS 3:5.9A)

1. The graph shows a few of the streets in Harpersfield.

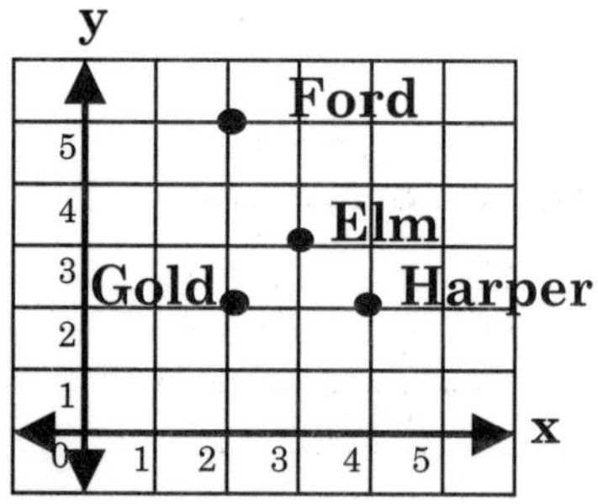

Which ordered pair best represents the point on the graph labeled "Elm Street"?

A (3, 3)
B (4, 3)
C (3, 4)
D (4, 4)

---

2. The graph shows some of the area stores in Palmer.

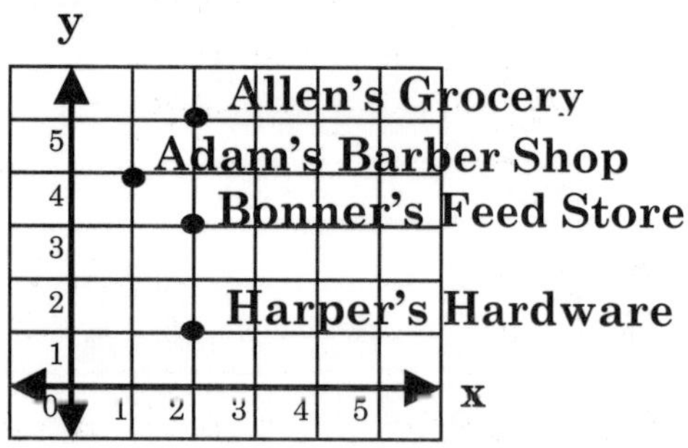

Which ordered pair best represents the point on the graph labeled "Harper's Hardware"?

A (2, 3)
B (1, 2)
C (2, 1)
D (2, 2)

3. The graph shows some of the playground equipment at the city park.

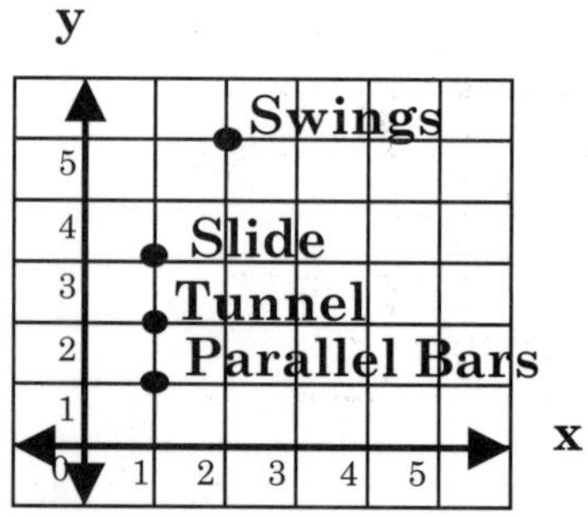

Which ordered pair best represents the point on the graph labeled "Slide"?

A (1, 1)
B (1, 2)
C (2, 1)
D (1, 3)

---

4. The graph shows T.M.'s pasture.

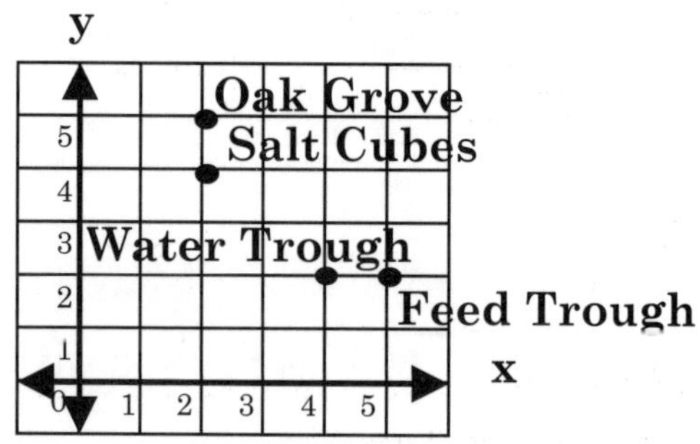

Which ordered pair best represents the point on the graph labeled "Feed Trough"?

A (5, 2)
B (4, 2)
C (2, 5)
D (5, 2)

Geometry: Step Four B

The student is expected to locate and name points on a coordinate grid using ordered pairs of whole numbers. (TAKS 3:5.9A)

1. Which pair of coordinates shows the location of point N?

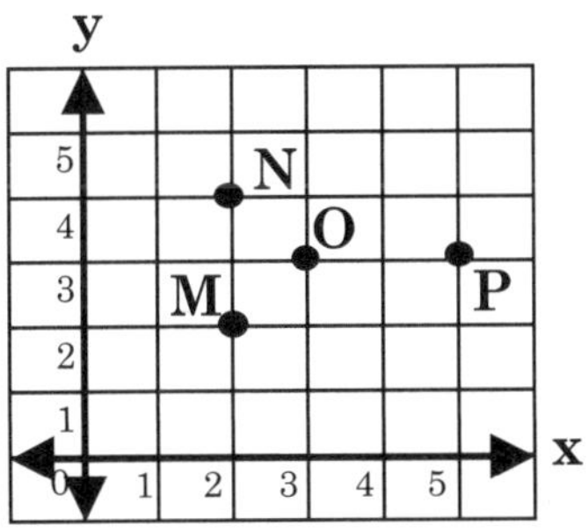

A (2, 2) C (2, 4)
B (3, 3) D (4, 4)

2. Which pair of coordinates shows the location of point F?

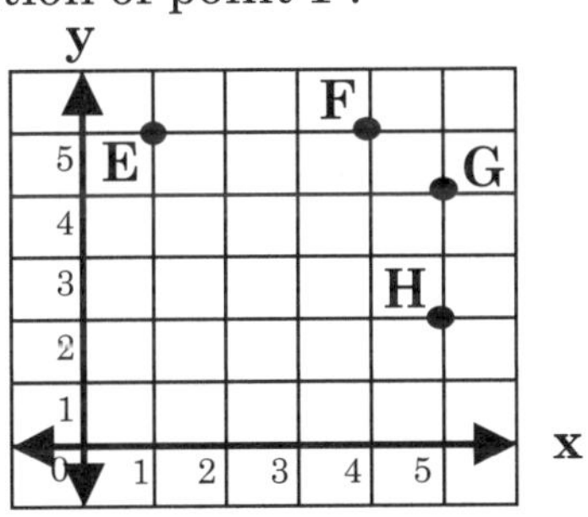

A (4, 5) C (1, 5)
B (5, 4) D (5, 1)

3. Which pair of coordinates names the location of point O?

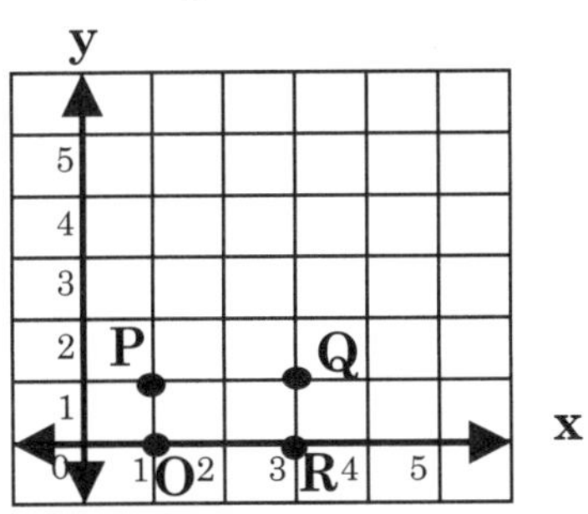

A (1, 0) C (0, 1)
B (1, 1) D (3, 1)

4. Which pair of coordinates shows the location of point L?

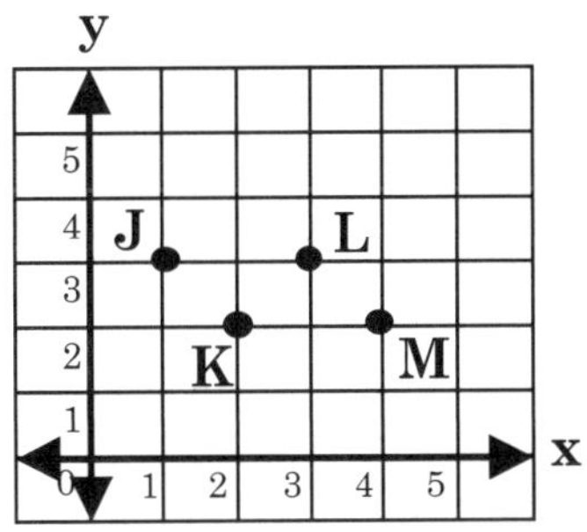

A (2, 4) C (4, 2)
B (3, 3) D (1, 3)

5. Which pair of coordinates shows the location of point I?

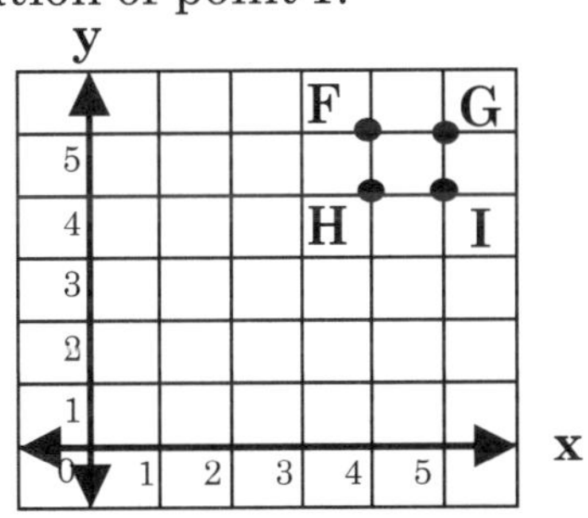

A (4, 5) C (5, 5)
B (5, 4) D (4, 4)

6. Which pair of coordinates names the location of point Q?

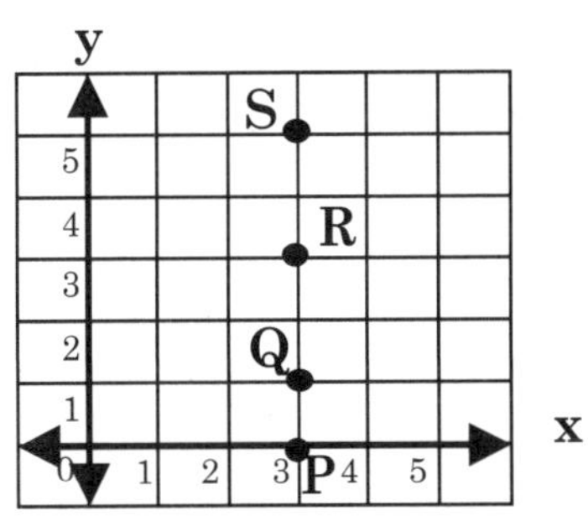

A (1, 3) C (3, 3)
B (1, 1) D (3, 1)

Geometry: Step Four C

The student is expected to use tables of related number pairs to make line graphs. (TAKS 5:5.13A)
The student is expected to graph a given set of data using an appropriate graphical representation such as picture or line. (TAKS 5:5.13C)

1. The chart shows the coordinates of 3 points.

Point	x	y
D	4	3
E	5	4
F	9	7

Which graph shows the line containing these points?

A
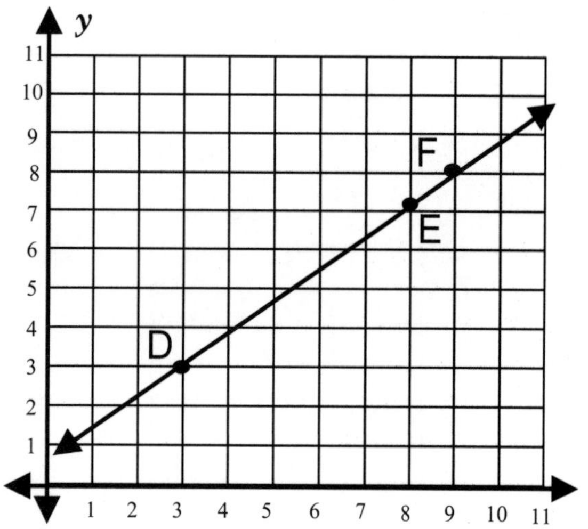

C
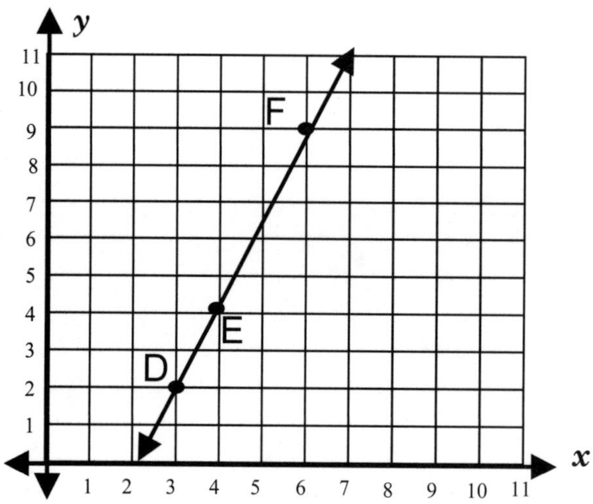

B
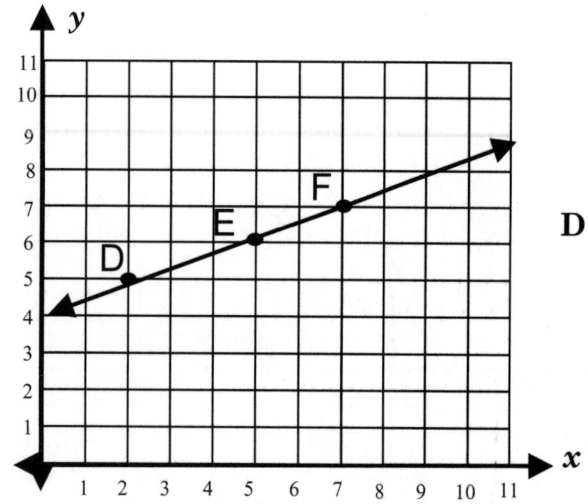

D
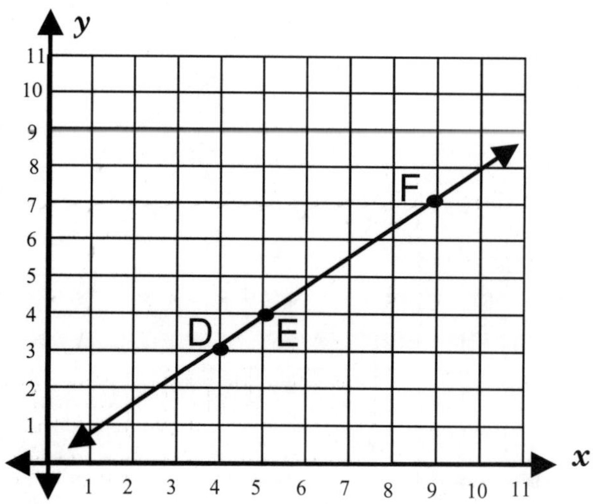

Geometry: Step Four D

The student is expected to use tables of related number pairs to make line graphs. (TAKS 5:5.13A)
The student is expected to graph a given set of data using an appropriate graphical representation such as picture or line. (TAKS 5:5.13C)

1. The chart shows the coordinates of 3 points.

Point	x	y
D	4	6
E	7	4
F	8	3

Which graph shows the line containing these points?

A

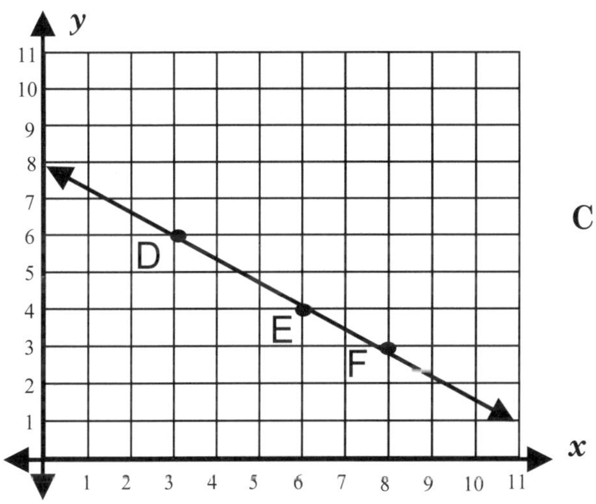

C

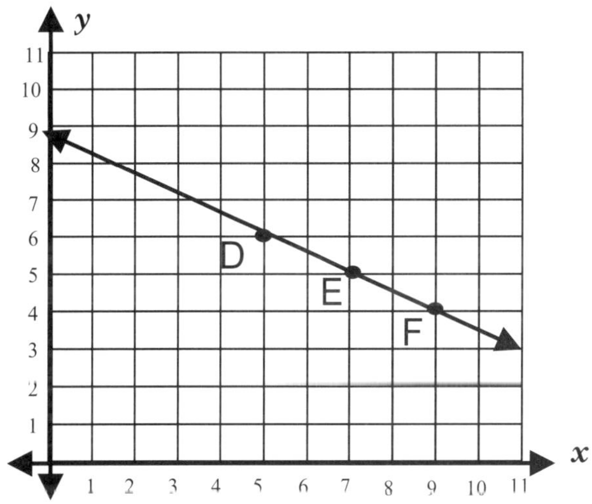

B

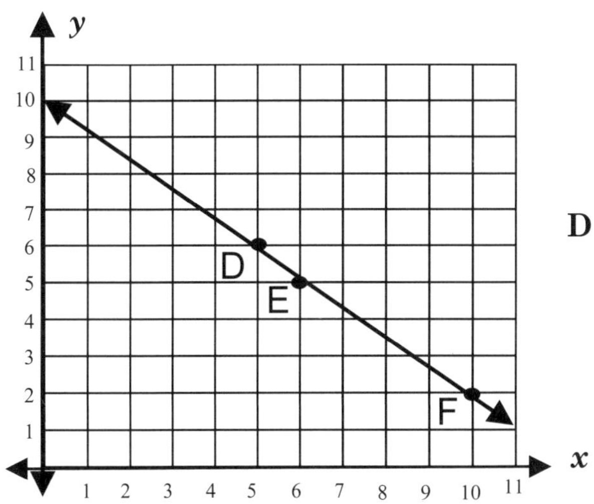

D

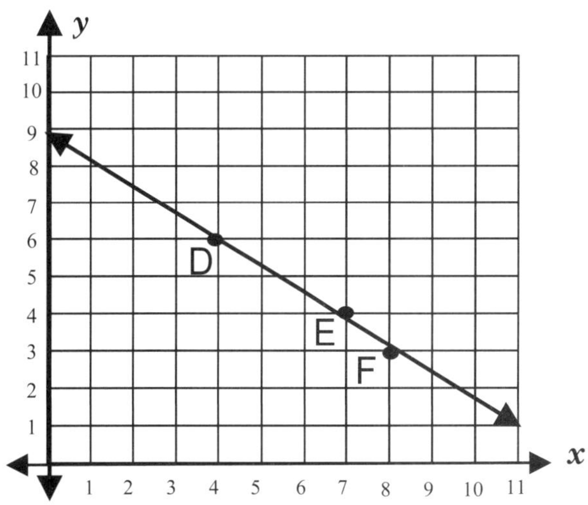

Geometry: Step Four E

The student is expected to use tables of related number pairs to make line graphs. (TAKS 5:5.13A)
The student is expected to graph a given set of data using an appropriate graphical representation such as picture or line. (TAKS 5:5.13C)

1. The line graph below shows 4 points.

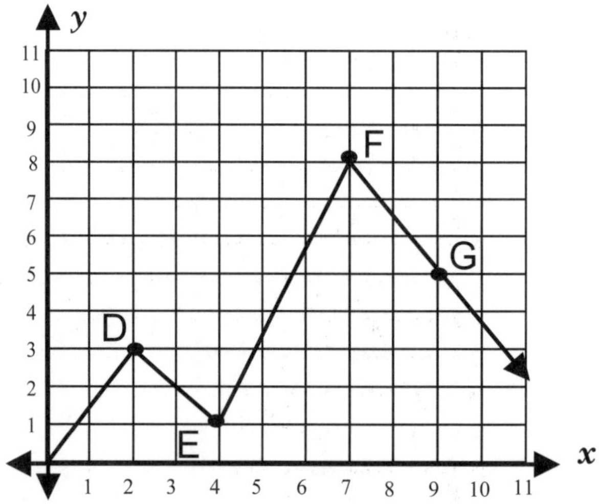

Which table shows the coordinates of the points on the line graph above?

A

Point	x	y
D	3	2
E	1	4
F	8	7
G	5	9

C

Point	x	y
D	2	3
E	4	1
F	7	8
G	5	9

B

Point	x	y
D	2	3
E	1	4
F	7	8
G	9	5

D

Point	x	y
D	2	3
E	4	1
F	7	8
G	9	5

Geometry: Step Four F

The student is expected to use tables of related number pairs to make line graphs. (TAKS 5:5.13A)
The student is expected to graph a given set of data using an appropriate graphical representation such as picture or line. (TAKS 5:5.13C)

1. The line graph below shows 4 points.

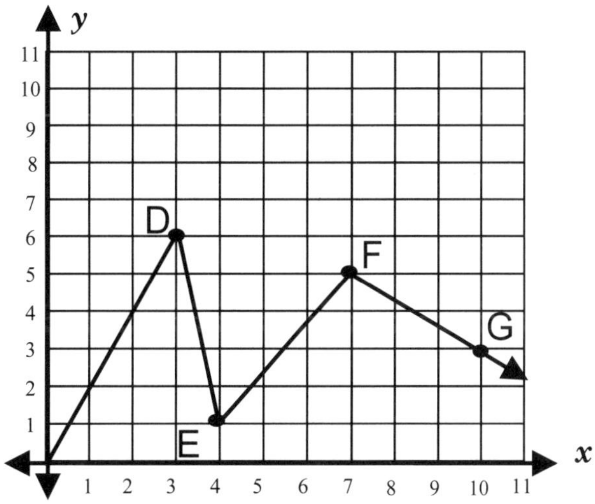

Which table shows the coordinates of the points on the line graph above?

A

Point	x	y
D	6	3
E	1	4
F	5	7
G	3	10

C

Point	x	y
D	3	6
E	4	1
F	7	5
G	10	3

B

Point	x	y
D	3	6
E	4	1
F	7	5
G	3	9

D

Point	x	y
D	3	6
E	4	1
F	8	7
G	10	3

Geometry: Assessment

TAKS Objectives: 3:5.7A, 3:5.7B, 3:5.8A, 3:5.8B, 3:5.9A, 5:5.13A, 5:5.13C

1. Which term could ***not*** be used to describe this figure?

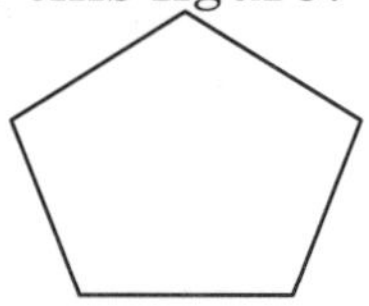

A regular polygon
B quadrilateral
C polygon
D pentagon

---

2. The figure below is a rectangular pyramid.

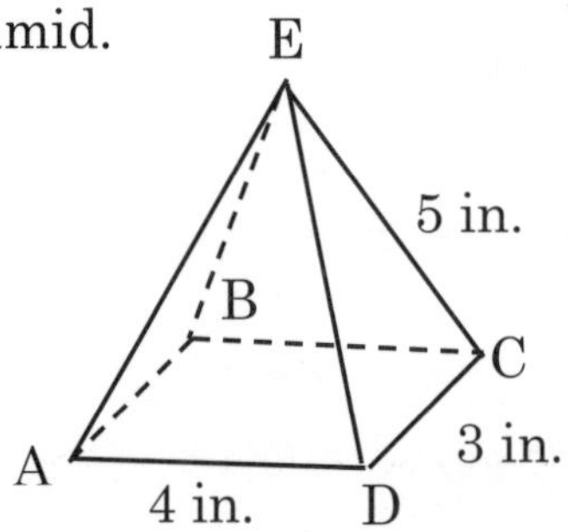

Which statement is true?

A Face ADE is congruent to ABCD.
B Face ABE is congruent to DCE.
C Face BCE is congruent to DCE.
D Face ADE is congruent to ABE.

---

3. Square **JKLM** is inscribed inside square **STUV**.

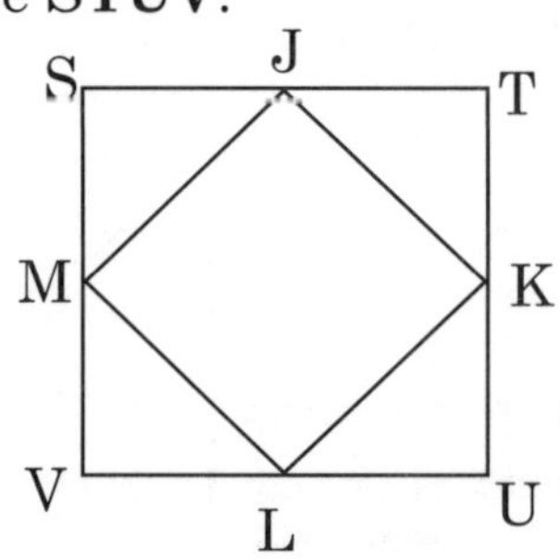

Which line segments are parallel?

A ML and JT
B MJ and LK
C SV and ST
D JT and MV

4. Which figures appear to be congruent?

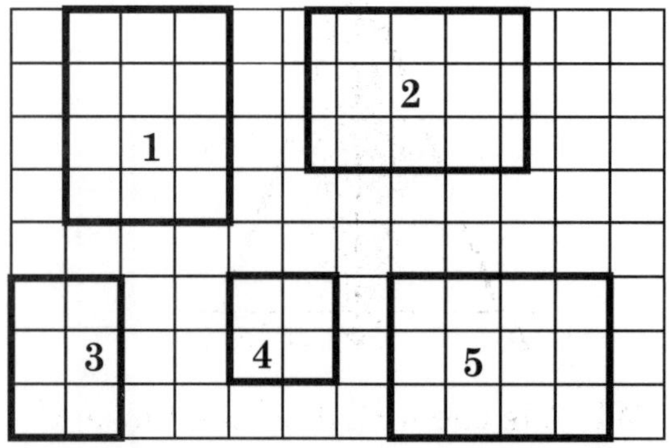

A 3 and 5
B 4 and 5
C 1,2, and 5
D 3 and 4

---

5. If the 2 polygons below are congruent, then—

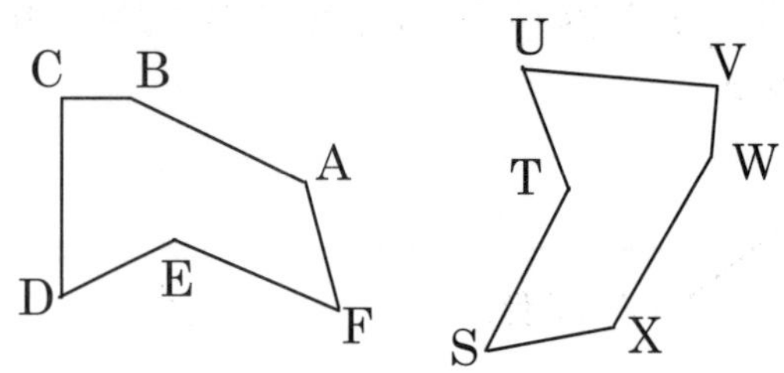

A BC is congruent to UT
B AF is congruent to VU
C UT is congruent to DE
D ST is congruent to ED

---

6. **ABCD** is a square.

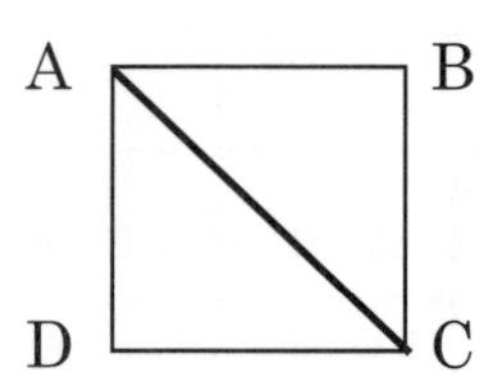

Which statement is true?

A AC = AB
B BC = AD
C AD < DC
D AB > BC

7. A ribbon tied from each side of a bottle and taped to the surface of the table. A line of symmetry can be drawn through the bottle.

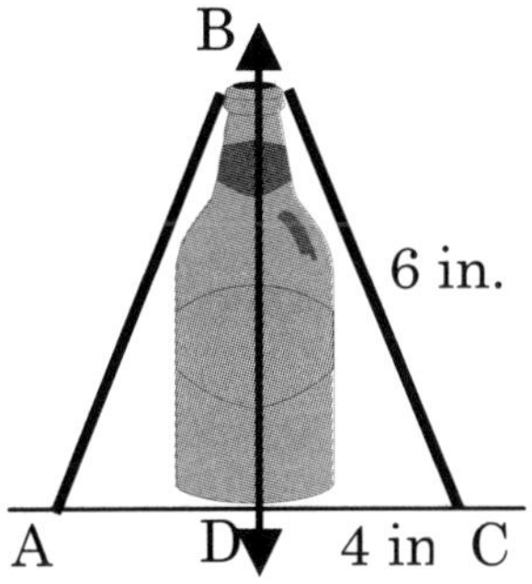

What is the length of the piece of Ribbon AB?

A 4 in.
B 6 in.
C 8 in.
D 10 in.

---

8. Triangle **ABC** is congruent to triangle **MNO**.

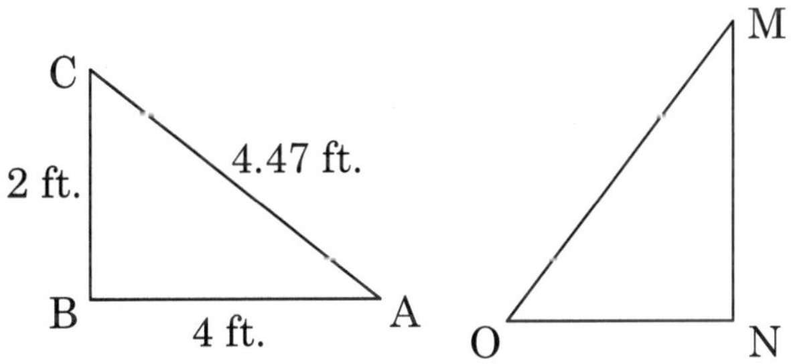

What is the length of segment OM?

A 2 ft
B 4 ft
C 4.47 ft
D 6 ft

9. Which of the following shows an example of a reflection?

A

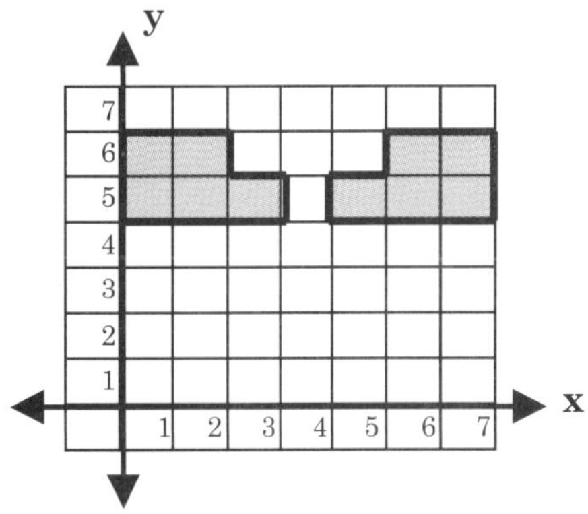

B

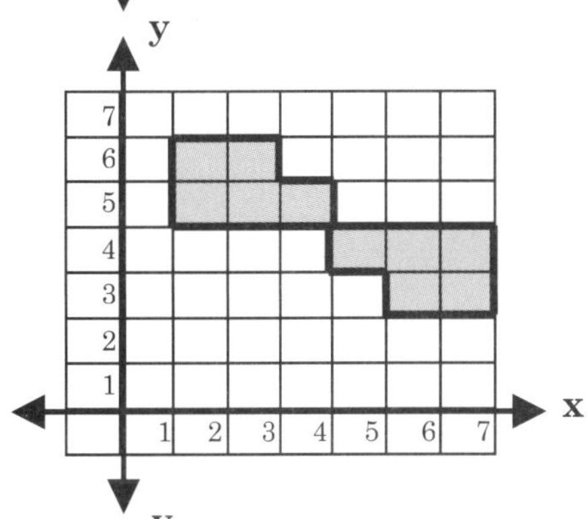

C

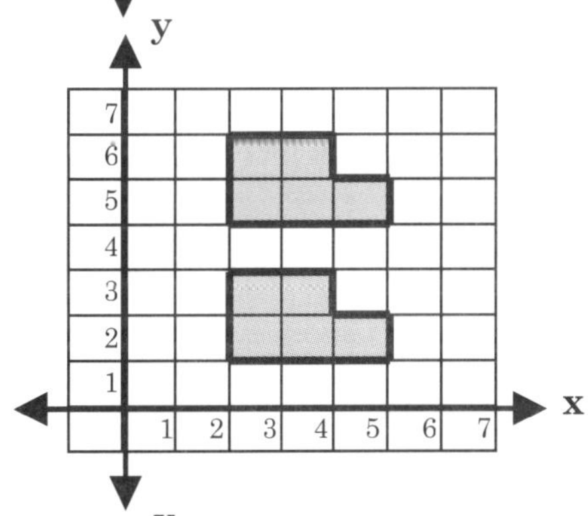

D

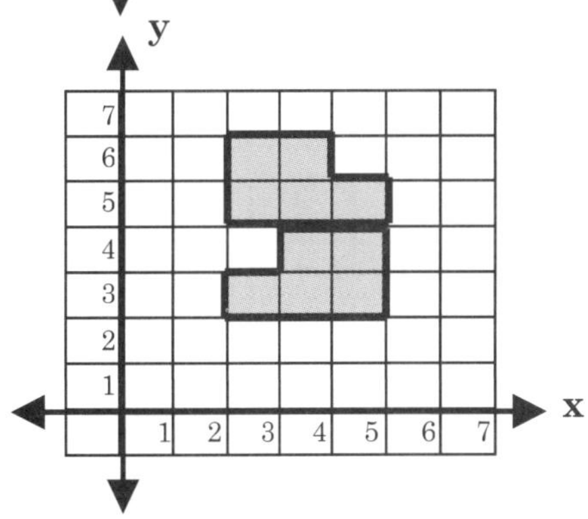

10. The line graph below shows 4 points.

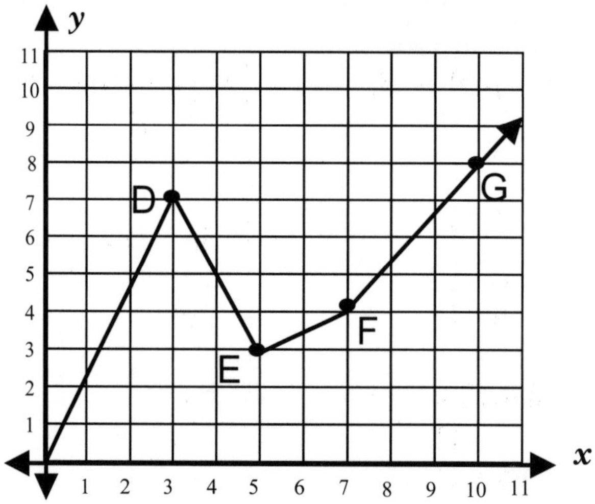

Which table shows the coordinates of the points on the line graph above?

A

Point	x	y
D	3	7
E	3	5
F	4	7
G	10	8

C

Point	x	y
D	3	7
E	5	3
F	7	4
G	10	8

B

Point	x	y
D	7	3
E	5	3
F	7	4
G	10	8

D

Point	x	y
D	3	3
E	5	2
F	7	5
G	9	8

Geometry: Answer Key

Step One A
1. B
2. D
3. C
4. C
5. A
6. B
7. D
8. D
9. D

Step One B
1. D
2. B
3. C
4. A
5. B
6. C
7. B

Step One C
1. D
2. A
3. A
4. D
5. D
6. B

Step Two A
1. C
2. C
3. B
4. C
5. B
6. C

Step Two B
1. D
2. C
3. B
4. D
5. C
6. B

Step Two C
1. C
2. B
3. A
4. C
5. B
6. B

Step Two D
1. B
2. C
3. C
4. D
5. C
6. D

Step Three A
1. A
2. A

Step Three B
1. A
2. B

Step Three C
1. B
2. D

Step Three D
1. B
2. B
3. C
4. A
5. C
6. A

Step Four A
1. A
2. C
3. D
4. D

Step Four B
1. C
2. A
3. A
4. B
5. B
6. D

Step Four C
1. D

Step Four D
1. D

Step Four E
1. D

Step Four F
1. C

Assessment
1. B
2. B
3. B
4. C
5. C
6. B
7. B
8. C
9. A
10. C

Measurement

The student is expected to measure to solve problems involving length (including perimeter), weight, capacity, time, temperature, and area. **(TEKS 5.11A) (TAKS 4)** *Measurement units or their abbreviations will be used with numerical answers as appropriate. Students will find perimeter or area using the information in verbal or pictorial representations. Some measurements may be missing but can be identified using the attributes of the geometric figures. Problems involving weight, capacity, or time may require conversion of units and may have pictorial representations to aid the student in finding a solution. The student should be able to measure with the ruler on the Mathematics Chart only if the item specifically instructs them to use the ruler. (Note: The formula chart has the area of a square, rectangle and triangle.)*

The student is expected to describe numerical relationships between units of measure within the same measurement system, such as an inch is one-twelfth of a foot. **(TEKS 5.11B) (TAKS 4)** *Students will match a unit of measure with a rational representation of its relationship to another unit. The relationship may be written as a fraction, mixed number, or whole number. Students will compare the relative sizes of two different measures within the same system (e.g., less than, greater than, equal to) or choose the measurement that fits a given relationship (e.g., 90 minutes is ½ of 3 hours). The student should be able to compare two different units of measure within the same system, either customary or metric, and choose the unit of measure that fits a given relationship (for example, 18 inches can be expressed as 1½ feet or ½ yard).*

The student is expected to measure volume using models of cubic units. **(TEKS 5.10A) (TAKS 4)**

Suggested Sequence
Simple to Complex

Step One .... Customary Measurement (TAKS 4:5.11A, 4:5.11B)
Step Two .... Metric Measurement (TAKS 4:5.11A)
Step Three .... Mixed Application of Customary and Metric Measurement (TAKS 4:5.11A)
Step Four .... Perimeter (TAKS 4:5.11A)
Step Five .... Area of a Square and Rectangle (TAKS 4:5.11A)
Step Six.................. Area of a Triangle (TAKS 4:5.11A)
Step Seven............. Measuring with a Ruler (TAKS 4:5.11A)
Step Eight.............. Area and Perimeter Problems (TAKS 4:5.11A)
Step Nine .... Volume (TAKS 4:5.10A)
Assessment

Vocabulary:

- 🕮 Kilometers
- 🕮 Meter
- 🕮 Centimeter
- 🕮 Millimeter
- 🕮 Mile
- 🕮 Yard
- 🕮 Foot
- 🕮 Inch
- 🕮 Liter
- 🕮 Milliliter
- 🕮 Gallon
- 🕮 Quart
- 🕮 Ounce
- 🕮 Pint
- 🕮 Cup
- 🕮 Ton
- 🕮 Pound
- 🕮 Kilogram
- 🕮 Gram
- 🕮 Milligram
- 🕮 Year
- 🕮 Month
- 🕮 Week
- 🕮 Day
- 🕮 Hour
- 🕮 Minute
- 🕮 Second
- 🕮 Weight
- 🕮 Height
- 🕮 Perimeter
- 🕮 Area
- 🕮 Volume
- 🕮 Polygon
- 🕮 Square Unit

Grade 5 Mathematics Chart

Inch Ruler

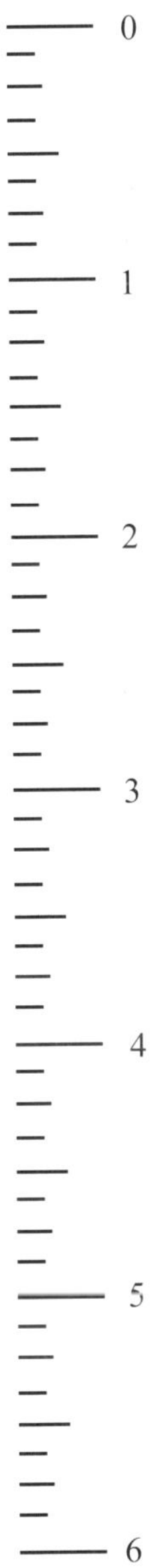

Centimeter Ruler

LENGTH

Metric	Customary
1 kilometer = 1000 meters	1 mile = 1760 yards
1 meter = 100 centimeters	1 mile = 5280 feet
1 centimeter = 10 millimeters	1 yard = 3 feet
	1 foot = 12 inches

CAPACITY AND VOLUME

Metric	Customary	
1 liter = 1000 milliliters	1 gallon = 4 quarts	1 pint = 2 cups
	1 gallon = 128 ounces	1 cup = 8 ounce
	1 quart = 2 pints	

MASS AND WEIGHT

Metric	Customary
1 kilogram = 1000 grams	1 ton = 2000 pounds
1 gram = 1000 milligrams	1 pound = 16 ounces

TIME

1 year = 365 days	1 day = 24 hours
1 year = 12 months	1 hour = 60 minutes
1 year = 52 weeks	1 minute = 60 seconds
1 week = 7 days	

Perimeter

square	$P = 4s$
rectangle	$P = 2l + 2w$ or $P = 2(l + w)$

Area

square	$A = s^2$
rectangle	$A = lw$ or $A = bh$
triangle	$A = \frac{1}{2}bh$ or $A = \frac{bh}{2}$

Measurement Information Sheet

If there are 3 feet in a yard, then a foot is one-third of a yard.
(1 feet = $\frac{1}{3}$ of a yard)

If there are 12 inches in a foot, then an inch is one-twelfth of a foot.
(1 inch = $\frac{1}{12}$ of a foot)

If there are 4 quarts in a gallon, then a quart is one-fourth of a gallon.
(1 quart = $\frac{1}{4}$ of a gallon)

If there are 2 pints in a quart, then a pint is one-half of a quart.
(1 pint = $\frac{1}{2}$ of a quart)

If there are 2 cups in a pint, then a cup is one-half of a pint.
(1 cup = $\frac{1}{2}$ of a pint)

If there are 8 ounces in a cup, then an ounce is one-eighth of a cup.
(1 ounce = $\frac{1}{8}$ of a cup)

If there are 16 ounces in a pound, then an ounce is one-sixteenth of a pound. (1 ounce = $\frac{1}{16}$ of a pound)

If there are 12 months in a year, then a month is one-twelfth of a year.
(1 month = $\frac{1}{12}$ of a year)

If there are 7 days in a week, then a day is one-seventh of a week.
(1 day = $\frac{1}{7}$ of a week)

If there are 24 hours in a day, then an hour is one-twenty fourth of a day. (1 hour = $\frac{1}{24}$ of a day)

If there are 60 minutes in an hour, then a minute is one-sixtieth of an hour. (1 minute = $\frac{1}{60}$ of an hour) (1 second = $\frac{1}{60}$ of an minute)

Measurement: Step One A

The student is expected to describe numerical relationships between units of measure within the same measurement system such as an inch is one-twelfth of a foot. (TAKS 4:5.11B)

1. John needed 28 inches of rope. This could also be written as _______

   A $2\frac{1}{3}$ feet
   C $\frac{28}{100}$ feet
   B $2\frac{8}{10}$ feet
   D 2.8 feet

2. It took 90 minutes for Ken's parents to drive him to Grandpa's house. This could also be written as _______

   A 9 hours
   C $1\frac{1}{2}$ hours
   B $9\frac{1}{10}$ hours
   D $1\frac{1}{3}$ hours

3. Sean drank 5 pints of water. This could also be written as _______

   A $1\frac{1}{4}$ gallons
   C $2\frac{1}{2}$ quarts
   B $1\frac{1}{2}$ quarts
   D $2\frac{1}{4}$ quarts

4. Maria played with her dolls for 45 minutes. This could also be written as _______

   A $\frac{45}{100}$ hours
   C $\frac{1}{3}$ hour
   B $\frac{3}{4}$ hour
   D $\frac{1}{4}$ hour

5. Bryan rode his bicycle around the track. It is measured in yards. He rode 880 yards. This could also be written as _______

   A 1 mile
   C $\frac{1}{2}$ mile
   B $\frac{3}{4}$ mile
   D $\frac{1}{3}$ mile

6. Kara needs $\frac{3}{4}$ of a foot of ribbon for a project. This could also be written as _______

   A 4 inches
   C 7 inches
   B 6 inches
   D 9 inches

7. Dad's riding lawn mower weighs 500 pounds. This could also be written as _______

   A 5 tons
   C $\frac{1}{4}$ ton
   B $\frac{1}{2}$ ton
   D $\frac{1}{5}$ ton

8. Lee's parents left the sprinklers on while they were gone on a trip. The lawn was flooded when they returned. It had been on for 84 hours. This could also be written as _______

   A $8\frac{1}{4}$ days
   C 3 days
   B $3\frac{1}{2}$ days
   D $2\frac{1}{2}$ days

9. The recipe calls for $1\frac{1}{2}$ cups of water. This could also be written as _______

   A 4 ounces
   C 10 ounces
   B 8 ounces
   D 12 ounces

10. The roast weighed $3\frac{1}{4}$ pounds. This could also be written as _______

    A 52 ounces
    C 26 ounces
    B 34 ounces
    D 12 ounces

Measurement: Step One B

The student is expected to measure to solve problems involving length (including perimeter), weight, capacity, time, temperature, and area. (TAKS 6:5.11A)

1. The distance from Kathleen's house to the road is 6,483 feet. How many yards is this?

   A 19,449 yd
   B 6,483 yd
   C 2,161 yd
   D 1,081 yd

---

2. Matthew participated in a rocking chair marathon. He rocked for 23 hours and 17 minutes. How many minutes did he rock?

   A 2,317 min
   B 1,397 min
   C 1,380 min
   D 293 min

---

3. Rachel's dog weighs 32 pounds. How many ounces does the dog weigh?

   A 6 oz
   B 384 oz
   C 512 oz
   D 518 oz

---

4. The puppy drank 1 gallon and 2 quarts of water. How many quarts of water did he drink?

   A 10 qt
   B 8 qt
   C 6 qt
   D 4 qt

---

5. Rachel had been asking her daddy for a puppy for exactly 1 year and 39 weeks. About how many weeks is this?

   A 39 wk
   B 52 wk
   C 81 wk
   D 91 wk

6. The puppy's leash is 7 feet 9 inches long. How many inches long is the leash?

   A 79 in.
   B 84 in.
   C 93 in.
   D 97 in.

---

7. The puppy's bathtub holds 63 gallons of water. How many ounces is this?

   A 11,340 oz
   B 8,082 oz
   C 8,064 oz
   D 6,318 oz

---

8. When measured from nose to tail, Rachel's puppy is 2 inches more than 3 feet long. How many inches is this?

   A 23 in.
   B 36 in.
   C 38 in.
   D 72 in.

---

9. Rachel's puppy grew very fast. On his first birthday, the puppy weighed 24 pounds. How many ounces is this?

   A 1.5 oz
   B 16 oz
   C 284 oz
   D 384 oz

---

10. Rachel and the puppy played outside for 2 hours and 14 minutes. How many minutes did they play?

    A 106 min
    B 120 min
    C 134 min
    D 214 min

Measurement: Sample for Analysis

The student is expected to measure to solve problems involving length (including perimeter), weight, capacity, time, temperature, and area. (TAKS 6:5.11A)

Customary Measurement Problems

Nathan's father is 3 inches less than 6 feet tall. How many inches is this?

A 57 in. **B** 69 in. **C** 72 in. **D** 75 in.

Strategy:

1. Look at the important numbers in the problem and underline them.
   <u>3 inches less than 6 feet</u>

2. How many inches are in 6 feet?
   1 foot = 12 inches
   6 feet = (6) (12 inches)
   72 inches

3. Don't stop now! Remember, Nathan's dad is 3 inches <u>less than</u> 6 feet tall.
   72 inches — 3 inches = 69 inches

4. Check for the reasonableness of your answer. An adult man could be 69 inches tall.

5. Find 69 inches in the answer choice.

6. Mark answer choice B on your answer sheet.

Hint: Remember to <u>read carefully</u>. Look for key words such as less, more, and units of measure.

Measurement: Step One C

The student is expected to measure to solve problems involving length (including perimeter), weight, capacity, time, temperature, and area. (TAKS 6:5.11A) (TAKS 4:5.11B)

1. Yvonne's dining room table is 6 inches longer than 4 feet. How many inches is this?

   A 42 in. **C** 54 in.
   B 48 in. **D** 60 in.

2. Yvonne is making punch for a party. Her recipe calls for 12 quarts of water. How many pints are equivalent to 12 quarts?

   A 1.2 pt **C** 24 pt
   B 6 pt **D** 48 pt

3. Yvonne's kitchen counter is 6 inches less than 3 feet tall. How many inches is this?

   A 24 in. **C** 36 in.
   B 30 in. **D** 42 in.

4. The party lasted for 10 minutes short of 3 hours. How many minutes is this?

   A 170 min **C** 120 min
   B 160 min **D** 105 min

5. Maria had 10 inches less than the yard of ribbon she needed to make a bow. How many inches is this?

   A 2 inches **C** 30 inches
   B 26 inches **D** 46 inches

6. Timmy was 3 minutes late for his 2:15 doctors appointment. What time did he arrive?

   A 3:15 **C** 2:13
   B 2:18 **D** 2:12

7. Yvonne and her friends planned another party to take place in 3 weeks and 4 days. How many days will it be until their next party?

   A 21 days **C** 28 days
   B 25 days **D** 32 days

8. On the way home, Yvonne saw a 2 ton pickup truck on the side of the road. How many pounds are equivalent to 2 tons?

   A 2,000 lb **C** 4,000 lb
   B 2,500 lb **D** 4,500 lb

9. When she arrived home, Yvonne saw that Cheryl had left her a 25 pound, 12 ounce bag of sugar. How many ounces of sugar was this?

   A 400 oz **C** 2,5000 oz
   B 412 oz **D** 1,280 oz

10. Yvonne decided to use the sugar to make maple syrup. She made 10 gallons of syrup. How many ounces are equivalent to 10 gallons?

    A 40 oz **C** 128 oz
    B 80 oz **D** 1,280 oz

11. Alberto ran out of gas $\frac{3}{4}$ of a mile from the gas station. How far is this?

    A 1,320 yards **C** 1,760 yards
    B 1,730 yards **D** 3,960 yards

Measurement: Step One D

The student is expected to describe numerical relationships between units of measure within the same measurement system such as an inch is one-twelfth of a foot. (TAKS 4:5.11B)

1. Mrs. Harper made 1 gallon of ice cream. She used 3 quarts of ice cream as a dessert for supper. What is the relationship between the ice cream served at supper and the ice cream she made?

A She used $\frac{3}{4}$ of the ice cream she made.

B She used $\frac{1}{3}$ of the ice cream she made.

C She used $\frac{2}{3}$ of the ice cream she made.

D She used $\frac{1}{2}$ of the ice cream she made.

---

2. Kevin bought 1 yard of rope. He used 18 inches of the rope to tie up his dog. What is the relationship between the rope he used and the rope he bought?

A He used $\frac{1}{18}$ of the rope he bought.

B He used $\frac{1}{36}$ of the rope he bought.

C He used $\frac{3}{4}$ of the rope he bought.

D He used $\frac{1}{2}$ of the rope he bought.

---

3. Carmen is making cookies. She needs 1 cup of cooking oil. She only has 3 ounces. What is the relationship between the cooking oil she has and the cooking oil she needs?

A She has $\frac{2}{3}$ of the oil she needs.

B She has $\frac{3}{4}$ of the oil she needs.

C She has $\frac{3}{8}$ of the oil she needs.

D She has $\frac{1}{3}$ of the oil she needs.

4. Rene is making a scarf. She bought a yard of fabric, but she only needs 2 feet of the fabric for the scarf. What is the relationship between what she needs for the scarf and what she bought?

A She used $\frac{1}{3}$ of the fabric she bought.

B She used $\frac{3}{4}$ of the fabric she bought.

C She used $\frac{1}{2}$ of the fabric she bought.

D She used $\frac{2}{3}$ of the fabric she bought.

---

5. Patty has to practice 1 hour a day on the piano. She has 15 minutes more until her hour is up. What is the relationship between how much longer she has to practice and how long she must practice?

A She has $\frac{1}{4}$ of an hour of practice to go.

B She has $\frac{3}{4}$ of an hour of practice to go.

C She has $\frac{1}{5}$ of an hour of practice to go.

D She has $\frac{9}{15}$ of an hour of practice to go.

---

6. Elizabeth's mom bought a gallon of punch. Elizabeth took a quart to school to share with her friends. What is the relationship between how much is left in the gallon container and what was bought?

A She has $\frac{1}{4}$ of the punch left.

B She has $\frac{1}{2}$ of the punch left.

C She has $\frac{3}{8}$ of the punch left.

D She has $\frac{3}{4}$ of the punch left.

Measurement: Step One E

The student is expected to measure to solve problems involving length (including perimeter), weight, capacity, time, temperature, and area. (TAKS 4:5.11A)

1. Lynn bought 4 yards of fabric. She used 8 feet 6 inches to make curtains. How much fabric did she have left?

   A 4 ft 4 in.   C 3 ft 6 in.
   B 4 ft 6 in.   D 2 yd 6 in.

2. The Women's Guild recently sponsored a community coffee. They prepared 19 gallons of coffee. There were 3 quarts 1 pint left. How much coffee did they drink?

   A 73 ½ qt   C 16 ½ qt
   B 72 ½ qt   D 15 ½ qt

3. Quinn is exactly 2 years old. His friend is 6 months younger than Quinn. How old is his friend?

   A 8 mo   C 14 mo
   B 10 mo   D 18 mo

4. Tom made 5 pounds of fudge. He ate 2 pounds and 8 ounces How much fudge was left?

   A 3 ½ lb   C 1 ½ lb
   B 2 ½ lb   D ½ lb

5. Kim and her sister visited their grandparents during the summer. Kim spent 3 weeks and 4 days with her grandparents. Her sister had a doctors appointment and had to leave early. She spent 6 days less than Kim. How long was her sister at her grandparents?

   A 2 weeks 5 days   C 3 weeks 5 days
   B 2 weeks 8 days   D 4 weeks 3 days

6. Shelley practiced on her piano for 30 minutes a day for 2 weeks. How many hours did Shelley practice the piano during the last 2 weeks?

   A 6 h   C 14 h
   B 7 h   D 60 h

7. Heather and Brandon are going to the movies. It starts at 7:15 P.M. and it lasts 150 minutes. What time will they get out of the movies?

   A 8:15 P.M.   C 9:45 P.M.
   B 9:15 P.M.   D 10:15 P.M.

8. Melanie is mixing paint. The instructions call for 7 quarts of paint. She bought 2 gallons of paint. How much will she have left?

   A 1 qt   C 5 qt
   B 2 qt   D 9 qt

9. Cassie is making ice cream. She wants to make 3 gallons of ice cream for a party. Her freezer makes 6 quarts. How many freezers will she have to make for the party?

   A 2   C 4
   B 3   D 5

Measurement: Step One F

The student is expected to measure to solve problems involving length (including perimeter), weight, capacity, time, temperature, and area. (TAKS 4:5.11A)

1. Tammie worked at the hospital as a volunteer from 9:45 to 2:30. How many service hours did she work?

   A 5 ¾ hours
   B 4 ¾ hours
   C 4 ½ hours
   D 3 ¾ hours

2. Tomorrow Tammie will work from 1:30 to 6:15. How many service hours will she work?

   A 4 ½ hours
   B 6 ¾ hours
   C 5 ¾ hours
   D 4 ¾ hours

3. Ricky must practice his violin 5 hours a week. He has already practiced 2 hours and 45 minutes. How much longer does he need to practice?

   A 3 hrs 15 min
   B 2 hrs 45 min
   C 2 hrs 35 min
   D 2 hrs 15 min

4. Malcom usually works from 10:00 to 5:00 everyday. Today he had to leave for 2 hours and 30 minutes for a doctors appointment. How long did he work?

   A 4 ½ hours
   B 5 hours
   C 2 ½ hours
   D 7 ½ hours

5. Carmen woke up and looked at the thermometer outside her window. It read 45°F. The weatherman said it would be freezing by noon. How much will the temperature drop by noon?

   A 12°F
   B 13°F
   C 15°F
   D 32°F

6. Summer had finally arrived. The morning temperature was 75°F. At noon it was 95°F and by 3:00 it was 102°F. How much more did the temperature increase in the morning than the afternoon?

   A 7°F
   B 13°F
   C 20°F
   D 27°F

7. The thermometer must read 45°F before the class can play outside for recess. At 9:00 it was 37°F. How much will it have to increase before they can go out to play?

   A 8°F
   B 12°F
   C 18°F
   D 82°F

8. Today they said the temperature would reach 100°F for the first time in the year 2003. By 8:00 AM it was 76°F. It reached 100°F at 3:00 PM. It went back down to 76°F at 10:00 PM. How long did it take the temperature to go from 76°F back down to 76°F?

   A 2 hours
   B 12 hours
   C 14 hours
   D 16 hours

Measurement: Sample for Analysis

The student is expected to measure to solve problems involving length (including perimeter), weight, capacity, time, temperature, and area. (TAKS 4:5.11A)

Metric Measurement Problems

Rachel's science textbook weighs 1,589 grams. How many milligrams does the science text weigh?

A 1,589 mg
B 15.89 mg
C 158,900 mg
D 1,589,000 mg

Strategies:

1. Read the problem carefully to determine the conversion you must make.

2. You need to convert grams to milligrams.

3. Refer to the conversion table in the text booklet:
   1 gram = 1000 milligrams

4. To find out how many milligrams are in 1,589 grams, multiply 1,589 by 1000.

5. You can do this by moving the decimal point 3 places to the right.
   1,589 X 1,000 = 1,589,000 or you can just move the decimal point over three places. 1,589.000 ➡ 1,589,000

6. Check for the reasonableness of your answer:
   1 milligram is approximately equal to the weight of 1 grain of salt.

7. Compare this with your answer and the other answer choices. The answer is found in choice **D**.

Measurement: Step Two A

The student is expected to measure to solve problems involving length (including perimeter), weight, capacity, time, temperature, and area. (TAKS 6:5.11A)
The student is expected to describe numerical relationships between units of measure within the same measurement system such as an inch is one-twelfth of a foot. (TAKS 4:5.11B)

1. How many meters are equivalent to 4,753 centimeters?

   A 4.753 m **C** 475.3 m
   B 47.53 m **D** 47,530 m

2. Which unit of measurement is $\frac{1}{100}$ of a meter?

   A 1 centimeter **C** 1 millimeter
   B 1 decimeter **D** 1 kilometer

3. How many centimeters are equivalent to 768 millimeters?

   A 0.768 cm **C** 76.8 cm
   B 7.68 cm **D** 7680 cm

4. A meter is one-thousandths of a _____.

   A centimeter **C** millimeter
   B decimeter **D** kilometer

5. How many milliliters are equivalent to 87 liters?

   A 0.087 ml **C** 8,700 ml
   B 0.87 ml **D** 87,000 ml

6. How many kilograms are equivalent to 72 grams?

   A 0.072 kg **C** 7,200 kg
   B 0.72 kg **D** 72,000 kg

7. A gram is one-thousandths of a ______.

   A centimeter **C** milligram
   B kilogram **D** kilometer

8. How many meters are equivalent to 3 kilometers?

   A 3,000,000 m **C** 3,000 m
   B 300,000 m **D** 300 m

9. How many liters are equivalent to 574 milliliters?

   A 0.574 l **C** 57.4 l
   B 5.74 l **D** 5740 l

10. Which unit of measurement is $\frac{1}{1000}$ of a liter?

    A 1 milliliter **C** 1 milligram
    B 1 gram **D** 1 kilometer

11. How many grams are equivalent to 56 kilograms?

    A 0.0056 g **C** 5,600 g
    B 0.056 g **D** 56,000 g

12. How many meters are equivalent to 9,874 millimeters?

    A 98.74 m **C** 0.9874 m
    B 9.874 m **D** 0.09874 m

13. How many liters are equivalent to 6,850 milliliters?

    A 685.0 l **C** 6.85 l
    B 68.5 l **D** 0.685 l

Measurement: Step Two B

The student is expected to measure to solve problems involving length (including perimeter), weight, capacity, time, temperature, and area. (TAKS 4:5.11A)

1. The smallest diamond with a brilliant cut and 57-facets had a diameter of only 12 millimeters. How many centimeters is the diameter of the diamond?

   A 0.0012 cm **C** 1.2 cm
   B 0.12 cm **D** 120 cm

2. The gateway to the West Arch in St. Louis is the tallest monument in the world. It rises to a height of 110 meters. How many centimeters is the height of this monument?

   A 11.0 cm **C** 1,100 cm
   B 110 cm **D** 11,000 cm

3. The largest guitar ever built weighed 140,286 grams. How many kilograms did this guitar weigh?

   A 14.0268 kg **C** 1,402.86 kg
   B 140.286 kg **D** 14,028,600 kg

4. The metropolitan Opera House in New York City has a stage that is 71 meters wide. How many millimeters wide is this stage?

   A 0.071 mm **C** 7,100 mm
   B 0.71 mm **D** 71,000 mm

5. On May 31, 1975, Peter Dowdeswell of England drank 1,020 milliliters of milk in 3.2 seconds. How many liters of milk did he drink?

   A 0.102 *l* **C** 1.20 *l*
   B 1.02 *l* **D** 102 *l*

6. On July 14, 1986, Tony Dowdeswell ate 1,532.25 grams of unmelted ice cream in 31.37 seconds. How many milligrams of ice cream was this?

   A 1,532,250 mg **C** 15.3225 mg
   B 153,225 mg **D** 1.53225 mg

7. Syd weighs 81.82 kilograms. His brother David, weighs 92.27 kilograms. How many grams does Syd weigh?

   A 92,270 g **C** 9,227 g
   B 81,820 g **D** 8,182 g

8. Mrs. Hanna had a pencil which weighed 5.8 grams. How many kilograms did the pencil weigh?

   A 0.0058 kg **C** 58 kg
   B 0.58 kg **D** 5800 kg

Measurement: Step Two C

The student is expected to measure to solve problems involving length (including perimeter), weight, capacity, time, temperature, and area. (TAKS 4:5.11A)

1. Kasey prepared 4 liters of punch for her birthday party. She had 75 milliliters left. How much punch did they drink at the party?

   A 3,925 ml
   B 4,075 ml
   C 3,025 ml
   D 2,025 ml

2. Kevin and Kelyn have 14 kilograms of candy to pass out as party favors. They had 500 grams left. How much candy did they pass out at the party?

   A 14,500 g
   B 13,500 g
   C 12,500 g
   D 10,500 g

3. Yesterday, Polly bought 4.36 meters of fabric to make a dress. She got her pattern out and found that she needed 25 more centimeters of fabric. How many total centimeters of fabric were needed to make the dress?

   A 461 cm
   B 4.61 cm
   C 411 cm
   D 361 cm

4. Manuel ran 3.465 kilometers. Sammy ran 635 meters further. How far did Sammy run in meters?

   A 410 m
   B 4.100 m
   C 4,100 m
   D 4,110 m

5. Tim rode his bicycle 4.236 kilometers to Tommy's house and then went back home. How far in meters did he ride his bicycle?

   A 4.236 m
   B 8.472 m
   C 4,236 m
   D 8,472 m

6. Rodney needed 5 meters of rope. The rope came in packages of 7.50 meters. How much rope will he have left in centimeters?

   A 25 cm
   B 2.5 cm
   C 250 cm
   D 150 cm

7. Kevin, Kasey and Kelyn have a dog named Missy. Missy's leash is 2.47 meters long. They need to shorten it 35 centimeters. How many centimeters long will Missy's leash be after they shorten it?

   A 2.12 cm
   B 212 cm
   C 2,120 cm
   D 2,220 cm

8. Tyler's dog had 4 puppies. The biggest weighed 5.5 kilograms and the smallest weighed 3.2 kilograms. What is the difference in weight from the largest to the smallest in grams?

   A 2.3 g
   B 23 g
   C 2,300 g
   D 23,000 g

Measurement: Step Three A

The student is expected to measure to solve problems involving length (including perimeter), weight, capacity, time, temperature, and area. (TAKS 4:5.11A)

1. Claire is 65 inches tall. Patrick is 70 inches tall. Louis is 73 inches tall. How much taller is Patrick than Claire?

   A 3 in. **C** 8 in.
   B 5 in. **D** 10 in.

2. Louis, Patrick, and Carl competed in a long-jump contest. Patrick jumped 2.8 meters and Louis jumped 1.9 meters. Carl's long jump measured 3.1 meters. How much further did Carl jump than Louis?

   A 5.0 m **C** 1.2 m
   B 5.7 m **D** 0.3 m

3. John and Greg Rice are the world's shortest living twins. They live in West Palm Beach, Florida. Each brother is 34 inches tall. What is the combined height of the two brothers?

   A 34 in. **C** 68 in.
   B 64 in. **D** 69 in.

4. David weighs 205 pounds, Syd weighs 180 pounds, and Rachel weighs 20 pounds. If Syd, David, and Rachel all stepped on a scale at the same time what would their combined weight be?

   A 200 lb **C** 385 lb
   B 225 lb **D** 405 lb

5. Cheryl is making spaghetti sauce for her class. Cheryl will need 48 ounces of tomatoes for the recipe. The cans of tomatoes that Cheryl bought each weigh 8 ounces. How many cans of tomatoes will Cheryl need to make the spaghetti sauce?

   A 6 cans **C** 40 cans
   B 8 cans **D** 48 cans

6. Cheryl bought spaghetti noodles. Each bag of noodles weighed 2 kilograms and cost $0.79. If Cheryl bought 7 bags of spaghetti noodles, how many kilograms of noodles did she have?

   A 9 kg **C** 27 kg
   B 14 kg **D** 79 kg

7. Mrs. Ruth Kistler was born in 1899. Her granddaughter Suzan was born in Glendale, California, in 1956. How old was Mrs. Kistler when Suzan was born?

   A 55 yr **C** 67 yr
   B 57 yr **D** 99 yr

8. Mrs. Murad spends 4 months of every year living with her son, Louis. If Mrs. Murad continues this for 12 years, how many years will she have spent living with Louis?

   A 4 yr **C** 11 yr
   B 5 yr **D** 48 yr

9. The monkey that has lived the longest was named "Bobo" and he lived in Pearl River, New York. Bobo was 53 years old when he died in 1988. In what year was Bobo born?

   A 1988 **C** 1935
   B 1953 **D** 1923

10. Dru practices the piano for 45 minutes each day. How many hours does Dru practice in 8 days?

    A 4 hr **C** 8 hr
    B 6 hr **D** 45 hr

11. Teddy wanted to go to summer camp. The session for 5th grade boys lasted for 3 weeks. How many days would Teddy be at camp if he went to this session?

    A 3 days **C** 15 days
    B 14 days **D** 21 days

12. The first human heart transplant operation was performed on December 3, 1967. The man who received the heart lived for 18 days after the operation. On what day did this man die?

    A January 21, 1968
    B December 21, 1967
    C December 18, 1967
    D November 15, 1967

Measurement: Step Three B

The student is expected to measure to solve problems involving length (including perimeter), weight, capacity, time, temperature, and area. (TAKS 4:5.11A)

1. It took Lenora and her mother 3 days to prepare the beds for their fall garden. On Monday, they prepared a bed that was 14 meters long. On Tuesday they prepared a 12.5 meter long bed. On the third day, they prepared the last bed which was 8.9 meters long. Which expression could be used to find the total length of the three garden beds?

   A 14 + 12.5 - 8.9
   B (14 x 12.5) ÷ 8.9
   C 14 + 12.5 + 8.9
   D (14 - 12.5) + 8.9

---

2. A 6-ton African elephant eats about 350 pounds of food per day. Which expression could be used to find how many pounds of food is eaten per week?

   A 6 x 350
   B 7 x 350
   C 350 ÷ 7
   D 350 ÷ 6

---

3. Jacob bought 3 liters of gasoline for his lawnmower. He used 1.33 liters of the gasoline mowing his yard. Which expression could be used to find out how much gasoline Jacob had left?

   A 3 - 1.33
   B 3 + 1.33
   C 3 x 1.33
   D 3 ÷ 1.33

4. Hilda tries to swim each day. For four days, she recorded how much time she spent swimming. She swam for 55 minutes on Monday, 45 minutes on Tuesday, 25 minutes on Wednesday, and 75 minutes on Thursday. Which expression could be used to find the total amount of time Hilda spent swimming?

   A 4 x 55
   B (55 + 45 + 25 + 75) ÷ 4
   C (55 + 45) - (25 + 75)
   D 55 + 45 + 25 + 75

---

5. Rob was cooking a roast for dinner. He set the temperature of the oven for 250 degrees. After 2 hours, Rob increased the temperature to 375 degrees. Which expression could be used to find out how many degrees higher the temperature of the oven was after Rob changed it?

   A 250 + 375
   B 375 ÷ 250
   C 375 - 250
   D 375 ÷ 2

---

6. Syd had an 18 meter length of rope that he was going to use to tie down a tarp over his canoe. Since the tarp had 6 places to attach the rope, he divided the rope into 6 equal pieces. Which expression could be used to find the length of each piece of rope?

   A 18 x 6
   B 18 ÷ 6
   C 18 - 6
   D 18 + 6

Measurement: Sample for Analysis

The student is expected to measure to solve problems involving length (including perimeter), weight, capacity, time, temperature, and area. (TAKS 4:5.11A)

Perimeter

Rachel had a beautiful pink bath towel that Graham had given her for her birthday. Graham decorated the bath towel with a border of pink and white polka-dotted ribbon. To make the corners look neat, Graham cut the ribbon as shown in the drawing.

24 inches

36 inches

How many inches of polka-dotted ribbon did Graham use on Rachel's towel?

A 50 in. **B** 60 in. **C** 120 in. **D** 144 in.

Strategy:

1. Read the problem carefully. A border of ribbon goes all the way around the towel.
2. You are looking for the perimeter of the towel. The perimeter is the distance around a shape. The perimeter of a shape is the sum of the length of its sides.
3. The bath towel has two long sides and two short sides.
4. Add the lengths of all 4 sides:

$$\begin{array}{r} 24 \\ 24 \\ 36 \\ +\ 36 \\ \hline 120 \end{array}$$

5. Look for 120 in. among the choices. Choice C

Measurement: Step Four A

The student is expected to measure to solve problems involving length (including perimeter), weight, capacity, time, temperature, and area. (TAKS 4:5.11A)

1. How many yards are in the perimeter of this polygon?

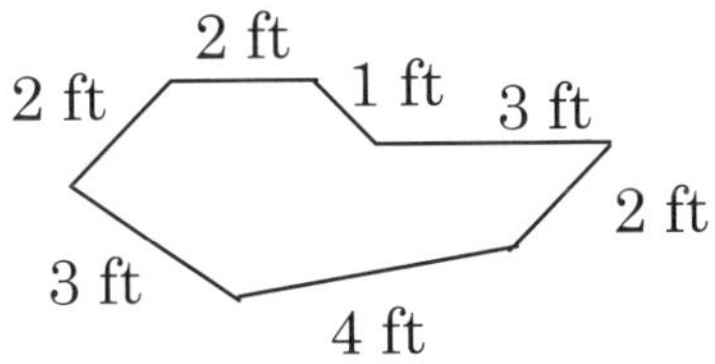

A $4\frac{3}{4}$ yards

B $5\frac{1}{2}$ yards

C $5\frac{2}{3}$ yards

D 17 yards

---

2. Martin wanted to build three birdhouses. He cut a rectangular piece of wood to use for the floor of the birdhouse, and then attached a rain gutter as shown in the drawing.

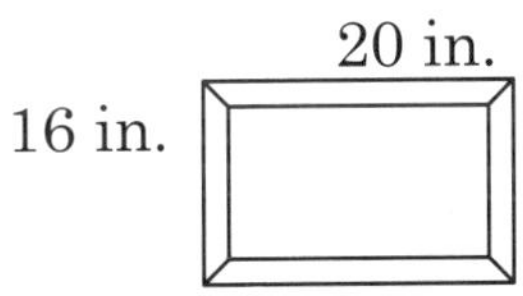

How many yards of gutter did Marty use on the floor of each birdhouse?

A 2 yd

B $1\frac{1}{2}$ yd

C 1 yd

D $\frac{3}{4}$ yd

---

3. Brittany went on a trip from San Antonio to Austin. The distance from San Antonio to New Braunfels is 27 miles. The distance from New Braunfels to Kyle is 38 miles, and there are 17 miles between Kyle and Austin.

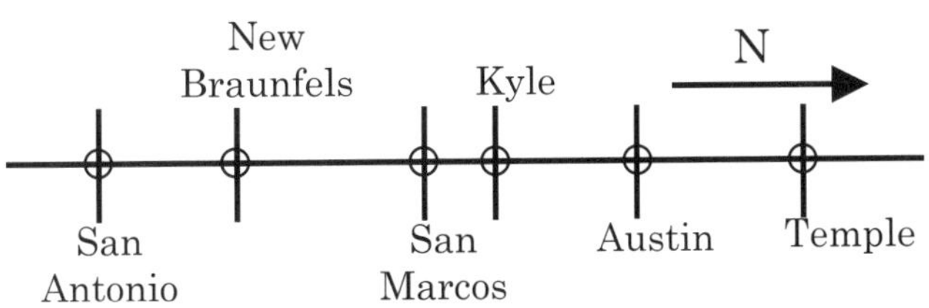

What distance did Brittany travel from San Antonio to Austin?

A 55 mi

B 65 mi

C 82 mi

D 90 mi

4. Aaron is using his building blocks to make a miniature space station. Aaron left a door for satellites in the side of the space station.

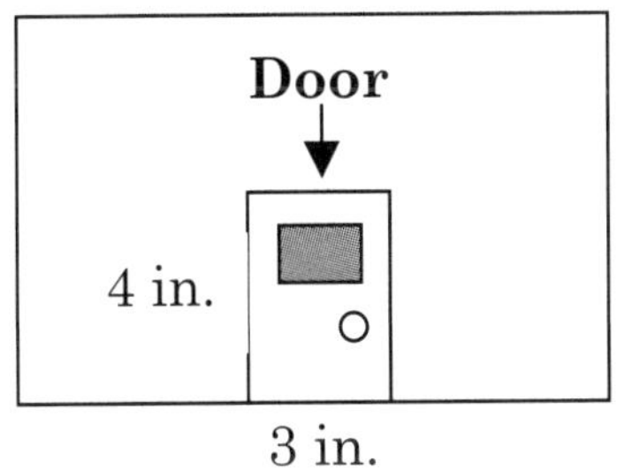

What is the perimeter of the satellite door?

A $\frac{1}{6}$ feet

B $\frac{3}{4}$ feet

C $1\frac{1}{6}$ feet

D $1\frac{1}{2}$ feet

---

5. Aaron laid a bath towel down on his bedroom floor. The towel marked the size of the space station floor.

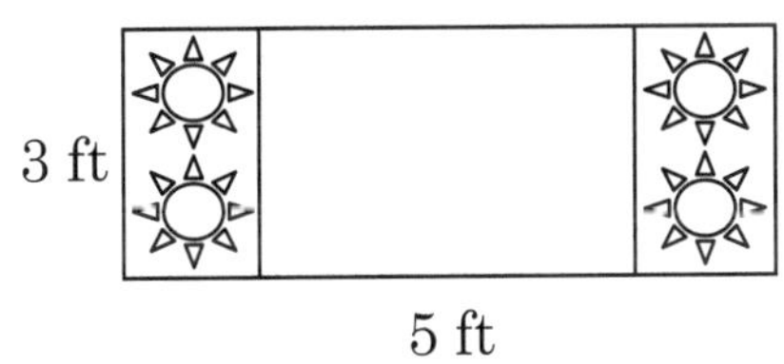

What is the perimeter of the floor of the space station?

A 5 ft

B 8 ft

C 15 ft

D 16 ft

---

6. How many yards are in the perimeter of this rectangle?

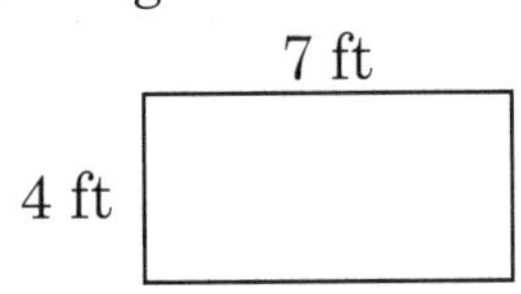

A $28\frac{1}{2}$ yd

B $7\frac{1}{3}$ yd

C $6\frac{3}{4}$ yd

D $5\frac{1}{3}$ yd

Measurement: Step Four B

The student is expected to measure to solve problems involving length (including perimeter), weight, capacity, time, temperature, and area. (TAKS 4:5.11A)

1. Brenda bought an album at the variety store. She covered it with flowered fabric and trimmed the edges with blue ribbon. She cut the ribbon as shown in the drawing.

How many feet of blue ribbon did Brenda use to trim the cover of her photo album?

A 43 ft
B 21 ft
C $3\frac{3}{4}$ ft
D $3\frac{1}{2}$ ft

2. Eric ran 1,760 yards around the track at the high school. The track is shown in the diagram below.

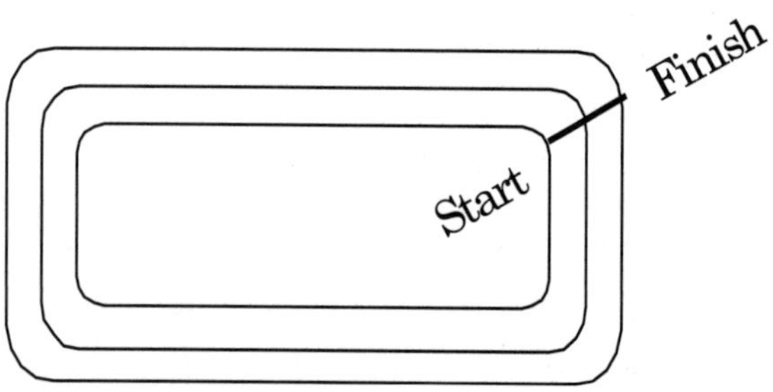

If Eric ran around the track 4 times for a total of 1,760 yards, what is the distance around the track 1 time?

A 220 yds
B 400 yds
C 415 yds
D 440 yds

3. Kathleen knew she needed to exercise. She decided to measure the roads around her neighborhood, so she could keep track of how far she rides her bike. A map of the neighborhood is shown below.

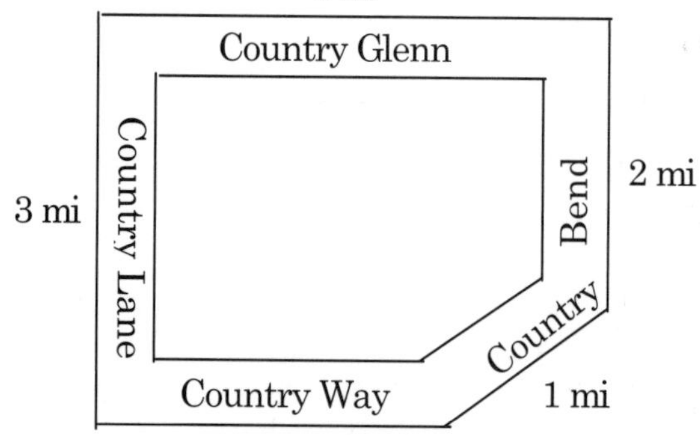

If Kathleen rode her bicycle around the neighborhood 1 time, how many miles would she travel?

A 7 mi
B 9 mi
C 13 mi
D 26 mi

4. Marty had an irregular shaped field on his farm. He wanted to string an electric fence around this field. The field is shown in this drawing.

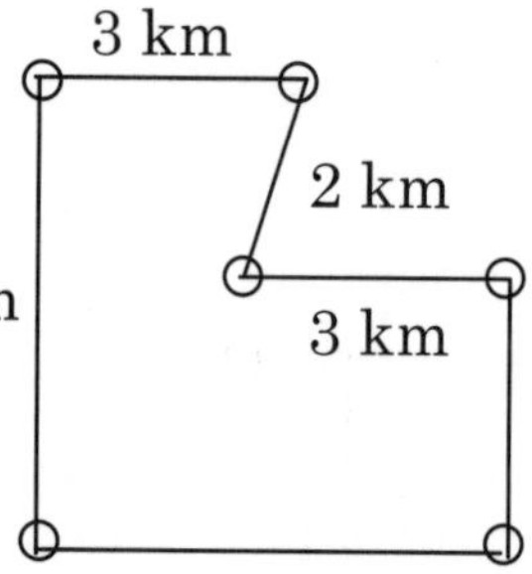

How many kilometers of electric wire did Marty use to fence this field?

A 15 km
B 20 km
C 21 km
D 25 km

Measurement: Step Four C

The student is expected to measure to solve problems involving length (including perimeter), weight, capacity, time, temperature, and area. (TAKS 4:5.11A)

1. Which of the following rectangles has a perimeter of 22 centimeters?

A 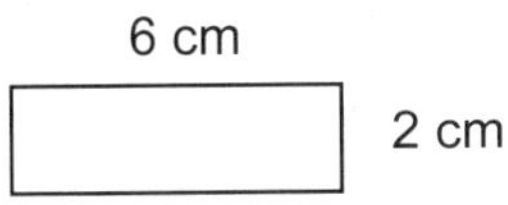

B 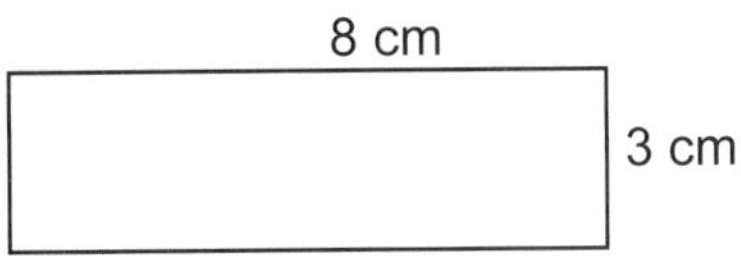

C 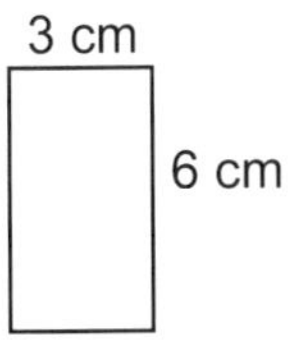

D 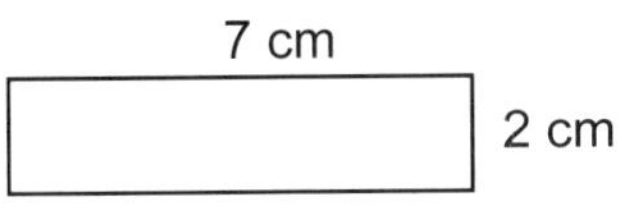

2. Which of the following squares has a perimeter of 20 centimeters?

A 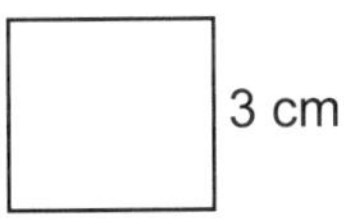

B 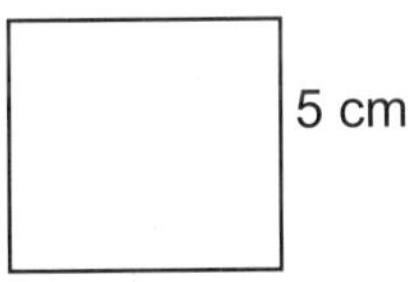

C 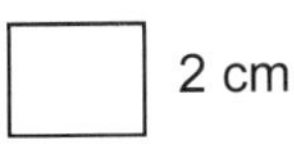

D 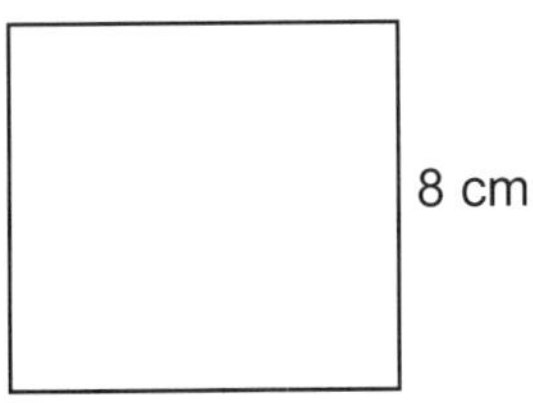

3. Which of the following rectangles has a perimeter of 20 inches?

A 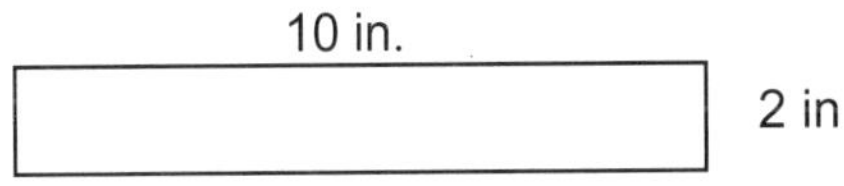

B 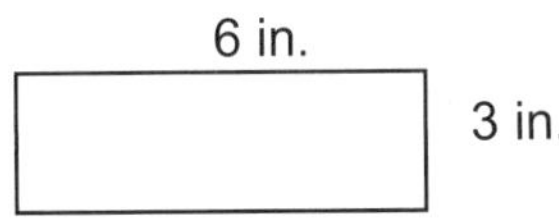

C 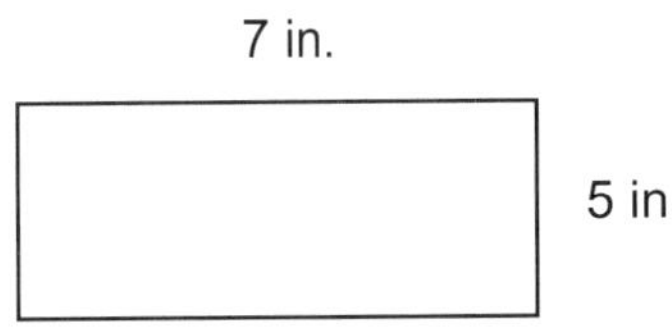

D 

4. Which of the following squares has a perimeter of 12 inches?

A 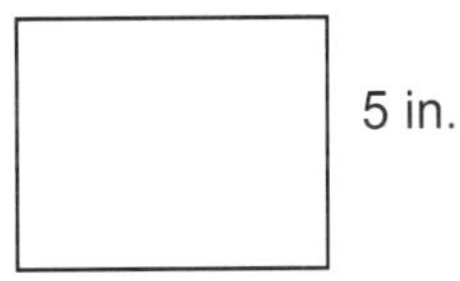

B 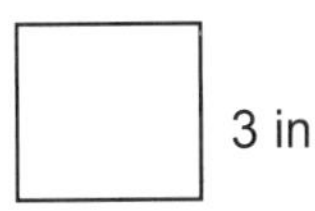

C 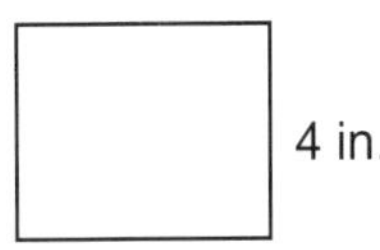

D 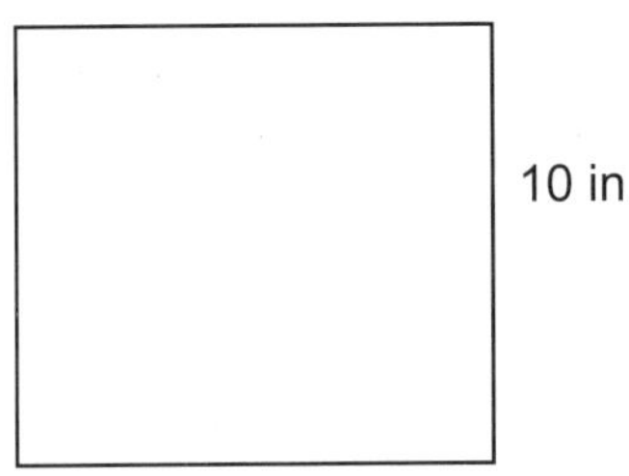

Measurement: Sample for Analysis

The student is expected to measure to solve problems involving length (including perimeter), weight, capacity, time, temperature, and area. (TAKS 4:5.11A)

Perimeter

Kevin was building a rectangular fence. His dad told him that the perimeter of the fence was 30 feet. He knew that he would use 6 feet on the front of the fence and 6 feet on the back of the fence , but he could not get to the other 2 sides because of the bushes. How much fencing will he need for one of the remaining sides?

A 24 ft **B** 18 ft **C** 10 ft **D** 9 ft

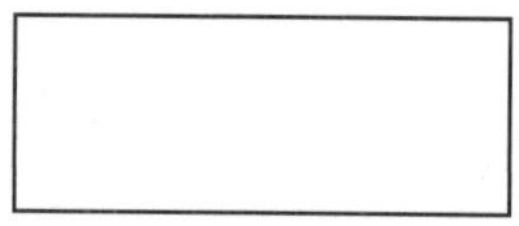

6 feet

Strategy:

1. What do you know about a rectangle? Opposite sides are equal. If the front and back are 6 and 6, then we have used 12 feet of the 30 feet that makes up the perimeter. 30 - 12 = 18.
2. 18 feet are left and we know the remaining two sides are also equal since it is a rectangle. 18 ÷ 2 = 9 so each of the two remaining sides is 9 feet.
3. Now what was the question? How many feet will he need for one of the remaining sides? That is easy—9 feet.

Watch out for those tricky wrong answers!

A 24 feet If you did not read carefully and thought it was a square instead of a rectangle, you might have done this: 6 + 6 + 6 + 6 = 24

B 18 feet If you worked the problem perfectly and forgot the last step, to divide 18 by 2 to split the sides, then you would have answered 18 feet.

C 12 feet If you added only the 2 sides you knew, 6 + 6, you might have gotten 12.

D 9 feet If you did everything right, you would have gotten **D**!

Measurement: Sample for Analysis

The student is expected to measure to solve problems involving length (including perimeter), weight, capacity, time, temperature, and area. (TAKS 4:5.11A)

Perimeter

Amy's mom told her to draw a square on the board that has a perimeter of 32 inches. Before she can do this she has to know how long the sides are. How long is one of the sides?

A 4 in. **B** 6 in. **C** 8 in. **D** 128 in.

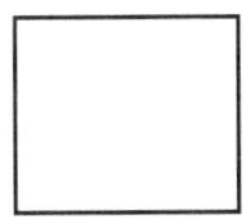

32 inches perimeter

Strategy:

1. What do you know about a square? A square has 4 equal sides. If you need to know the length of each side, then you need to divide the whole (perimeter) into equal parts (sides). Divide!! 32 divided by 4 is 8.

2. Now what was the question? How many inches is each side? That is easy—8 inches.

Watch out for those tricky wrong answers!

A 4 inches It has 4 sides, but that does not mean the answer is 4.

B 6 inches 32 divided by 4 is not 6.

C 8 inches 32 divided by 4 is 8.

D 128 inches You do not multiply 32 by 4, you divide 32 by 4.

Measurement: Step Four D

The student is expected to measure to solve problems involving length (including perimeter), weight, capacity, time, temperature, and area. (TAKS 4:5.11A)

1. The perimeter of a rectangular garden is 40 feet. If the width of the garden is 8 feet, what is the length?

8 ft
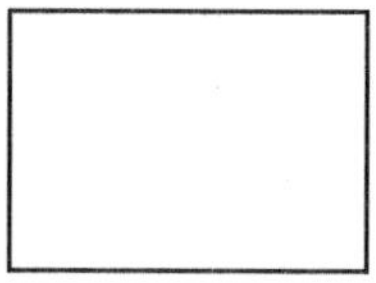

A 12 ft B 16 ft C 24 ft D 40 ft

2. The perimeter of a square frame is 48 inches. What is the length of one of the sides?

A 6 in. B 12 in. C 16 in. D 24 in.

3. The perimeter of a regular polygon with three sides is 24 centimeters. How long is one of the sides? (Hint: What is the definition of a regular polygon?)

A 12 cm B 10 cm C 8 cm D 6 cm

4. The perimeter of a rectangular sandbox is 24 feet. The width of the sandbox is 5 feet. What is the length of one of the sides?

A 6 ft B 7 ft C 14 ft D 21 ft

5. The perimeter of a square window is 16 feet. What is the length of one of the sides?

A 64 ft B 12ft C 8 ft D 4 ft

6. The perimeter a rectangular storage room is 48 ft. The front and back walls are each 8 feet. What is the length of one of the other sides?

A 16 ft B 40 ft C 56 ft D 192 ft

7. The perimeter of a regular polygon with three sides is 42 centimeters. How long is one of the sides?

A 8 cm B 10 cm C 14 cm D 16 cm

8. The perimeter of a square is 56 centimeters. How long is one of the sides?

A 14 cm B 16 cm C 18 cm D 20 cm

Measurement: Step Four E

The student is expected to measure to solve problems involving length (including perimeter), weight, capacity, time, temperature, and area. (TAKS 4:5.11A)

1. Lynne ran and finished a 36 mile race. The race course forms a triangle as shown in the diagram. The distance along the Martindale Road was 9 miles and the distance along Maxwell Road was 15 miles.

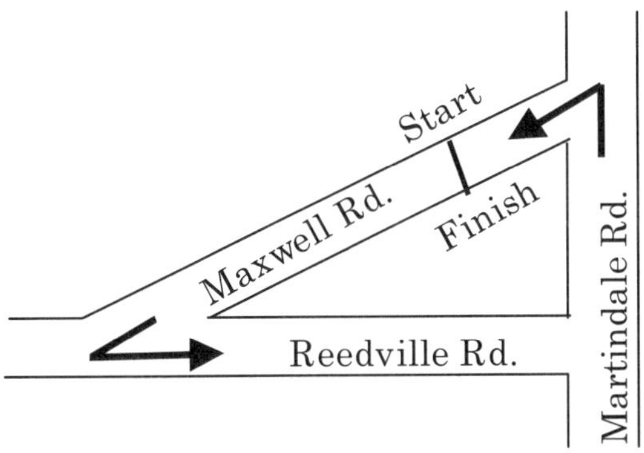

What distance did Lynne run along Reedville Road?

A 8 mi **B** 10 mi **C** 12 mi **D** 30 mi

2. The perimeter of this polygon is 54 centimeters. What is the length of the unmarked side?

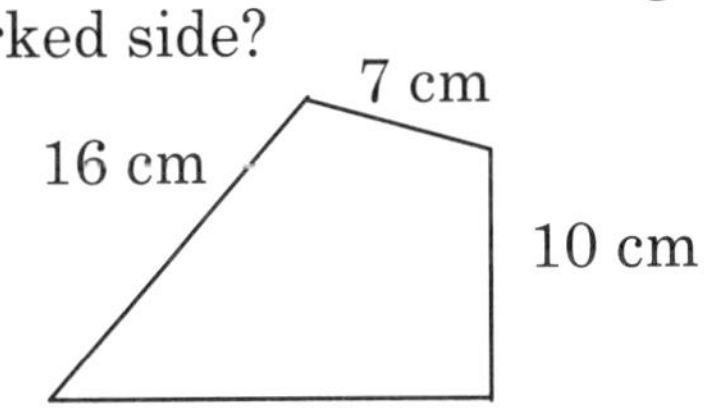

A 16 cm **B** 21 cm **C** 23 cm **D** 33 cm

3. The perimeter of this quadrilateral is 33 in. What is the length of the unmarked side?

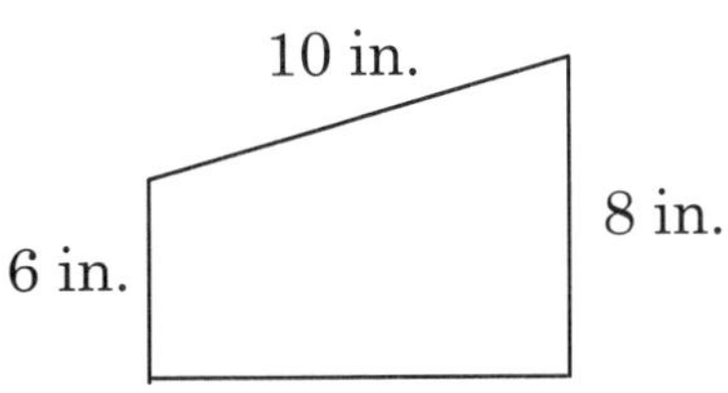

A 6 in. **B** 8 in. **C** 9 in. **D** 10 in.

4. Jayla glued 85 inches of trim on a triangular piece of paper as shown in the diagram. She used 36 inches of trim on side A and used 23 inches of trim on side B.

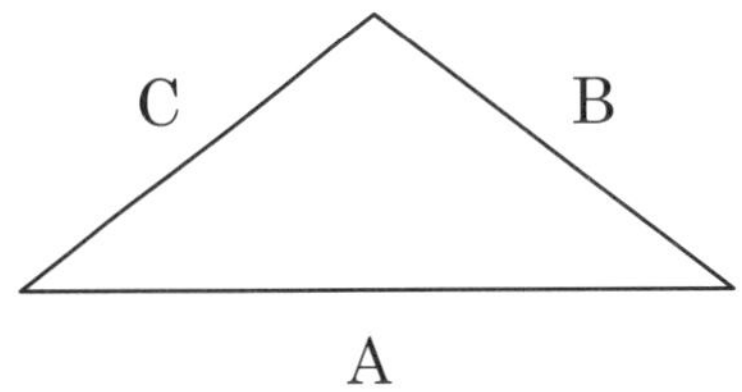

How much trim did Jayla glue on Side C of the paper?

A 26 in. **B** 23 in. **C** 16 in. **D** 13 in.

5. The perimeter of this triangle is 27 inches. What is the length of the unmarked side?

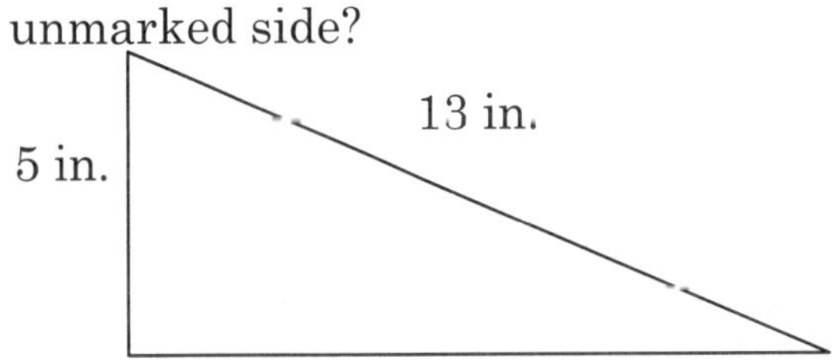

A 18 in. **B** 11 in. **C** 9 in. **D** 8 in.

6. The perimeter of this quadrilateral is 33 in. What is the length of the unmarked side?

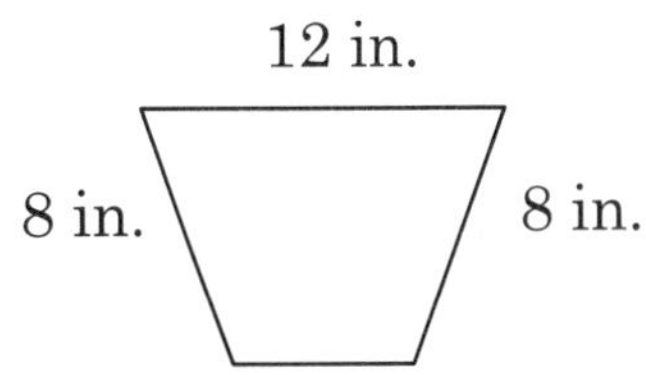

A 5 in. **B** 6 in. **C** 7 in. **D** 28 in

Measurement: Sample for Analysis

The student is expected to measure to solve problems involving length (including perimeter), weight, capacity, time, temperature, and area. (TAKS 4:5.11A)

Area of Square and Rectangle

Kenneth is going to tile the storeroom floor. The floor is rectangular and measures 6 feet long and 8 feet wide. What is the area of the room?

A 14 square feet **B** 28 square feet **C** 42 square feet **D** 48 square feet

Strategy:

1. Look at the formula chart for the formula of the area of a rectangle. The Area of a Rectangle = Length x Width or $A = lw$.

2. The length is 6 and the width is 8. 6 x 8 = 48.

Draw a picture if you need to.

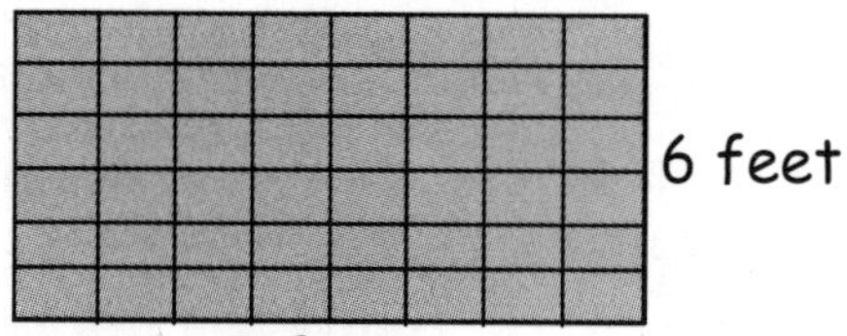

Watch out for tricky wrong answers!

A 14 feet Adding the two sides will only give you one row of tile on one side and one row of tile on the second side. That is not a completely tiled floor.

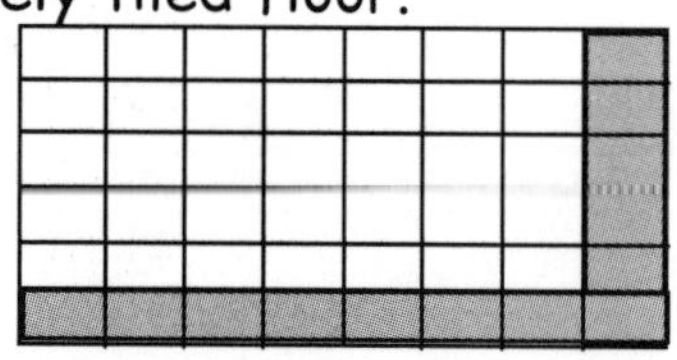

B 28 feet 28 is the perimeter of the room. We are looking for the area of the room.

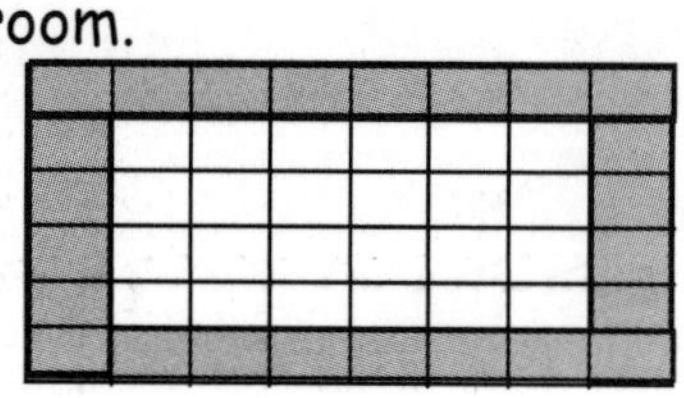

C 42 feet 6 x 7 = 42 and 6 x 8 = 48 Make sure you know your facts.

Measurement: Step Five A

The student is expected to measure to solve problems involving length (including perimeter), weight, capacity, time, temperature, and area. (TAKS 4:5.11A)

1. Jody is measuring her floor for new carpet. The diagram below shows a drawing of her floor.

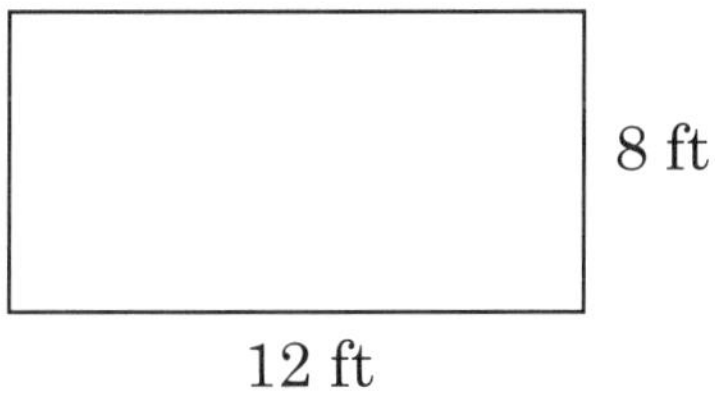

How many square feet of carpet does she need to order?

A 20 square feet **C** 40 square feet
B 36 square feet **D** 96 square feet

---

2. Mr. James is measuring his bulletin board to determine how much kraft paper he needs to cover it. The bulletin board is shown below.

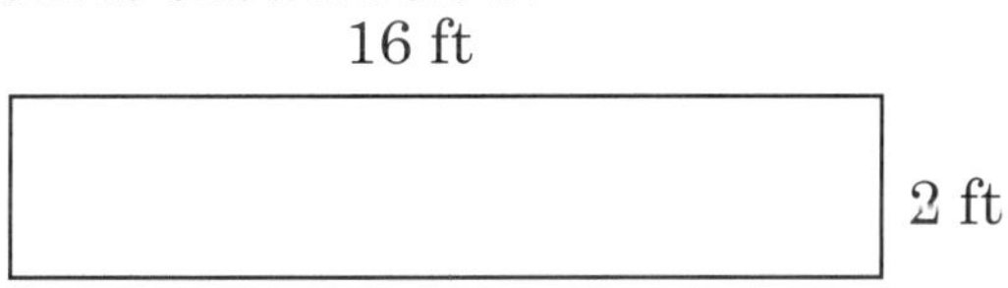

How many square feet does he need to purchase?

A 36 square feet **C** 24 square feet
B 32 square feet **D** 18 square feet

---

3. The city is planning to construct a city park. The square area of land for the baseball field with stands is shown in a diagram below.

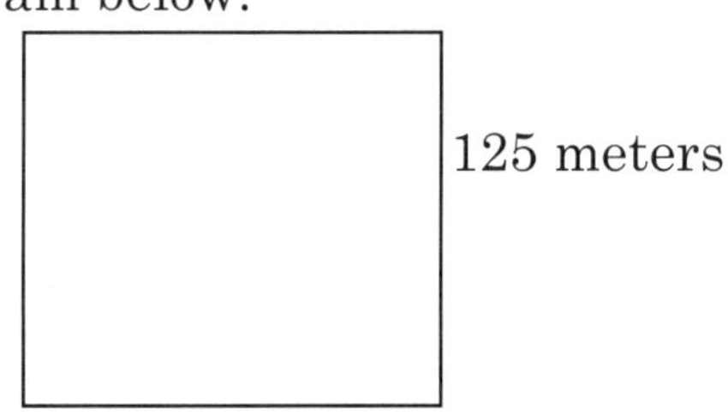

How many square meters will be used for the baseball field?

A 250 sq m **C** 1,562 sq m
B 500 sq m **D** 15,625 sq m

4. The city park will also have a soccer field with stands. A diagram of the soccer field is show below.

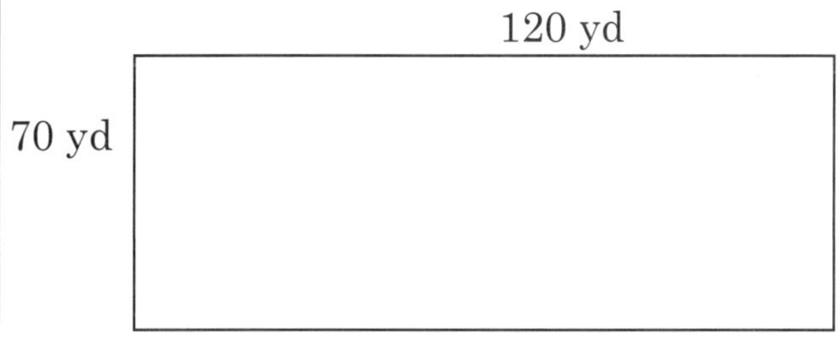

How many square yards of land will be used for the soccer field?

A 8,400 sq yd **C** 380 sq yd
B 840 sq yd **D** 190 sq yd

---

5. The city is planning a big square picnic area among the trees. This area is shown in the diagram below.

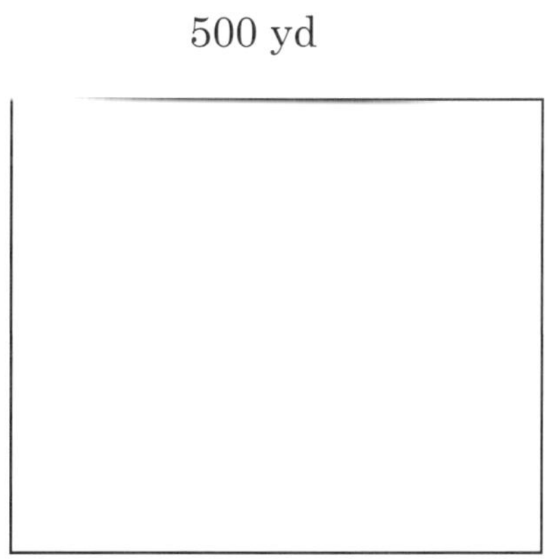

How many square yards of land will be used for the picnic area?

A 250,000 sq yd **C** 1,500 sq yd
B 2,000 sq yd **D** 1,000 sq yd

Measurement: Step Five B

The student is expected to measure to solve problems involving length (including perimeter), weight, capacity, time, temperature, and area. (TAKS 4:5.11A)

1. Lance is shopping for a rectangular rug in a catalog. The rugs are listed under the area they cover. He wants a rug that is 7 feet long and 3 feet wide. What is the area of the rug?

   A 10 square feet **C** 21 square feet
   B 20 square feet **D** 24 square feet

2. Lillie is going to cover a rectangular bulletin board with kraft paper. If the bulletin board is 4 feet wide and 8 feet long, what is the area of the bulletin board?

   A 32 square feet **C** 16 square feet
   B 24 square feet **D** 12 square feet

3. Jennifer is purchasing glass for a window that was broken by a flying baseball. The square pane is 36 centimeters long. What is the area of the pane of glass?

   A 72 square centimeters
   B 144 square centimeters
   C 360 square centimeters
   D 1,296 square centimeters

4. Kent is placing wallpaper on one wall in the bedroom. The wall is 8 feet tall and 12 feet wide. How many square feet of wallpaper does he need to buy?

   A 20 square feet
   B 40 square feet
   C 86 square feet
   D 96 square feet

5. Rosa needs a pad to go on the dining table. The table is 7 feet long and 5 feet wide. What is the area of the table top?

   A 12 square feet **C** 35 square feet
   B 24 square feet **D** 49 square feet

6. Thomas is going to pour concrete in the backyard for a patio that is square. One of the sides is 15 feet. What is the area of the patio he wants to build?

   A 30 square feet **C** 60 square feet
   B 45 square feet **D** 225 square feet

7. Patsy is digging an area for a flowerbed. She has measured off a bed that is 24 feet long and 12 feet wide. What is the area of the flowerbed?

   A 288 square feet
   B 172 square feet
   C 72 square feet
   D 36 square feet

8. Albert is trying to purchase of piece of land to raise cattle. It is a square plot of land that is 50 yards long. What is the area of the plot of land?

   A 2,500 square yards
   B 1,500 square yards
   C 1,000 square yards
   D 500 square yards

Measurement: Step Five C

The student is expected to measure to solve problems involving length (including perimeter), weight, capacity, time, temperature, and area. (TAKS 4:5.11A)

1. Tony has been hired to paint a mural of a square wall that is 144 square feet. What is the length of one of the walls?

   A 12 feet
   B 14 feet
   C 38 feet
   D 72 feet

2. Justin is going to plant a rectangular garden with an area of 56 square feet. If the width is 7 feet, how long is the length?

   A 392 feet
   B 63 feet
   C 9 feet
   D 8 feet

3. Tyson is going to build a fence in his backyard. He has 100 square feet in his backyard. If his yard is square, how many feet of fencing does he need to fence in the yard?

   A 40 feet
   B 30 feet
   C 20 feet
   D 10 feet

4. Randy has a rectangular tarp to put on four poles to use as a shade for a picnic. The tarp has an area of 63 square feet. If the length is 9 feet, what is the width of the tarp?

   A 567 feet
   B 74 feet
   C 8 feet
   D 7 feet

5. Mr. Ruiz has a new square garden fountain in their backyard. The fountain covers 81 square feet of their backyard. What is the length of one of the sides of the fountain?

   A 162 feet
   B 41 feet
   C 20 feet
   D 9 feet

6. Mrs. Neighbors has a rectangular patio deck that has an area of 54 square feet. If the length is 9, what is the perimeter of the deck?

   A 6 feet
   B 30 feet
   C 130 feet
   D 260 feet

7. Billie is painting a rectangular wall that has a perimeter of 30 feet. If the length of one side is 7, what is the area that he will paint?

   A 8 square feet
   B 56 square feet
   C 210 square feet
   D 270 square feet

8. Heather is going to paper a square wall with an area of 49 square feet. What is the perimeter of this wall?

   A 7 feet
   B 14 feet
   C 28 feet
   D 32 feet

Measurement: Sample for Analysis

The student is expected to measure to solve problems involving length (including perimeter), weight, capacity, time, temperature, and area. (TAKS 4:5.11A)

Area of a Triangle

What is the area of this triangle?

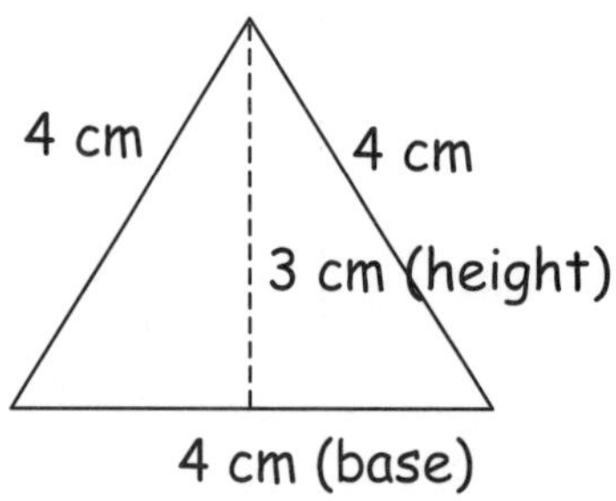

A 6 sq cm **B** 12 sq cm **C** 15 sq cm **D** 64 sq cm

Strategy:

1. Look at the formula chart and find the formula for the area of a triangle. $\frac{1}{2}$ bh which means to multiply the base of the triangle (4) times the height of the triangle (3). 4 x 3 = 12 The area is $\frac{1}{2}$ of 12 which is 6. Answer choice A. Now that was easy.

Try it again.

What is the area of this triangle?

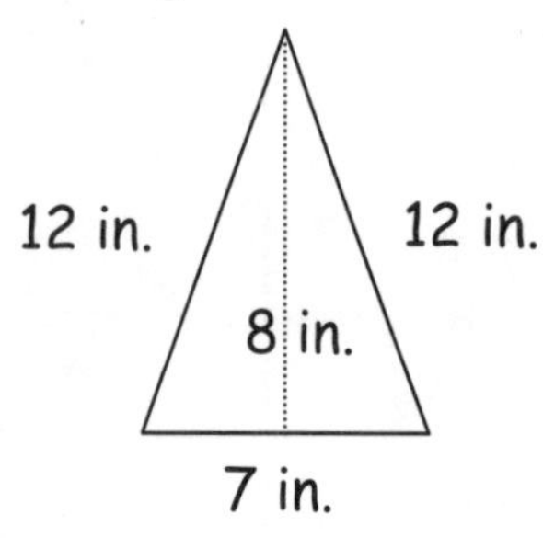

A 15 sq in. **B** 24 sq in. **C** 28 sq in. **D** 56 sq in.

Did you get choice C? You are good!!

Measurement: Step Six A

The student is expected to measure to solve problems involving length (including perimeter), weight, capacity, time, temperature, and area. (TAKS 4:5.11A)

1. What is the area of this triangle?

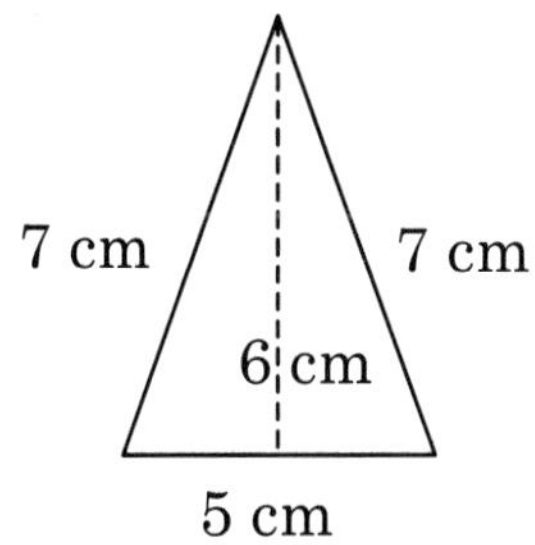

A 25 square cm
B 19 square cm
C 15 square cm
D 11 square cm

---

2. What is the area of this triangle?

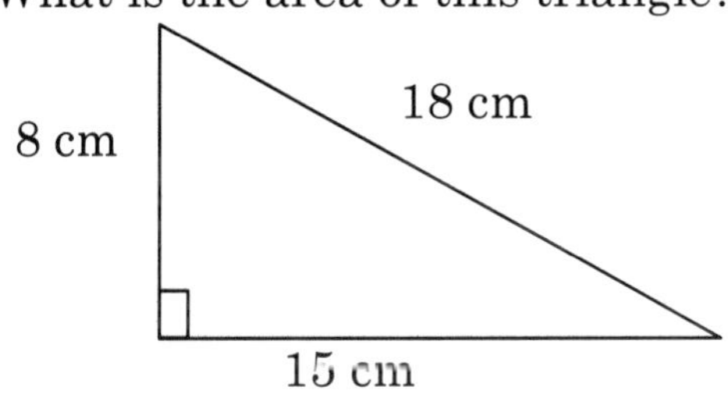

A 120 square cm
B 60 square cm
C 41 square cm
D 23 square cm

---

3. What is the area of this triangle?

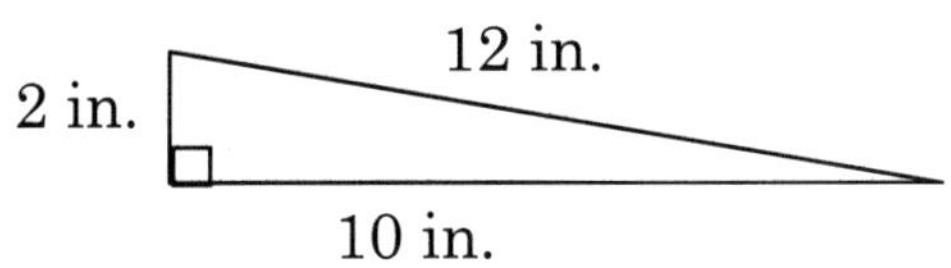

A 120 square in.
B 11 square in.
C 10 square in.
D 5 square in.

4. What is the area of this triangle?

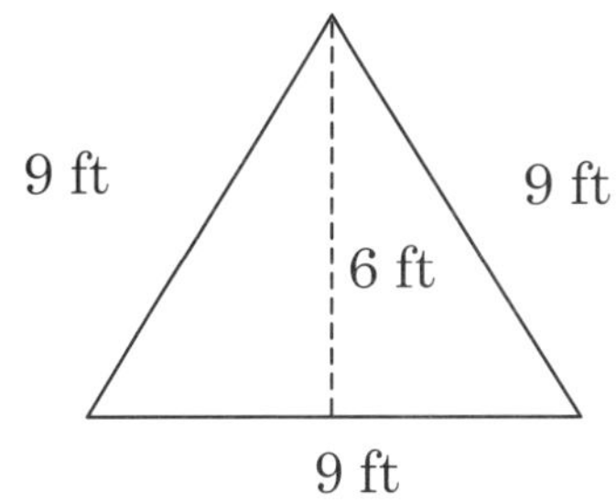

A 40 square ft
B 27 square ft
C 15 square ft
D 7.5 square ft

---

5. What is the area of this triangle?

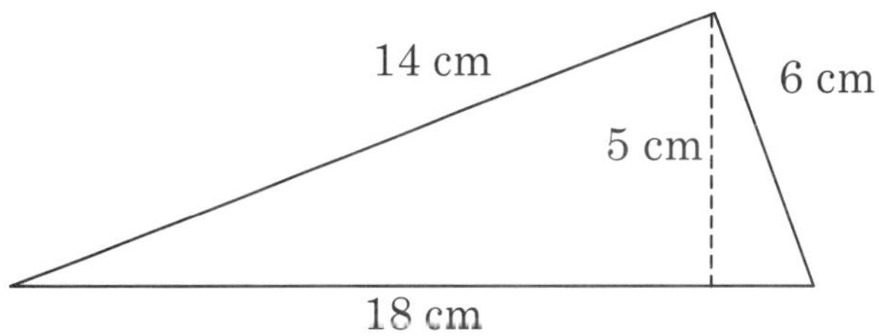

A 45 square cm
B 54 square cm
C 60 square cm
D 126 square cm

---

6. What is the area of this triangle?

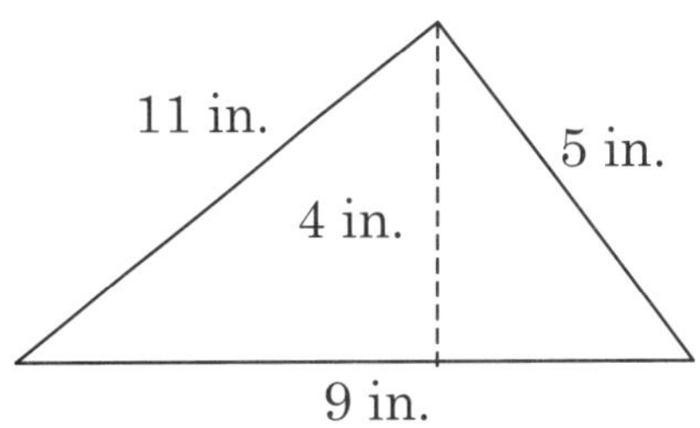

A 45 square in.
B 29 square in.
C 22 square in.
D 18 square in.

Measurement: Step Six B

The student is expected to measure to solve problems involving length (including perimeter), weight, capacity, time, temperature, and area. (TAKS 4:5.11A)

1. What is the area of this triangle?

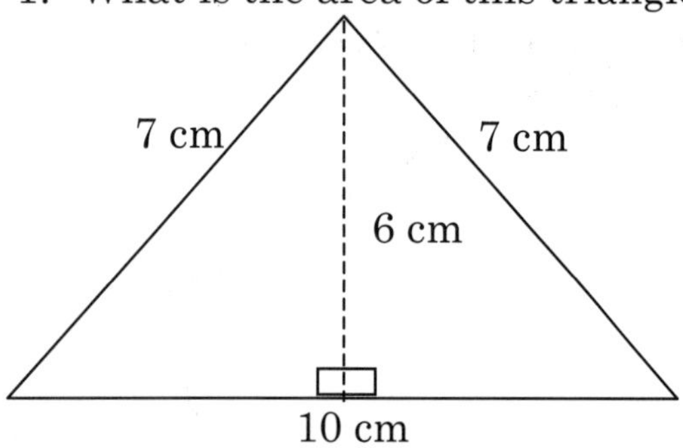

A 30 square cm
B 24 square cm
C 16 square cm
D 14 square cm

---

2. What is the area of this triangle?

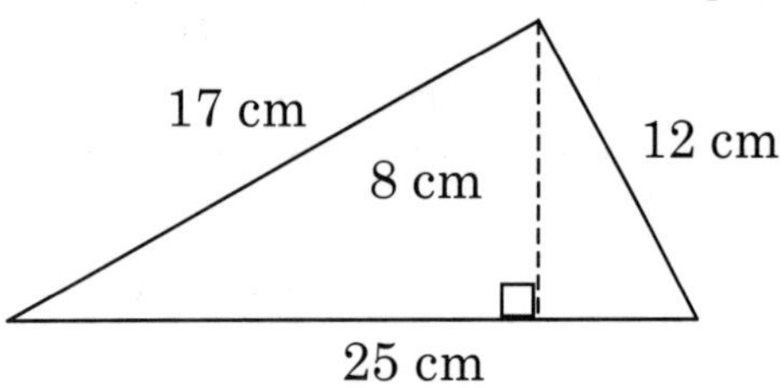

A 200 square cm
B 150 square cm
C 100 square cm
D 62 square cm

---

3. What is the area of this triangle?

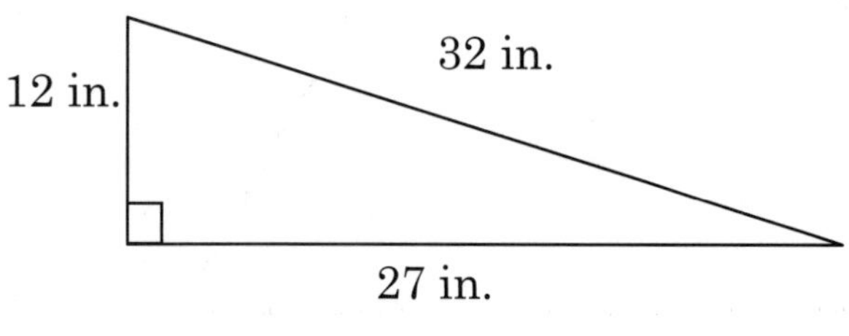

A 432 square in.
B 162 square in.
C 71 square in.
D 39 square in.

4. What is the area of this triangle?

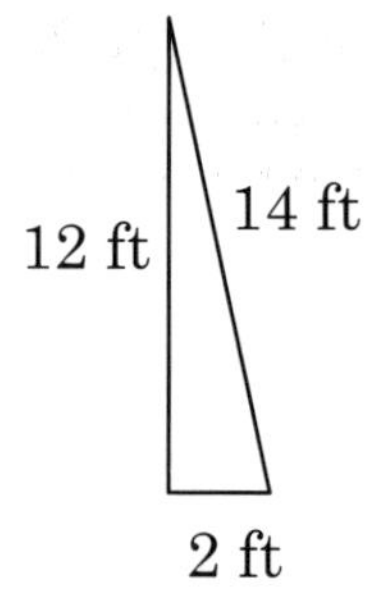

A 28 square ft
B 26 square ft
C 14 square ft
D 12 square ft

---

5. What is the area of this triangle?

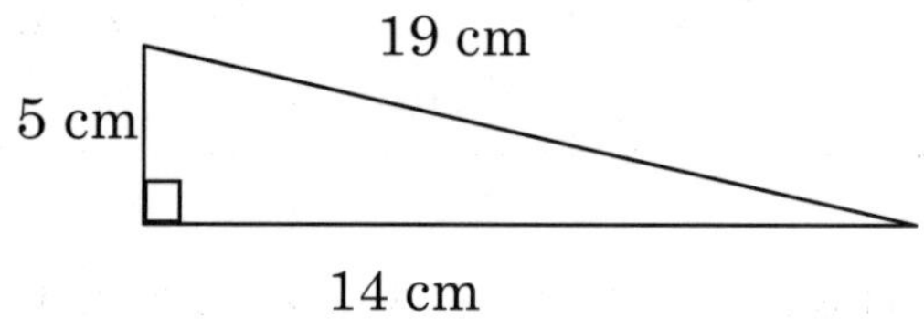

A 133 square cm
B 38 square cm
C 35 square cm
D 33 square cm

---

6. What is the area of this triangle?

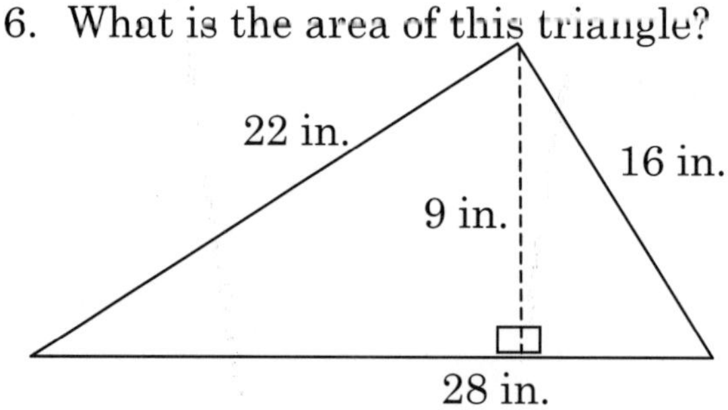

A 126 square in.
B 176 square in.
C 224 square in.
D 308 square in.

Measurement: Step Seven A

The student is expected to measure to solve problems involving length (including perimeter), weight, capacity, time, temperature, and area. (TAKS 4:5.11A)

1. Use the ruler on the Mathematics Chart to measure the perimeter of these two polygons. Measure to the nearest centimeter.

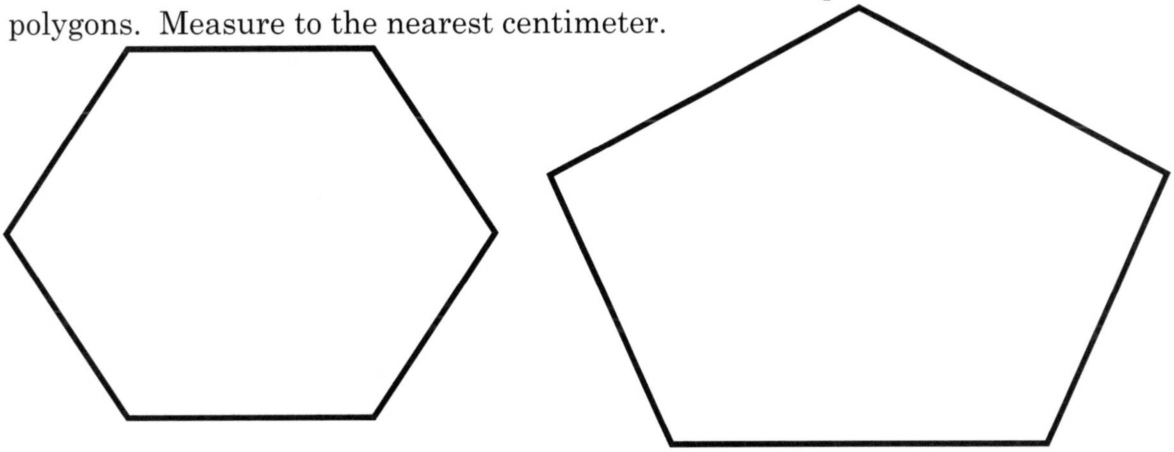

What is the difference to the nearest centimeter of the perimeter of the two polygons?

A 5 cm **B** 15 cm **C** 18 cm **D** 23 cm

---

2. Use the ruler on the Mathematics Chart to measure the perimeter of these two triangles. Measure to the nearest inch.

What is the difference to the nearest inch of the perimeter of the two polygons?

A 0 in. **B** 1 in. **C** 2 in. **D** 3 in.

Measurement: Step Seven B

The student is expected to measure to solve problems involving length (including perimeter), weight, capacity, time, temperature, and area. (TAKS 4:5.11A)

1. Use the ruler on the Mathematics Chart to measure to find the area of these two polygons. Measure to the nearest centimeter.

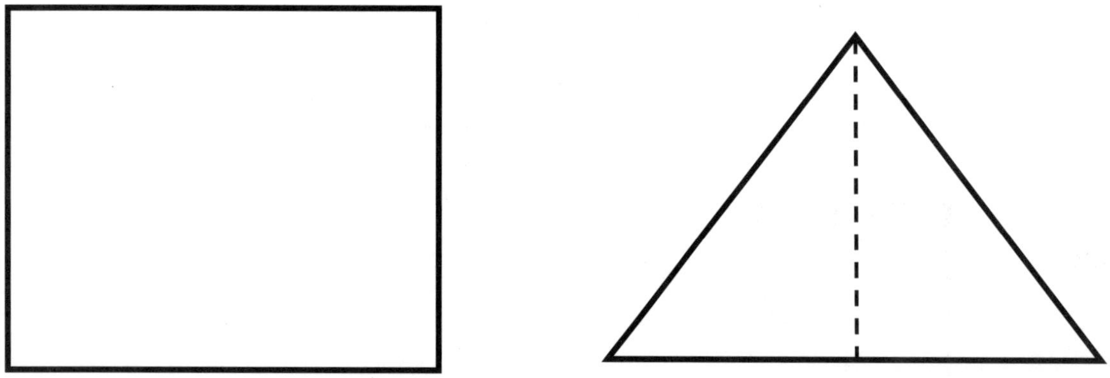

What is the difference to the nearest centimeter of the area of the two polygons?

A 14 sq cm **B** 15 sq cm **C** 24 sq cm **D** 30 sq cm

---

2. Use the ruler on the Mathematics Chart to measure to find the area of these two polygons. Measure to the nearest inch.

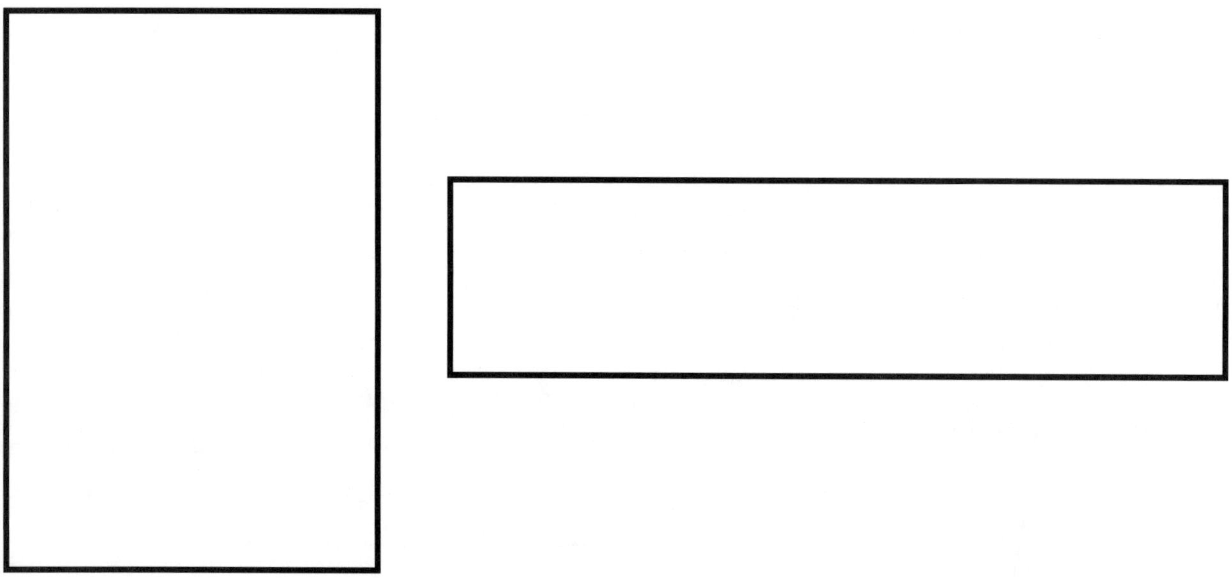

What is the difference to the nearest inch of the area of the two polygons?

A 10 sq in. **B** 6 sq in. **C** 4 sq in. **D** 2 sq in.

Measurement: Sample for Analysis

The student is expected to measure to solve problems involving length (including perimeter), weight, capacity, time, temperature, and area. (TAKS 4:5.11A)

Area and Perimeter Problems

Which is one way to find the area of the polygon?

One Way

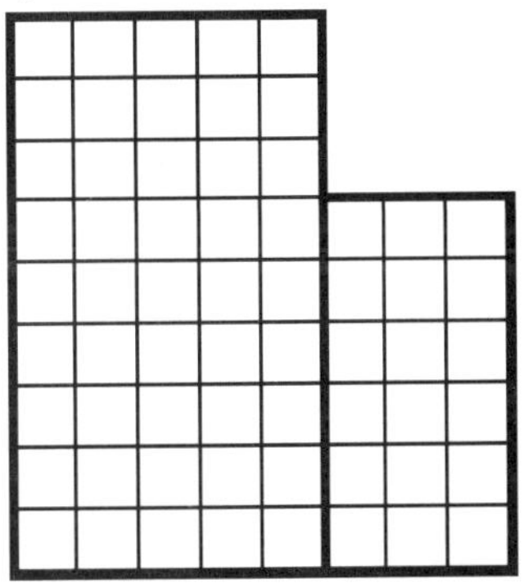

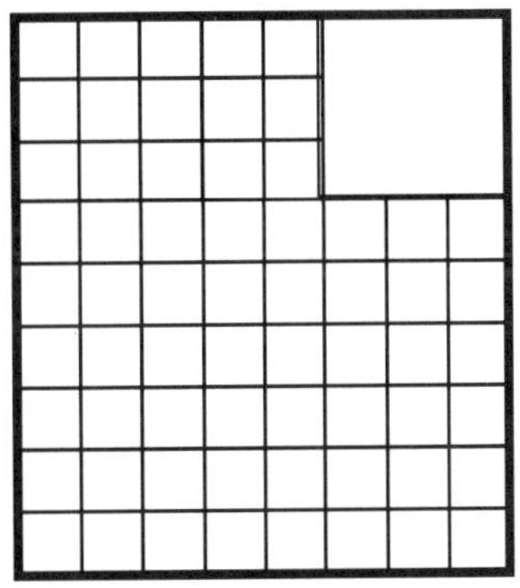

Another Way

A (8 x 9) - (3 x 3) **B** (8 x 9) + (3 x 3) **C** (5 x 9) + (3 x 3) **D** (8 x 6)

Strategy: Make It Simpler—Objective 6 5.14C

1. Look at the polygon. You want to determine the area of the polygon.
2. You can do this in three ways—
   a. Count all of the squares.
   b. Find the area of each section and add them together: (5 x 9) + (3 x 6), or
   c. Find the area of the figure as if it were one complete rectangle and then subtract the area of the "cut-out" portion: (8 x 9) - (3 x 3)
3. Look at the answer choices. Find the answer choice which matches one of your equations.
4. Choice A matches the equation you found when using method 2 c. Therefore, choice A is the correct answer.

Tips: There will often be more than one way to find the area of a polygon.

Measurement: Step Eight A

The student is expected to measure to solve problems involving length (including perimeter), weight, capacity, time, temperature, and area. (TAKS 4:5.11A)

1. Which is one way to find the area of the polygon?

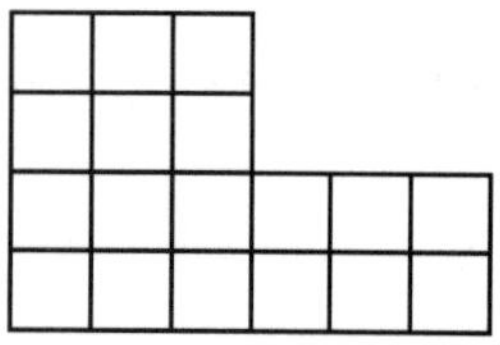

A (4 x 6) - (4 x 3) C (3 x 4) x (2 x 3)
B (3 x 4) + (2 x 3) D (3 x 2) + (2 x 3)

---

2. Which is one way to find the perimeter of the triangle?

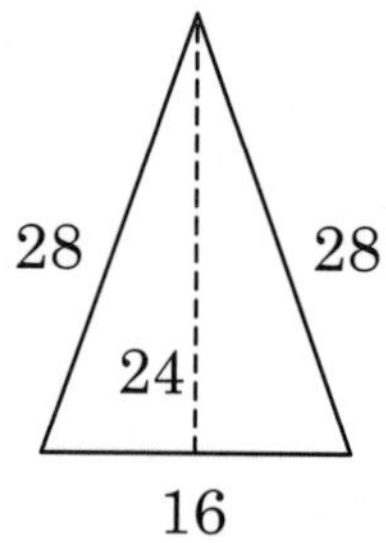

A (24 x 16) ÷ 2
B 28 + 16 + 28
C 28 x 16
D 28 + 16 + 28 + 24

---

3. Which is one way to find the area of the polygon?

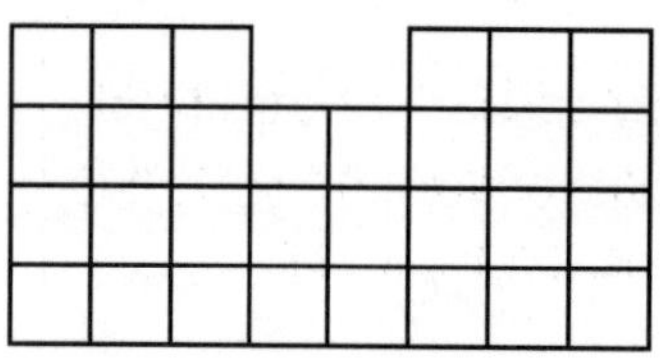

A (6 x 4) + (2 x 4)
B (3 x 4) + (2 x 4) + (3 x 4)
C 6 x 4
D (8 x 4) – 2

---

4. Which is one way to find the perimeter of the polygon?

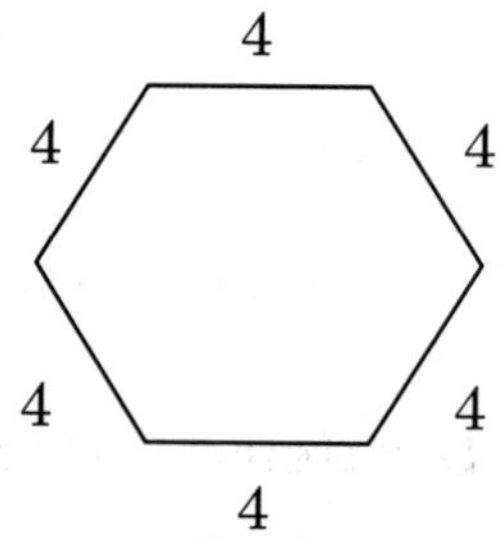

A 6 x 4 C (4 x 4 x 4) + (4 x 4)
B 4 x 8 D 6 + (4 x 1)

---

5. Which is one way to find the area of the triangle?

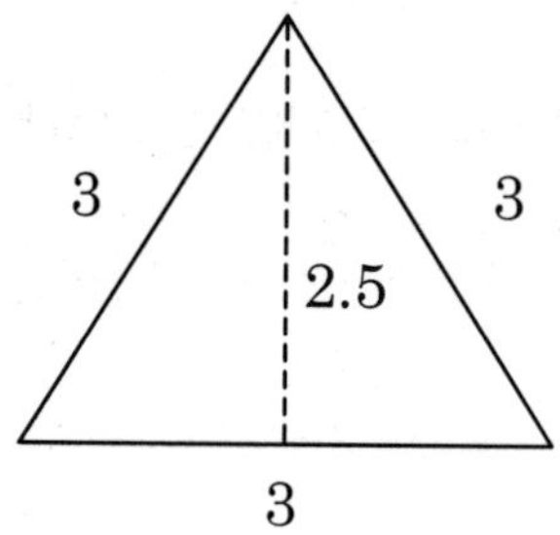

A 3 + 3 + 3
B 3 x 2.5
C (3 x 2.5) ÷ 2
D 3 + 3 + 3 + 2.5

---

6. Which is one way to find the perimeter of the polygon?

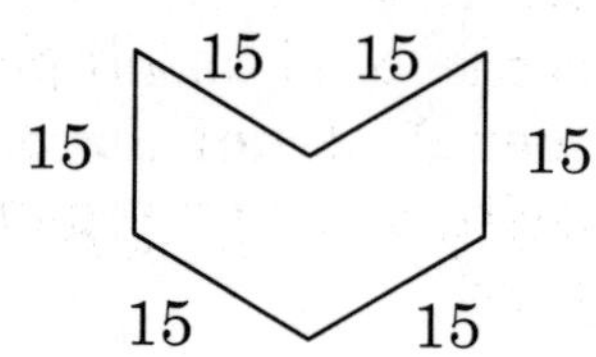

A 15 x 15
B 15 + 15 + 15 + 15 + 15
C 15 x 6
D (15 x 15 x 15) + (15 x 15 x 15)

Measurement: Sample for Analysis

The student is expected to measure to solve problems involving length (including perimeter), weight, capacity, time, temperature, and area. (TAKS 4:5.11A)

Area and Perimeter Problems

The area of a square room is 9 square feet. What is the perimeter of the room?

A 3 feet **B** 4 feet **C** 12 feet **D** 18 feet

Strategy: Draw a Picture--Objective 6 5.14C

Understand the Problem

What is the question?

What is the perimeter of the room?

What is the important information?

Area of square that is 9 square feet

Step 1

Choose a Plan

Draw a Picture

Draw a picture of a square that is 9 square feet. When you find an area of a square, you multiply the two sides. In a square those two sides have to be the same number. What number can be multiplied by itself to get 9? Right 3 x 3. Draw a square with 3 on the top and 3 down the side.

Step 2

Work the Problem

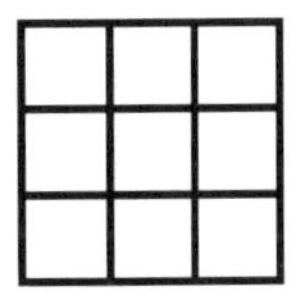

Now count the number of squares around the square room or add 3 + 3 + 3 + 3 for the four sides.

Step 3

Is this the Right Answer?

Write a sentence answering the question.

A square room with an area of 9 square feet has a perimeter of 12 feet.

Does it make sense? (Yes) No

Step 4

Measurement: Step Eight B

The student is expected to measure to solve problems involving length (including perimeter), weight, capacity, time, temperature, and area. (TAKS 4:5.11A)

1. The area of a square table is 49 square feet. What is the perimeter of the table?

   A 2,401 ft
   B 196 ft
   C 28 ft
   D 7 ft

2. The area of a square piece of fabric is 16 square centimeters. What is the perimeter of the fabric?

   A 256 cm
   B 16 cm
   C 8 cm
   D 4 cm

3. The area of a square board is 25 square inches. What is the perimeter of the board?

   A 5 in.
   B 12 in.
   C 20 in.
   D 100 in.

4. The area of a square sandbox is 144 square inches. What is the perimeter of the sandbox?

   A 12 in.
   B 24 in.
   C 42 in.
   D 48 m

5. The perimeter of a square rug is 16 inches. What is the area of the rug?

   A 16 sq in.
   B 32 sq in.
   C 64 sq in.
   D 256 sq in.

6. The perimeter of a square tablecloth is 36 centimeters. What is the area of the tablecloth?

   A 4 sq cm
   B 9 sq cm
   C 18 sq cm
   D 81 sq cm

7. The perimeter of a square table is 24 feet. What is the area of the table?

   A 6 sq ft
   B 12 sq ft
   C 24 sq ft
   D 36 sq ft

8. The perimeter of a square playing court is 40 feet. What is the area of the playing court?

   A 100 sq ft
   B 40 sq ft
   C 10 sq ft
   D 4 sq ft

Measurement: Sample for Analysis

The student is expected to measure volume using models of cubic units. (TAKS 4:5.10A)

Volume

A square prism made of 1-inch cubes is shown below.

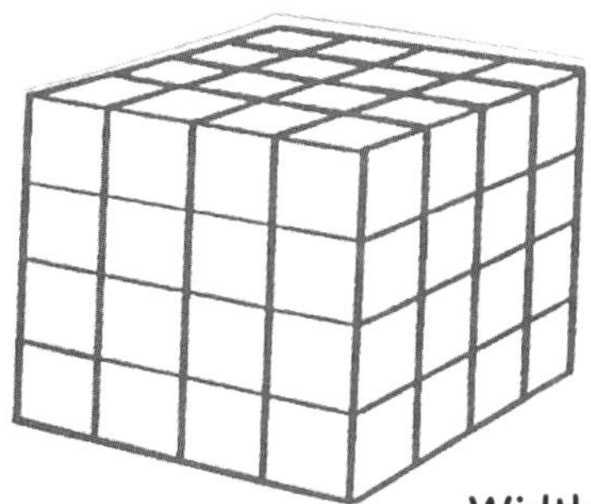

What is the volume of this square prism?

A 4 in.^{3} **B** 16 in.^{3} **C** 32 in.^{3} **D** 64 in.^{3}

Strategy:

1. A square prism is a three-dimensional figure. You have to use your imagination and turn this two-dimensional picture into a three-dimensional prism. Volume is the amount of space inside each cube. Since each cube is 1 cubic inch then the total number of cubes will be the volume of this figure in cubic inches.

2. The formula for volume is: Length x Width x Height. Length (4) x Width (4) x Height (4) = Volume 64

3. The answer is 64 cubic inches or 64 in.^{3}

Measurement: Step Nine A

The student is expected to measure volume using models of cubic units. (TAKS 4:5.10A)

1. A rectangular prism made of 1-inch cubes is shown below.

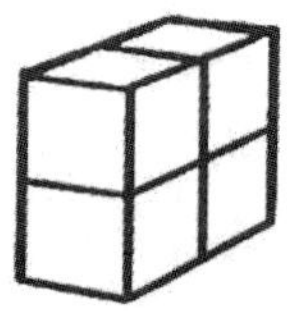

What is the volume of this rectangular prism?

A 8 in.^{3} **C** 5 in.^{3}

B 6 in.^{3} **D** 4 in^3

2. A figure made of 1-inch cubes is shown below.

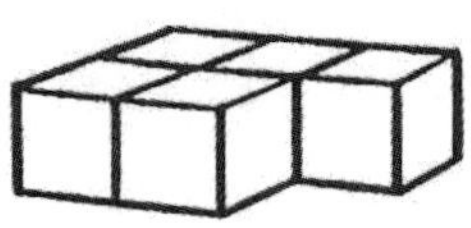

What is the volume of this figure?

A 15 in.^{3} **C** 6 in.^{3}

B 10 in.^{3} **D** 5 in.^{3}

3. The rectangular prism below is made of 1-inch cubes.

What is the volume of this rectangular prism?

A 6 in.^{3} **C** 10 in.^{3}

B 8 in.^{3} **D** 11 in.^{3}

4. A rectangular prism made of 1-inch cubes is shown below.

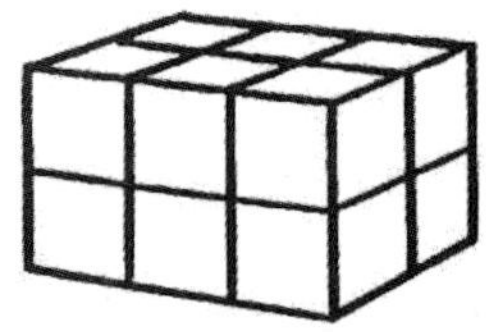

What is the volume of this rectangular prism?

A 16 in.^{3} **C** 10 in.^{3}

B 12 in.^{3} **D** 9 in.^{3}

5. A square prism made of 1-inch cubes is shown below.

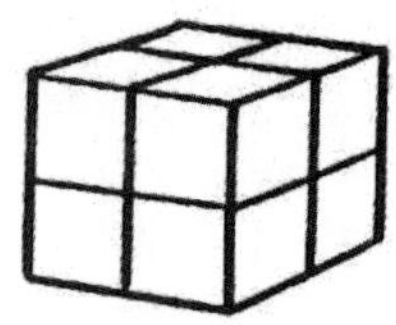

What is the volume of this square prism?

A 8 in.^{3} **C** 12 in.^{3}

B 10 in.^{3} **D** 16 in.^{3}

6. The square prism below is made of 1-inch cubes.

What is the volume of this square prism?

A 120 in.^{3} **C** 48 in.^{3}

B 64 in.^{3} **D** 24 in.^{3}

Measurement: Step Nine B

The student is expected to measure volume using models of cubic units. (TAKS 4:5.10A)

1. A square prism made of 1-inch cubes is shown below.

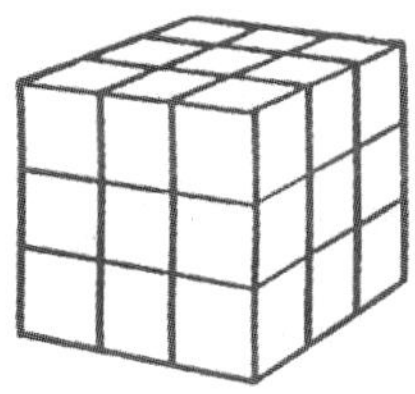

What is the volume of this square prism?

A 6 in.^{3} C 18 in.^{3}

B 9 in.^{3} D 27 in^3

2. A rectangular prism made of 1-inch cubes is shown below.

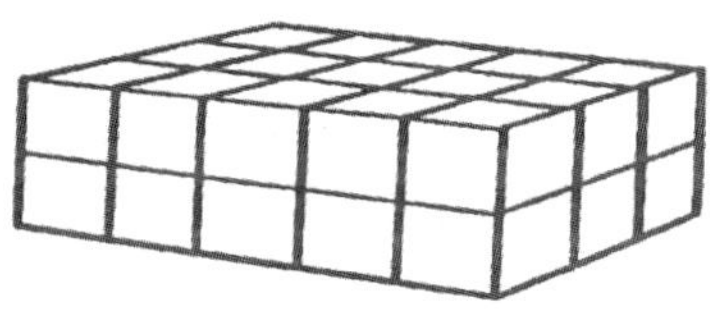

What is the volume of this rectangular prism?

A 5 in.^{3} C 18 in.^{3}

B 10 in.^{3} D 30 in.^{3}

3. The figure below is made of 1-inch cubes.

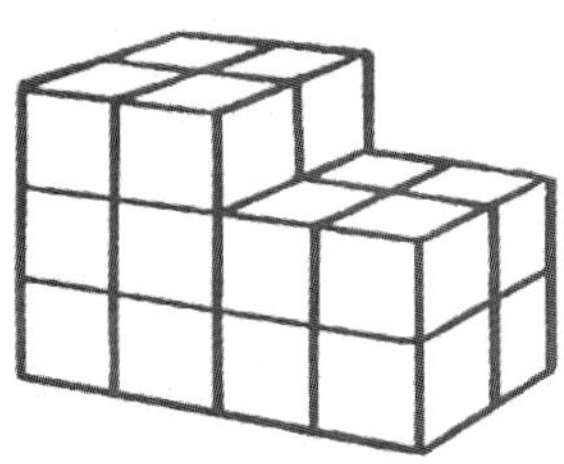

What is the volume of this figure?

A 8 in.^{3} C 20 in.^{3}

B 12 in.^{3} D 24 in.^{3}

4. A figure made of 1-inch cubes is shown below.

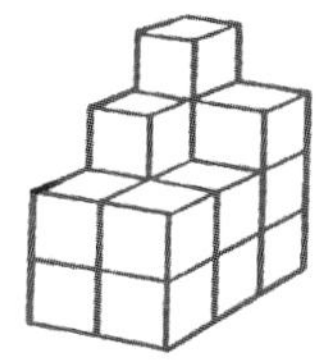

What is the volume of this figure?

A 16 in.^{3} C 10 in.^{3}

B 15 in.^{3} D 9 in.^{3}

5. A rectangular prism made of 1-inch cubes is shown below.

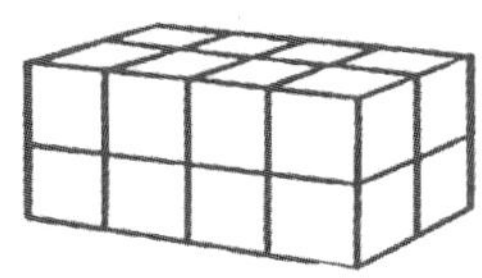

What is the volume of this rectangular prism?

A 8 in.^{3} C 18 in.^{3}

B 16 in.^{3} D 20 in.^{3}

6. The rectangular prism below is made of 1-inch cubes.

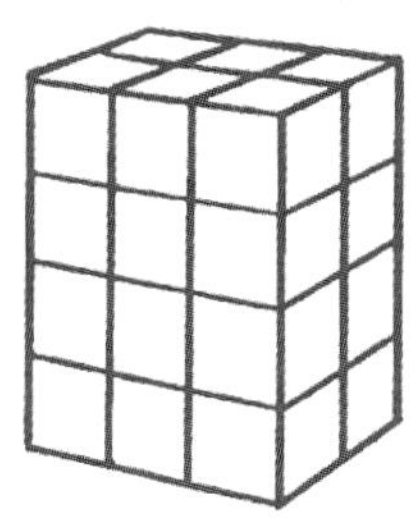

What is the volume of this rectangular prism?

A 26 in.^{3} C 36 in.^{3}

B 32 in.^{3} D 24 in.^{3}

Measurement: Assessment

TAKS Objectives: 4:5.10A, 4:5.11A, 4:5.11B

1. The area of a square rug is 36 square feet. What is the perimeter of the rug?

   A 6 ft **C** 36 ft
   B 24 ft **D** 48 ft

2. Richard has a sign shop. Recently he made a sign with an arrow as shown below.

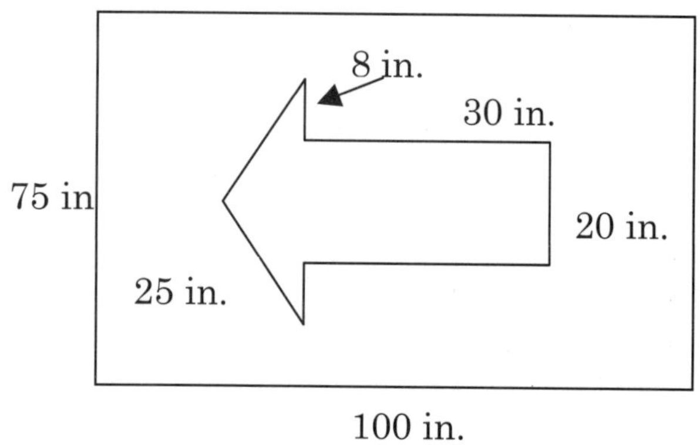

   What is the perimeter of the arrow?

   A 83 in. **C** 166 in.
   B 146 in. **D** 350 in.

3. The perimeter of a square room is 32 feet. What is the area of the square room?

   A 72 sq ft **C** 320 sq ft
   B 64 sq ft **D** 8 sq ft

4. Which unit of measurement is $\frac{1}{100}$ of a meter?

   A 1 centimeter **C** 1 millimeter
   B 1 decimeter **D** 1 kilometer

5. Juan held his breath for 1 minute and 10 seconds. Tony held his breath for 2 minutes. How much longer did Tony hold his breath than Juan?

   A 30 min 10 sec **C** 1 min 50 sec
   B 1 min 10 sec **D** 50 sec

6. How many centimeters are in 357 meters?

   A 3.57 cm **C** 3,570 cm
   B 35.7 cm **D** 35,700 cm

7. The library book weighs 1,456 grams. How many kilograms does the book weigh?

   A 1.456 kg **C** 145,600 kg
   B 14.56 kg **D** 1,456,000 kg

8. What fractional part of a quart is a ounce?

   A $\frac{1}{2}$ **B** $\frac{1}{4}$ **C** $\frac{1}{16}$ **D** $\frac{1}{32}$

9. Dad's riding lawn mower weighs 500 pounds. This could also be written as ______

   A 5 tons **C** $\frac{1}{4}$ ton
   B $\frac{1}{2}$ ton **D** $\frac{1}{5}$ ton

10. Ted's jump rope is 5 inches shorter than 12 feet. How many inches is this?

    A 60 in. **C** 144 in.
    B 139 in. **D** 149 in.

11. Elisa weighs 74 pounds, 14 ounces. How many total ounces is this?

A 88 oz
B 888 oz
C 1,184 oz
D 1,198 oz

---

12. Jan ran 12 miles on a rectangular course. She ran 2 miles down Ave. B and 4 miles down 1st Street. How many miles did Jan run on Ave. A?

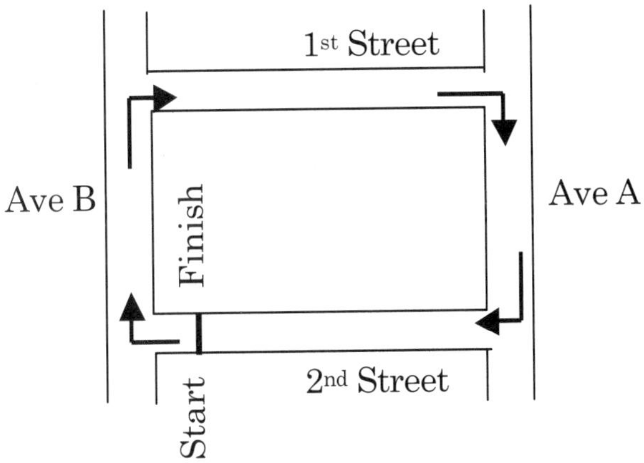

A 2 miles
B 4 miles
C 6 miles
D 8 miles

---

13. Which is one way to find the area of the polygon?

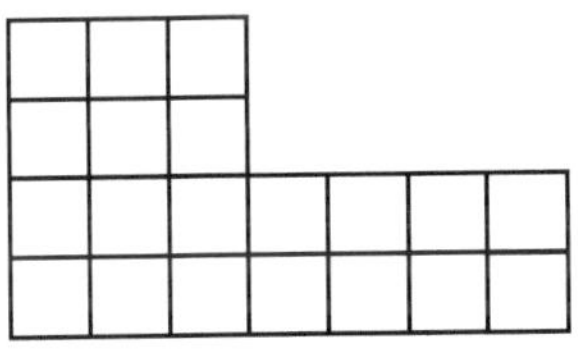

A (4 x 6) - (4 x 3)
B (3 x 4) + (2 x 4)
C (3 x 4) x (2 x 4)
D (3 x 2) + (2 x 4)

---

14. The area of Jinna's quilt is 120 square feet. The quilt is 10 feet wide. Which number sentence could be used to find the length of Jinna's quilt?

A 129 – 10 = □
B 120 + 10 = □
C 120 x 10 = □
D 120 ÷ 10 = □

15. Gene had a dentist appointment at 10:45 AM on Saturday morning. He was in the dentist's office for 2 hours and 30 minutes. What time did Gene leave the dentist office?

A 12:45 PM
B 1:00 PM
C 1:15 PM
D 2:15 PM

---

16. What is the area of this triangle?

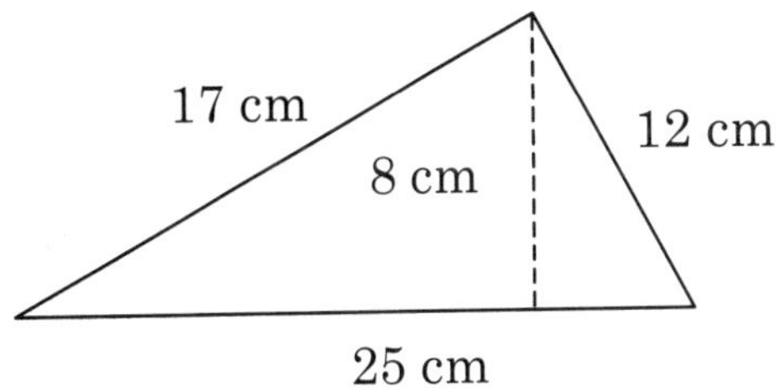

A 200 square cm
B 150 square cm
C 100 square cm
D 62 square cm

---

17. The square prism below is made of 1-inch cubes.

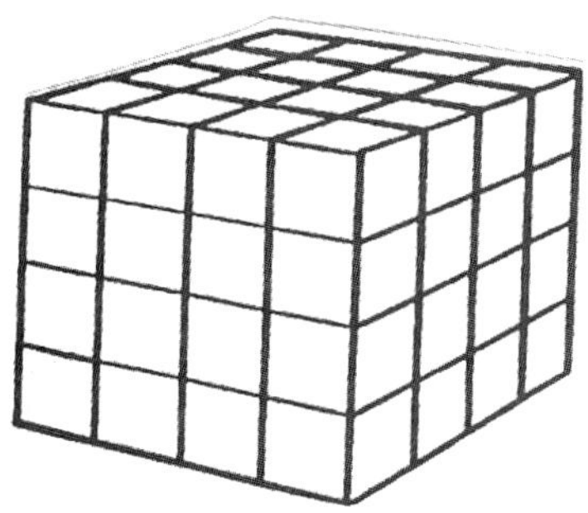

What is the volume of this square prism?

A 16 in.^{3}
B 32 in.^{3}
C 64 in.^{3}
D 128 in.^{3}

Measurement: Answer Key

Step One A
1. A
2. C
3. C
4. B
5. C
6. D
7. C
8. B
9. D
10. A

Step One B
1. C
2. B
3. C
4. C
5. D
6. C
7. C
8. C
9. D
10. C

Step One C
1. C
2. C
3. B
4. A
5. B
6. B
7. B
8. C
9. B
10. D
11. A

Step One D
1. A
2. D
3. C
4. D
5. A
6. D

Step One E
1. C
2. B
3. D
4. B
5. A
6. B
7. C
8. A
9. A

Step One F
1. B
2. D
3. D
4. A
5. B
6. B
7. A
8. C

Step Two A
1. B
2. A
3. C
4. D
5. D
6. A
7. B
8. C
9. A
10. A
11. D
12. B
13. C

Step Two B
1. C
2. D
3. B
4. D
5. B
6. A
7. B
8. A

Step Two C
1. A
2. B
3. A
4. C
5. D
6. C
7. B
8. C

Step Three A
1. B
2. C
3. C
4. D
5. A
6. B
7. B
8. A
9. C
10. B
11. D
12. B

Step Three B
1. C
2. B
3. A
4. D
5. C
6. B

Step Four A
1. C
2. A
3. C
4. C
5. D
6. B

Step Four B
1. D
2. D
3. C
4. C

Step Four C
1. B
2. B
3. D
4. B

Step Four D
1. A
2. B
3. C
4. B
5. D
6. A
7. C
8. A

Step Four E
1. C
2. B
3. C
4. A
5. C
6. A

Step Five A
1. D
2. B
3. D
4. A
5. A

Step Five B
1. C
2. A
3. D
4. D
5. C
6. D
7. A
8. A

Step Five C
1. A
2. D
3. A
4. D
5. D
6. B
7. B
8. C

Step Six A
1. C
2. B
3. C
4. B
5. A
6. D

Step Six B
1. A
2. C
3. B
4. D
5. C
6. A

Step Seven A
1. A
2. A

Step Seven B
1. B
2. D

Step Eight A
1. B
2. B
3. D
4. A
5. C
6. C

Step Eight B
1. C
2. B
3. C
4. D
5. A
6. D
7. D
8. A

Step Nine A
1. D
2. D
3. A
4. B
5. A
6. B

Step Nine B
1. D
2. D
3. C
4. A
5. B
6. D

Assessment
1. B
2. B
3. B
4. A
5. D
6. D
7. A
8. D
9. C
10. B
11. D
12. A
13. B
14. D
15. C
16. C
17. C

Probability and Statistics

The student is expected to use pictures to make generalizations about determining all possible combinations. **(TEKS 5.5A) (TAKS 2)** *Students will determine possible combinations using verbal and/or pictorial representations of choices. The pictorial representations may be drawings, diagrams, or lists. Students will select the number or possible combinations, a pictorial representation of the possible combinations, a combination that is possible, or a combination that is NOT possible.*

The student is expected to use lists, tables, charts, and diagrams to find patterns and make generalizations, such as a procedure for determining equivalent fractions. **(TEKS 5.5B) (TAKS 2)** *When matching data with appropriate graphical representation, students will represent all the data points accurately, use correct labels, show whether data is discrete or continuous, and determine that the graphical representation contains all the information provided by the set of data. Graphical representation may include, but are not limited to, pictographs, bar graphs, number-line graphs, broken graphs, Venn diagrams, and scatterplots. Data may be embedded in text or may be organized in a list, table, or tally chart.*

The student is expected to use experimental results to make predictions. **(TEKS 5.12B) (TAKS 5)** *Information will be listed in the text of the item or will be given in a table or chart. Students will be asked to find the fractional part that a given outcome represents, to identify the probability that the next outcome will be a given outcome, or to use an experimental probability to predict the number of times a given outcome will occur in a given total number of outcomes..*

The student is expected to describe characteristics of data presented in tables and graphs including the shape and spread of the data and the middle number. **(TEKS 5.13B) (TAKS 5)** *Students will match the median or the range with a given set of data provided in a table or graph, or will describe characteristics of the data in word form or in number form, such as how many more or how many less. Students may also identify characteristics that do NOT fit the data.*

The student is expected to graph a given set of data using an appropriate graphical representation such as a picture or line. **(TEKS 5.13C) (TAKS 5)** *Students will match a table of related number pairs to a graph of a line (such as ordered pairs on a coordinate grid) or a broken-line graph.*

Suggested Sequence
Simple to Complex

Step One .... Pattern and Generalizations (TAKS 2:5.5B)
Step Two .... Characteristics of Data (TAKS 5:5.13B)
Step Three .... Probability (TAKS 2:5.5A, 5:5.12B)
Step Four .... Possible Combinations (TAKS 2:5.5A)
Step Five .... Appropriate Graphical Representation (TAKS 5:5.13C)
Assessment

"Patterns" is a strong concept in Objective 2 because of the patterns in algebraic expressions. It is also a strong concept in Objective 6 because "patterns" is one of the most used strategies in problem solving. It is placed under Probability and Statistics in this book because it is such a strong concept in evaluating the data to determine the probability that the occurrence will continue.

Vocabulary:

- 🕮 Probably
- 🕮 Possible Combinations
- 🕮 Greatest Number of Times
- 🕮 Graph
- 🕮 Possible Outcomes
- 🕮 Least Number of Times
- 🕮 Probability
- 🕮 Possible Combinations
- 🕮 Mean (Average)
- 🕮 Chart
- 🕮 Line graph
- 🕮 Bar Graph
- 🕮 Venn Diagraph
- 🕮 Middle (Median) Number
- 🕮 Prediction
- 🕮 Spread (Range)
- 🕮 Digit
- 🕮 Scatterplot
- 🕮 Broke-Graph

Probability and Statistics: Step One A

The student is expected to use lists, tables, charts, and diagrams to find patterns and make generalizations. (TAKS 2:5.5B)

1. The chart shows the price of candy bars for sale at the local store.

Candy Sales

Number of Candy Bars	Cost (includes tax)
2	$0.25
4	$0.50
6	$0.75
8	$1.00

If the pattern continues, exactly how many candy bars can Sean buy with $2.00?

A 10 **C** 14
B 12 **D** 16

2. Carbonated drinks are on sale this weekend at the grocery store. The chart shows the cost of six packs of drinks, including tax.

Carbonated Drinks

Six Packs	Total Cost
3	$5
6	$7
9	$9
12	$11

If the pattern continues, exactly how many six packs can Sean buy with $15?

A 13 **C** 16
B 14 **D** 18

3. The chart shows the price of balloons for sale at the local store.

Balloons

Number of Balloons	Cost
2	$0.75
4	$1.50
6	$2.25
8	$3.00

If the pattern continues, exactly how many balloons can Maria buy with $5.25?

A 10 **C** 14
B 12 **D** 16

4. Action characters are on sale this weekend at the mall. The chart shows the cost of action characters, including tax.

Action Characters

Number of Action Characters	Total Cost
1	$5
5	$8
9	$11
13	$14

If the pattern continues, exactly how many action characters can Sean buy with $20?

A 21 **C** 17
B 19 **D** 15

Probability and Statistics: Step One B

The student is expected to use lists, tables, charts, and diagrams to find patterns and make generalizations. (TAKS 2:5.5B)

1. The chart shows the number of hotdog buns in different numbers of packages.

Packages of Hotdog Buns

Number of Packages	3	5	7	8
Total Number of Buns	24	40	56	64

If the pattern continues, which method can be used to find the total number of hotdog buns in 15 packages?

A Multiply 15 and 9
B Multiply 15 and 8
C Multiply 15 and 7
D Add 64 and 15

---

2. Mrs. Ramos is baking cookies for a bake sale. She is going to make several batches of cookies. The chart shows the number of eggs needed for different batches of cookies.

Batches of Cookies

Number of Batches	4	6	9	12
Number of Eggs Needed	8	12	18	24

If the pattern continues, which method can be used to find the total number of eggs needed for 16 batches of cookies?

A Multiply 16 and 24
B Multiply 16 and 12
C Multiply 16 and 2
D Add 16 and 24

---

3. Tiffany is making beaded necklaces. The chart shows how long it takes her to make different numbers of necklaces.

Necklaces

Number of Necklaces	2	5	6	8
Total Minutes to Make	12	30	36	48

If the pattern continues, which method can be used to find the total number of minutes it will take her to make 12 necklaces?

A Add 12 and 48
B Multiply 12 and 8
C Add 12 and 8
D Multiply 12 and 6

Probability and Statistics: Step One C

The student is expected to use lists, tables, charts, and diagrams to find patterns and make generalizations. (TAKS 2:5.5B)

1. Manuel is planning a long enduring bicycle ride. The table shows how many miles he can ride during different lengths of time. The numbers form a pattern.

Manuel's Long Ride

Number of Hours	2	3	4	5	6
Number of Miles	53	79.5	106		

Find the missing numbers in the table.

A 132.5 mi and 158 mi
B 132.5 mi and 159 mi
C 122.5 mi and 149 mi
D 108 mi and 126 mi

---

2. Mrs. Ramos is making curtains for her home. The table shows how many yards of fabric she needs for the windows. The numbers form a pattern.

Fabric for Window Curtains

Number of Windows	2	3	4	5	6
Number of Yards of Fabric	9	13.5	18		

Find the missing numbers in the table.

A 21.5 yd and 25 yd
B 21.5 yd and 37 yd
C 22.5 yd and 27 yd
D 20.5 yd and 23 yd

---

3. Melissa is making tile covered boxes to sell at the craft show. The table shows how many tiles she needs for the boxes. The numbers form a pattern.

Tile Box Project

Number of Boxes	2	3	4	5	6
Number of Tiles	13.5	20	26.5		

Find the missing numbers in the table.

A 33 and 39.5
B 27.5 and 30
C 36.5 and 40
D 39.5 and 40

Probability and Statistics: Sample for Analysis

The student is expected to describe characteristics of data presented in tables and graphs including the shape and spread of the data and the middle number. (TAKS 5:5.13 B)

Characteristic of Data

(Mean)

Martin raises cattle. Yesterday, he sold 3 cows at the local cattle auction. The first cow sold for $879. The second cow sold for $762, and the third cow went for a price of $912. What was the mean (average) price of each of these cows?

A $638 **B** $851 **C** $879 **D** $2,553

Strategy:

1. The mean price is the price that you would get if you added the price of all the cows and then divided this total by the number of cows. It can also be called the "average" price.

2.

```
  $879          $851
  $762       3|$2553
+ $912         24
------         --
$2,553          15
                15
                --
                 3
                 3
                --
                 0
```

3. The mean (average) price of each cow is $851. Mark answer choice B on your answer sheet.

Tip: A mean (average) number will never be less than the smallest number or greater than the largest number.

Probability and Statistics: Step Two A

The student is expected to describe characteristics of data presented in tables and graphs including the shape and spread of the data and the middle number. (TAKS 5:5.13 B)

1. Mrs. Valdez had a parent conference with 5 parents today. She spent 20 minutes with the first and last parents, 35 minutes with the second parent, 5 minutes with the third parent, and 1 hour with the fourth parent. What was the mean (average) amount of time she spent with each parent?

   A 16 min **C** 24 min
   B 20 min **D** 28 min

2. David played 4 games of Scrabble. His scores were 192, 185, 219, and 176. What was his mean (average) score?

   A 155 **C** 193
   B 183 **D** 197

3. At the "All-You-Can-Eat Pancake Feast", Scott ate 34 pancakes, Randy ate 30 pancakes, and Robert ate 50 pancakes. What is the mean (average) number of pancakes eaten by these three men?

   A 36 **C** 57
   B 38 **D** 114

4. Rene took 4 tests in her math class. Her scores were 98, 87, 92, and 84. What was her mean (average) score rounded to the nearest whole number?

   A 90 **C** 92
   B 91 **D** 361

5. In 1987, it rained 27 inches in Utopia, Texas. In 1988, the rainfall for the year totaled 35 inches, while it rained only 19 inches in 1989. What was the mean (average) annual rainfall in Utopia, Texas during this 3-year period?

   A 19 in. **C** 27 in.
   B 20 in. **D** 81 in.

6. Julie performed a gymnastics routine at a tournament. The 5 judges gave her scores of 9, 7, 5, 8, and 6. What was Julie's mean (average) score?

   A 5 **C** 8
   B 7 **D** 35

7. David was shopping for a new coat. He liked a wool coat that cost $179. He also found a nylon jacket for $22 and a cloth coat for $63. What was the mean (average) price of these 3 coats?

   A $88 **C** $121
   B $100 **D** $264

8. Kathleen exercised 45 minutes Monday, 1 hour Tuesday and 54 minutes on Wednesday. What was the mean (average) amount of time that Kathleen exercised?

   A 159 min **C** 53 min
   B 100 min **D** 33 min

Probability and Statistics: Sample for Analysis

The student is expected to describe characteristics of data presented in tables and graphs including the shape and spread of the data and the middle number. (TAKS 5:5.13 B)

Characteristic of Data
(Median)

The attendance for Mrs. Newman's fifth grade class for a week is shown below. What is the median (middle) attendance for the week?

Fifth Grade Daily Attendance	
Day	**Number of Students**
Monday	24
Tuesday	22
Wednesday	25
Thursday	20
Friday	18

A 25 **B** 24 **C** 22 **D** 18

Strategy:

1. The question is asking for the median which is the middle number and that is exactly what it means.
2. Arrange the numbers from least to greatest:

   18
   20
   (22)
   24
   25
3. Circle the number in the middle.
4. That is what they are asking: "What is the number in the middle?"
5. The middle number is 22, choice C.

Tip: Do not forget to arrange them in order from least to greatest or greatest to least and then circle the middle number.

Tip: If there are an even number of entries, then you would use the average of the two middle numbers.

Probability and Statistics: Step Two B

The student is expected to describe characteristics of data presented in tables and graphs including the shape and spread of the data and the middle number. (TAKS 5:5.13 B)

1. Connie had a lemonade stand in her front yard for 5 days, which is shown below. What is the median (middle) sales for the 5-day period?

Lemonade Sales	
Day	**Money Made**
Monday	$15
Tuesday	$18
Wednesday	$8
Thursday	$12
Friday	$16

A $8 **C** $16
B $15 **D** $18

2. Timmy's basketball team is on a winning streak. Below are the number of points his team scored in the last 5 games. What is the median (middle) points for the 5 games?

Timmy's Team	
Game	**Points**
First	32
Second	54
Third	26
Fourth	35
Fifth	43

A 26 **C** 35
B 32 **D** 43

3. Karla's scouts were selling cookies. She recorded her group's sells for a 5 week period. What is the median (middle) sales for the 5 week period?

Cookie Sales	
Week	**Sales**
First	$78
Second	$94
Third	$83
Fourth	$54
Fifth	$67

A $67 **C** $83
B $78 **D** $94

4. Mollie's softball team is planning to go to state. Below are the number of points her team scored in the last 5 games. What is the median (middle) points for the 5 games?

Mollie's Team	
Game	**Points**
First	16
Second	8
Third	18
Fourth	12
Fifth	14

A 8 **C** 14
B 12 **D** 16

Probability and Statistics: Sample for Analysis

The student is expected to describe characteristics of data presented in tables and graphs including the shape and spread of the data and the middle number. (TAKS 5:5.13 B)

Characteristic of Data

(Range or Spread)

The high temperature for Wylie, Texas, on the third day of July over the last 10 years is given in the table.

Year	Temperature
1993	92° F
1994	93° F
1995	95° F
1996	96° F
1997	93° F
1998	96° F
1999	91° F
2000	98° F
2001	95° F
2002	96° F

What is the range of these temperatures?

A 7° F **B** 94.5° F **C** 91° F **D** 96° F

Strategy:

1. Carefully examine the table before reading the problem.
2. Read the problem for understanding.
3. Find the range.
4. The range is the difference between the highest temperature and lowest temperature. 98 - 91 = 7
5. The correct answer is the first choice.
6. Choice B is the median temperature.
7. Choice C is the lowest temperature.
8. Choice D is the temperature that occurs most often.

Probability and Statistics: Step Two C

The student is expected to describe characteristics of data presented in tables and graphs including the shape and spread of the data and the middle number. (TAKS 5:5.13 B)

1. Carmen sold Girl Scout Cookies in her neighborhood. Below is a chart listing the number of boxes she sold each day. What is the range of the number of boxes she sold in a five day period?

Cookies	
Day	**Boxes Sold**
Monday	16
Tuesday	15
Wednesday	7
Thursday	14
Friday	8

A 5 **C** 14
B 9 **D** 60

2. For the last two weeks Martha has been studying fractions in her math class. Below is a list of her grades on five of her tests in the last two weeks. What is the range of her grades?

Martha's Math Tests	
Test	**Grade**
First	72
Second	65
Third	86
Fourth	83
Fifth	87

A 22 **C** 157
B 83 **D** 786

3. Ricky is raising a calf for the stock show. Below is a chart listing his calf's weight as it nears time for the show. What is the range of the weight of the calf during the 5 weeks before the show?

Calf's Weight	
Week	**Pounds**
First	555
Second	595
Third	642
Fourth	675
Fifth	697

A 142 lb **C** 642 lb
B 150 lb **D** 633 lb

4. Wylie had rain for 5 days straight. Below is the amount of rain for each of the five days. What is the range of the amount of rain during those five days?

Wylie's Rainy Days	
Day	**Inches of Rain**
Sunday	5
Monday	4
Tuesday	6
Thursday	2
Friday	3

A 24 in. **C** 4 in.
B 20 in. **D** 2 in.

Probability and Statistics: Step Two D

The student is expected to describe characteristics of data presented in tables and graphs including the shape and spread of the data and the middle number. (TAKS 5:5.13 B)

The graph shows David's math quiz scores for a 6-week period.

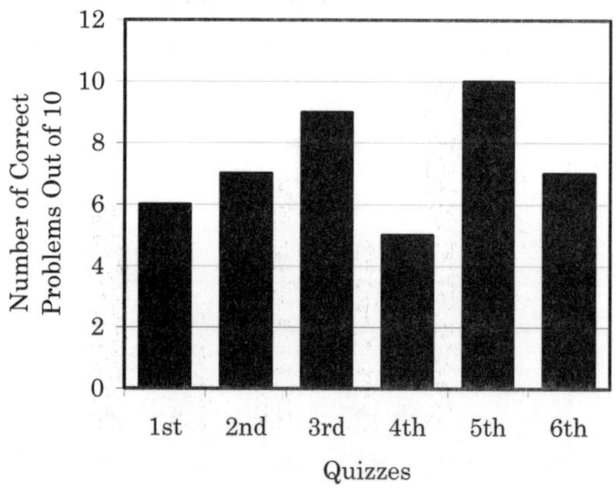

1. What was David's second best score?

A 9 **C** 7
B 8 **D** 6

---

2. What was the range of the David's scores?

A 5 **C** 7
B 6 **D** 8

---

3. What is David's median (middle) score?

A 5 **C** 7
B 6 **D** 8

---

4. What is David's mean (average) rounded to the nearest whole number?

A 5 **C** 7
B 6 **D** 8

The graph shows chocolate doughnut sales at Dave's Doughnuts and Delights.

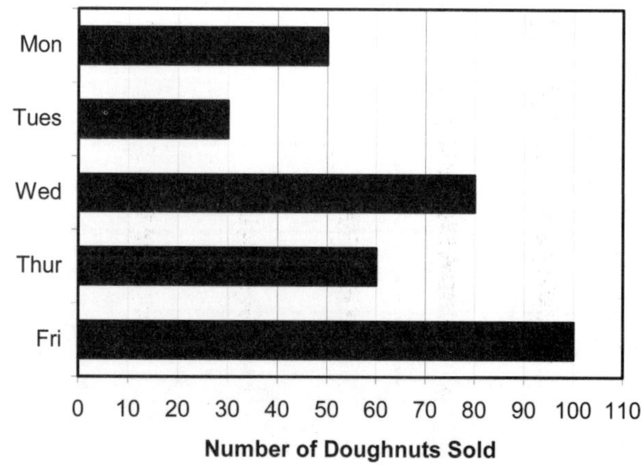

5. What is the mean (average) of the doughnuts sold?

A 60 **C** 75
B 64 **D** 80

---

6. What is the median (middle) amount of the doughnuts sold?

A 60 **C** 75
B 64 **D** 80

---

7. How many doughnuts were sold on Monday, Tuesday, and Wednesday?

A 160 **C** 110
B 130 **D** 80

---

8. What is the range of the doughnuts sold?

A 80 **C** 60
B 70 **D** 50

Probability and Statistics: Step Two E

The student is expected to describe characteristics of data presented in tables and graphs including the shape and spread of the data and the middle number. (TAKS 5:5.13 B)

The graph shows Ed's math test scores during a 6-week grading period.

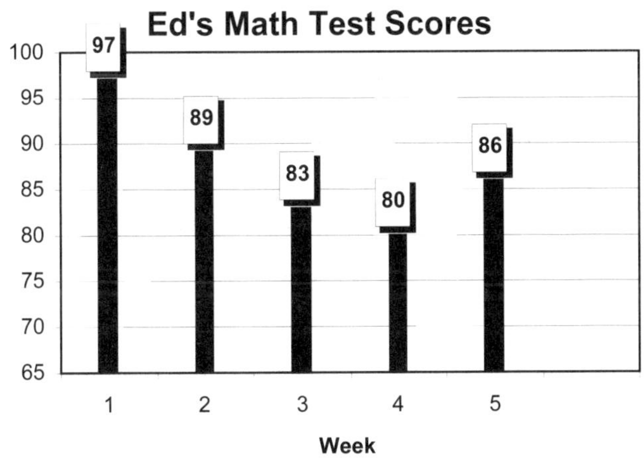

1. What is Ed's math test mean (average) rounded to the nearest whole number?

   A 86
   B 87
   C 89
   D 91

2. Which statement best describes Ed's test scores for the grading period?

   A Ed's scores improved after the fourth grading period.
   B Ed's scores stayed the same throughout the 6 weeks.
   C Ed's scores went down from the first week until the last.
   D Ed's scores improved throughout the 6 weeks.

3. What is Ed's median (middle) score for his math tests?

   A 87
   B 86
   C 83
   D 80

The graph shows the heights of 5 children in Mr. Ruiz class.

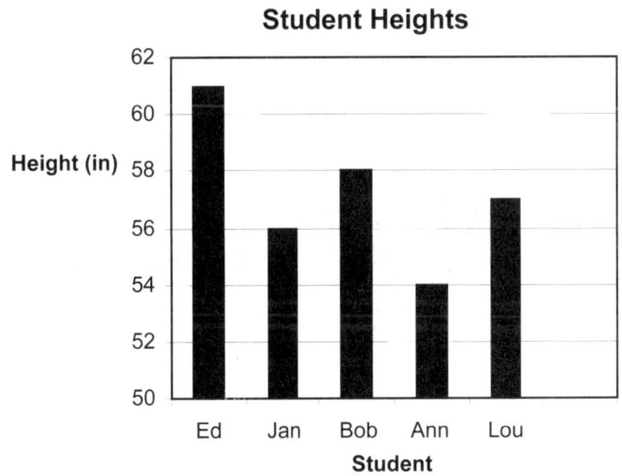

4. What is the mean (average) height of the 5 students rounded to the nearest whole number?

   A 54
   B 56
   C 57
   D 58

5. What is the median (middle) heights of the 5 students?

   A 54
   B 56
   C 57
   D 58

6. How many students are taller than 4 feet 8 inches?

   A 1
   B 2
   C 3
   D 4

7. What is the range of the heights of the students?

   A 63
   B 54
   C 7
   D 5

Probability and Statistics: Step Three A

The student is expected to use pictures to make generalizations about determining all possible combinations. (TAKS 2:5.5A)
The student is expected to use experimental results to make predictions. (TAKS 5:5.12B)

1. The cards shown below will be placed facedown.

If a card is picked, it is most likely to be a _____ .

A 1
B 3
C 4
D 5

---

2. In a total of 10 spins, which number will the spinner probably point to the greatest number of times?

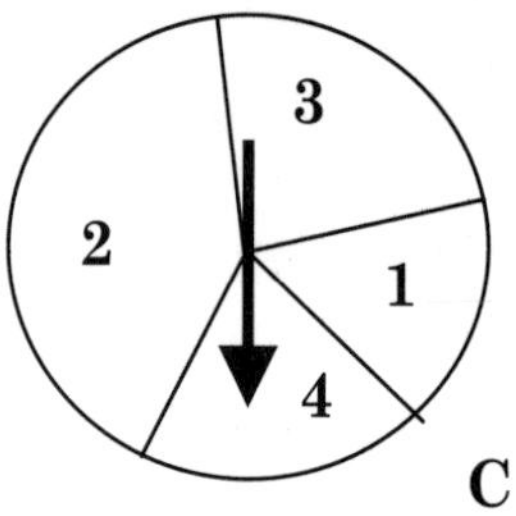

A 1
B 2
C 3
D 4

---

3. In a total of 200 spins, which color will the spinner probably point to the least number of times?

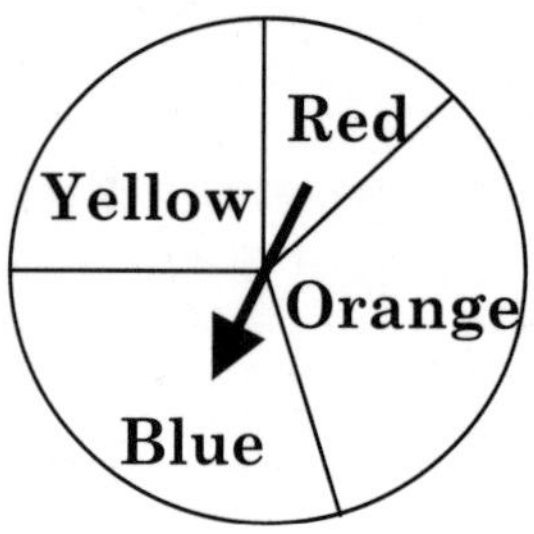

A Red
B Orange
C Blue
D Yellow

4. The cards shown below are placed facedown.

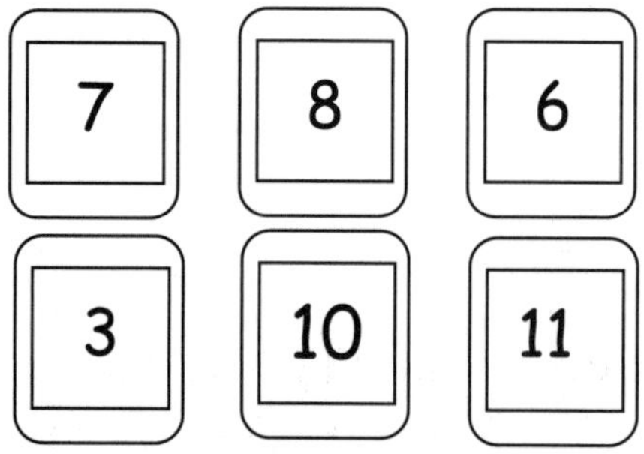

If you pick 1 card, it is most likely to be a_____.

A 1-digit number
B 2-digit number
C number less than 8
D number greater than 10

---

5. Michael has 3 different pairs of shoes that he can wear with jeans. His plan is to choose a pair of shoes at random using a game spinner. Which spinner should he use so that each pair of shoes has an equal chance of being selected?

A
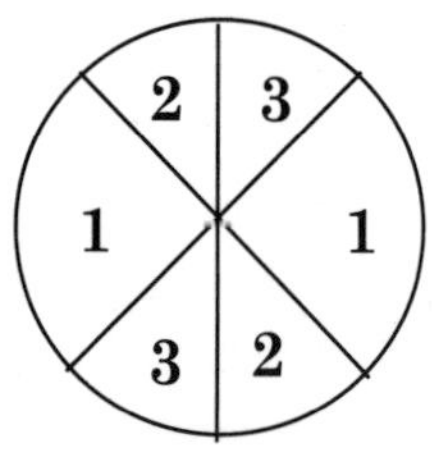

C
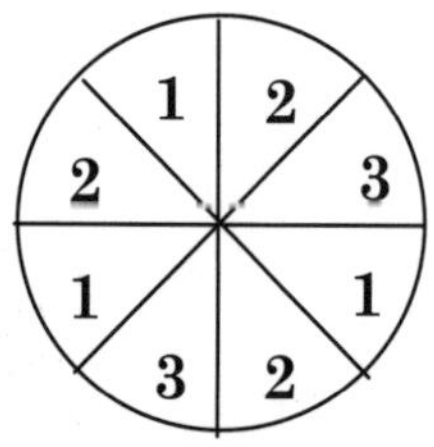

B
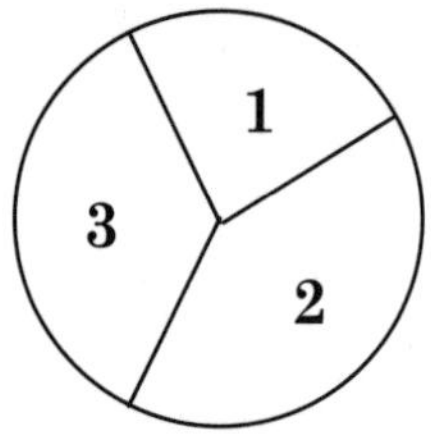

D
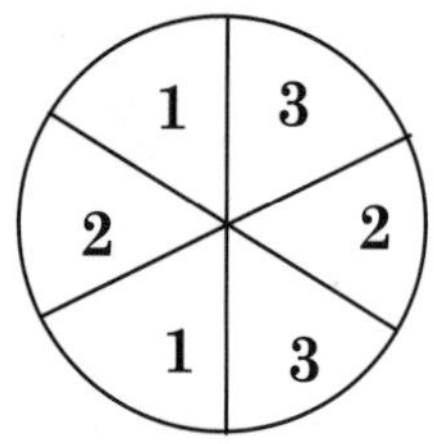

Probability and Statistics: Sample for Analysis

The student is expected to use pictures to make generalizations about determining all possible combinations. (TAKS 2:5.5A)
The student is expected to use experimental results to make predictions. (TAKS 5:5.12B)

Fractional Probability

Each section of the spinner below is the same size.

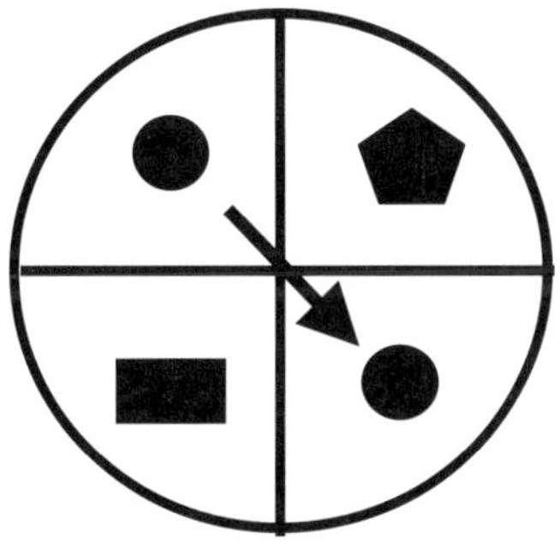

What is the probability of the spinner landing on a circle?

A $\frac{1}{4}$ **B** $\frac{1}{3}$ **C** $\frac{1}{2}$ **D** $\frac{2}{2}$

Strategy:

1. You want to find the probability that the spinner will land on the circle.
2. Since all 4 sections of the spinner are the same size, it is equally likely that the spinner could land in any section.
3. Notice that TWO of the sections of the spinner have a circle on them.
4. The probability could be expressed as a fraction:

$$\frac{\textit{Number of sections of spinner with circle}}{\textit{Number of sections in the spinner}} = \frac{2}{4} = \frac{1}{2}$$

5. Choice **C** is the correct answer.

Tip: Be sure to check all the sections of the spinner carefully. Reduce all fractions to their lowest terms.

Probability and Statistics: Step Three B

The student is expected to use pictures to make generalizations about determining all possible combinations. (TAKS 2:5.5A)
The student is expected to use experimental results to make predictions. (TAKS 5:5.12B)

1. Each section of the spinner below is the same size.

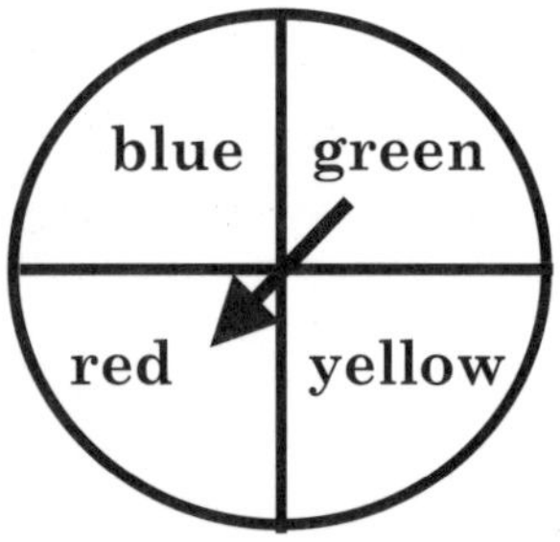

What is the probability of the spinner landing on the red section?

A $\frac{1}{4}$ **C** $\frac{1}{2}$

B $\frac{1}{3}$ **D** $\frac{3}{4}$

---

2. Each section of the spinner below is the same size.

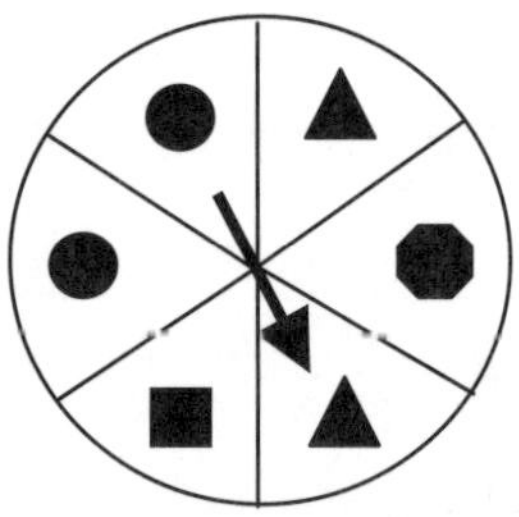

What is the probability of the spinner landing on the triangle?

A $\frac{1}{6}$ **C** $\frac{1}{3}$

B $\frac{1}{4}$ **D** $\frac{2}{3}$

3. Each section of the spinner below is the same size.

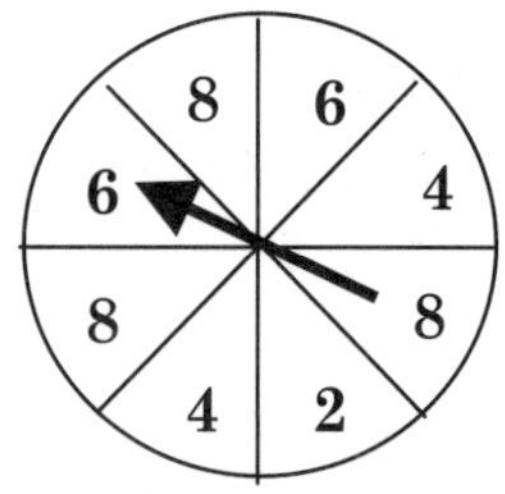

What is the probability of the spinner landing on the number 8?

A $\frac{1}{8}$ **C** $\frac{3}{5}$

B $\frac{3}{8}$ **D** $\frac{6}{7}$

---

4. Each section of the spinner below is the same size.

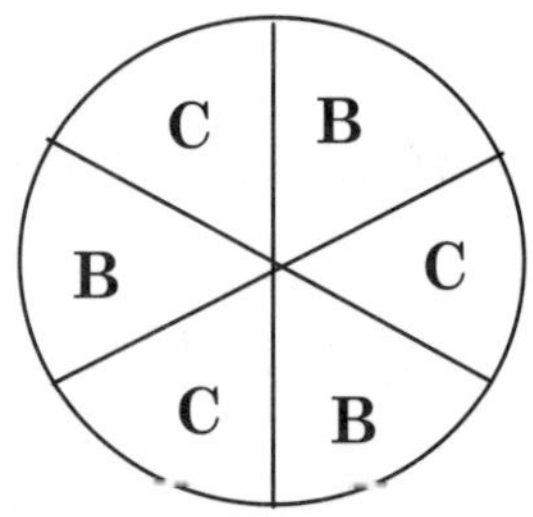

What is the probability of the spinner landing on C?

A $\frac{1}{6}$ **C** $\frac{1}{3}$

B $\frac{1}{4}$ **D** $\frac{1}{2}$

Probability and Statistics: Sample for Analysis

The student is expected to use pictures to make generalizations about determining all possible combinations. (TAKS 2:5.5A)
The student is expected to use experimental results to make predictions. (TAKS 5:5.12B)

A grocery store cart contains 8 cans of green beans, 6 cans of carrots, 4 cans of corn and 2 cans of pickled beets. The cans are all the same size and shape. If a can is chosen from the cart without looking, what is the probability that it will be a can of corn?

A $\frac{4}{16}$ **B** $\frac{1}{5}$ **C** $\frac{5}{20}$ **D** $\frac{1}{4}$

Strategy:

1. You want to find out what the chance is that a can of corn will be chosen when it is equally likely that any can could be chosen.
2. The probability can be expressed as a fraction.

$$\frac{\text{Number of cans of corn}}{\text{Total number of cans on shelf}} = \frac{4}{20}$$

3. The chances are, out of 20 possible choices, 4 are corn.
4. Mark answer Choice **B**, since $\frac{4}{20} = \frac{1}{5}$.

Tip: Always reduce fractions to lowest terms!
A fractional probability is always determined as follows:

$$\frac{\text{Number of successful outcomes}}{\text{Total number of outcomes}}$$

Probability and Statistics: Step Three C

The student is expected to use pictures to make generalizations about determining all possible combinations. (TAKS 2:5.5A)
The student is expected to use experimental results to make predictions. (TAKS 5:5.12B)

1. Patrick owns a fencing company. He checked the records of the fences he built last month. Of the 15 fences built, 1 was barbed wire, 5 were chain link, 6 were cedar, and 3 were redwood. If Patrick randomly chose to inspect 1 of these fences, what is the probability that it would be a chain-link fence?

   A $\frac{1}{3}$ **B** $\frac{1}{5}$ **C** $\frac{5}{10}$ **D** $\frac{3}{12}$

2. A box contains 1 white bow, 2 yellow bows, 3 red bows, and 6 green bows. The bows are all the same size and shape. If Patricia reaches in the box and pulls out a bow without looking, what is the probability that it will be yellow?

   A $\frac{1}{12}$ **B** $\frac{2}{10}$ **C** $\frac{1}{6}$ **D** $\frac{1}{4}$

3. Martin's wallet contains 1 \$20 bill, 2 \$5 bills, 9 \$1 bills, and 4 \$10 bills. If Martin reaches into his wallet and pulls out a bill without looking, what is the probability that it will be a \$5 bill?

   A $\frac{5}{49}$ **B** $\frac{1}{8}$ **C** $\frac{5}{16}$ **D** $\frac{5}{20}$

4. Of 20 customers who were asked to name their favorite type of cookie, 4 chose peanut butter, 6 chose oatmeal, 8 chose chocolate chip, and 2 chose butter cookies. If one customer is selected at random from this group, what is the probability that his favorite cookie will be chocolate chip?

   A $\frac{1}{8}$ **B** $\frac{8}{12}$ **C** $\frac{20}{8}$ **D** $\frac{2}{5}$

5. Nick has a collection of baseball caps. He takes pride in wearing different colors with different logos each and every day. He has 3 green caps, 4 red caps, 5 blue caps and 6 white caps. If he were to select a cap at random from this group, what is the probability that he will pick a green cap?

   A $\frac{1}{6}$ **B** $\frac{3}{9}$ **C** $\frac{3}{15}$ **D** $\frac{1}{18}$

6. Irma is trying to get a flight out of Corpus Christi to Dallas as soon as possible. There are 4 flights at 8:00 am, 3 flights at 9:30 am and 2 flights at 11:00 am. If she randomly selects a flight, what are her chances of getting a flight out at 8:00 am?

   A $\frac{4}{5}$ **B** $\frac{4}{9}$ **C** $\frac{2}{3}$ **D** $\frac{1}{4}$

Probability and Statistics: Step Three D

The student is expected to use pictures to make generalizations about determining all possible combinations. (TAKS 2:5.5A)
The student is expected to use experimental results to make predictions. (TAKS 5:5.12B)

1. Each student in Tammie's class selected a marble out of a bag without looking, recorded the color, and put the marble back into the bag. The results are shown on the chart below.

Tammie's Class

Color	Tally
Black	𝍸 |||
Blue	𝍸 𝍸 ||
Red	𝍸 |||
Green	𝍸 |

Based on the results, what fraction of the marbles selected was red?

A $\frac{8}{35}$ B $\frac{3}{5}$ C $\frac{8}{25}$ D $\frac{4}{17}$

2. Each person in the class selected a flavor of ice cream. The results are shown on the chart below.

Student Selections

Flavor	Tally
Strawberry	𝍸 ||
Peach	𝍸 𝍸 |
Chocolate	𝍸 |
Vanilla	𝍸 𝍸

Based on the results, what fraction of the flavors selected was peach?

A $\frac{7}{34}$ B $\frac{11}{34}$ C $\frac{6}{34}$ D $\frac{5}{6}$

3. All the players on the baseball team selected a color for their uniforms. The results are shown on the chart below.

Uniform Colors

Color	Tally
Blue	|||
Purple	𝍸 ||
Orange	||||
Green	𝍸 |

Based on the results, what fraction of the uniform colors selected was green?

A $\frac{4}{20}$ B $\frac{3}{10}$ C $\frac{8}{25}$ D $\frac{5}{20}$

4. Mr. Neal's class is having a pizza party. The results are shown on the chart below.

Pizza Choices

Pizza	Tally
Pepperoni	𝍸 ||
Sausage	𝍸 |
Cheese	𝍸
Mushroom	||

Based on the results, what fraction of the pizzas selected was mushroom?

A $\frac{2}{2}$ B $\frac{2}{15}$ C $\frac{1}{10}$ D $\frac{2}{5}$

Probability and Statistics: Step Three E

The student is expected to use pictures to make generalizations about determining all possible combinations. (TAKS 2:5.5A)
The student is expected to use experimental results to make predictions. (TAKS 5:5.12B)

1. Betty's track coach used a stopwatch to find out how long it took Betty to run one lap around the field. The times of four of Betty's laps are listed on the table.

Betty's Time

Lap	Time (seconds)
1	58.2
2	62.4
3	48.2
4	49.9

Based on these results, what is the probability that Betty will run her next lap in less than 50 seconds?

A $\frac{1}{2}$ **C** $\frac{2}{50}$

B $\frac{3}{4}$ **D** $\frac{1}{4}$

2. Jason has hit at least one home run at every baseball game. The number of home runs for each game is listed on the chart below.

Jason's Home Runs

Game	Home Runs
1	2
2	3
3	2
4	4

Based on these results, what is the probability that Jason will hit 4 home runs in the next game?

A $\frac{1}{2}$ **C** $\frac{4}{4}$

B $\frac{3}{4}$ **D** $\frac{1}{4}$

3. David, Ben, and Mike are on the track team. They throw the shot put. They keep a record of how many times they throw the shot over 25 feet. The chart shows how each boy did last week.

Shot Put Record

Name	Number of Throws	Number of Throws over 25 feet
David	9	3
Ben	12	4
Mike	7	6

What is the probability that Ben will get the next throw over 25 feet?

A $\frac{6}{7}$ **B** $\frac{1}{3}$ **C** $\frac{1}{2}$ **D** $\frac{1}{4}$

4. Sara, Pam, and Claire are on the tennis team. They have been practicing their serve. They keep a record of the number of times they keep their serve within the serving lines. The chart shows how each girl did last week.

Tennis Serve Record

Name	Number of Tries	Number of Successful Serves
Sara	20	11
Pam	17	9
Claire	18	6

What is the probability that Claire's serve will be successful?

A $\frac{2}{3}$ **B** $\frac{1}{3}$ **C** $\frac{1}{2}$ **D** $\frac{1}{9}$

Probability and Statistics: Step Three F

The student is expected to use pictures to make generalizations about determining all possible combinations. (TAKS 2:5.5A)
The student is expected to use experimental results to make predictions. (TAKS 5:5.12B)

1. Camie and her friends sold Girl Scout Cookies in her neighborhood. The table shows the data from the sales.

Cookies Sold

Girls	Camie	Lena	Micah	Lindsey	Celia	Ana
Number of Boxes Sold	8	6	3	5	7	3

Which fraction represents the number of boxes that Camie sold?

A $\frac{8}{12}$ **B** $\frac{3}{8}$ **C** $\frac{1}{4}$ **D** $\frac{4}{32}$

---

2. The area lake is swarming with frogs. Ricky's dad is going to have a frog leg fry. The table shows the data of how many frogs Ricky and his friend captured.

Frog Safari

Hunters	Randy	Ben	Ricky	Alberto	Lennie
Number of Frogs Captured	6	2	9	5	5

Which fraction represents the number of frogs that Ricky captured?

A $\frac{3}{27}$ **B** $\frac{5}{9}$ **C** $\frac{10}{27}$ **D** $\frac{1}{3}$

---

3. Greta is making potholders for her relatives as presents. The table shows the data of how many potholders she has made in the last few months.

Potholder Project

Months	April	May	June	July	August
Number of Potholders	6	6	9	5	4

Which fraction represents the number of potholders that Greta made in August?

A $\frac{2}{15}$ **B** $\frac{3}{27}$ **C** $\frac{4}{32}$ **D** $\frac{1}{6}$

Probability and Statistics: Sample for Analysis

The student is expected to use pictures to make generalizations about determining all possible combinations. (TAKS 2:5.5A)
The student is expected to use experimental results to make predictions. (TAKS 5:5.12B)

Ratio

There are 8 pair of socks in the laundry basket. 2 pair are blue. 3 pair are white. There are 2 green pairs and 1 red pair. If Rachel pulls a pair of socks out of the laundry basket without looking, what is the probability that she will get a green pair of socks?

A 1 in 10 **B** 1 in 8 **C** 1 in 5 **D** 1 in 4

Strategy:

1. There are 8 pair of socks in the laundry basket.
2. The question is asking for only the green pair of socks.
3. There are 2 pair of green socks from a total of 8 pair of socks.
4. That means 2 in 8. As a fraction that would be $\frac{2}{8}$ which could be reduced to $\frac{1}{4}$. $\frac{1}{4}$ means 1 in 4.
5. Answer choice **D** is 1 in 4. YES!

Probability and Statistics: Step Three G

The student is expected to use pictures to make generalizations about determining all possible combinations. (TAKS 2:5.5A)
The student is expected to use experimental results to make predictions. (TAKS 5:5.12B)

1. Ruth asked each of the 24 students in her class to choose a favorite sport. The chart shows the students' choices.

Favorite Sports		
Sport	Number of Students	
Soccer	𝍸 I	6
Football	III	3
Basketball	𝍸 III	8
Track	𝍸	5
Swimming	II	2
	Total	24

If a student from the class is selected at random, what is the probability that the student's favorite sport will be football?

A 1 in 24 **C** 1 in 6
B 1 in 8 **D** 3 in 21

2. It is Ishmael's turn to spin in a game he is playing with his friends.

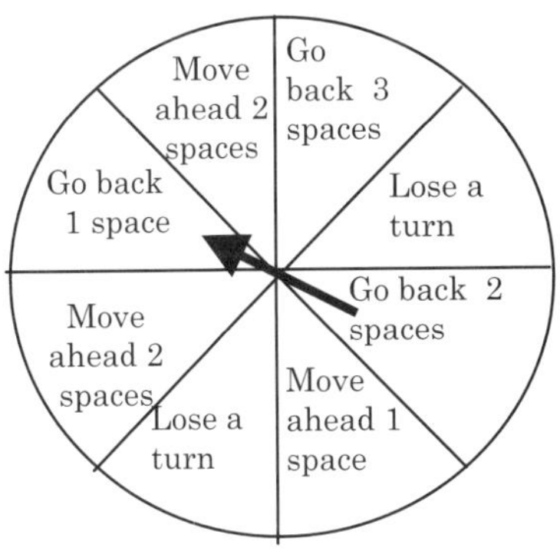

What is the probability that Ishmael will have to go back in this spin?

A 5 in 8 **C** 1 in 2
B 3 in 8 **D** Not Here

3. James was playing baseball. Out of the past 21 times at bat, James has hit 3 home runs. If this ratio continues, what is the probability that he will hit a home run his next time at bat?

A 1 in 2 **C** 1 in 5
B 1 in 3 **D** 1 in 7

4. Syd has a bag of 24 marbles that are all the same size. 4 marbles are red and 6 are yellow. 12 of the marbles are multi-colored and 2 marbles are blue. If Syd randomly chooses a marble out of the bag, what is the probability that it will be yellow?

A 1 in 2 **C** 1 in 6
B 1 in 4 **D** 1 in 12

5. There are 10 fifth grade math teachers at Andrew's school. Andrew especially likes 2 of them. When a computer randomly selects Andrew's math teacher, what is the probability that the teacher will be one whom Andrew especially likes?

A 1 in 10 **C** 1 in 6
B 1 in 8 **D** 1 in 5

Probability and Statistics: Step Three H

The student is expected to use pictures to make generalizations about determining all possible combinations. (TAKS 2:5.5A)
The student is expected to use experimental results to make predictions. (TAKS 5:5.12B)

1. There are 12 people who work in the aquarium at Sea World. 4 have blonde hair, 6 have brown hair, and 2 have red hair. If one employee's name is drawn out of a hat, what is the probability that the employee will have red hair?

A 1 in 12 C 1 in 6
B 1 in 10 D 1 in 4

2. Ann recently surveyed 36 of her classmates to find what activity they most often participated in after school. The results are shown in the chart below.

After School Activities	
Activity	Number of Students
Watching TV	18
Bike Riding	8
Skateboarding	4
Doing Chores	6

If Ann randomly calls one person from the group after school on Tuesday, what is the probability that this person will be a person who marked watching T.V. on the survey?

A 1 in 36 C 1 in 8
B 1 in 18 D 1 in 2

3. Leah asked each of the 18 cousins in her family to choose a favorite season of the year. The chart shows the cousins' choices.

Favorite Seasons		
Season	Number of Cousins	
Winter	𝍸	5
Spring	|||	3
Summer	𝍸 |||	8
Fall	||	2
	Total	18

If a cousin from the family is selected at random, what is the probability that the cousin's favorite season will be fall?

A 1 in 9 C 5 in 18
B 1 in 6 D 4 in 9

4. In a class of 22 children, there are 12 girls and 10 boys. If the teacher randomly calls on a student, what is the probability that the student will be a girl?

A 2 of 11 C 1 of 10
B 6 of 11 D 1 of 12

Probability and Statistics: Sample for Analysis

The student is expected to use pictures to make generalizations about determining all possible combinations. (TAKS 2:5.5A)

Patricia has 3 chairs in her living room. She placed them in a straight line against the south wall of the living room. In how many ways can Patricia arrange the chairs in a straight line against the south wall of her living room?

A 1 **B** 3 **C** 6 **D** 24

Strategy:

1. There are 3 positions for the chairs.
   Left Middle Right
2. The left position has 3 possibilities because there are 3 chairs to be placed.
3. The middle section has 2 possibilities because there are 2 chairs left to be placed after one has already been placed in the left position.
4. The right section has only 1 possibility because the other 2 chairs have already been placed in the left and middle position.
5.

Places:	Left		Middle		Right		
Possibilities:	**3**	**x**	**2**	**x**	**1**	**=**	**6 possibilities**

Tip: You can draw a picture or diagram to help you visualize the possibilities.

Probability and Statistics: Step Four A

The student is expected to use pictures to make generalizations about determining all possible combinations. (TAKS 2:5.5A)

1. Omar has 3 animal pictures. He placed them in a straight line on his bedroom wall. In how many ways can he arrange the pictures in a straight line on his bedroom wall?

A 24 **B** 6 **C** 3 **D** 1

---

2. How many different ways can these 5 balls be arranged in a row?

A 120 **B** 60 **C** 20 **D** 15

---

3. Lin has 4 coins. He placed them in a straight line on his kitchen table. In how many ways can he arrange the coins in a straight line on his kitchen table?

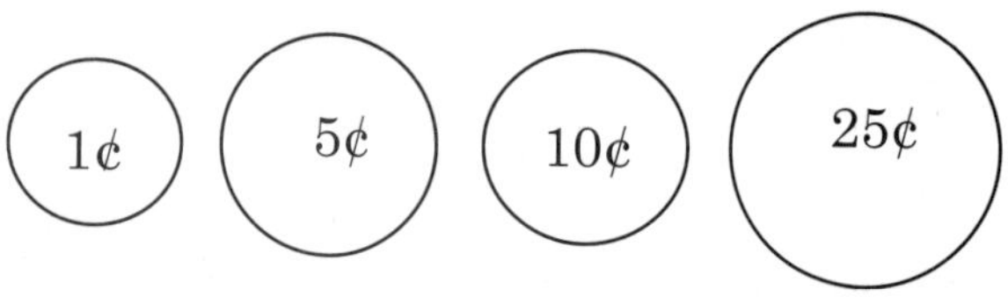

A 4 **B** 8 **C** 16 **D** 24

---

4. Kenny has 6 wooden shapes. How many ways can he arrange the wooden shapes in a straight line?

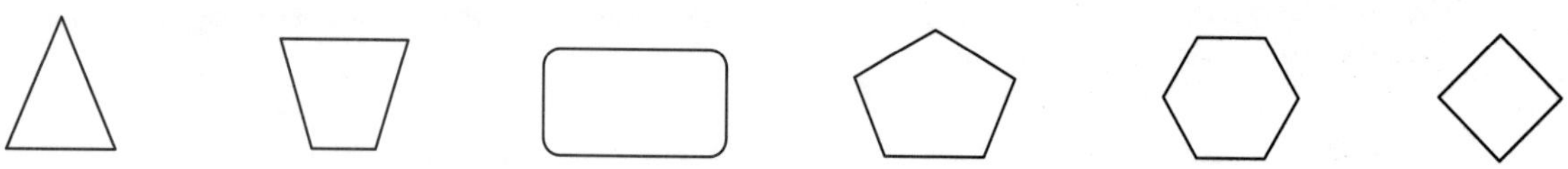

A 240 **B** 360 **C** 720 **D** 840

Probability and Statistics: Sample for Analysis

The student is expected to use pictures to make generalizations about determining all possible combinations. (TAKS 2:5.5A)

Different Combinations

Arlana is trying to decide what to do on Saturday. She wants to pick a game, a musical instrument, and a place to go from the activities shown.

How many different combinations of a game, a musical instrument, and a place to go could she choose?

A 6 **B** 11 **C** 15 **D** 45

Strategy:

1. There are 3 choices of games to play so write a 3 above the pictures of games.
2. There are 5 choices of musical instruments to play so write a 5 above the musical instruments.
3. There are 3 choices of places to go so write a 3 above the places to go.
4. Now multiply the three numbers.
5. **Choices: Games Instruments Places**

   Possibilities: 3 × 5 × 3 = 45 possibilities

6. The answer is 45, choice **D**.

Probability and Statistics: Step Four B

The student is expected to use pictures to make generalizations about determining all possible combinations. (TAKS 2:5.5A)

1. If Rosa chooses 1 type of ice cream, 1 number of scoops, and 1 type of cone for dessert, how many different combinations could she choose?

Ice Cream Cones		
Flavors	**Number of Scoops**	**Type of Cone**
Vanilla Chocolate Strawberry	1 2 3	Cake Sugar Waffle

A 6
B 9
C 27
D 81

2. If Ronnie chooses 1 type of drink, 1 type of food, and 1 type of candy, how many different combinations could he choose to eat at the ballgame?

Eating at the Game		
Drinks	**Food**	**Candy**
Grape Orange Strawberry	Nachos Hotdog	Sucker Chocolate

A 7
B 9
C 12
D 16

3. If Trevor chooses 1 meat, 1 vegetable, 1 fruit, and 1 beverage for dinner, how many different combinations could he choose?

Friday's Dinner			
Meat	**Vegetable**	**Fruit**	**Beverage**
Steak	Corn	Apple	Milk
Fish	Beans	Orange	Juice
Chicken	Carrots	Banana	Water
Ham		Grapes	

A 256
B 144
C 24
D 14

4. Syd is designing a new resort community. From the signs shown, he wants to choose a traffic sign, an indoor sign, and a recreation sign.

How many different combinations of a traffic sign, an indoor sign, and a recreation sign could be made?

A 8
B 16
C 24
D 120

Probability and Statistics: Step Four C

The student is expected to use pictures to make generalizations about determining all possible combinations. (TAKS 2:5.5A)

1. Martha cut out fabric into various shapes to make a quilt. She cut out 3 hexagons, 2 octagons, 1 pentagon, and 3 squares. She wants to sew 4 pieces of fabric in a design. Which combination of fabric shapes is *not* possible?

A
B
C
D

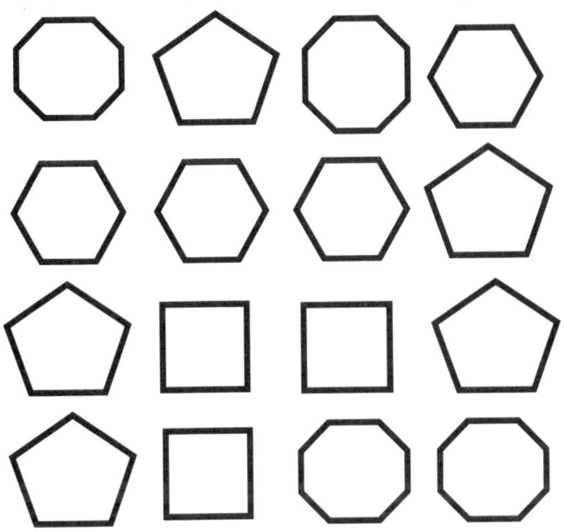

2. Michael made labels to use on a poster. He has 3 green labels, 2 red labels, 4 blue labels, and 1 purple label. He is only going to use 4 on each poster. Which combination of labels is *not* possible for one of the posters?

A Green Blue Blue Blue

B Green Green Green Red

C Purple Green Green Purple

D Red Green Blue Purple

3. Maria bought 8 stars to decorate her room. Her mom told her she could only use 3 of them. She has 3 gold, 2 blue, 1 red, and 2 purple. Which combination of stars could she select to hang in her room?

A Red Gold Red

B Purple Purple Purple

C Blue Red Red

D Red Gold Gold

4. Tammy cut out 10 hearts to make a Valentine. She cut out 2 red, 4 pink, and 4 white. She can only fit 4 on her card. Which combination of labels is *not* possible for one of the posters?

A Red Pink White White

B Pink Pink White White

C Red Red White White

D Red Pink Red Red

Probability and Statistics: Step Four D

The student is expected to use pictures to make generalizations about determining all possible combinations. (TAKS 2:5.5A)

1. Rachel has 2 jackets, 7 skirts and 5 blouses. How many different combinations of jacket, skirt and blouse can she make?

   A 14 B 17 C 19 D 70

2. Raul has 2 bats, 5 baseballs and 2 gloves. How many different combinations of bat, baseball and glove can he use?

   A 9 B 12 C 20 D 22

3. Rene has 4 bows and 6 hair clips. How many different combinations of bow and hair clip can she wear?

   A 24 B 10 C 6 D 4

4. Rollie has 3 red marbles, 4 green marbles and 2 black marbles. How many different combinations of marbles can he play with?

   A 12 B 24 C 26 D 28

5. Rennie has 6 pairs of socks, 2 pairs of dress shoes and 3 pairs of slacks. How many different combinations of socks, shoes and slacks can he wear?

   A 11 B 12 C 15 D 36

6. Rocky has 4 pairs of shorts, 5 T-shirts, and 2 pairs of running shoes. How many different combinations of short, shirt and shoes can he wear?

   A 20 B 30 C 40 D 50

7. Rosey has 3 dresses, 5 pairs of socks and 2 pairs of dress shoes. How many different combinations of dress, socks, and shoes can she wear?

   A 10 B 15 C 20 D 30

8. Ricky is having a party. He has 2 kinds of ice cream, 2 kinds of cakes, and 3 kinds of sandwiches. How many different combinations of ice cream, cake, and sandwich can his guests eat?

   A 4 B 12 C 16 D 18

Probability and Statistics: Sample for Analysis

The student is expected to use pictures to make generalizations about determining all possible combinations. (TAKS 2:5.5A)

Lena is making a sandwich for lunch. The chart shows the things she could place in her sandwich.

Sandwich Extras
Tomatoes
Pickles
Lettuce
Onions
Cheese

If Lena chooses 3 different toppings, how many combinations are possible?

Strategy 1:Create an Organized List Objective 6 5.14C

1. Creating an organized list is probably the best strategy for this problem.
2. Follow the strategy in the way this list was created:
   Tomatoes, Pickles, Lettuce
   Tomatoes, Pickles, Onions
   Tomatoes, Pickles, Cheese
   Tomatoes, Lettuce, Onions
   Tomatoes, Lettuce, Cheese
   Tomatoes, Onions, Cheese
   Pickles, Lettuce, Onions
   Pickles, Lettuce, Cheese
   Pickles, Onions, Cheese
   Lettuce, Onions, Cheese
3. How many possible combinations? 10

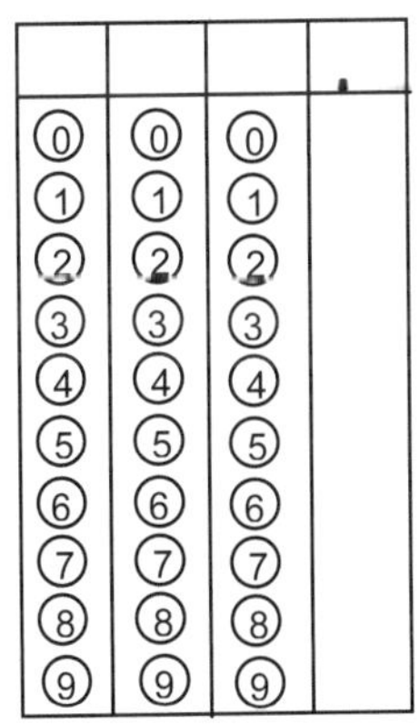

Probability and Statistics: Step Four E

The student is expected to use pictures to make generalizations about determining all possible combinations. (TAKS 2:5.5A)

1. Rosa is making a hamburger for lunch. The chart shows the extras she can place in her hamburger.

Hamburger Extras
Lettuce
Tomato
Onion
Pickles

If Rosa chooses 2 different extras, how many combinations are possible?

2. Millie is painting her room. The chart shows the different colors of paint she could use.

Paints
Red
Blue
Yellow
Green

If Millie chooses 3 different paints, how many combinations are possible?

3. Tony is making a banana split. The charts shows the types of syrup he can place on each of the scoops of ice cream.

Syrup
Chocolate
Strawberry
Caramel
Peach
Marshmallow

If Tony chooses 3 different syrups, how many combinations are possible?

4. Carmen is making a pizza for lunch. The chart shows the toppings she can use.

Pizza Toppings
Pepperoni
Beef
Sausage
Mushrooms
Peppers

If Carmen chooses 2 different toppings, how many combinations are possible?

Probability and Statistics: Sample for Analysis

The student is expected to use pictures to make generalizations about determining all possible combinations. (TAKS 2:5.5A)

Possible Combinations

John has 5 coins in his pocket: 3 pennies, 1 nickel, and 1 dime. If he takes 3 coins out of his pocket, which is a possible amount they could total?

A \$0.24 **B** \$0.16 **C** \$0.15 **D** \$0.02

Strategy 1:

1. If you added the value of all the coins, the total would be: 1 + 1 + 1 + 5 + 10 = 18; therefore, \$0.24 could not be possible. Remember, he is only taking 3 coins from his pocket.
2. If he pulled out the 3 pennies, that would be the lowest amount; therefore, \$0.02 **is not possible.**
3. The only way he could get \$0.15 would be by only pulling out two coins: 5 + 10 = 15. One or two pennies with the nickel or dime will not add to \$0.15; therefore, \$0.15 is not possible.
4. What about \$0.16? Yes, 5 + 10 + 1 = \$0.16.

   Three coins and \$0.16, Right!!!

Strategy 2:

1. Look at your coins.
2. Try to take the numbers 1, 1, 1, 5, and 10 and make one of those answers using 3 numbers.

1 + 1 + 1 = 3
1 + 1 + 5 = 7
1 + 1 + 10 = 12
1 + 5 + 10 = 16 YES, YES, YES!

Probability and Statistics: Step Four F

The student is expected to use pictures to make generalizations about determining all possible combinations. (TAKS 2:5.5A)

1. Allen has 4 coins in his pocket: 1 nickel, 1 penny, and 2 dimes. If he takes 3 coins out of his pocket, which is a possible amount they could total?

   A \$0.11 **C** \$0.21
   B \$0.15 **D** \$0.26

2. Larry has 5 coins in his pocket: 2 pennies, 2 nickels, and 1 dime. If he takes 3 coins out of his pocket, which is a possible amount they could total?

   A \$0.22 **C** \$0.15
   B \$0.20 **D** \$0.06

3. Lennie has 3 coins in his pocket: 1 penny, 1 nickel, and 1 dime. If he takes 2 coins out of his pocket, which is a possible amount they could total?

   A \$0.05 **C** \$0.11
   B \$0.07 **D** \$0.17

4. Laura has 4 coins in her school box: 1 penny and 3 nickels. If she takes 3 coins out of her box, which is a possible amount they could total?

   A \$0.16 **C** \$0.13
   B \$0.15 **D** \$0.10

5. Gina has 3 coins in her purse: 2 dimes and 1 penny. If she takes 2 coins out of her purse, which is a possible amount they could total?

   A \$0.20 **C** \$0.10
   B \$0.18 **D** \$0.08

6. Gary has 5 coins in his pocket: 2 nickels, 1 penny, and 2 dimes. If he takes 3 coins out of his pocket, which is a possible amount they could total?

   A \$0.08 **C** \$0.16
   B \$0.12 **D** \$0.18

7. Jack has 4 coins in his pocket: 3 dimes and 1 nickel. If he takes 2 coins out of his pocket, which is a possible amount they could total?

   A \$0.10 **C** \$0.22
   B \$0.20 **D** \$0.24

8. Joe has 3 coins in his pocket: 2 nickels and 1 dime. If he takes 2 coins out of his pocket, which is a possible amount they could total?

   A \$0.05 **C** \$0.20
   B \$0.10 **D** \$0.25

Probability and Statistics: Step Four G

The student is expected to use pictures to make generalizations about determining all possible combinations. (TAKS 2:5.5A)

1. The Wylie Cafe serves ham, chicken and beef sandwiches. Each sandwich comes with wheat, white or rye bread. If only combinations of 1 bread and 1 meat are shown, which drawing shows each combination exactly 1 time?

A
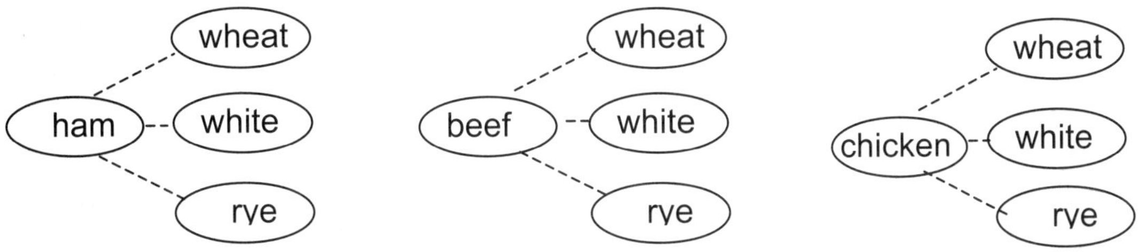

B
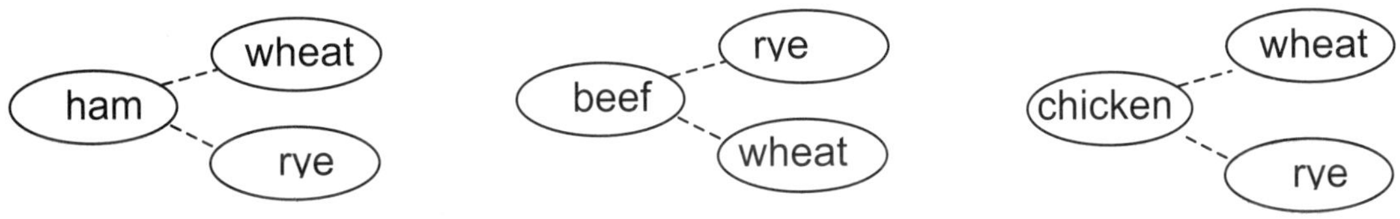

C
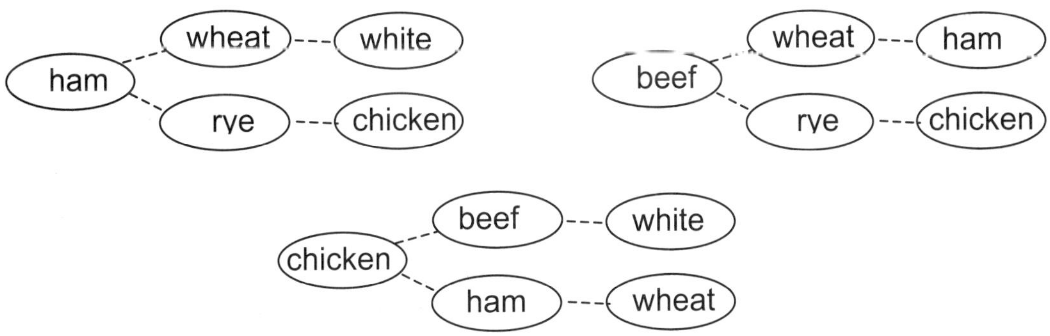

D
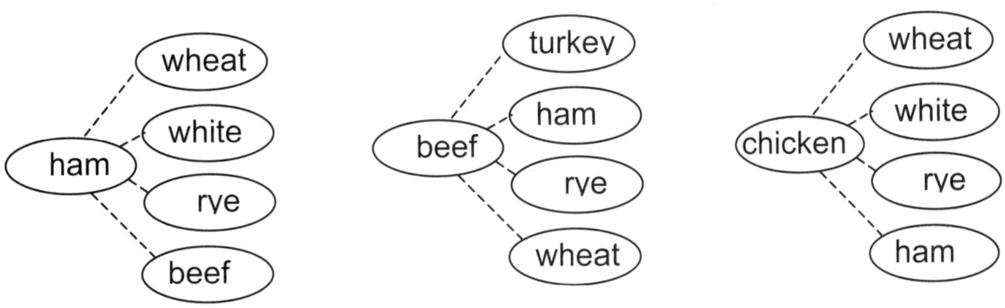

Probability and Statistics: Step Four H

The student is expected to use pictures to make generalizations about determining all possible combinations. (TAKS 2:5.5A)

1. The Sandwich Shop sells cola, tea and lemonade. Each drink is available in a small size, medium size, and large size. If only combinations of 1 drink and 1 size are shown, which drawing shows each combination exactly 1 time?

A
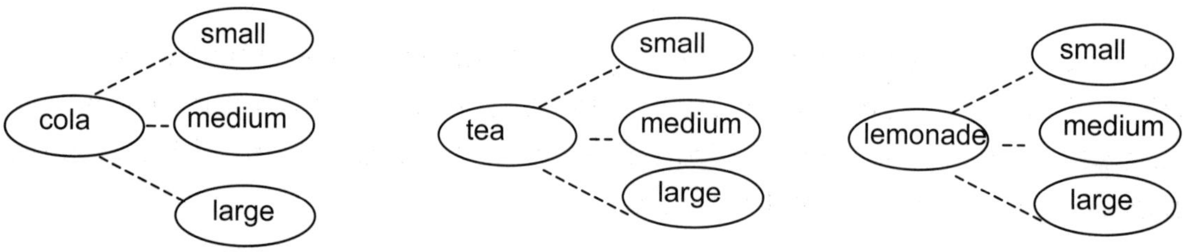

B
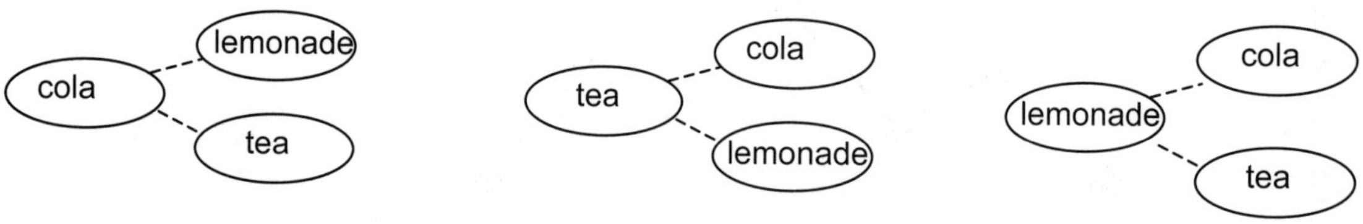

C
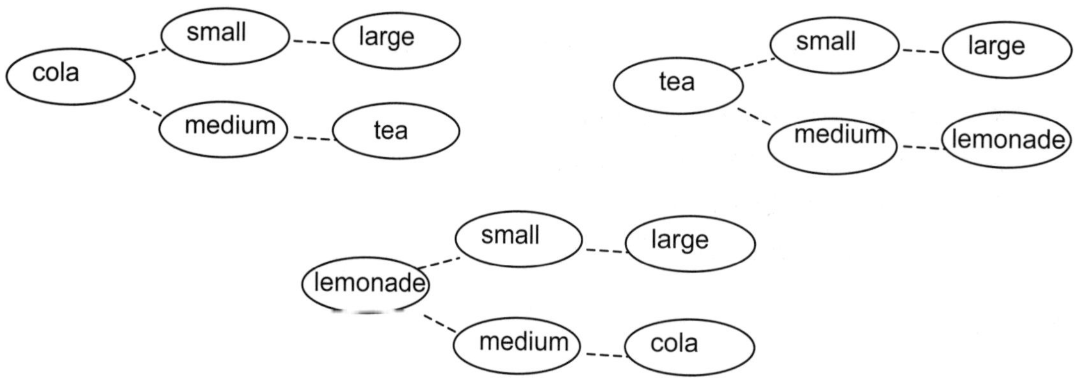

D
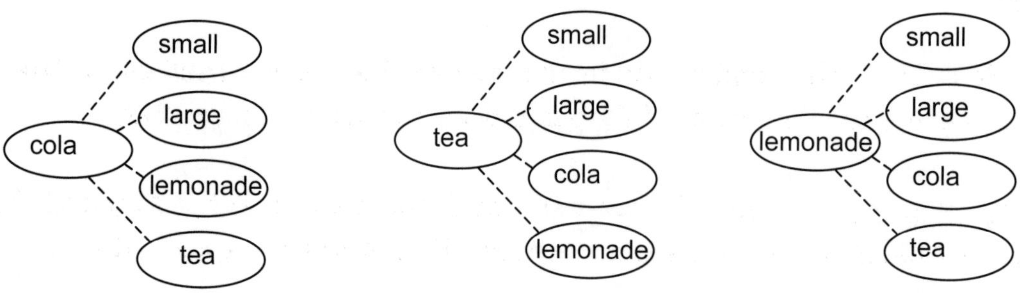

Probability and Statistics: Sample for Analysis

The student is expected to graph a given set of data using an appropriate graphical representation such as a picture or line. (TAKS 5:5.13 C)

Broken Line Graph

Mrs. Newman asked Peter to create a line graph using her class attendance information. Peter made only one mistake from the information in creating his graph. Listed in the answer choice is the information she gave him. Which choice is ***not*** represented correctly on the graph?

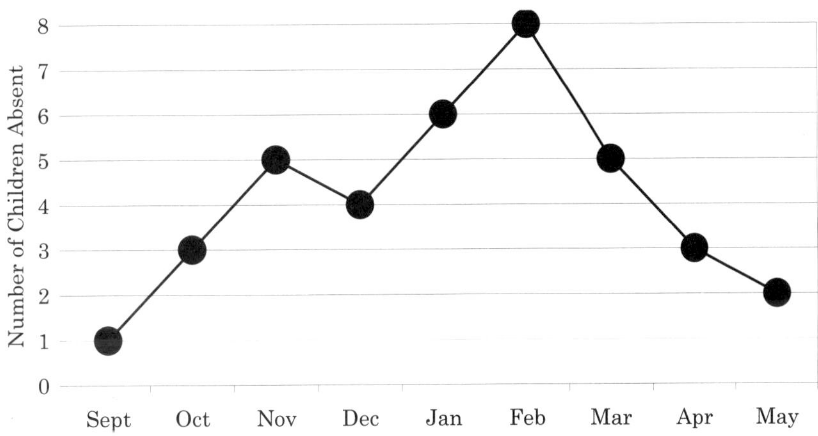

A 6 children absent in January
B 8 children absent in February
C 3 children absent in May
D 3 children absent in October

Strategy:

1. Double check the information and see which one Peter missed on the graph.
2. Circle each number and month in the answer choices and then circle the information on the graph. Which one does not match correctly?
3. Look carefully at choice C. Peter placed 2 children absent in May and the information is 3 children absent in May. This is where he missed it.

Probability and Statistics: Sample for Analysis

The student is expected to graph a given set of data using an appropriate graphical representation such as a picture or line. (TAKS 5:5.13 C)

The cooking teacher asked Connie to keep a record of the number of cookies baked by the students each day. She created a picture graph. Her teacher checked her graph with the information she gave her and she only found one mistake. Which choice is ***not*** represented correctly on the graph?

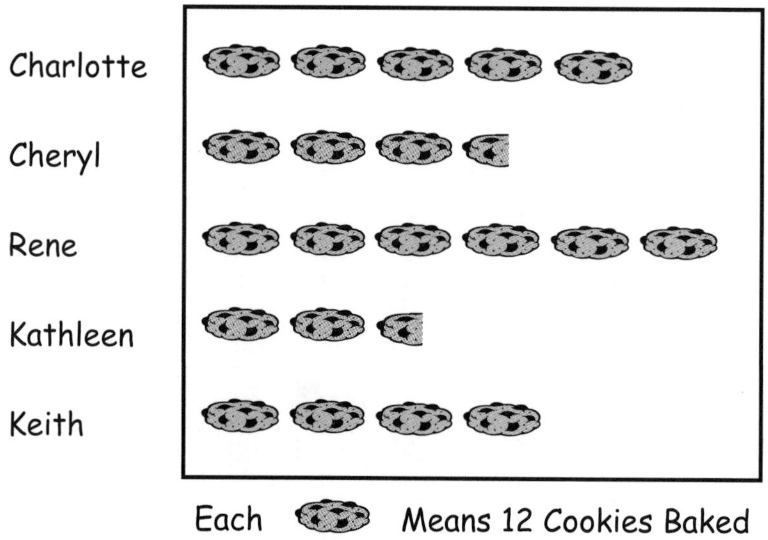

A Charlotte baked 60 cookies.
B Rene baked 6 dozen cookies.
C Keith baked 48 cookies.
D Kathleen baked 36 cookies.

Strategy:

1. Double check Connie's graph.
2. On the graph write the number each person baked.
3. Look at the scale. Each cookie represents 12 cookies. Watch out!
4. Now check it with the information the teacher gave Connie.
5. Where did Connie miss it?
6. Choice D--What does a half cookie represent and what does a whole cookie represent?

Probability and Statistics: Step Five A

The student is expected to graph a given set of data using an appropriate graphical representation such as a picture or line. (TAKS 5:5.13 C)

The chart shows the number of flowers sold by 4 florists on one day.

Flower Sales		
Florist	**Carnations**	**Roses**
Flowerland	7	5
Flowers and Friends	5	6
Smith's Florist	12	8
Springtown Flower Market	4	1

1. Which information does ***not*** match the graph?

A Flowerland sold a total of 12 carnations and roses.
B Smith's Florist sold 4 more carnations than roses.
C Springtown sold 4 times more carnations than roses.
D Flowers and Friends sold a total of 30 carnations and roses.

---

2. How many more carnations than roses were sold by all 4 florists?

A 8
B 12
C 20
D 28

The chart shows the number of cars sold by 5 salesmen last month.

NEW CAR

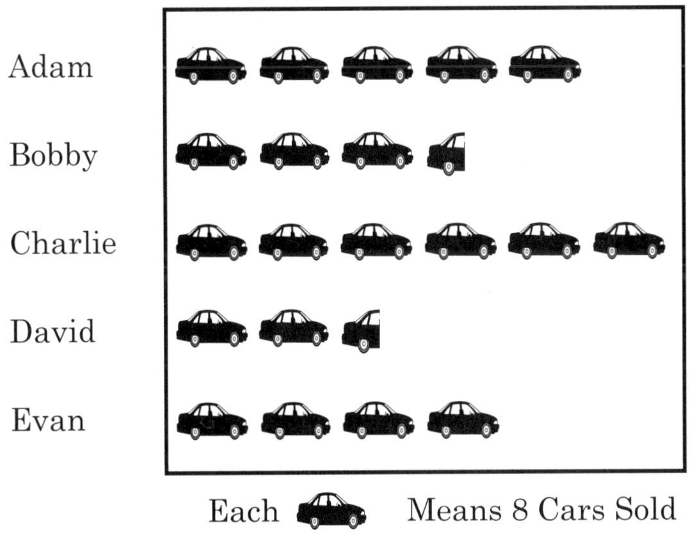

3. Which information does ***not*** match the graph?

A Adam sold 40 cars.
B Bobby sold 32 cars.
C David sold 20 cars.
D Charlie sold 48 cars.

---

4. Which two salesmen sold a combined total of 48 cars?

A Adam and Charlie
B Bobby and David
C Charlie and Evan
D Evan and David

---

5. How many cars did Adam, Bobby, and Evan sell?

A 11 **C** 88
B 56 **D** 100

Probability and Statistics: Step Five B

The student is expected to graph a given set of data using an appropriate graphical representation such as a picture or line. (TAKS 5:5.13 C)

The graph shows how many children attended the movie during each show time.

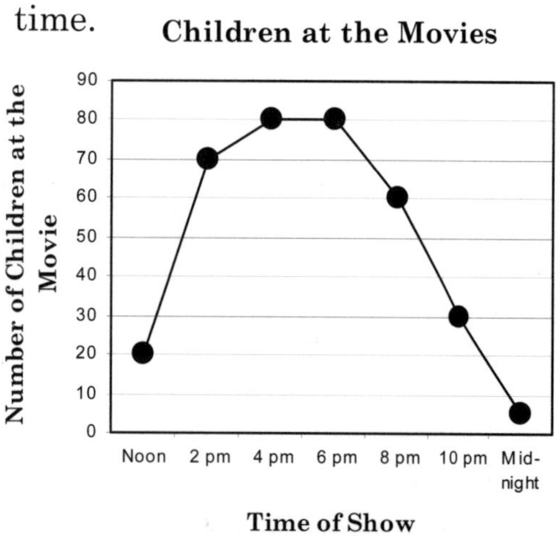

1. During which two shows did the least number of children attend the movie?

   A Noon and 10 pm
   B Midnight and 10 pm
   C Noon and Midnight
   D 4 pm and 6 pm

---

2. Which statement best describes the attendance of children at the movies?

   A No children attended the midnight showing of the movie.
   B Attendance rose until 4 pm and then went down after 6 pm.
   C More children attended the 10 pm show.
   D Attendance at the movies rose from noon until 8 pm.

---

3. How many shows did less than a total of 65 children attend?

   A 4 **C** 2
   B 3 **D** 1

Cecelia has been digging up earthworms to use for fishing bait. The graph shows how many earthworms Cecelia dug each day last week.

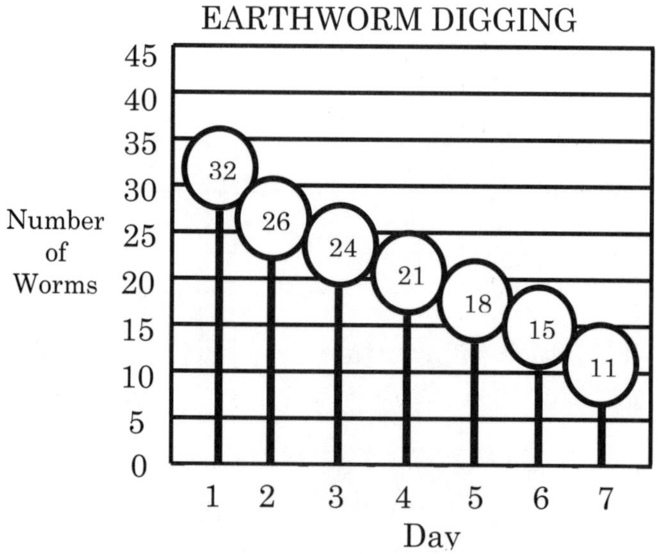

4. On the 3 days she dug the fewest earthworms, how many worms did Cecelia dig?

   A 26 **C** 44
   B 33 **D** 82

---

5. Which statement best describes Cecelia's earthworm digging for the week?

   A Cecelia caught more worms each day than she did the day before.
   B Cecelia didn't catch any earthworms on day 8.
   C Cecelia's earthworm count stayed the same from day 1 through day 7.
   D Cecelia's earthworm count went down from the first day until the last.

Probability and Statistics: Step Five C

The student is expected to graph a given set of data using an appropriate graphical representation such as a picture or line. (TAKS 5:5.13 C)

The chart shows the mass (weight) of 5 fifth-grade students on four different graphs.

One

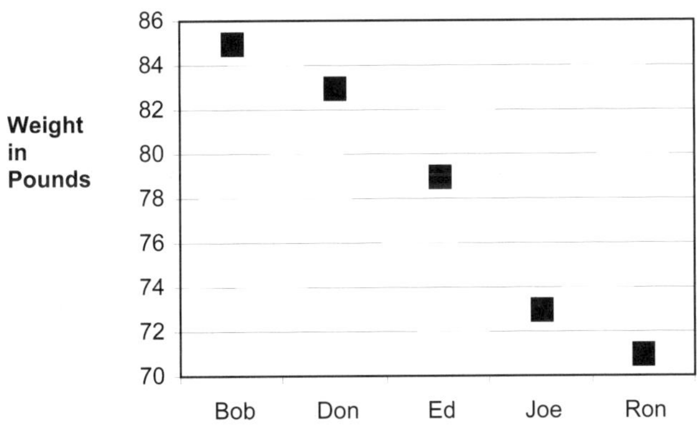

Two

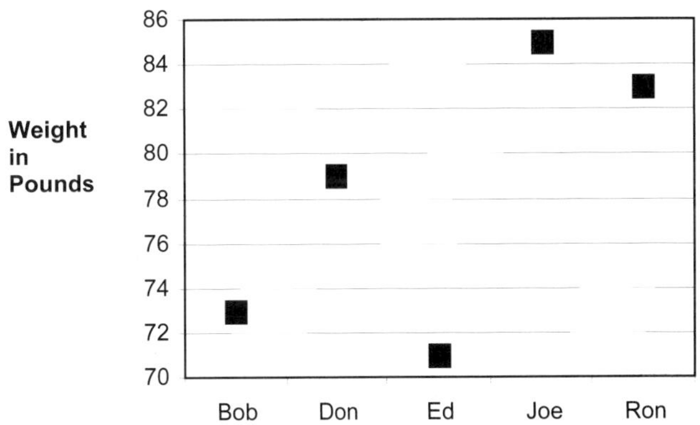

Three

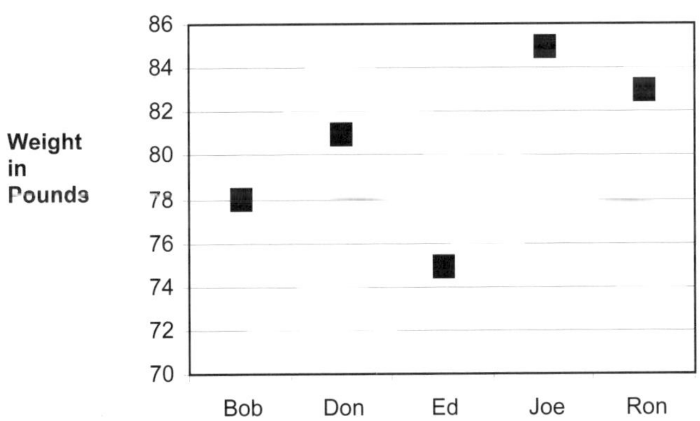

Four

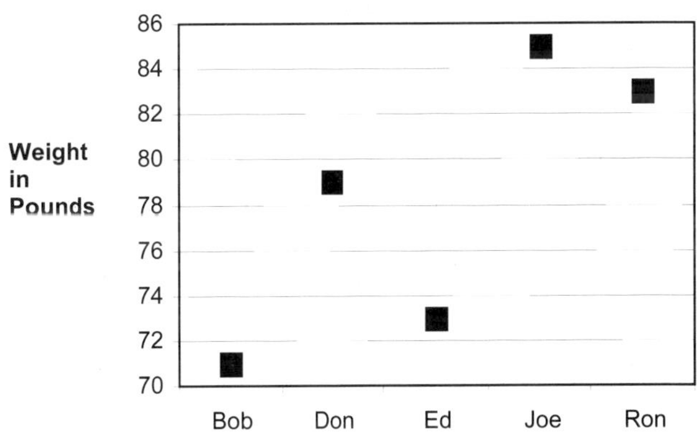

1. Which graph shows Bob weighing 73 pounds?

   A One
   B Two
   C Three
   D Four

2. Which graph shows Ed weighing 75 pounds?

   A One
   B Two
   C Three
   D Four

Probability and Statistics: Step Five D

The student is expected to graph a given set of data using an appropriate graphical representation such as a picture or line. (TAKS 5:5.13 C)

The chart shows the life span of 5 different animals on four different graphs.

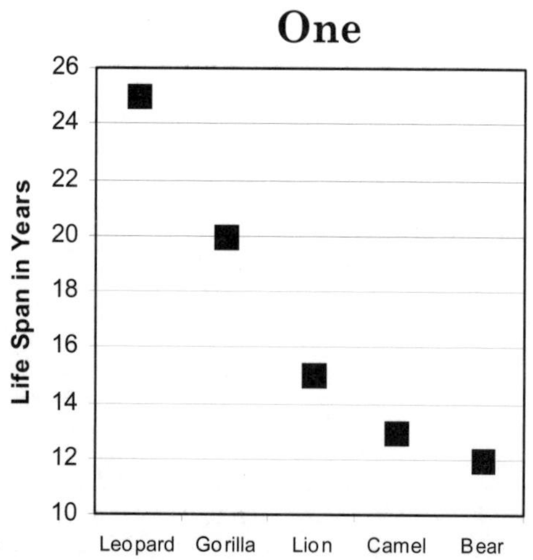

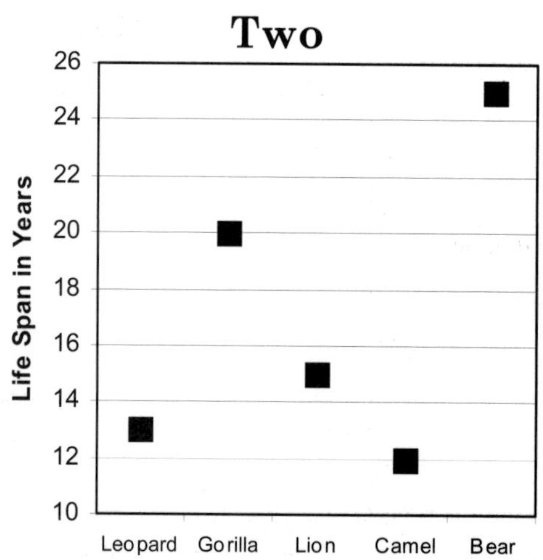

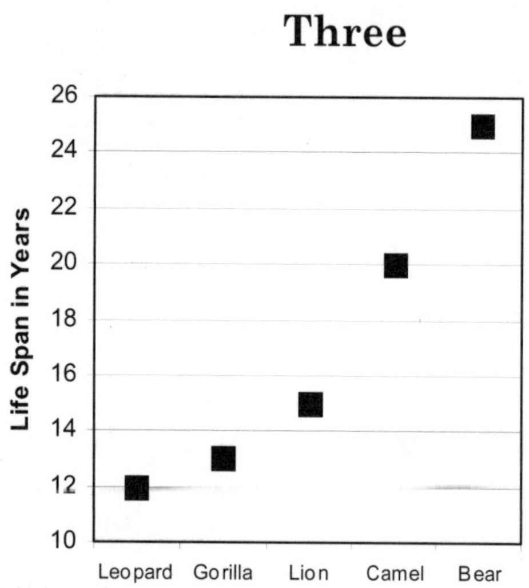

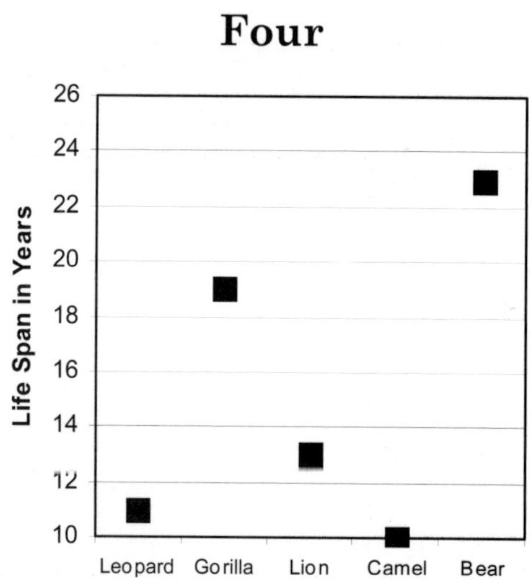

1. Which graph shows the lion with a life span of 13 years?

   A One
   B Two
   C Three
   D Four

2. Which graph shows the camel with a life span of 12 years?

   A One
   B Two
   C Three
   D Four

Probability and Statistics: Step Five E

The student is expected to graph a given set of data using an appropriate graphical representation such as a picture or line. (TAKS 5:5.13 C)

The chart shows the speed of 5 different running animals on four different graphs.

One

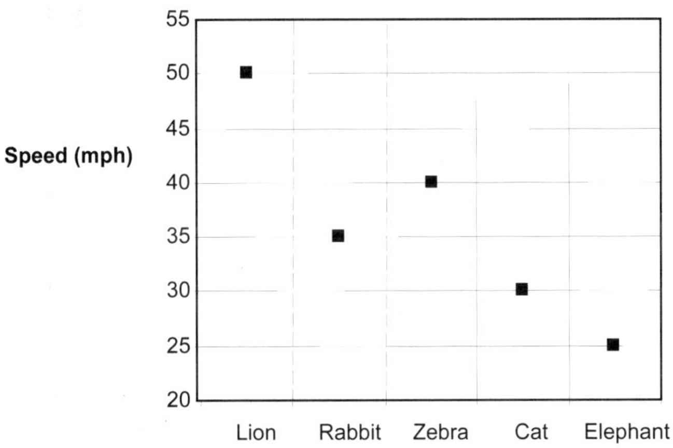

Two

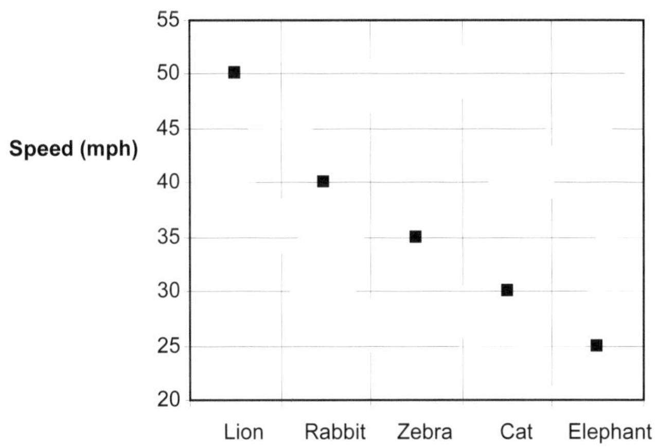

Three

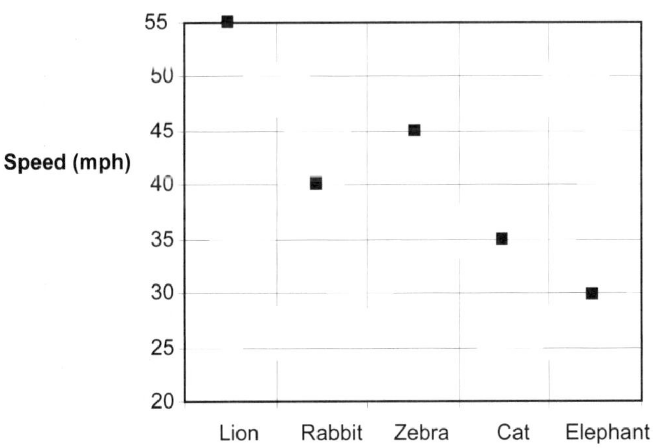

Four

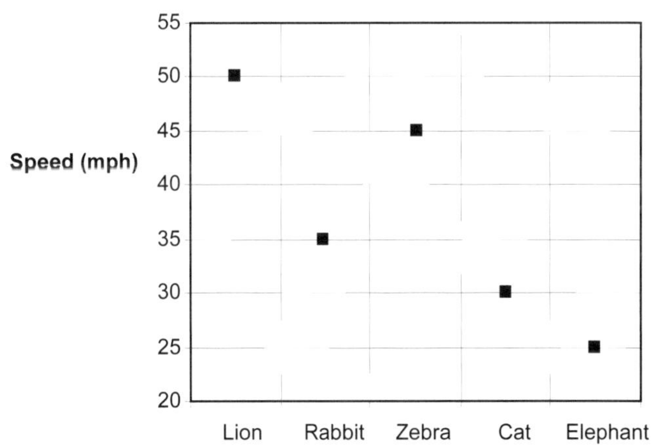

1. Which graph shows the zebra at a speed of 40 miles per hour?

   A One
   B Two
   C Three
   D Four

2. Which graph shows the cat at a speed of 35 miles per hour?

   A One
   B Two
   C Three
   D Four

Probability and Statistics: Step Five F

The student is expected to graph a given set of data using an appropriate graphical representation such as a picture or line. (TAKS 5:5.13 C)

Mrs. Ruiz's fifth grade class conducted a survey of pizzas. Some students liked more than one type of pizza.

PIZZA

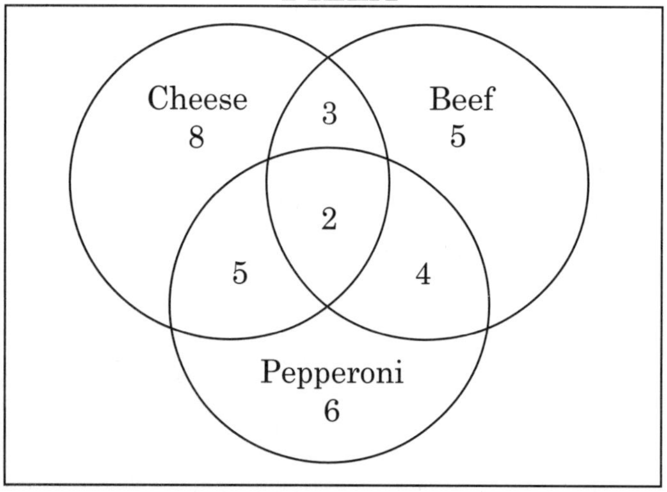

1. How many students liked all three kinds?

   A 2 **B** 3 **C** 6 **D** 5

2. How many students liked both cheese and pepperoni?

   A 2 **B** 5 **C** 7 **D** 24

3. How many students liked only beef?

   A 2 **B** 3 **C** 4 **D** 5

4. How many students liked only cheese?

   A 3 **B** 5 **C** 6 **D** 8

5. How many total students were surveyed?

   A 33 **B** 19 **C** 14 **D** 11

Probability and Statistics: Step Five G

The student is expected to graph a given set of data using an appropriate graphical representation such as a picture or line. (TAKS 5:5.13 C)

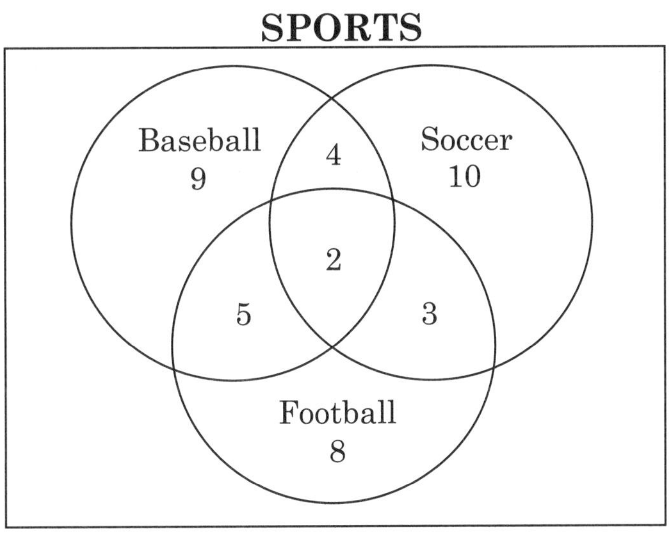

1. How many students played both baseball and football?

   A 9 **B** 7 **C** 5 **D** 2

---

2. How many students played all three sports?

   A 4 **B** 2 **C** 5 **D** 10

---

3. How many students only played football?

   A 8 **B** 5 **C** 4 **D** 3

---

4. How many students played soccer and football?

   A 10 **B** 8 **C** 5 **D** 2

---

5. How many total students were surveyed?

   A 14 **B** 27 **C** 41 **D** 45

"Most Appropriate Graph"

Line graphs are used to show changes or trends over periods of time. Line Graphs are used when gradual changes in data need to be seen.

Bar Graphs are used when data needs to be compared. Bar Graphs are used to compare several different quantities.

Charts are used to list quantities.

Circle graphs are useful for showing how a whole quantity is divided into parts. Circle Graphs are used to show different proportions, amounts, sizes, or numbers of data.

Pictographs or **Picture Graphs** are used when data needs to be displayed. Picture Graphs cannot show exact figures unless symbols stand for very small amounts.

Probability and Statistics: Sample for Analysis

The student is expected to graph a given set of data using an appropriate graphical representation such as a picture or line. (TAKS 5:5.13 C)

Hector identified the amount of sodium in a serving of 4 different kinds of crackers. Which represents the most appropriate way to show the number of milligrams of sodium in each kind of cracker?

A

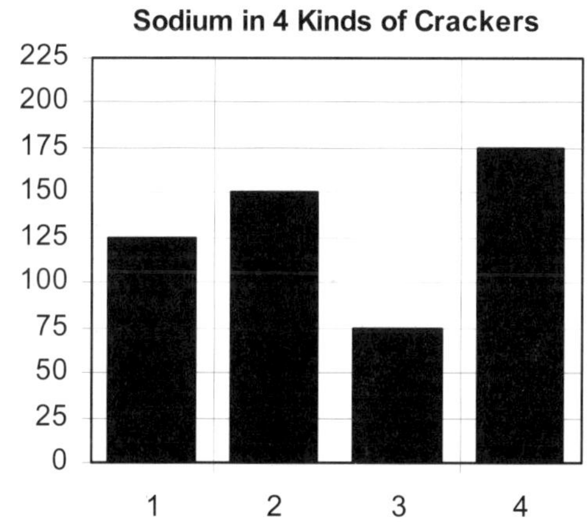

C

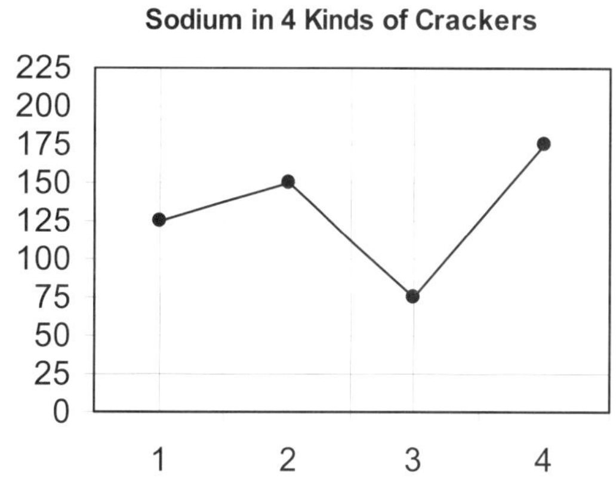

B

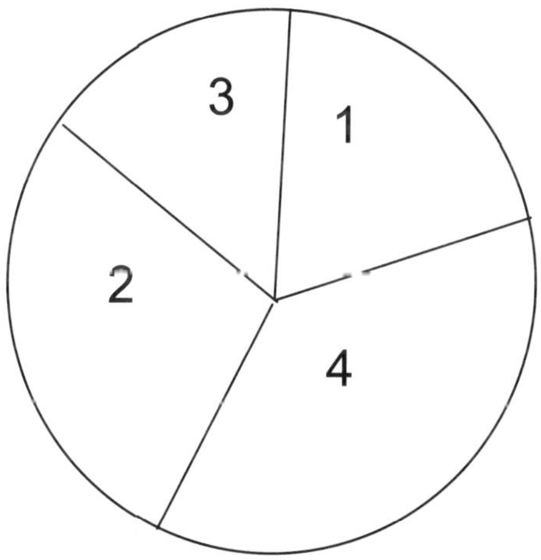

D

Sodium in 4 Kinds of Crackers

Cracker	Number of Milligrams of Sodium
1	125
2	150
3	75
4	175

Strategy:

1. Carefully examine the data in the chart and the graphs.
2. Hector is comparing the amount of sodium in 4 different types of crackers.
3. Choice A is a bar graph. It appropriately compares the 4 types of crackers.
4. Choice B is a circle graph. There are 4 separate crackers being compared. The 4 crackers are not part of a whole.
5. Choice C is a line graph. Line graphs are used to show changes or trends over periods of time. Since we are comparing 4 types of crackers and time is not involved in the comparison, the line graph is not the most appropriate way to show the number of milligrams of sodium in each kind of cracker.
6. Choice D is a chart. It states the differences in numbers, but the comparison is not as appropriate as the bar graph.

Probability and Statistics: Step Five H

The student is expected to graph a given set of data using an appropriate graphical representation such as a picture or line. (TAKS 5:5.13C)

1. The Plaza Pizza Pantry sold 300 pizzas last night. Which represents the least appropriate way to show the number of each type of pizza sold?

A
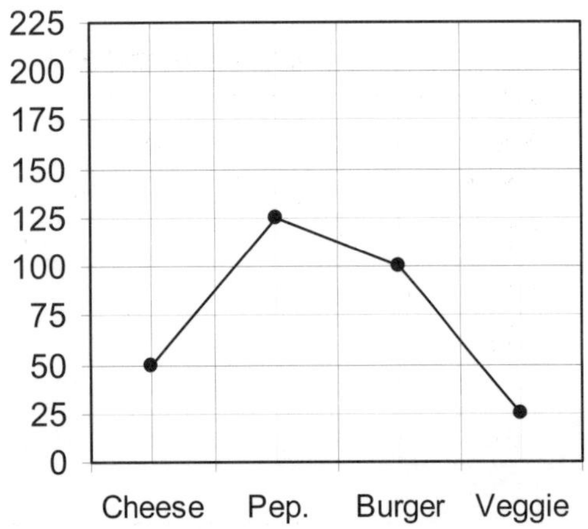

C
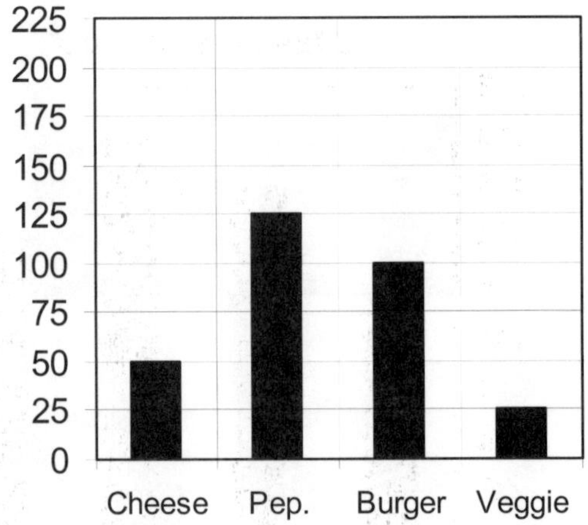

B
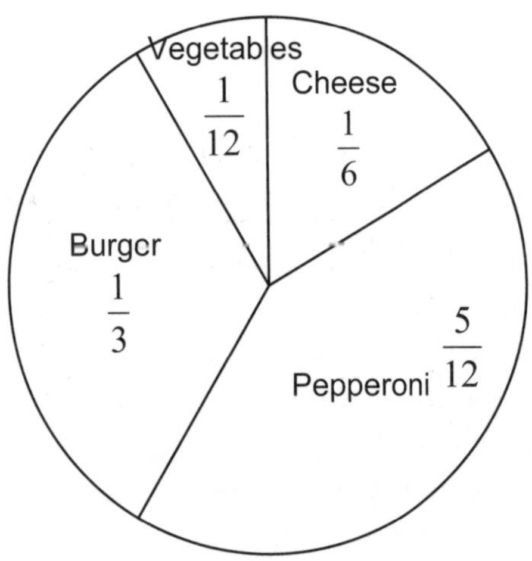

D
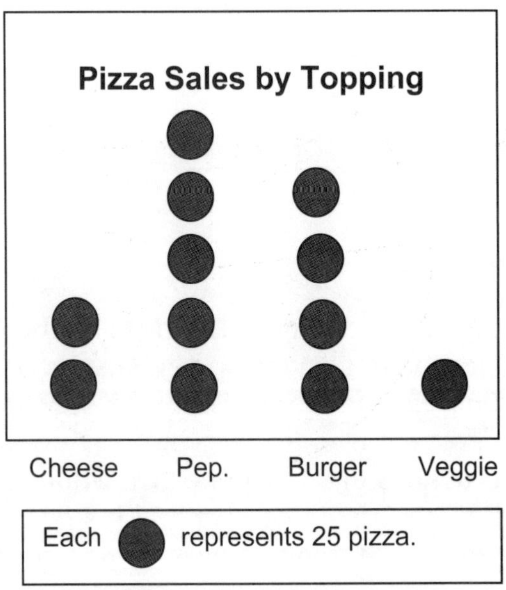

Probability and Statistics: Step Five I

The student is expected to graph a given set of data using an appropriate graphical representation such as a picture or line. (TAKS 5:5.13C)

1. The Paris Community Theater performed the play *The Sound of Music* 4 nights last week. Which represents the most appropriate way to show the number of people attending the performance on each night?

A

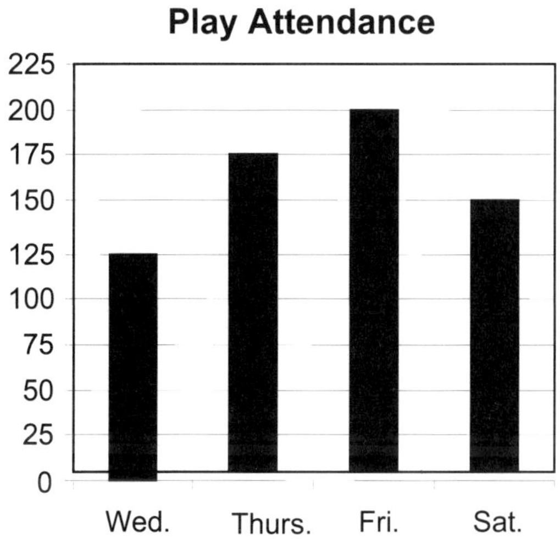

C

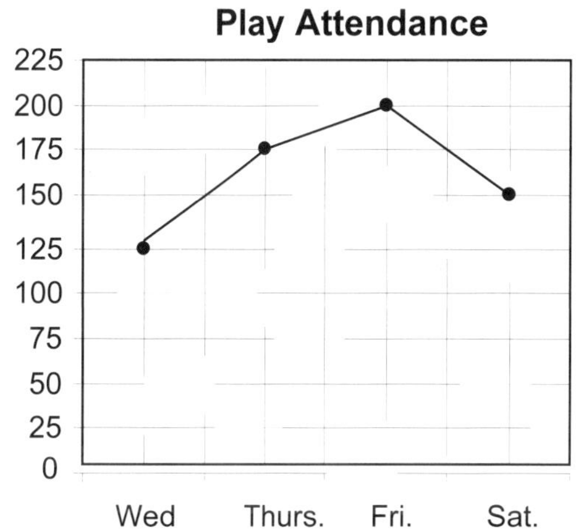

B

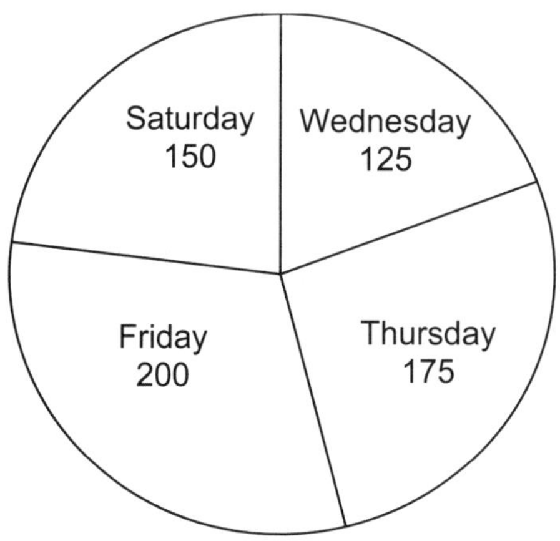

D

Play Attendance

Day	Number of People
Wednesday	125
Thursday	175
Friday	200
Saturday	150

Probability and Statistics: Assessment

TAKS Objectives: 2:5.5A, 2:5.5B, 2:5.6A, 5:5.12B, 5:5.13B, 5:5.13C

The chart shows the price of candy bars for sale at the local store.

Candy

Number of Candy Bars	Cost
2	$0.75
4	$1.50
6	$2.25
8	$3.00

1. If the pattern continues, exactly how many candy bars can Lewis buy with $6.75?

   A 14 **B** 16 **C** 18 **D** 20

2. In a total of 100 spins, which 2 shapes will the spinner probably point to the least number of times?

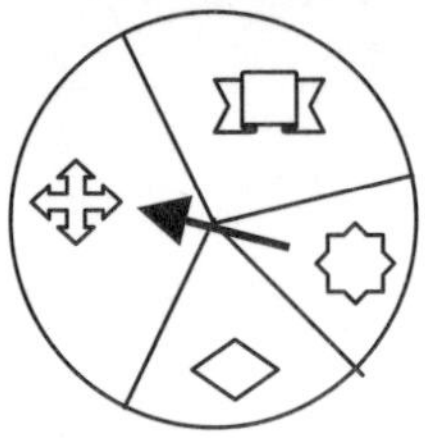

A 

C 

B 

D 

3. Each section of the spinner below is the same size.

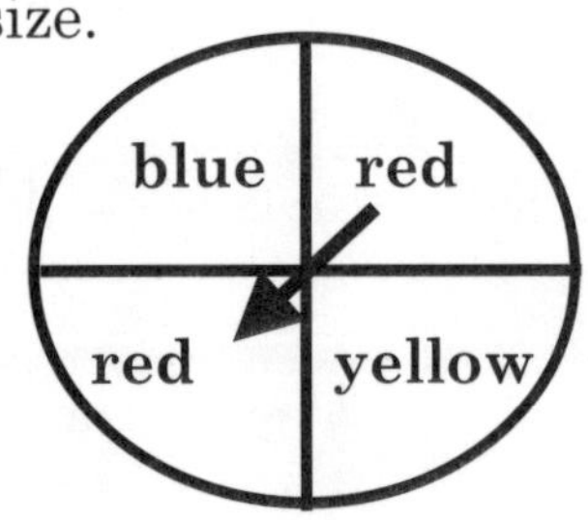

What is the probability of landing on the red section?

A $\frac{1}{4}$ **B** $\frac{1}{3}$ **C** $\frac{1}{2}$ **D** $\frac{1}{1}$

4. Ricardo has 6 different jackets that he can wear to school. His plan is to choose a jacket at random using a game spinner. Which spinner should he use so that each jacket has an equal chance of being selected?

A 

C 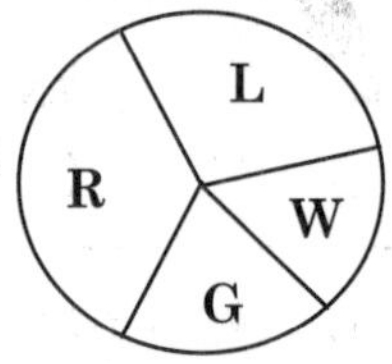

B 

D 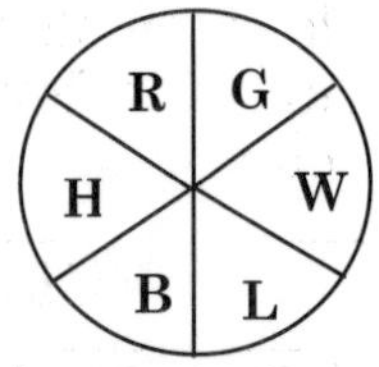

5. Jo Ann is an artist. She had a showing of several of her paintings. Of the 15 paintings that were displayed, 3 were oils, 5 were watercolors, 6 were landscapes, and 1 was a portrait. If Jo Ann randomly chose to sell 1 of these paintings, what is the probability that it would be an oil painting?

   A $\frac{1}{3}$ **C** $\frac{5}{10}$

   B $\frac{1}{5}$ **D** $\frac{1}{15}$

6. Amelia has 4 different fruits that she wants to arrange in a straight line on the serving table. How many different ways can the fruits be arranged in a straight line on the serving table?

   A 4 **C** 12

   B 8 **D** 24

7. How many different ways can these 5 people be arranged in a row?

A 25 **B** 60 **C** 120 **D** 240

8. If Mrs. James chooses 1 bathroom cleaner, 1 furniture polish, and 1 kitchen cleaner from the list below, how many different combinations could she choose?

Cleaning Supplies		
Bath Cleaner	Kitchen Cleaner	Furniture Polish
Scrub n' Shine	Grease Cutter	Shimmer
Squeaky Clean	No More Mess	Glisten
Super Soap	Wash Away	Smudge-Buster
	Kitchen Magic	

A 10 **B** 24 **C** 36 **D** 64

9. The hair color of 36 students is recorded in the chart below.

Hair Color		
Color	Number of People	
Brown	卌 卌 ||	12
Black	卌 卌	10
Blonde	卌 ||||	9
Red	卌	5
	Total	36

If one of these students is selected at random, what is the probability the student will have black hair?

A 1 in 36
B 5 in 18
C 1 in 4
D 1 in 3

10. Bebe is designing a photo display. From the pictures shown below, Bebe wants to choose 1 form of transportation, 1 person and 1 building to put in her display.

How many different combinations of a form of transportation, a place, and a person could Bebe select?

A 11
B 24
C 48
D 121

11. Donna played 4 games of dominoes. Her scores were 105, 225, 350, and 420. What was her mean (average) score?

A 250
B 275
C 367
D 1100

12. The cards shown below will be placed facedown.

7	3	5	7	7
3	7	4	3	5

If a card is picked, it is most likely to be a _____ .

A 3
B 4
C 5
D 7

It is Shamika's turn to spin in a game she is playing with her friends.

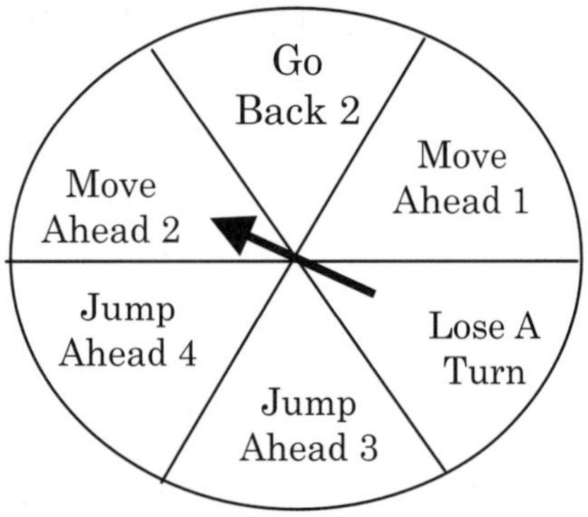

13. What is the probability that Shamika will be able to jump ahead on this spin?

A 1 in 6 **C** 1 in 3
B 1 in 2 **D** 2 in 3

The graph shows after school activities chosen by students.

AFTER-SCHOOL ACTIVITIES

Each ☆ represents 5 students	
Sport	☆☆☆☆☆☆☆☆
Music Lesson	☆☆☆☆☆
Scout	☆☆☆
Service Project	☆☆☆☆

14. How many students participated in the 2 most popular activities?

A 13 **C** 40
B 15 **D** 65

The graph shows the distances run by 5 children in a 12-minute time period.

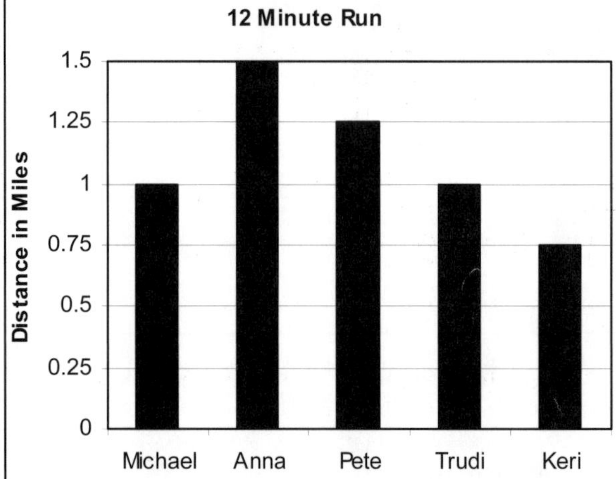

15. What is the range of distances?

A 1.5 miles **C** 0.50 miles
B 0.75 miles **D** 0.25 miles

---

16. What is the median (middle) of the distances?

A 1.5 miles **C** 1 miles
B 1.25 miles **D** 0.75 miles

The graph shows the water level of the Blanco River during a twelve-hour period.

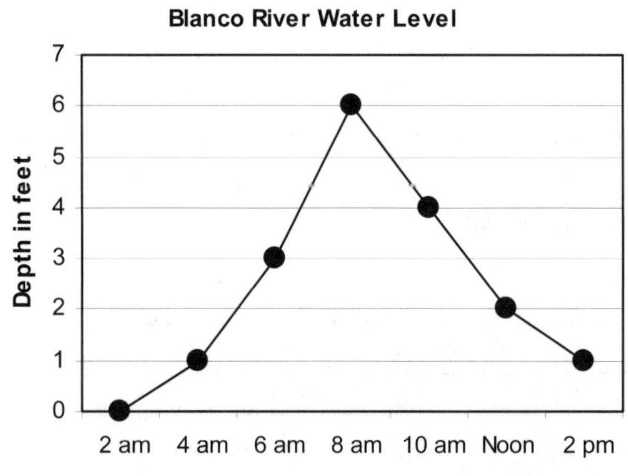

17. During what time period did the water level rise the most?

A 12 noon to 2 pm
B 2 am to 4 am
C 4 am to 6 am
D 6 am to 8 am

The cards shown below are placed facedown.

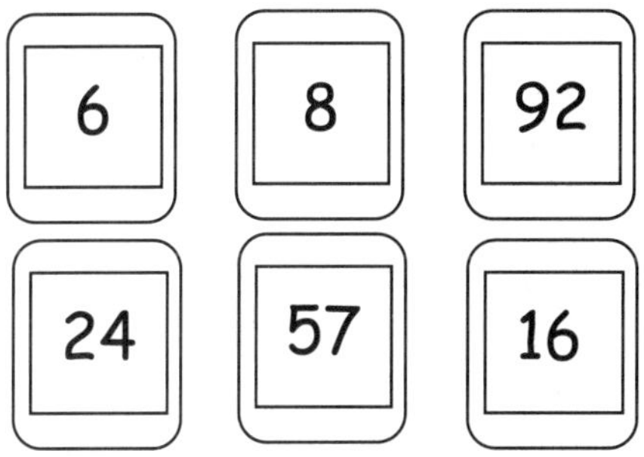

18. If you pick 1 card, it is most likely to be a _______.

A 1-digit number
B 2-digit number
C number less than 8
D number greater than 16

---

19. Alice has 4 coins in her pocket: 1 nickel, 1 penny, and 2 dimes. If she takes 3 coins out of her pocket, which is a possible amount they could total?

A \$0.11 **C** \$0.26
B \$0.16 **D** \$0.31

---

20. Karen's friends were selling cookies for the hospital charity. She recorded her group's sales for a 5 week period. What is the median (middle) sales for the 5 week period?

Cookie Sales

Week	Sales
First	\$76
Second	\$93
Third	\$81
Fourth	\$56
Fifth	\$69

A \$76 **C** \$81
B \$69 **D** \$93

21. If the number of packages and number of cookies continue in the pattern shown, how many cookies will there be in 6 packages?

Cookies

Number of Packages	1	2	3					
Number of Cookies	7	14	21					

A 6 **C** 42
B 35 **D** 48

Mr. Davis conducted a survey of students that participated in a sport after school. Some students participated in more than one sport.

Sport

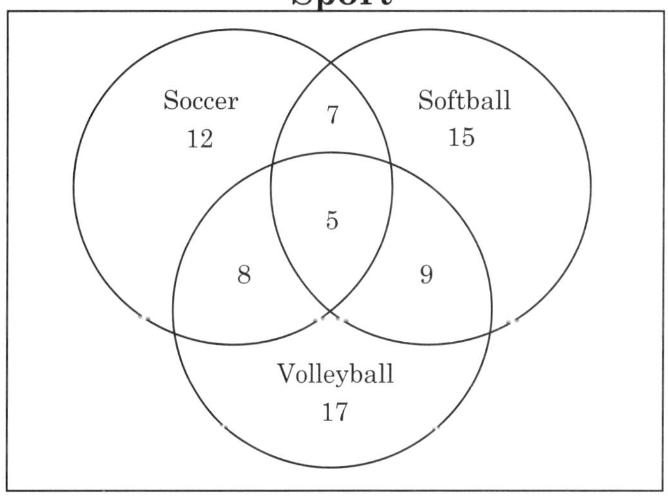

22. How many students participated in all three sports?

A 29 **B** 22 **C** 12 **D** 5

---

23. How many students participated in just softball?

A 36 **B** 31 **C** 15 **D** 9

---

24. How many students participated in both soccer and volleyball?

A 5 **B** 8 **C** 13 **D** 20

The chart shows the average speed of 5 different race cars during a recent race on four different graphs.

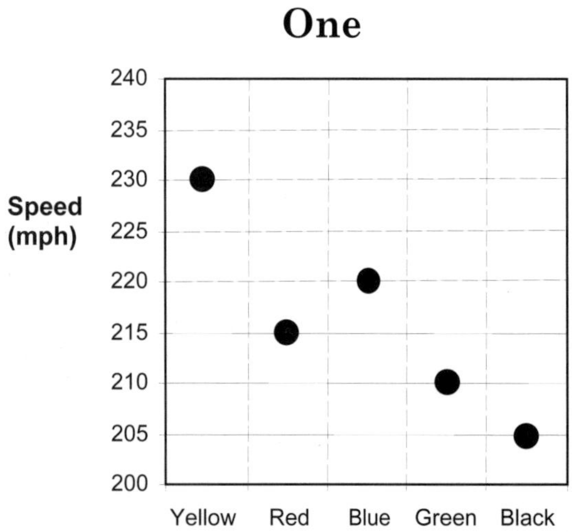

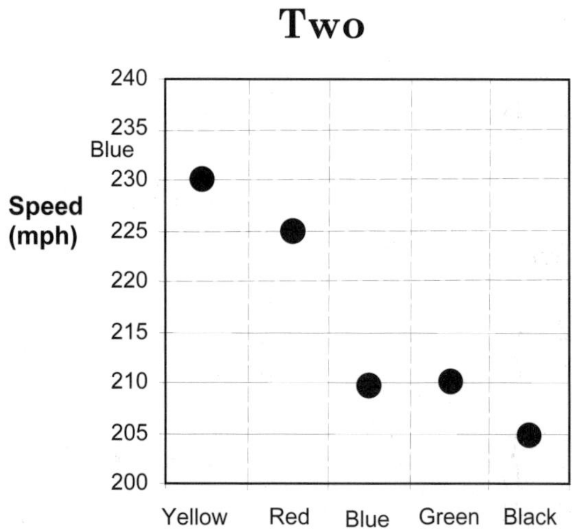

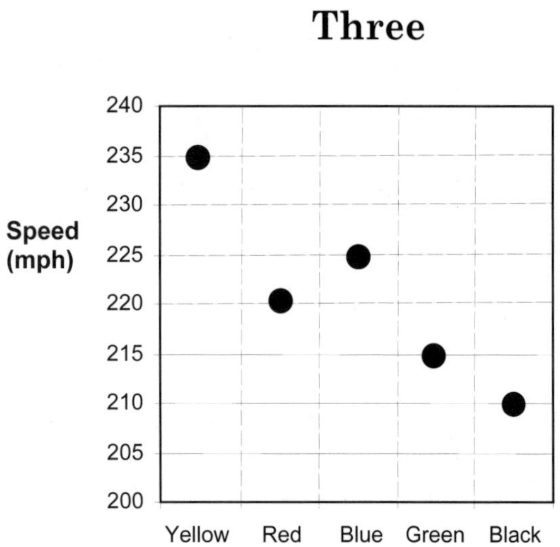

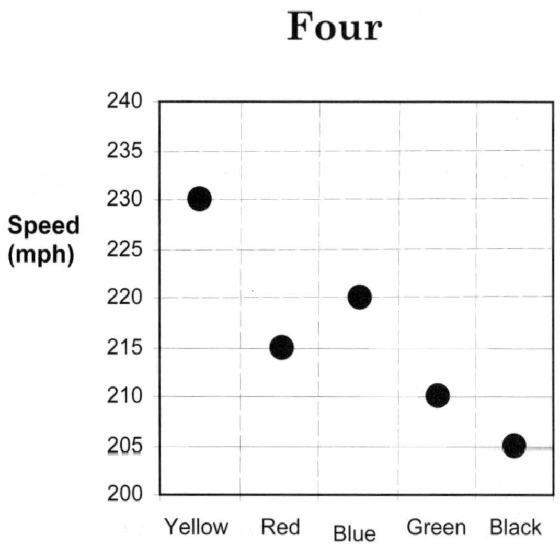

25. Which graph shows the yellow car at a speed of 235 miles per hour?

A One
B Two
C Three
D Four

26. Which graph shows the red car at a speed of 220 miles per hour?

A One
B Two
C Three
D Four

Probability and Statistics: Answer Key

Step One A
1. D
2. D
3. C
4. A

Step One B
1. B
2. C
3. D

Step One C
1. B
2. C
3. A

Step Two A
1. D
2. C
3. B
4. A
5. C
6. B
7. A
8. C

Step Two B
1. B
2. C
3. B
4. C

Step Two C
1. B
2. A
3. A
4. C

Step Two D
1. A
2. A
3. C
4. C
5. B
6. A
7. A
8. B

Step Two E
1. B
2. A
3. B
4. C
5. C
6. C
7. C

Step Three A
1. B
2. B
3. A
4. A
5. D

Step Three B
1. A
2. C
3. B
4. D

Step Three C
1. A
2. C
3. B
4. D
5. A
6. B

Step Three D
1. D
2. B
3. B
4. C

Step Three E
1. A
2. D
3. B
4. B

Step Three F
1. C
2. D
3. A

Step Three G
1. B
2. B
3. D
4. B
5. D

Step Three H
1. C
2. D
3. A
4. B

Step Four A
1. B
2. A
3. D
4. C

Step Four B
1. C
2. C
3. B
4. B

Step Four C
1. C
2. C
3. D
4. D

Step Four D
1. D
2. C
3. A
4. B
5. D
6. C
7. D
8. B

Step Four E
1. 6
2. 4
3. 10
4. 10

Step Four F
1. C
2. B
3. C
4. B
5. A
6. C
7. B
8. B

Step Four G
1. A

Step Four H
1. A

Step Five A
1. D
2. A
3. B
4. B
5. D

Step Five B
1. C
2. B
3. A
4. C
5. D

Step Five C
1. B
2. C

Step Five D
1. D
2. B

Step Five E
1. A
2. C

Step Five F
1. A
2. C
3. D
4. D
5. A

Step Five G
1. B
2. B
3. A
4. C
5. C

Step Five H
1. B

Step Five I
1. A

Assessment
1. C
2. C
3. C
4. D
5. B
6. D
7. C
8. C
9. B
10. C
11. B
12. D
13. C
14. D
15. B
16. C
17. D
18. B
19. B
20. A
21. C
22. D
23. C
24. C
25. C
26. C

Problem Solving

The student is expected to identify the mathematics in everyday situations. **(TEKS 5.14A) (TAKS 6)** *The students should be able to select the description of a mathematical situation when provided a written or pictorial prompt.*

The student is expected to use a problem-solving model that incorporates understanding the problem, making a plan, carrying out the plan, and evaluating the solution for reasonableness. **(TEKS 5.14B) (TAKS 6)** *The students should be able to identify the information that is needed to solve a problem. The students should be able to select or describe the next step or a missing step that would be most appropriate in a problem-solving situation. The students should be able to identify the question that is being asked or answered.*

The student is expected to select or develop an appropriate problem-solving strategy, including drawing a picture, looking for a pattern, systemic guessing and checking, acting it out, making a table, working a simpler problem, or working backwards to solve a problem. **(TEKS 5.14C) (TAKS 6)**

The student is expected to make generalizations from patterns or sets of examples and nonexamples. **(TEKS 5.16A) (TAKS 6)** *The students should be able to select the generalization of the common characteristic among examples. The students should be able to select an example from among nonexamples or a nonexample from among examples based on a given characteristic. A nonexample is a counterexample or an example that shows a general statement to be false.*

The student is expected to relate informal language to mathematical language and symbols. **(TEKS 5.15B) (TAKS 6)**

The student is expected to select from and use diagrams and number sentences to represent real-life situations. **(TEKS 5.6A) (TAKS 2)**

Suggested Sequence
Simple to Complex

Step One.........Generalization from Patterns, Examples and Nonexamples (TAKS 6:5.16A)
Step Two ....Mathematics in Everyday Situations (6:5.14C) (2:5.6A) (6:5.14A)
Step Three.....Process of Problem Solving (TAKS 6:5.14B)
Step Four ....Problem Solving Strategies (TAKS 6:5.14C)
Step Five ....Mathematical Language and Symbols (TAKS 6:5.15B)
Assessment

Vocabulary

- 🕮 Logical Reasoning
- 🕮 Work Simpler Problem
- 🕮 Organized List
- 🕮 Quotient
- 🕮 Product
- 🕮 Sum
- 🕮 Difference
- 🕮 Generalization
- 🕮 Example
- 🕮 Nonexample

Problem Solving: Sample for Analysis

The student is expected to make generalizations from patterns or sets of examples and nonexamples. (TAKS 6:5.16A)

Look for the pattern in the sequence of numbers below.

72, 65, 70, 63, 68, 61

Which number comes next in the pattern?

A 54 **C** 66
B 56 **D** 68

Strategy:

Very Important Tip: Do not just subtract the first two numbers and think that the difference is repeated with every number. Evaluate each sequence and establish a rule.

1. What is the difference in 72 and 65? The pattern is going down so the difference is being subtracted. (72 - 65 = 7) *So 7 is subtracted.*

2. What is the difference in 65 and 70? The pattern is going up so the difference is being added. (70- 65 = 5) *So 5 is added.*

3. What is the difference in 70 and 63? The pattern is going down so the difference is being subtracted. (70 - 63 = 7) *So 7 is subtracted.*

4. What is the difference in 63 and 68? The pattern is going up so the difference is being added. (68 - 63 = 5) *So 5 is added.*

5. What is the difference in 68 and 61? The pattern is going down so the difference is being subtracted. (68 - 61 = 7) *So 7 is subtracted.*

6. Can you see the pattern now? Subtract 7, add 5, subtract 7, add 5, subtract 7, then you will add 5. 61 + 5 = 66 Choice ***C***

Problem Solving: Sample for Analysis

The student is expected to make generalizations from patterns or sets of examples and nonexamples. (TAKS 6:5.16A)

Look for the pattern in the sequence of numbers below.

38, 44, 41, 47, 44, 50

Which rule describes this pattern best?

A Add 9, subtract 3
B Add 6, add 3
C Add 6, subtract 3
D Add 4, subtract 3

Strategy:

Very Important Tip: Do not just subtract the first two numbers and think that the difference is repeated with every number. Evaluate each sequence and establish a rule.

1. What is the difference in 38 and 44? The pattern is going up so the difference is being added. (44 - 38 = 6) *So 6 is added.*

2. What is the difference in 44 and 41? The pattern is going down so the difference is being subtracted. (44 - 41 = 3) *So 3 is subtracted.*

3. What is the difference in 41 and 47? The pattern is going up so the difference is being added. (47 - 41 = 6) *So 6 is added.*

4. What is the difference in 47 and 44? The pattern is going down so the difference is being subtracted. (47 - 44 = 3) *So 3 is subtracted.*

5. What is the difference in 44 and 50? The pattern is going up so the difference is being added. (50 - 44 = 6) *So 6 is added.*

6. Do you know the rule now? Add 6, subtract 3, add 6, subtract 3, add 6
   Add 6, subtract 3 Choice ***C***

Problem Solving: Step One A

The student is expected to make generalizations from patterns or sets of examples and nonexamples. (TAKS 6:5.16A)

1. Look for the pattern in the sequence of numbers below.

73, 75, 79, 85, 93, 103

Which number comes next in this pattern?

A 115
B 113
C 109
D 105

---

2. Look for the pattern in the sequence of numbers below.

16, 25, 28, 37, 40, 49

Which number comes next in the pattern?

A 36
B 37
C 40
D 52

---

3. Look for the pattern in the sequence of numbers below.

53, 45, 51, 43, 49, 41

Which number comes next in the pattern?

A 49
B 47
C 45
D 33

---

4. Look for the pattern in the sequence of numbers below.

51, 56, 63, 72, 83, 96

Which number comes next in the pattern?

A 111
B 105
C 103
D 101

5. Look for the pattern in the sequence of numbers below.

38, 46, 42, 50, 46, 54

Which rule describes this pattern best?

A Add 16, subtract 8
B Add 4, subtract 8
C Add 8, subtract 4
D Add 8, subtract 6

---

6. Look for the pattern in the sequence of numbers below.

27, 37, 32, 42, 37, 47

Which rule describes this pattern best?

A Add 10, subtract 5
B Add 5, subtract 10
C Add 20, subtract 10
D Add 15, subtract 10

---

7. Look for the pattern in the sequence of numbers below.

22, 29, 34, 41, 46, 53

Which rule describes this pattern best?

A Add 31, subtract 7
B Add 7, subtract 5
C Add 7, add 5
D Add 12

Problem Solving: Step One B

The student is expected to make generalizations from patterns or sets of examples and nonexamples. (TAKS 6:5.16A)

1. Mr. James gave his fifth-grade math class two sets of numbers that were sorted according to a certain rule. The numbers that followed the rule were put in Set A, and the numbers that did not follow the rule were put in Set B.

Set A	45.36, 63.57, 37.93, 85.25, 57.73
Set B	73.3, 3.603, 52.9, 33.2, 207.7

Based on this information, all the numbers in Set A_____

A include the digit 7
B are written to the hundredths place
C have an odd number in the tenths place
D have an odd number in the hundredths place

---

2. Mr. James gave his fifth-grade math class two sets of numbers that were sorted according to a certain rule. The numbers that followed the rule were put in Set A, and the numbers that did not follow the rule were put in Set B.

Set A	25.16, 46.345, 0.229, 127.28, 11.76
Set B	13.37, 22.633, 38.97, 99.21, 7.758

Based on this information, all the numbers in Set A_____

A have an even number in the hundredths place
B are written to the thousandths place
C have an odd number in the ones place
D include the digit 1

Problem Solving: Sample for Analysis

The student is expected to make generalizations from patterns or sets of examples and nonexamples. (TAKS 6:5.16A)

These are examples of dordies.

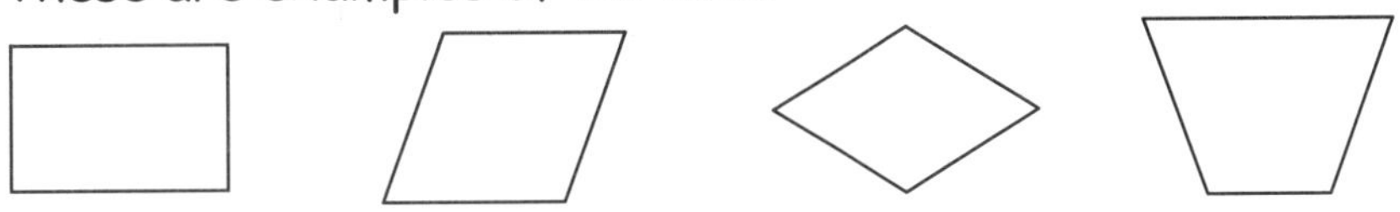

These are not examples of dordies.

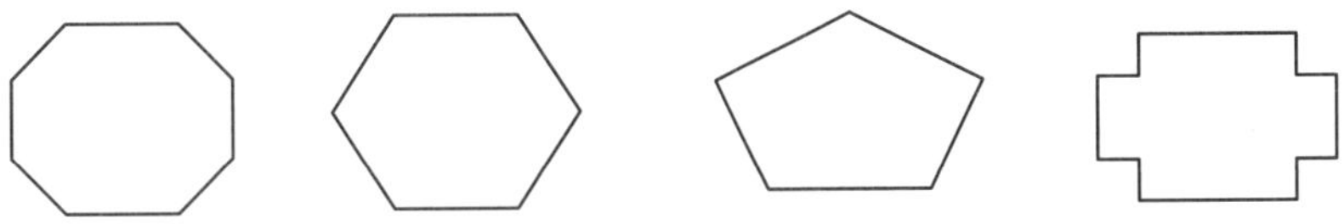

Which figure below is **NOT** a dordy?

A 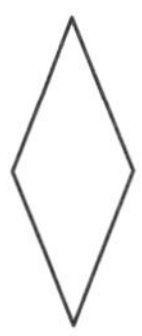

B 

C 

D 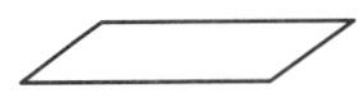

Strategy: Logical Reasoning

1. Examine the attributes of the dordy.
   straight lines no curves
   first one has 4 sides—second has 4 sides
   third has 4 sides—fourth has 4 sides
   They are all polygons
2. Examine the attributes of the figures that are not dordies.
   straight lines no curves
   first has 8 sides—second has 6 sides
   third has 5 sides—fourth has 12 sides
   They are all polygons
3. Compare the attributes and see what each has in common and what is different from a dordy and one that is not.
4. Answer choice A has straight lines and 4 sides.
   Answer choice B has straight lines and 4 sides.
   Answer choice C has straight lines and 5 sides.
   Answer choice D has straight lines and 4 sides.
5. All dordies have 4 sides. All that are not dordies do not have 4 sides. Now which answer choice is **NOT** a dordy? Answer Choice C

Problem Solving: Step One C

The student is expected to make generalizations from patterns or sets of examples and nonexamples. (TAKS 6:5.16A)

1. These are examples of tanzies.

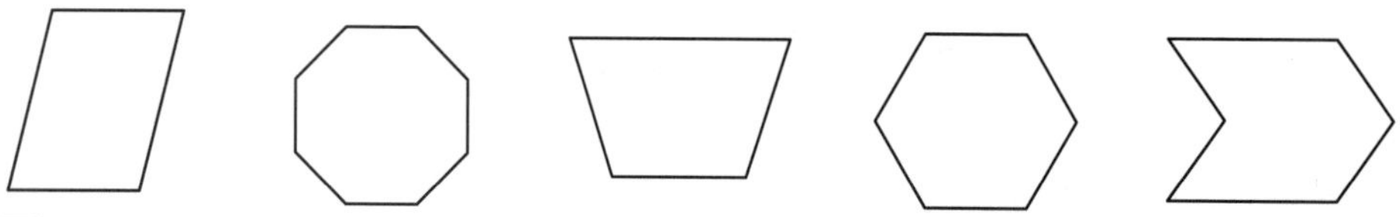

These are not examples of tanzies.

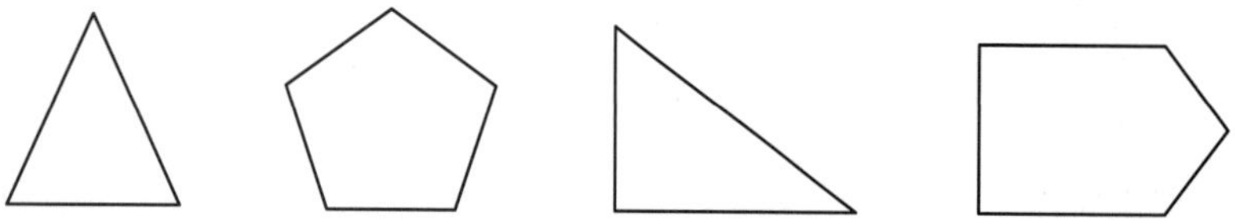

Which figure below is a tanzy?

A 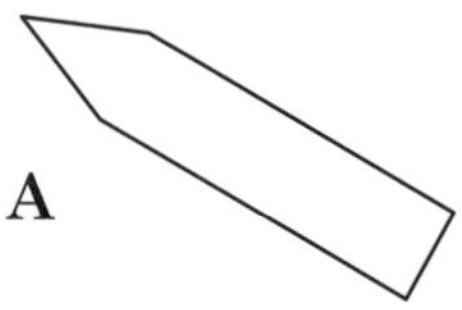 B 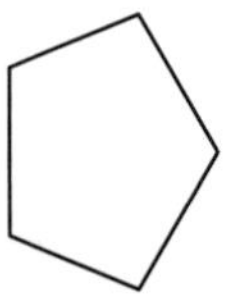 C 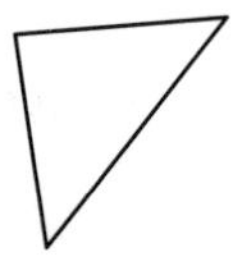 D 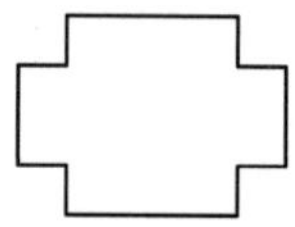

---

2. These are examples of arrowinks.

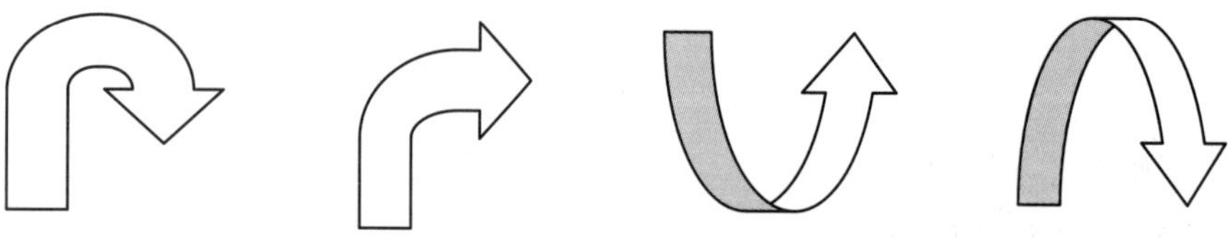

These are not examples of arrowinks.

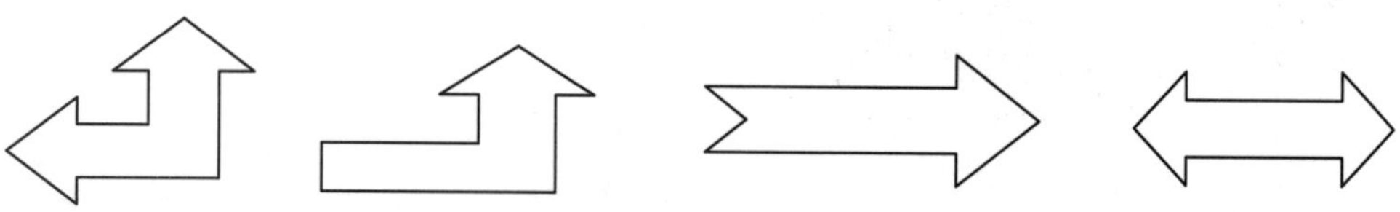

Which figure below is an arrowink?

A 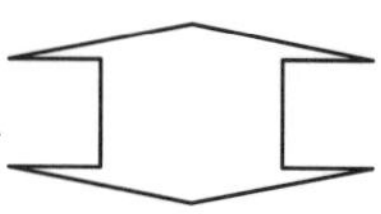 B 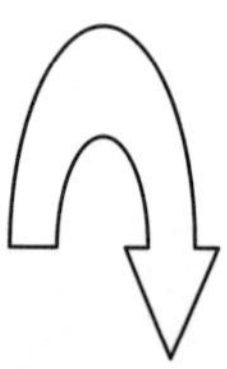 C 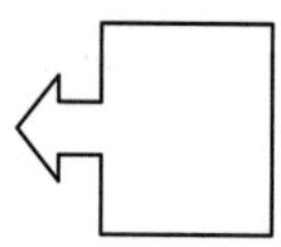 D 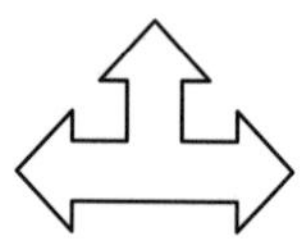

Problem Solving: Step One D

The student is expected to make generalizations from patterns or sets of examples and nonexamples. (TAKS 6:5.16A)

1. **These are examples of zalios.**

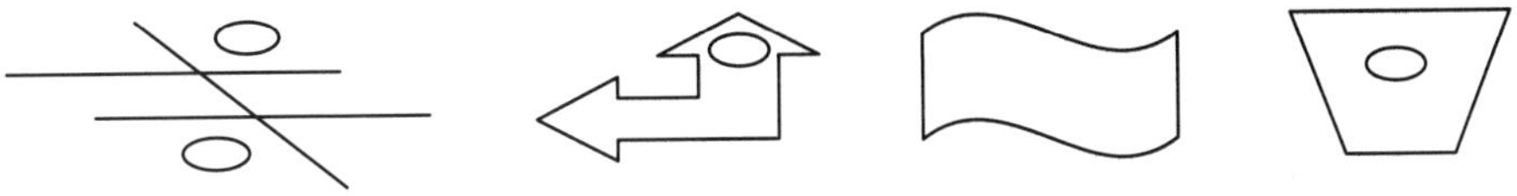

These are not examples of zalios.

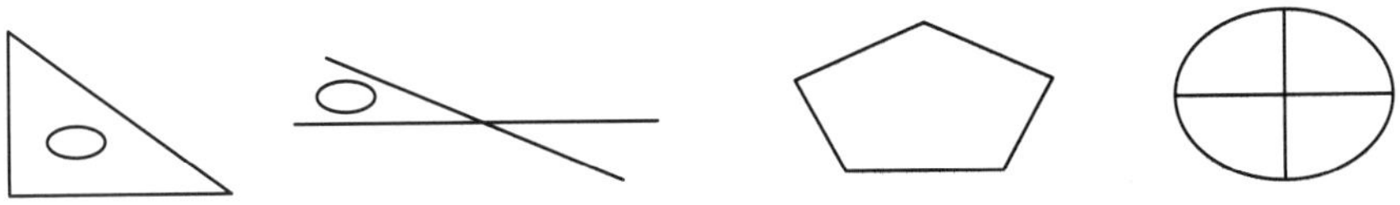

Which figure below is NOT a zalio?

A 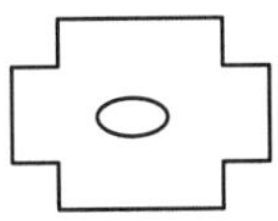 **B** 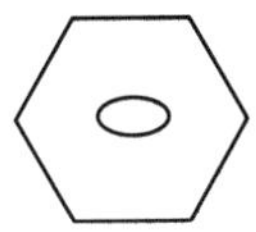 **C** 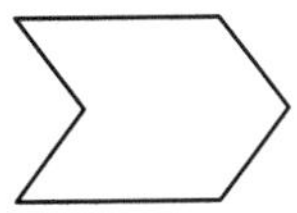 **D** 

---

2. **These are examples of grainylos.**

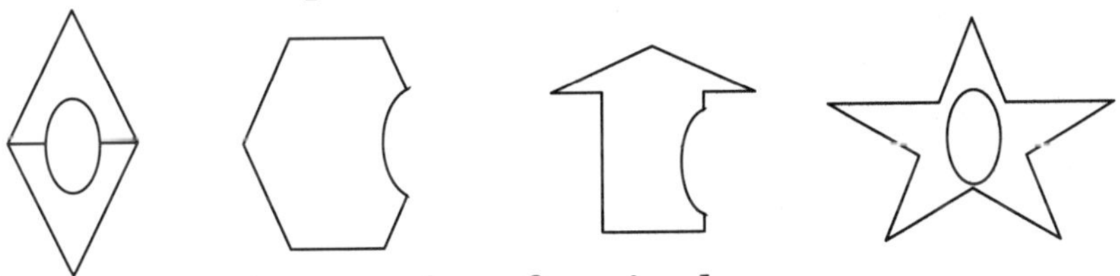

These are not examples of grainylos.

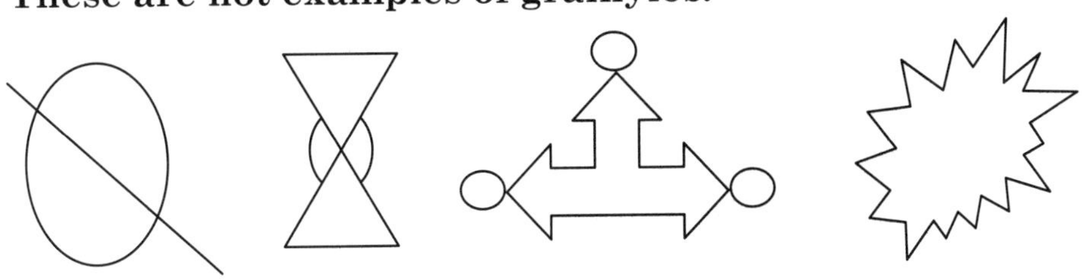

Which figure below is a grainylos?

A 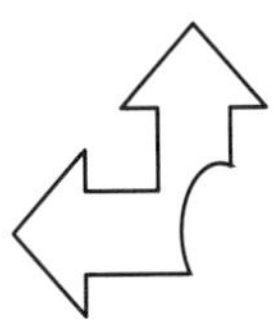 **B**  **C** 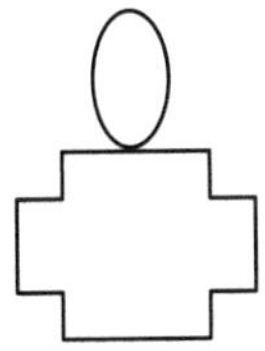 **D** 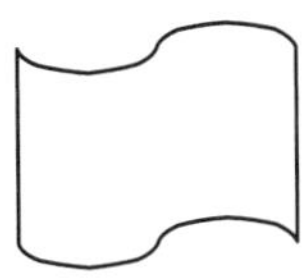

Problem Solving: Your Turn

The student is expected to make generalizations from patterns or sets of examples and nonexamples. (TAKS 6:5.16A)

Create your own.

1. **These are examples of** ________________.

These are not examples of ________________.

Which figure below is NOT a ________________?

A

C

B

D

Problem Solving: Step Two A

The student is expected to identify the mathematics in everyday situations.
(TAKS 6:5.14A)

A sign above a rack of shirts is shown below. The price tag on a shirt is shown below.

Gigantic Sale

The Price Marked Is
75% off
Regular Price

1. Which problem matches the purchase of a shirt?

A The regular price of the shirt is \$8.00. If Joe buys a shirt, 75% will be taken off the price of \$8.00. What will be the cost of the shirt?

B The regular price of the shirt is \$75. \$8.00 will be taken off that price as a part of the Gigantic Sale. What will be the cost of the shirt?

C The sales price of the shirt is \$8.00. \$0.75 will be taken off that price as a part of the Gigantic Sale. What will be the cost of the shirt?

D The shirt has already been marked down 75% of the regular price. The shirt is on sale for \$8.00. What will be the cost of the shirt?

A sign shown on a computer printer is shown below.

Factory Rebate of \$25
Computer Printer Only \$199

Regular Price \$224

2. Which problem matches the purchase of the computer printer?

A The price of the computer printer is \$199. The clerk will take \$25 off of the \$199 at the register. What will be the cost of the computer printer?

B The price of the computer printer is \$224. The clerk will take \$25 off of the \$224 at the register. What will be the cost of the computer printer?

C The price of the computer printer is \$224. The customer will need to send the receipt to the factory to receive a rebate of \$25. What will be the cost of the computer printer?

D The computer printer has been marked down from \$224 to \$199 and now the factory has marked it down to \$25. What will be the cost of the computer printer?

Problem Solving: Step Two B

The student is expected to identify the mathematics in everyday situations. (TAKS 6:5.14A)

1. Mrs. Currin is cutting hair ribbons for her three daughters. Mary Beth's ribbon needs to be twice as long as Kathleen's ribbon and 3 times as long as Claire's ribbon. What additional information does Mrs. Currin need to find out how much ribbon she needs?

   A The number of inches in 4 feet
   B The length of ribbon cut for Claire
   C The number of centimeters in a meter
   D The number of inches in a roll of ribbon

2. Willie is planning a 75 mile trip to El Paso. He wants to find his arrival time if he leaves at 3:00 PM. What additional information does he need?

   A The distance from El Paso to the New Mexico
   B The number of miles on the odometer of the car he will drive
   C The number of feet in a mile
   D The speed he will be driving most of the trip

3. The Newman family went on a trip to Abilene. They drove from San Marcos to Abilene in 5 ½ hours. What other information do you need to determine the time the Newmans arrived in Abilene?

   A The amount of gasoline they used
   B The road conditions
   C The distance from San Marcos to Abilene
   D The time they left San Marcos

4. Mrs. Currin is cutting roses from her garden. Her pink rose bush is 7 inches taller than her yellow rose bush. The yellow rose bush is 4 inches taller than her red rose bush. What other information could be used to find the heights of each of Mrs. Currin's rose bushes?

   A The height of the yellow rose bush
   B The ages of all the rose bushes
   C The number of roses Mrs. Currin cut from each bush
   D The size of Mrs. Currin's rose garden

5. Mr. Currin is 1 year older than Mrs. Currin. Mrs. Currin was 25 years old when their daughter, Kathleen, was born. What information do you need to find how old Mr. Currin is now?

   A The age of Mr. Currin when Kathleen was born
   B The age of the Currin's other children
   C The age of Kathleen when she was born
   D The year that Kathleen was born

6. Jason bought two new baseball cards. His "Mickey Mantle" baseball card cost \$0.75 less than his "Babe Ruth" card. What other information could be used to determine how much Jason spent for both baseball cards?

   A The age of the "Mickey Mantle" card
   B The cost of a package of baseball cards
   C The amount of money his dad gave him
   D The cost of the "Babe Ruth" card

Problem Solving: Step Two C

The student is expected to identify the mathematics in everyday situations. (TAKS 6:5.14A)

1. Jana's doctor told her to drink plenty of liquids to get over her cold. She drank 3 glasses of water, 2 glasses of orange juice and 3 glasses of grape juice. She wants to find out how much she drank during the day. What additional information does she need?

   A The number of ounces in the glass

   B The amount of pulp in the orange juice

   C The number of quarts in 2 gallons

   D The number of ounces in a pound

---

2. Maria has worked a day at her new job. She worked a total of 6 hours. She wants to find out how much she made. What additional information does she need?

   A The number of minutes in an hour

   B The number of hours in a work day

   C The amount she is being paid an hour

   D The amount of time she spent doing each task

---

3. Jennifer is going to buy dog food for the week. She knows that 20 pounds of food is in every bag. She feeds her dog two bowls of food a day. She needs to know how many bags to buy. What additional information does she need?

   A The cost of the dog food

   B The number of pounds in a ton

   C The length of time it takes the dog to eat each bowl

   D The amount of dog food the bowl will hold

4. Marcus is going to the movies. The movie starts at 6:00. His mother needs to know what time to pick him up. What additional information does she need?

   A The running time of the movie

   B The number of times the movie shows during the day

   C The time the movies beside it starts

   D The capacity of the theater

---

5. Rosa is going to Kinkos to have the programs copied for the piano recital of her students. They charge \$0.10 a copy. She will need 80 programs copied. She needs to know how much it will cost. What additional information does she need?

   A The number of parents attending

   B The number of copies needed for one program

   C The number of \$0.10 in a \$1.00

   D The number of papers in a package of paper

Problem Solving: Step Three A

The student is expected to use a problem-solving model that incorporates understanding the problem, making a plan, carrying out the plan, and evaluating the solution for reasonableness. (TAKS 6:5.14B)

1. Pat made 2 quarts of hot chocolate. Only 3 cups of hot chocolate were left after breakfast. What fractional part of Pat's hot chocolate did her family drink for breakfast?

   A $\frac{3}{5}$ **C** $\frac{3}{4}$

   B $\frac{3}{8}$ **D** $\frac{5}{8}$

Show Your Work

2. Catrina bought 2 yards of fabric. She used 45 inches to make a table scarf. What fractional part of the piece of fabric she bought does she have left?

   A $\frac{5}{8}$ **C** $\frac{4}{5}$

   B $\frac{1}{4}$ **D** $\frac{3}{8}$

Show Your Work

3. Tony's tree is 9 yards tall. The trunk is 3 feet tall. What fractional part of the tree has branches?

   A $\frac{2}{3}$ **C** $\frac{7}{9}$

   B $\frac{1}{3}$ **D** $\frac{8}{9}$

Show Your Work

4. Carmen spent 1 hour at the swimming pool. She had to play with her little cousin 12 minutes of that time. What fractional part of her time at the pool did she have without her cousin?

   A $\frac{4}{5}$ **C** $\frac{1}{10}$

   B $\frac{2}{12}$ **D** $\frac{1}{5}$

Show Your Work

Problem Solving: Step Three B

The student is expected to use a problem-solving model that incorporates understanding the problem, making a plan, carrying out the plan, and evaluating the solution for reasonableness. (TAKS 6:5.14B)

1. Katie bought a candy bar for $0.63. She received $0.37 in change. What is the least number of coins she could have received?

   A 3 **C** 5
   B 4 **D** 6

Show Your Work

2. Lonnie wanted change for a $20 bill. He needed at least one $10, $5, and $1 bill. What is the greatest number of bills he could have received?

   A 5 **C** 7
   B 6 **D** 10

Show Your Work

3. Margaret has $2.00 to spend on bows. She wants to get as many bows as possible for her money. The two-color bows are 3 for $.75. The 10 looped bows are 2 for $0.90. The bright-colored bows are 4 for $0.80. What is the greatest number of bows she can buy with $2.00?

   A 4 **C** 8
   B 6 **D** 10

Show Your Work

4. Judy has 2 quarters, 3 dimes, 6 nickels, and 4 pennies. She has bought 3 pencils and her bill is $0.72. What is the greatest number of coins she could use to pay exactly $0.72 for the pencils?

   A 8 **C** 12
   B 10 **D** 14

Show Your Work

Problem Solving: Step Three C

The student is expected to use a problem-solving model that incorporates understanding the problem, making a plan, carrying out the plan, and evaluating the solution for reasonableness. (TAKS 6:5.14B)

1. Kima is helping her mother out at the bakery. The customer wants a total of 120 cupcakes. There must be 1 chocolate cupcake for every 7 white cupcakes. Kima has to make the chocolate cupcakes. How many chocolate cupcakes should she make?

   A 28 **C** 17
   B 24 **D** 15

Show Your Work

2. Tyson is helping his dad put up a picket fence. For every 6 fence-boards there has to be 1 post. The first and last parts of the fence must be a post. Dad came home with a total of 36 pieces of wood for the picket-fence. How many of the pieces of wood were posts?

   A 6 **C** 10
   B 8 **D** 12

Show Your Work

3. Mrs. Byrd is planning an art project for her class. She needs 1 red piece of construction paper for every 8 green pieces of construction paper for each project. She bought 63 pieces of construction paper. How many projects will be made with the 63 pieces of paper?

   A 12 **C** 7
   B 9 **D** 6

Show Your Work

Problem Solving: Sample for Analysis

The student is expected to select or develop an appropriate problem solving strategy, including drawing a picture, looking for a pattern, systematic guessing and checking, acting it out, making a table, working a simpler problem, or working backwards to solve a problem.(TAKS 6:5.14C)

The sale price for gum is 8 for $1.25. Reba wants to buy 12 pieces of gum. Which is a reasonable total cost Reba will pay?

A Less than $1.00
B Between $1.00 and $1.50
C Between $1.50 and $2.00
D More than $2.00

Strategy: Work a Simpler Problem

Understand the Problem

What is the question?

Which is a reasonable total cost Reba will pay?

What is the important information?

8 for $1.25
12 pieces

Step 1

Choose a Plan

Logical Reasoning

12 = 8 + 4 4 is half of 8

The cost would be $1.25 for 8 and then one half of $1.25 or about $0.62 for 4. $1.25 + $0.62 = $1.87

That is between $1.50 and $2.00

Or it could be worked another way------

Step 2

Work the Problem

Work a Simpler Problem

Break the pieces up to find how much each piece costs and then extend that cost. To find how much each costs, divide.

$1.25 ÷ 8 = 0.156 rounded to .16
At 16 cents a piece, how much would 12 pieces cost? 12 x .16 = $1.92
$1.92 is between $1.50 and $2.00

Step 3

Is this the Right Answer?

Write a sentence answering the question.

If 8 pieces cost $1.25, then 12 pieces would cost between $1.50 and $2.00.
Since 12 pieces must cost more than 8 pieces, this is a reasonable answer.

Does it make sense? **(Yes)** **No**

Step 4

Problem Solving: Step Four A

The student is expected to select or develop an appropriate problem solving strategy, including drawing a picture, looking for a pattern, systematic guessing and checking, acting it out, making a table, working a simpler problem, or working backwards to solve a problem. (TAKS 6:5.14C)

1. The sale price for canned fruit is 4 cans for \$3.25. Rebecca wants to buy 6 cans of fruit. Which is a reasonable cost for 6 cans of fruit?

   A Less than \$4
   B Between \$4 and \$5
   C Between \$5 and \$6
   D More than \$7

Show Your Work

Think about it:
\$3.25 divided by 4—Round \$3.25 to \$3.20 because that will go into 4 evenly and that will give you the approximate price for each. The answer would be \$0.80 a can. \$0.80 x 6 = ?

2. Ken and 4 friends are going to put their money together to buy candy bars. The price of the candy bars is listed as 3 for \$1.25. Which is a reasonable total cost for Ken and his friends if they each want 1 candy bar?

   A Less than \$2
   B Between \$2 and \$3
   C Between \$3 and \$4
   D More than \$5

Show Your Work

Think about it:

3. The sale price for chili is 5 cans for \$5.50. Dale wants to buy 3 cans of chili. Which is a reasonable cost for 3 cans of chili?

   A Less than \$3
   B Between \$3 and \$4
   C Between \$4 and \$5
   D More than \$5

Show Your Work

Think about it:

4. Oranges are on sale at 6 for \$1.15. If Lana wants to buy 8 oranges, what is a reasonable cost?

   A Less than \$1.00
   B Between \$1.00 and \$1.50
   C Between \$1.50 and \$2.00
   D More than \$2.00

Show Your Work

Think about it:

Problem Solving: Step Four B

The student is expected to select or develop an appropriate problem solving strategy, including drawing a picture, looking for a pattern, systematic guessing and checking, acting it out, making a table, working a simpler problem, or working backwards to solve a problem. (TAKS 6:5.14C)

1. The sale price for shirts is 3 for $7.00. Juan wants to buy 1 shirt. Which is a reasonable cost Juan will pay for the 1 shirt?

   A Less than $2
   B Between $2 and $3
   C Between $3 and $4
   D More than $4

Show Your Work

Think about it:

2. They are having a sale of 5 roast beef sandwiches for $4.00. Tim and Tom want to buy 2 sandwiches each. Which is a reasonable total cost for Tim's and Tom's sandwiches?

   A Less than $2
   B Between $2 and $3
   C Between $3 and $4
   D More than $4

Show Your Work

Think about it:

3. The sale price for apples is 5 apples for $2.25. Dan wants to buy 8 apples to make caramel apples. Which is a reasonable cost for 8 apples?

   A Less than $2
   B Between $2 and $3
   C Between $3 and $4
   D More than $4

Show Your Work

Think about it:

4. At the drive-thru, apple pies are on sale for 3 for $1.00. Kim wants to buy 8. Which is a reasonable total cost for the eight pies?

   A Less than $2
   B Between $2 and $3
   C Between $3 and $4
   D More than $4

Show Your Work

Think about it:

Problem Solving: Step Four C

The student is expected to select or develop an appropriate problem solving strategy, including drawing a picture, looking for a pattern, systematic guessing and checking, acting it out, making a table, working a simpler problem, or working backwards to solve a problem. (TAKS 6:5.14C)

1. Mr. Davis assigned 12 problems for extra credit. They could choose the ones they wanted to do and do as many as they wanted to do. Each student would receive a point for every problem solved correctly. Matt received 4 more points than Brandon. Rene received twice as many points as Brandon. Which table shows a reasonable set of points each student received?

A

Student	Points
Matt	5
Brandon	1
Rene	4

B

Student	Points
Matt	6
Brandon	2
Rene	12

C

Student	Points
Matt	8
Brandon	4
Rene	8

D

Student	Points
Matt	9
Brandon	5
Rene	8

2. Stephanie's volleyball team won the volleyball game. Millie, Stephanie and Rosa scored most of the points for their team. Millie scored a third as many points as Stephanie. Rosa scored twice as many as Millie. Which table shows a reasonable set of points each player scored?

A

Player	Points
Millie	3
Stephanie	9
Rosa	18

B

Player	Points
Millie	2
Stephanie	6
Rosa	12

C

Player	Points
Millie	2
Stephanie	6
Rosa	4

D

Player	Points
Millie	3
Stephanie	9
Rosa	2

Problem Solving: Sample for Analysis

The student is expected to select or develop an appropriate problem solving strategy, including drawing a picture, looking for a pattern, systematic guessing and checking, acting it out, making a table, working a simpler problem, or working backwards to solve a problem. (TAKS 6:5.14C)

Mrs. Ruiz class is going on a field trip. She is taking 12 girls and 12 boys on this trip. Before the trip she had them draw from a basket to determine which would be the leader for this trip. Which of the following would be true?

A The chance of a girl being the leader is better than a boy being the leader.
B The chance of a boy being the leader is better than a girl being the leader.
C The chance of the leader being a boy or girl is equal.
D The leader will be a boy.

Strategy: Logical Reasoning

Understand the Problem

What is the question?

Which of the following would be true?

What is the important information?

12 girls and 12 boys

Step 1

Choose a Plan

Logical Reasoning

If there are 12 girls and 12 boys, then there is an equal chance for each.

Step 2

Work the Problem

A The chance of a girl being picked is **not** better than a boy.

B The chance of a boy being the leader is **not** better than a girl.

C The chance of the leader being a boy or girl is equal.

D There is no evidence the leader will be a boy.

Step 3

Is this the Right Answer?

Write a sentence answering the question.

The chance of the leader being a boy or girl is equal.

Does it make sense? (Yes) **No**

Step 4

Problem Solving: Step Four D

The student is expected to select or develop an appropriate problem solving strategy, including drawing a picture, looking for a pattern, systematic guessing and checking, acting it out, making a table, working a simpler problem, or working backwards to solve a problem. (TAKS 6:5.14C)

1. Maria has 40 bingo markers numbered 1 through 40. If she chooses 1 of the markers out of the bin without looking, which of the following would be true?

   A The chance that the marker has an even number is the same as the chance that it has an odd number.

   B The chance that the marker has a 1-digit number is the same as the chance that it has a 2-digit number.

   C The marker most likely is the number 20.

   D The marker most likely has an odd number.

---

2. Before the football game, they always flip a coin to determine which team will begin the game in possession of the ball. Which of the following would be true when the coin is flipped?

   A The chance the coin will land on heads is better than the chance the coin will land on tails.

   B The chance the coin will land on tails is better than the chance the coin will land on heads.

   C The chance the coin will land on heads is equal to the chance the coin will land on tails.

   D The team that chooses heads is more likely to win the toss.

3. Regina worked in the garden yesterday. She spent $\frac{1}{4}$ hour planting beans, 35 minutes staking the tomato plant, and $\frac{1}{2}$ hour training the cucumber vines. What is a reasonable estimate of how much time Regina worked in the garden?

   A Less than 1 hour
   B Between 1 hour and 2 hours
   C Between 2 hours and 3 hours
   D More than 3 hours

---

4. Stan broke his leg. He has had a cast on for 2 months. The doctor took the cast off and told him to walk a little more each day until his muscles develop back to normal. He walked a $\frac{1}{4}$ of a mile the first, second and third day. The fourth and fifth day he walked $\frac{3}{4}$ of a mile. What is a reasonable estimate of the distance he walked in five days?

   A Less than 1 mile
   B Between 1 mile and 2 miles
   C Between 2 miles and 3 miles
   D More than 3 miles

---

5. When all the checkout lanes at the local discount store are being used, 31 customers can be checked out every 15 minutes. Which is a reasonable estimate of how many customers can be checked out in a $1\frac{1}{2}$ hour period?

   A 48 **C** 240
   B 180 **D** 465

Problem Solving: Sample for Analysis

The student is expected to select or develop an appropriate problem solving strategy, including drawing a picture, looking for a pattern, systematic guessing and checking, acting it out, making a table, working a simpler problem, or working backwards to solve a problem. (TAKS 6:5.14C)

Tina bought 4 items from the toy store. The lowest price toy, including tax, was \$4, and the highest price toy, including tax, was \$6. Which is a reasonable total for the toys?

A Less than \$5
B Between \$5 and \$10
C Between \$10 and \$15
D More than \$15

Strategy: Organized List/Logical Reasoning

Understand the Problem

What is the question?

Which is a reasonable total for the toys?

What is the important information?

4 items
Lowest toy \$4
Highest toy \$6

Step 1

Choose a Plan

Organized List/Logical Reasoning

Create a list of the lowest possible price and then a list of the highest possible price to create a logical answer.

Step 2

Work the Problem

Lowest total cost:

\$4 + \$4 + \$4 + \$6 = \$18

Highest total cost:

\$4 + \$6 + \$6 + \$6 = \$22

Step 3

Is this the Right Answer?

Write a sentence answering the question.

The cost was between \$18 and \$22.
That would be more than \$15 in the answer choices.

Does it make sense? (Yes) No

Step 4

Problem Solving: Step Four E

The student is expected to select or develop an appropriate problem solving strategy, including drawing a picture, looking for a pattern, systematic guessing and checking, acting it out, making a table, working a simpler problem, or working backwards to solve a problem. (TAKS 6:5.14C)

1. Rachel bought gifts for each of 4 family members. The lowest priced gift, including tax was $15, and the highest price gift was $18, including tax. Which is a reasonable total for the gifts?
   A Less than $60
   B Between $60 and $75
   C Between $75 and $90
   D more than $90

Show Your Work

2. Claire selected 4 items in a store. The lowest priced item was $4 and the highest priced item was $9. Before the tax is added, what is a reasonable total for the cost of the items?
   A Less than $9
   B Between $9 and $20
   C Between $21 and $35
   D More than $35

Show Your Work

3. Mrs. Pendleton owns a beauty shop. Haircuts cost $9 or $15, and hair coloring costs $25 or $30. What is a reasonable estimate of the price Cindy will pay to have her hair cut and colored?
   A Less than $30
   B Between $30 and $50
   C Between $50 and $70
   D More than $70

Show Your Work

4. Syd planted 10 rows of green beans with 12 to 15 plants in each row. What is the best estimate of the total number of bean plants he planted?
   A Less than 100
   B Between 100 and 120
   C Between 120 and 150
   D Between 150 and 170

Show Your Work

Problem Solving: Step Four F

The student is expected to select or develop an appropriate problem solving strategy, including drawing a picture, looking for a pattern, systematic guessing and checking, acting it out, making a table, working a simpler problem, or working backwards to solve a problem. (TAKS 6:5.14C)

1. Kathleen, Lisa, Amelia, and Regina went out to dinner. The meals they chose ranged in price from $9 to $12, tax included. Which is a reasonable total cost for the 4 meals?

   A Less than $30
   B Between $30 and $38
   C Between $38 and $46
   D More than $46

Show Your Work

2. Richard's test grades were 75, 88, 94, and 83. Which is a reasonable average for Richard's test scores?

   A Less than 70
   B Between 70 and 80
   C Between 80 and 90
   D More than 90

Show Your Work

3. Sonya sells shells at prices between $1.50 and $4.50. What is a reasonable total cost of 4 shells, not including tax?

   A Less than $6
   B Between $6 and $18
   C Between $18 and $25
   D More than $25

Show Your Work

4. Jason mowed lawns during the summer. In June he made $75, in July he made $90 and in August he made $85. Which is a reasonable average of Jason's income in the summer?

   A Less than $70
   B Between $70 and $80
   C Between $80 and $90
   D More than $90

Show Your Work

Problems Solving: Sample for Analysis

The student is expected to relate informal language to mathematical language and symbols. (TAKS 6:5.15B)

Charlie ate 2 cookies, Rene ate 7 cookies, Cheryl ate 4 cookies, and Keith ate 14 cookies. Which method could be used to find how many cookies they all ate?

A Add 2 and 7 and then subtract 4 from 14
B Add 2 and 7 and 4 and 14
C Multiply 2 by 4
D Subtract 7 from 14 and then add 6 to the difference

Strategy:

1. Read the problem carefully. DO NOT read the answer choices yet!

2. Decide what you want to find out from the information given.

3. You want to know how many cookies they ALL ate.

4. Write a number sentence to show how you would solve this problem.
   (2 + 7 + 4 + 14 = ?)
   *Write your equation.
   2 + 7 + 4 + 14 = ____________________
   Now verbalize your equation.
   Add 2 and 7 and 4 and 14 ____________________

5. Read the answer choices. Which one describes your description?
6. Answer B describes what you did since you added 2 and 7 and 4 and 14.

*This insert is not on the test, but is on the worksheets to have students verbalizing the process. TAKS 6:5.15B "informal language to mathematical language."

Problems Solving: Step Five A

The student is expected to relate informal language to mathematical language and symbols. (TAKS 6:5.15B)

1. Alicia has \$9 and Rosina has \$3. Diana has \$27. Which method could be used to find how much more money Diana has than Alicia and Rosina?

Write your equation.

____

Now verbalize your equation.

____

- **A** Subtract \$9 from \$27
- **B** Add \$9 and \$3 and then subtract the sum from \$27
- **C** Add \$9 and \$3 and \$27
- **D** Subtract \$3 from \$27

---

2. Mrs. McMullen has an egg farm. She is putting 132 eggs in cartons so they can be delivered to the store. Mrs. McMullen puts 12 eggs in each carton. Which method could be used to find how many cartons of eggs Mrs. McMullen must fill?

Write your equation.

____

Now verbalize your equation.

____

- **A** Divide 132 by 12
- **B** Multiply 12 times 5
- **C** Multiply 12 times 5 and then subtract the sum from 132
- **D** Subtract 12 from 132

3. Apples cost \$0.89 per pound. Mrs. Hightower eats 3 pounds which is 6 apples each week. Which method could be used to find how much Mrs. Hightower spends on apples in 52 weeks?

Write your equation.

____

Now verbalize your equation.

____

- **A** Multiply \$0.89 times 52
- **B** Add 6 and \$0.89
- **C** Multiply 3 times \$0.89 and then multiply the product by 52
- **D** Multiply 52 times 6 and then multiply the product by \$0.89

---

4. Paul and LuAnn went to the fireworks stand. They bought 2, \$5 packages of sparklers and 6, \$7 packages of bottle rockets. Which method could be used to determine how much Paul and LuAnn spent on fireworks?

Write your equation.

____

Now verbalize your equation.

____

- **A** Multiply 2 by 6, multiply \$5 by \$7, and then add their products
- **B** Add 2 and 6, add \$5 and \$7 and then multiply their sums
- **C** Multiply 2 by \$5, multiply 6 by \$7 and then add their products
- **D** Multiply 2 by \$5 and then multiply the product by \$7

Problem Solving: Step Five B

The student is expected to relate informal language to mathematical language and symbols. (TAKS 6:5.15B)

1. Garrick's dad told him he would pay him $10 an hour to work in the yard. Garrick worked for 2 hours pulling weeds in the flowerbed, 1.5 hours mowing the lawn and 3 hours pruning the trees. What method could be used to find how much his dad paid him at the end of the day?

Write your equation.

____

Now verbalize your equation.

____

A Add 2, 1.5, and 3 and then add the sum to $10

B Multiply 2 by $10, multiply 1.5 by $10, multiply 3 and $10 and then multiply their products

C Add 2, 1.5, and 3 and then subtract the sum from $10

D Add 2, 1.5, and 3 and then multiply the sum by $10

2. Kenny is going to plant 2 rows of tomato plants in his grandmother's garden. She wants 12 plants on each row. He is also going to plant 4 rows of tomato plants in his mother's garden. She wants 14 plants in each row. How many plants should he buy?

Write your equation.

____

Now verbalize your equation.

____

A Multiply 2 by 12, multiply 4 by 14 and then add the two products

B Add 2 and 4, add 12 and 14 and then multiply the two sums

C Add 2 and 12, add 4 and 14 and then multiply the two sums

D Divide 12 by 2, divide 14 by 4 and then add the two quotients

3. Tyson took Pudge to PetSmart to be groomed. The prices were: a bath $25, nails cut $5, brushing $4, and teeth brushed $4. Tyson had $40. Pudge had a bath, brushing, and his teeth brushed. Before Tyson left, he bought him a big chewy dog biscuit for $2.50. What method could be used to find how much money Tyson brought back to his dad?

Write your equation.

____

Now verbalize your equation.

____

A Add $25, $5, $4, $4, and $2.50 and then subtract the sum from $40

B Add $25, $5, $4, $40, and $2.50 and then subtract the sum from $40

C Add $25, $4, and $4 and then subtract the sum from $40

D Add $25, $4, $4, and $2.50 and then subtract the sum from $40

4. Mom has a week of activities. She needs 4 dozen cookies for the church bake sale on Monday. On Wednesday she needs 5 dozen cookies for the booster club bake sale. On Friday she needs 6 dozen cookies for the football concession stand. Her recipe makes 30 cookies. What method could be used to find how many batches of cookies she needs to make?

Write your equation.

____

Now verbalize your equation.

____

A Add 4, 5, and 6 and then multiply the sum by 12

B Add 4, 5 and 6, multiply the sum by 12 and then divide the product by 30

C Add 4, 5, and 6 and then add the sum to 30

D Add 4, 5, and 6 and then divide the sum by 30

Problem Solving: Step Five C

The student is expected to relate informal language to mathematical language and symbols. (TAKS 6:5.15B)

1. Rosa babysat her cousins for her aunt for $5 an hour. Her aunt said she would pay her an extra $10 if she washed the dishes and folded the clothes. Her aunt was gone for 4 hours. What method could be used to find how much her aunt paid her?

Write your equation.

____

Now verbalize your equation.

____

A Multiply $5 by 4 and then add $10 to the product
B Multiply 4 by $5, multiply 4 and $10 and then add the products
C Add $5 and $10 and then multiply the sum by 4
D Add $5 and $10 and then divide the sum by 4

---

2. Manuel needs to buy punch for his party. He thinks each person will drink 8 ounces of punch. He has 17 people coming to the party. The punch comes in gallon containers. He knows there are 128 ounces in a gallon. What method could be used to find how many gallons he needs to purchase?

Write your equation.

____

Now verbalize your equation.

____

A Add 2 and 8, multiply the answer by 17 and then divide the answer by 128
B Divide 128 by 4 and then multiply the answer by 17
C Multiply 8 by 17 and then divide the product by 128
D Multiply 2 by 8, add the answer to 17 and then divide the answer by 128

3. Mr. Ruiz had to use the copy machine to make copies of 2 tests. One test will take 2 pieces of paper and the other test will take 3 pieces of paper. There are 24 students in his class. What method could be used to find how much paper he will need to make these copies?

Write your equation.

____

Now verbalize your equation.

____

A Multiply 2 by 3 and then multiply the product by 24
B Add 2 and 3 and then multiply the sum by 2
C Divide 24 by 2, divide 24 by 3 and then add the two quotients
D Multiply 24 by 2, multiply 24 by 3 and then add the two products

---

4. Patty is a private tutor for math. She has 4 sessions on Monday, 5 sessions on Tuesday, 2 sessions on Wednesday, and 5 sessions each day, Thursday and Friday. She makes $20 a session. What method could be used to find how much money she will make during this week?

Write your equation.

____

Now verbalize your equation.

____

A Add 4, 5, 2 and 5 and then multiply the sum by $20
B Multiply 4 by $20 and add the product to the sum of 5, 2 and 5
C Add 4, 5, 2, 5, and 5 and then multiply the sum by $20
D Multiply 4, 5, 2, 5 and 5 and then add the product to $20

Problem Solving: Step Five D

The student is expected to relate informal language to mathematical language and symbols. (TAKS 6:5.15B)

1. Cassie had 25 pounds of dog food in a bag. After she fed her three dogs an equal amount of food at the end of the week, there were 9 pounds left in the bag. What should Cassie do to find how much each dog ate during the week?

Write your equation.

____

Now verbalize your equation.

____

A Divide 25 by 9 and then subtract the quotient from 3
B Subtract 9 from 25 and then divide the difference by 3
C Divide 25 by 7 and then divide by 3
D Subtract 9 from 25 and then multiply the difference by 3

---

2. Benny is training for a cross-country race. He must run a total of 100 miles in three weeks before the race. If he plans to run 5 days each week, what should he do to determine how many miles he needs to run each day?

Write your equation.

____

Now verbalize your equation.

____

A Divide 100 by 5 and then multiply by 21
B Multiply 5 by 21 and then divide by 100
C Divide 100 by 5 and then multiply by 15
D Multiply 5 by 3 and then divide 100 by the product

3. Timmy is planning a trip to Florida from Texas. It is 2,575 miles away. He is planning to be gone for 7 days. If he plans to spend 4 days driving and 3 days on the beach, what should he do to determine how many miles he needs to travel each day?

Write your equation.

____

Now verbalize your equation.

____

A Divide 2,575 by 2
B Divide 2,575 by 4
C Multiply 2,575 by 2 and then divide the product by 7
D Divide 2,575 by 7

---

4. Carla's mom gave her $25 to take to the carnival. She wants cotton candy. The rest she plans to spend on rides. If the cotton candy cost $1.25 and the tickets are 10 rides for $5, what does she need to do to determine how many tickets she can get?

Write your equation.

____

Now verbalize your equation.

____

A Subtract $1.25 from $25, divide the difference by $5 and then multiply the quotient by 10
B Subtract $5 from $25 and then divide the difference by 10
C Add $5 and $1.25 and then subtract the sum from $25
D Multiply 10 by $5 and then subtract the product from $25

Problem Solving: Step Five E

The student is expected to relate informal language to mathematical language and symbols. (TAKS 6:5.15B)

1. Callie wanted to find the total distance that she ran in the last two days. The first day she ran 5.26 miles, and the second day she ran 6.17 miles. She added 5 and 6. Compare Callie's estimate to the actual distance she ran. Explain why her estimate is more or less than the actual sum.

   A Less, because she rounded both numbers up

   B More, because she rounded both numbers up

   C Less, because she rounded both numbers down

   D More, because she rounded both numbers down

2. Zoey is keeping a time sheet of the hours she babysits during the summer while her neighbor is at work. The neighbor told her to just round the minutes to the nearest hour. Monday her time was 7 hours 25 minutes, Tuesday 8 hours 25 minutes, Wednesday 6 hours 25 minutes, Thursday 7 hours 25 minutes and Friday 8 hours and 20 minutes. She turned in 7 hours, 8 hours, 6 hours, 7 hours, and 8 hours. Explain why she might need to speak to her neighbor about her time sheet.

   A She is not being paid enough per hour.

   B She was not given credit for 2 hours of babysitting because she had to round down each time to the nearest hour.

   C She turned in more hours than she actually worked because she rounded to the nearest hour.

   D She should be paid overtime for the time over 8 hours.

3. Pam has to determine how much carpet she needs for her new bedroom. To calculate the amount of surface she needs to carpet, she multiples the length of the side of the floor by itself. Based on Pam's calculations, what do we know about the floor being carpeted?

   A It is rectangular, and she has calculated the area.

   B It is square, and she has calculated the area.

   C It is square, and she has calculated the perimeter.

   D It is rectangular, and she has calculated the perimeter.

4. Glen has been asked to create a banner for the football team. To calculate the amount of vinyl he needs, he multiples the length of the base of the banner by its height and then finds ½ of that product. Based on Glen's calculations, what do we know about the banner?

   A It is in the shape of a pentagon, and he has calculated the area.

   B It is in the shape of a triangle, and he has calculated the area.

   C It is in the shape of a triangle, and he has calculated the perimeter.

   D It is in the shape of a sphere, and he has calculated the area.

Problem Solving: Step Five F

The student is expected to select from and use diagrams and number sentences to represent real-life situations. (TAKS 2:5.6A)
The student is expected to relate informal language to mathematical language and symbols. (TAKS 6:5.15B)

1. Shelley is going to buy 3 hair bows that cost \$1.25 each and 4 barrettes that are\$1.50 each, including tax. Which number sentence can be used to find the total cost of 3 hair bows and 4 barrettes?

Write your equation.

____

A 3(4) + (\$1.25 + \$1.50) = □
B 3(\$1.50) + 4(\$1.25) = □
C 4(\$1.50) + 3(\$1.25) = □
D (\$1.50 + \$1.25) + (3 + 4) = □

2. Maria had \$55.50 to spend. She purchased 3 CDs for \$8.50 each. Which number sentence can be used to find how much money Maria had left?

Write your equation.

____

A \$55.50 – (\$8.50 + 3) = □
B \$55.50 – (\$8.50 – 3) = □
C \$55.50 – (3 x \$8.50) = □
D 3(\$8.50) – \$55.50 = □

3. Jean's pool holds a total of 58,452 gallons of water. The pool was low so Alex filled the pool by adding 985 gallons of water. Which number sentence could be used to find the number of gallons of water in the pool before Alex added the water?

Write your equation.

____

A 985 + □ = 58,452
B 58,452 ÷ □ = 985
C 58,452 x 985 = □
D 58,452 + □ = 985

4. Tyler spent \$4.86 for lunch and \$7.83 for supper. He had \$8.35 left at the end of the day. Which number sentence can be used to find how much money Tyler had before lunch?

Write your equation.

____

A \$4.86 + \$7.83 + \$8.35 = □
B (\$4.86 + \$7.83) – \$8.35 = □
C (\$4.86 + \$7.83) x \$8.35 = □
D \$8.35 – (\$4.86 + \$7.83) = □

5. Peggy went to the bookstore and bought 3 notebooks that cost \$2 each and 6 foam boards that cost \$3 each. Which number sentence can be used to find *C*, the total cost of all the items, not including tax?

Write your equation.

____

A 6(\$3) + 3(\$2) = *C*
B 2(6) + \$2(\$3) = *C*
C (3 + \$2) x (6 + \$3) = *C*
D 3(\$2) x 6(\$3) = *C*

6. In September there were 21 students in Jean's class. 2 students moved away in October. In November 3 new students joined the class. Which number sentence could be used to find, *S*, the number of students in Jean's class?

Write your equation.

____

A (21 + 2) + 3 = *S*
B 21 – (2 + 3) = *S*
C (21 – 2) + 3 = *S*
D 21 + (2 – 3) = *S*

Problem Solving: Step Five G

The student is expected to select from and use diagrams and number sentences to represent real-life situations. (TAKS 2:5.6A)

The student is expected to relate informal language to mathematical language and symbols. (TAKS 6:5.15B)

1. Terry has worked the first 78 problems on a worksheet that has a total of 130 problems. Which number sentence could be used to find the number of problems Terry must work before she is finished with the worksheet?

Write your equation.

____

A 130 ÷ 78 = □
B 130 – 78 = □
C 130 x 78 = □
D 130 + 78 = □

2. Dru read 5 books this month. Each book was 185 pages long. Last month he read 4 books with 170 pages each. Which number sentence could be used to find the total number of pages that Dru read in these 2 months?

Write your equation.

____

A 5(185) x 4(170) = □
B 4(5) + (185 x 170) = □
C 5(185) + 4(170) = □
D 5(185) – 4(170) = □

3. Mr. James scattered 100 pounds of grass seed on his front yard. He still had 4 bags of seed to scatter in his back yard. Each bag weighed 25 pounds. Which number sentence can be used to find *S*, the total number of pounds of seed Mr. James had for both his front and back yards?

Write your equation.

____

A *S* = 100 + 4(25) **C** *S* = 4(25) – 100
B *S* = 100 + (4 + 25) **D** *S* = 100 + (25–4)

4. Jean had an infection and was in the hospital for 9 days. The hospital bill came and the total charge for Jean's hospital room was $2,700. Which number sentence could be used to find out how much Jean was billed for each day she stayed in the hospital?

Write your equation.

____

A $2,700 x □ = 9 **C** 9 x □ = $2,700
B $2,700 x 9 = □ **D** $2,700 + 9 = □

5. Duke had cavities in 4 of his teeth. The dentist said that it would cost $300 to fill all 4 teeth. Which number sentence could be used to find the cost of each filling?

Write your equation.

____

A □ ÷ 4 = $300 **C** 75 + 4 = □
B □ x 4 – $300 **D** $300 – □ = 4

6. Mr. Harper poured 175 pounds of cement for a sidewalk in the front yard. He plans on using 9 bags of cement for a patio in the backyard. Each bag contained 30 pounds of cement. Which number sentence can be used to find *C* the total number of pounds of cement Mr. Harper had for his front and back yards?

Write your equation.

____

A 175 – 9(30) = *C* **C** 9(175 + 30) = *C*
B 175 + 9(30) = *C* **D** 9(30) – 175 = *C*

Problem Solving: Step Five H

The student is expected to select from and use diagrams and number sentences to represent real-life situations. (TAKS 2:5.6A)
The student is expected to relate informal language to mathematical language and symbols. (TAKS 6:5.15B)

1. Kylie's recipe calls for 2 cups of chocolate chips for 1 batch of chocolate chip cookies. She needs to make 4 batches. She also needs 3 cups of chocolate chips for each batch of peanut butter-chocolate balls. Her mom wants her to make 3 batches of peanut butter-chocolate balls. Which number sentence could be used to find the total cups of chocolate chips Kylie needs to make her goodies?

Write your equation.

____

A 2 + 1 + 4 + 3 + 3 = □
B 2(4) + 3(3) = □
C 2 x 4 x 3 x 3 = □
D 2(4) + 3 = □

2. Lucy and Christina found $0.63 when they cleaned out the closet. They found $0.97 in Joe's pants pocket when they did the laundry. When the ice cream truck came by, Lucy and Christina spent $0.79 each for 2 popsicles. Which number sentence could be used to find, *M*, the amount of money Lucy and Christina have now?

Write your equation.

____

A ($0.63 + $0.97) – 2($0.79) = *M*
B $0.63 + ($0.97 + $0.79) = *M*
C ($0.63 – $0.97) + $0.79 = *M*
D $0.63 – 2($0.97 + $0.79) = *M*

3. Adrienne rode her bike 2 miles every day for a 27-day period during the month of May. She rode her bike 3 miles every day for a 20-day period during the month of June. Which number sentence could be used to find the total miles that Adrienne rode her bike?

Write your equation.

____

A (2 + 3) x (27 + 20) = □
B 2 x 27 x 3 x 20 = □
C 2(27) + 3(20) = □
D 2(27) – 3(20) = □

4. Joe's uniform truck was packed with 316 uniforms. At his first stop, Joe delivered 46 clean uniforms and picked up 37 dirty uniforms. Which number sentence could be used to find, *U*, the number of uniforms on Joe's trucks after his first stop?

Write your equation.

____

A 316 – (46 + 37) = *U*
B (316 – 46) + 37 = *U*
C 316 + (46 + 37) = *U*
D 316 + (46 – 37) = *U*

5. Clay is a dentist. He placed 3 fillings in Mary Beth's teeth because she had 3 cavities. Mary Beth's dental bill was $146. Which number sentence could be used to find the cost of each of Mary Beth's fillings?

Write your equation.

____

A $146 x 3 = □
B $146 + 3 + 3 = □
C $146 ÷ 3 = □
D $146 – 3 = □

Problem Solving: Assessment

TAKS Objectives: 2:5.6A, 6:5.14A, 6:5.14B, 6:5.14C, 6:5.15B, 6:5.16A

1. Esther traveled on her bicycle for 5 days. The least amount of miles she traveled in one day was 15 miles, and the most she traveled in a day was 18 miles. Which is a reasonable total for the number of miles Esther traveled on her bike for all 5 days?

   A Less than 60 miles
   B Between 60 and 75 miles
   C Between 75 and 90 miles
   D More than 90 miles

2. Socks were on sale at 3 pairs for $5. Dave needs 5 new pairs of socks. Which of the following is a reasonable total for the cost of the 5 pairs of socks before the tax is added?

   A Less than $10
   B Between $10 and $15
   C Between $15 and $20
   D More than $20

3. Irma has to determine how much carpet she needs for her new bedroom. To calculate the amount of surface she needs to carpet, she multiples the length of the side of the floor by the width of the side of the floor. Based on Irma's calculations, what do we know about the floor being carpeted?

   A It is rectangular, and she has calculated the area.
   B It is square, and she has calculated the area.
   C It is square, and she has calculated the perimeter.
   D It is a rectangular, and she has calculated the perimeter

4. Mr. Perez is planning a field trip for several fifth grade classes. There are 78 children going and there must be 1 adult for every 15 children according to school policy. If there are three teachers going including himself, what should he do to determine how many additional adults he will need for the trip?

   A Divide 78 by 15 and subtract 3 from the quotient
   B Divide 78 by 15
   C Add 15 and 3 and divide 78 by the sum
   D Multiply 15 and 3 and divide the product by 78

5. In an assembly line, 36 employees can assemble 175 products in 20 minutes. How many products can be assembled in 3 hours?

   A 540
   B 720
   C 1,575
   D 3,500

6. Sandra and Heidi went to the movies. Heidi spent $0.85 for a soft drink and $0.55 for a candy bar. Sandra spent $0.95 for a large lemonade. Heidi gave the clerk $5 for her treats. Which method could be used to determine how much change Heidi received?

   A Add $0.55, $0.85, and $0.95 and then multiply the sum by $5
   B Add $0.85, $0.55, and $0.95, and subtract the sum from $5
   C Add $0.85 and $0.55, and subtract the sum from $5
   D Subtract $5 from the sum of $0.85 and $0.55

7. Jonquil is buying collars for her three cats. Max's collar needs to be twice as long as Florence's collar and three times as long as Fluffy's collar. What other information can be used to determine the length of Max's collar?

   A The length of a small collar
   B The length of Fluffy's collar
   C The cost of the collars
   D The material the collar is made of

8. Evangeline has 144 containers of paint in her art studio. She is organizing paint in her art studio so they can be stored neatly. Evangeline puts 12 containers in each small box. Which method could be used to find how many small boxes will be needed to store the containers?

   A Subtract 12 from 144
   B Multiply 12 times 12 and subtract the product from 144
   C Multiply 144 by 12
   D Divide 144 by 12

9. Mrs. Israel does volunteer work while Mr. Israel is in Guatemala. She works 16 hours a week at the local hospital. Which number sentence could be used to find, *H*, how many hours Mrs. Israel works at the hospital during a 4-week period?

   A $16 \times 4 = H$ **C** $16 \div 4 = H$
   B $16 \times 7 = H$ **D** $4 \times 7 \times 16 = H$

10. Brandon bought a rookie baseball card five years ago. He paid $1.50 for the package of 10 cards. He sold it to a sport's shop for $12.35. Which number sentence could be used to find, *P*, the profit he made from the one card?

   A $12.35 – ($1.50 ÷ 10) = *P*
   B ($12.35 + $1.50) ÷ 10 = P
   C ($12.35 ÷ 10) + $1.50 =P
   D $12.35 – ($1.50 x 10) = P

11. The Palmer Day Care 2 to 5 year olds are taking a field trip to the zoo. The policy requires 3 adults for every 6 children. The cafeteria workers are making 72 lunches. How many are adult lunches?

   A 24 **C** 9
   B 15 **D** 8

12. Lee's wooden floor hallway in his house is 9 yards long. A rug takes up 3 feet of the hall. What fractional part of the hall is not covered by the rug?

   A $\frac{2}{3}$ **C** $\frac{7}{9}$
   B $\frac{1}{3}$ **D** $\frac{8}{9}$

13. Ken and his brother are out buying school clothes. They found a sale on shirts: $15, buy one get one free. They bought 6 shirts with a $100. Which number sentence could be used to find how much they paid for the shirts?

   A $100 – ($15 x 6) =☐
   B $15 (6 – 3) = ☐
   C $15 (6 – 3) – $100 =☐
   D $100 – $15 (6 – 3) =☐

14. Cassie's dad gave her $10 to go to the movies. Her ticket cost $5. Popcorn cost $1.25 a bag, candy $0.75, drinks $1.25, and pickles $0.50. She bought a popcorn, drink, and pickle. What method could be used to determine how much money she spent?

   A Find the sum of $10, $5, $1.25, $1.25 and $0.50
   B Find the sum of $5, $1.25, $1.25 and $0.50
   C Find the sum of $5, $1.25, $1.25 and $0.50 and subtract it from $10
   D Find the sum of $5, $1.25 and $0.50

15. Mr. Pero gave his fifth-grade math class two sets of numbers that were sorted according to a certain rule. The numbers that followed the rule were put in Set A, and the numbers that did not follow the rule were put in Set B.

Set A	45.367, 63.57, 37.93, 75.25, 57.73
Set B	93.3, 3.603, 52.9, 33.2, 206.5

Based on this information, all the numbers in Set A_____

A include the digit 7
B are written to the hundredths place
C have an odd number in the tenths place
D have an odd number in the hundredths place

---

16. These are examples of zinnies.

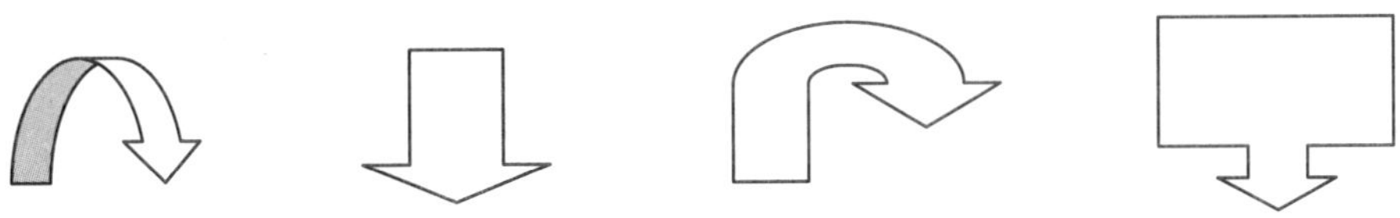

These are not examples of zinnies.

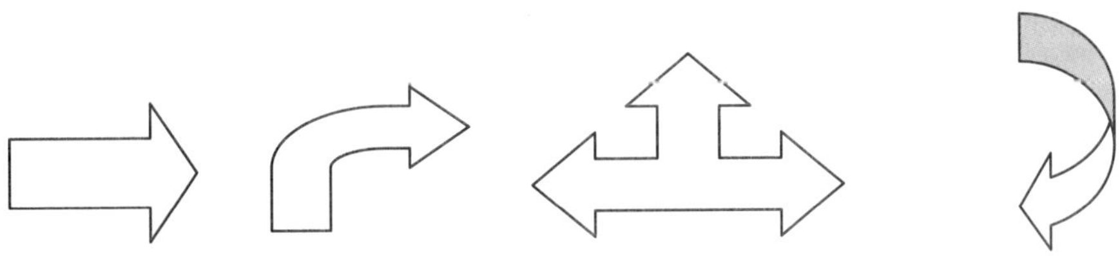

Which figure below is a zinny?

A 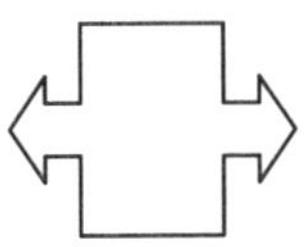 **B** 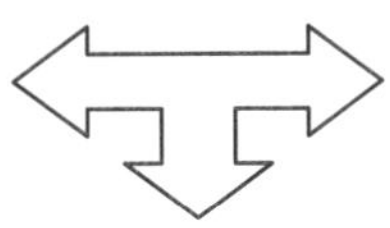 **C** 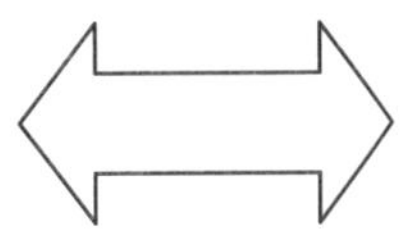 **D** 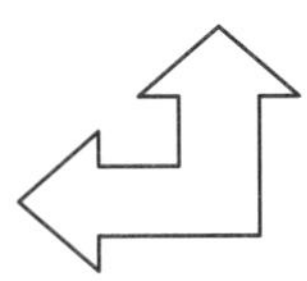

Problem Solving: Answer Key

Step One A
1. A
2. D
3. B
4. A
5. C
6. A
7. C

Step One B
1. B
2. A

Step One C
1. D even number sides
2. B curved

Step One D
1. D no parallel lines
2. A hole in figure

Step Two A
1. D
2. C

Step Two B
1. B
2. D
3. D
4. A
5. D
6. D

Step Two C
1. A
2. C
3. D
4. A
5. B

Step Three A
1. D
2. D
3. D
4. A

Step Three B
1. B
2. C
3. D
4. B

Step Three C
1. D
2. A
3. C

Step Four A
1. B
2. B
3. B
4. C

Step Four B
1. B
2. C
3. C
4. B

Step Four C
1. C
2. C

Step Four D
1. A
2. C
3. B
4. B
5. B

Step Four E
1. B
2. C
3. B
4. C

Step Four F
1. C
2. C
3. B
4. C

Step Five A
1. B
2. A
3. C
4. C

Step Five B
1. D
2. A
3. D
4. B

Step Five C
1. A
2. C
3. D
4. C

Step Five D
1. B
2. D
3. B
4. A

Step Five E
1. C
2. B
3. B
4. B

Step Five F
1. C
2. C
3. A
4. A
5. A
6. C

Step Five G
1. B
2. C
3. A
4. C
5. B
6. B

Step Five H
1. B
2. A
3. C
4. B
5. C

Assessment
1. C
2. A
3. A
4. A
5. C
6. C
7. B
8. D
9. A
10. A
11. A
12. D
13. B
14. B
15. A
16. B a zinny points down

Number Concepts: Review

TAKS Objectives: 1:5.1A, 1:5.1B, 1:5.4A, 1:5.4B

Use the information in the chart to answer the following questions.

Texas Counties' Population and Land Area		
County	Population	Land Area (square miles)
Brewster	8,159	6,169
King	358	914
Pecos	15,038	4,776
Presidio	5,608	3,857
Rockwall	24,583	128

1. What is the order of the populated areas from greatest number of people to least number of people of 4 of the above listed counties?

   A Brewster, Pecos, Presidio, King
   B Rockwall, Pecos, Brewster, Presidio
   C King, Presidio, Brewster, Pecos
   D King, Brewster, Pecos, Rockwall

2. Which conclusion can be drawn from this chart?

   A Rockwall County is a heavily populated area per square mile.
   B Everyone in King County owns land.
   C Pecos is located near Houston.
   D Presidio's population is twice its land area.

3. Which of the following counties has a population with a 5 in the thousands place?

   A Brewster
   B King
   C Rockwall
   D Pecos

Use the information in the chart to answer the following questions.

Distance of Planets from the Earth	
Mercury	57,000,000
Uranus	1,607,000,000
Saturn	762,700,000
Jupiter	390,700,000
Neptune	2,670,000,000
Pluto	2,680,000,000

4. What is the order of the distances from the Earth from the least distance to the greatest distance from 4 of the planets listed above?

   A Saturn, Neptune, Uranus, Pluto
   B Mercury, Neptune, Uranus, Pluto
   C Pluto, Neptune, Uranus, Saturn
   D Mercury, Jupiter, Saturn, Uranus

5. How would the distance from Earth to Pluto be written?

   A Two million, six hundred eighty thousand
   B Two billion, six hundred eighty million
   C Two billion, six hundred eighty hundred thousand
   D Two thousand, six hundred eighty

6. Which conclusion can be drawn from this chart?

   A Pluto has the largest land mass.
   B Mercury is smaller than Earth.
   C Pluto will probably be one of the last planets scientist will explore.
   D Saturn and Neptune are neighboring planets.

7. Micah has 5.2 yards of red yarn and 5.27 yards of blue yarn. She has 7.25 yards of yellow yarn and 5.22 yards of green yarn. Which of the following shows the colors of ribbon from longest to shortest?

A Yellow, blue, green, red
B Blue, yellow, green, red
C Yellow, blue, red, green
D Red, green, yellow, blue

---

8. Miguel bought a package of strawberry bubble gum and two packages of grape bubble gum. There were 125 pieces in each package. He also bought 12 pieces of sour apple bubble gum and 17 pieces of watermelon bubble gum. Which is the best estimate of the total pieces of bubble gum Miguel bought?

A 160 **C** 320
B 330 **D** 420

---

9. Tina had a babysitting job during the summer. She babysat 6 hours a day for 47 days. Which is the best estimate of the number of hours she babysat during the summer?

A Less than 200 hours
B Between 220 and 250 hours
C Between 250 and 280 hours
D More than 280

---

10. Malcom was figuring his mileage for his travel for one week. Monday he traveled 136 miles, Tuesday 178 miles, Wednesday 256 miles, Thursday 456 miles, and Friday 315 miles. What is the best estimate of the total miles he traveled during that week?

A Less than 1,000 miles
B Between 1,000 and 1,500 miles
C Between 1,500 and 2,000 miles
D More than 2,000 miles

11. Which group of decimals is in order from least to greatest?

A 7.037, 7.07, 7.307, 7.9
B 7.07, 7.307, 7.037, 7.9
C 7.9, 7.07, 7.037,7.307
D 7.9, 7.307, 7.07, 7.037

---

12. Maria and Karen went to the store to buy Heather a birthday gift. Together the 2 girls spent $12.95. Of this total, Karen spent $6.42. What is the best estimate of the amount of money Maria spent before tax to the nearest dollar?

A $5.00 **C** $7.00
B $6.00 **D** $8.00

---

13. Randy and his friends went snake hunting. The lengths of the snakes they caught are listed on the table below.

Hunters	Snake Lengths (Inches)
Randy	36.275
Lee	36.725
Manuel	36.095
Alberto	36.8

According to this table, who captured the longest snake?

A Randy **C** Manuel
B Lee **D** Alberto

---

14. Desiree was hired by the highway department to sit and count the cars traveling down a road. On Monday she counted 127, Tuesday 312, Wednesday 253, Thursday 189, and Friday 227. Which is the best estimate of how many cars traveled down the road during those five days?

A 1,100 **C** 800
B 900 **D** 700

Prime and Composite: Review

TAKS Objectives: 1:5.3D, 2:5.5C

1. Which group shows the prime factorization of the number 54?

   A 2 x 2 x 3 x 3
   B 2 x 3 x 3 x 3
   C 2 x 3 x 6
   D 2 x 2 x 3 x 4

2. Which group shows the prime factorization of the number 250?

   A 2 x 2 x 5 x 5
   B 2 x 5 x 10
   C 2 x 5 x 5 x 5
   D 2 x 3 x 5 x 5

3. What are the common factors of 3 and 12?

   A 1, 3
   B 1, 3, 4
   C 1, 2, 3, 4, 6
   D 1, 2, 3, 4, 6, 12

4. What are the common factors of 14 and 35?

   A 1, 2, 7, 14
   B 1, 2, 5, 7, 14, 35
   C 1, 7
   D 1, 5, 7, 35

5. Which is a prime factor of the composite number 56?

   A 3
   B 5
   C 7
   D 8

6. Which is a prime factor of the composite number 63?

   A 2
   B 5
   C 7
   D 9

7. Which number is ***not*** a prime number?

   A 3
   B 5
   C 7
   D 9

8. Which number is ***not*** a composite number?

   A 8
   B 7
   C 6
   D 4

9. Which group names all the whole number factors of a composite number?

   A 1, 19
   B 1, 2, 5, 10
   C 1, 3, 6, 9, 18
   D 1, 13

10. Which group names all the whole number factors of a composite number?

    A 1, 23
    B 1, 7, 49
    C 1, 2, 16
    D 1, 4, 6, 24

Fractions/Decimals: Review

TAKS Objectives: 1:5.2A, 1:5.2B, 1:5.2C, 1:5.3E, 2:5.5B, 5:5.12A

1. Which of the following fractions is *not* equivalent to $\frac{1}{4}$?

A $\frac{9}{36}$ **B** $\frac{7}{28}$ **C** $\frac{6}{8}$ **D** $\frac{3}{12}$

2. Which of the following fractions is equivalent to $\frac{4}{5}$?

A $\frac{12}{18}$ **B** $\frac{8}{10}$ **C** $\frac{3}{8}$ **D** $\frac{3}{7}$

3. Lisa picked 12 plums from the tree in her backyard. 6 of the plums were still green. Which fraction shows how many of the plums were still green?

A $\frac{1}{6}$ **B** $\frac{2}{5}$ **C** $\frac{1}{2}$ **D** $\frac{2}{3}$

4. Mrs. Green's class conducted an experiment on 8 plants. For one month they fed liquid plant food to 3 plants. Which fraction shows what part of the plants did not receive plant food?

A $\frac{5}{8}$ **B** $\frac{1}{3}$ **C** $\frac{2}{3}$ **D** $\frac{3}{4}$

5. Marcos sold $\frac{1}{9}$ of his tickets for the Christmas play. Amanda sold $\frac{1}{10}$ of her tickets. Which pair of fractions compares these two fractions correctly?

A $\frac{1}{9} > \frac{1}{10}$

B $\frac{1}{9} = \frac{1}{10}$

C $\frac{1}{9} < \frac{1}{10}$

D $\frac{9}{10} = \frac{1}{1}$

6. Harry had 8 one-dollar coins. His mom gave him 2 for his birthday and his grandfather gave him 4 for helping him on the farm. His dad gave him the rest. What fraction of the one-dollar coins did his dad give him?

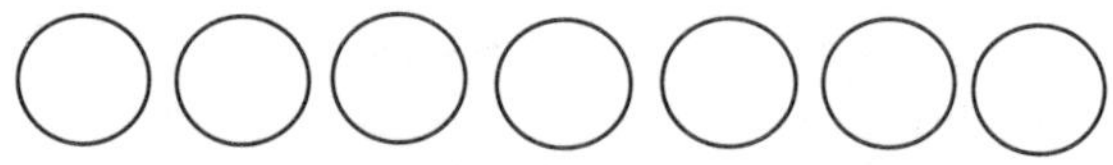

A $\frac{1}{4}$ **B** $\frac{3}{4}$ **C** $\frac{1}{2}$ **D** $\frac{1}{3}$

7. Rickie's mom made a pizza for supper. He ate $\frac{3}{8}$ of the pizza. His sister ate $\frac{1}{8}$ of the pizza. How much of the pizza did Rickie and his sister eat?

A $\frac{2}{5}$ **B** $\frac{4}{16}$ **C** $\frac{1}{2}$ **D** $\frac{3}{8}$

8. The model shaded shows 1.9.

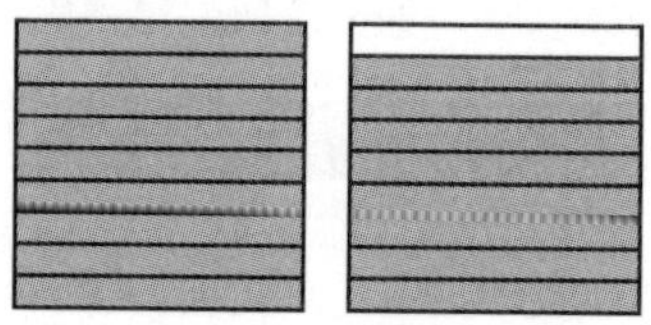

Which one of the answers below is equal to 1.9?

A $1\frac{9}{10}$ **B** $1\frac{2}{10}$ **C** $\frac{10}{9}$ **D** $1\frac{10}{10}$

9. Which fraction is larger than $\frac{3}{4}$?

A $\frac{7}{8}$ **B** $\frac{2}{3}$ **C** $\frac{3}{5}$ **D** $\frac{1}{2}$

Word Problems: Review

TAKS Objectives: 1:5.3A, 1:5.3B, 1:5.3C, 6:5.14A

1. Jamie read 10 books last summer. She can read 132 words a minute. At this rate, how many words could she read in 45 minutes?

   A 5,940 **C** 940
   B 5,840 **D** Not Here

2. Rene baked 148 cupcakes. She covered 36 with strawberry icing, 24 with chocolate icing, and 64 with coconut icing. The remaining cupcakes were covered with orange icing. How many cupcakes were covered with orange icing?

   A 24 **C** 124
   B 48 **D** Not Here

3. The cyclists were able to compete in a cross-country cycling race. They rode 146 miles during the first three days. The second part of their journey was a 600 mile stretch through the California mountains. The last part of the race was 249 miles of cycling in Washington State. How many miles had the cyclists ridden when they completed the race?

   A 995 mi **C** 985 mi
   B 986 mi **D** Not Here

4. Lennie and his dad were planning a cookout. Lennie invited 12 friends. Lennie planned to cook enough hotdogs for his 12 friends, his dad and himself to have 2 each. The weinners come 8 to a package. How many packages should be buy?

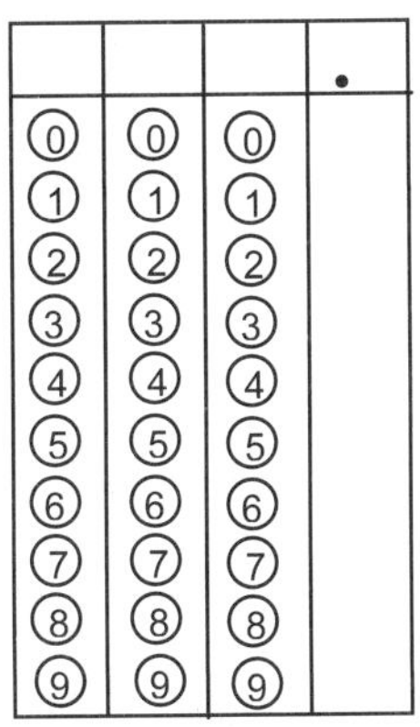

5. A module of cotton weighs 14.39 kilograms. A bushel of wheat weighs 19.46 kilograms. During one week Mr. Harper harvested 2 cotton modules and 2 wheat bushels. How many more kilograms of wheat than cotton did he harvest?

   A 10.14 kg **C** 38.92 kg
   B 28.78 kg **D** Not Here

6. David and his family went snow skiing for the Christmas holidays. David skied 10 miles on Friday morning and 4.6 miles Friday afternoon. He skied 3 miles Saturday morning and 6.3 miles on Saturday afternoon. How many more miles did David ski on Friday than Saturday?

   A 14.6 miles **C** 5.3 miles
   B 9.3 miles **D** 1 mile

7. Greta bought 4 pints of strawberries for $1.50 a pint at the market. She had a coupon for $0.75 off of the total cost. How much did she pay for the strawberries?

   A $6.75 **C** $5.25
   B $6.00 **D** $2.25

8. Jeff has $75 to spend on gifts for his mom and dad. He bought his mom a necklace for $24.92. He bought his dad a key chain with his name on it for $32.93. All prices include tax. How much money did he have left after purchasing these gifts?

   A $57.85 **C** $17.15
   B $18.15 **D** Not Here

Geometry: Review

TAKS Objectives: 3:5.7A, 3:5.7B, 3:5.8A, 3:5.8B, 3:5.9A, 5:5.13A, 5:5.13C

1. Which line segments are parallel?

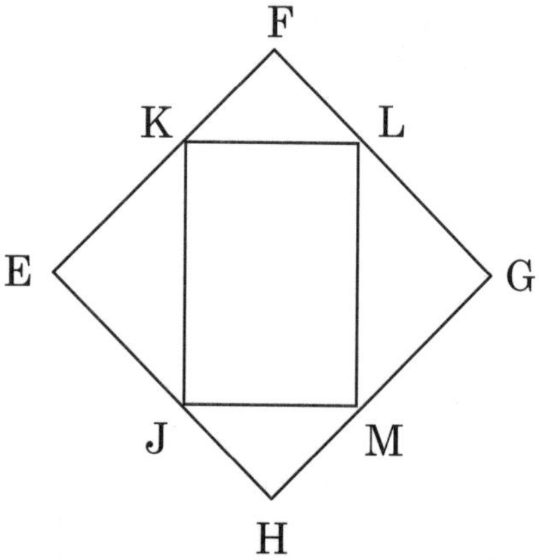

A KL and JM
B EK and GL
C FL and HM
D JH and MH

2. Which figures appear to be congruent?

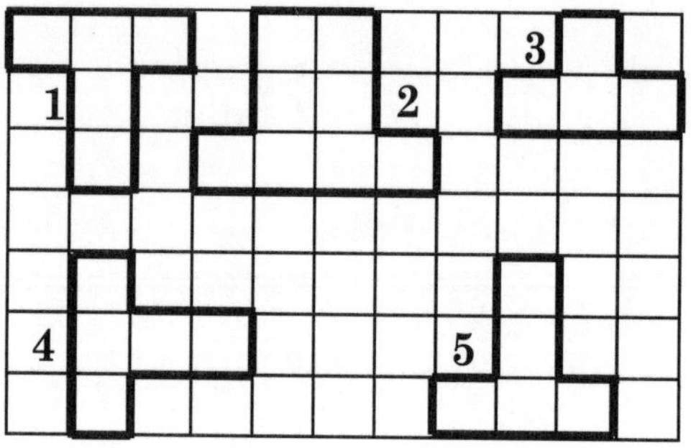

A 1 and 3
B 1 and 5
C 3 and 4
D 1, 4, and 5

3. A wire is tied from each side of a tree to a stake in the ground to keep the tree straight while it is young. A line of symmetry can be drawn through the tree.

What is the length of the piece of wire AB?

A 2 ft
B 6 ft
C 8 ft
D 16 ft

4. Which of these shapes could never have parallel lines?

A Square
B Pentagon
C Octagon
D Triangle

5. Which of these shapes has an odd number of sides?

A Octagon
B Quadrilateral
C Pentagon
D Hexagon

6. Which of these figures has 2 more edges than faces?

A

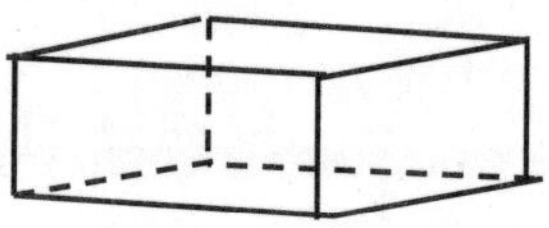

C

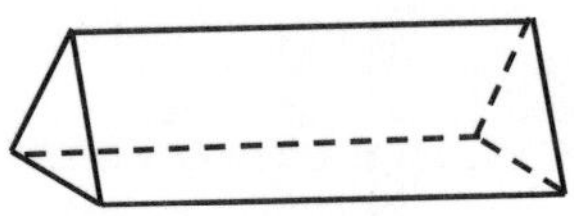

B

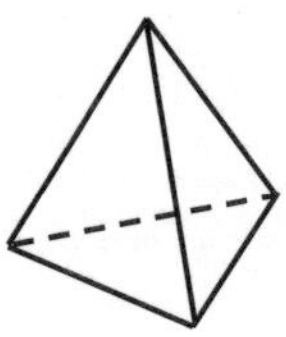

D

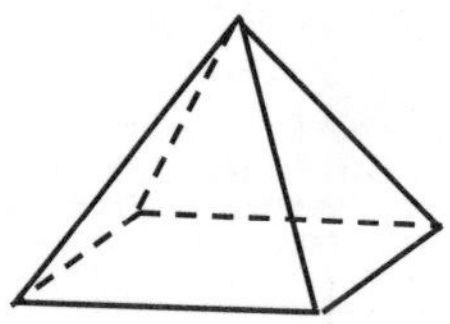

7. Which of the following shows an example of rotation?

A

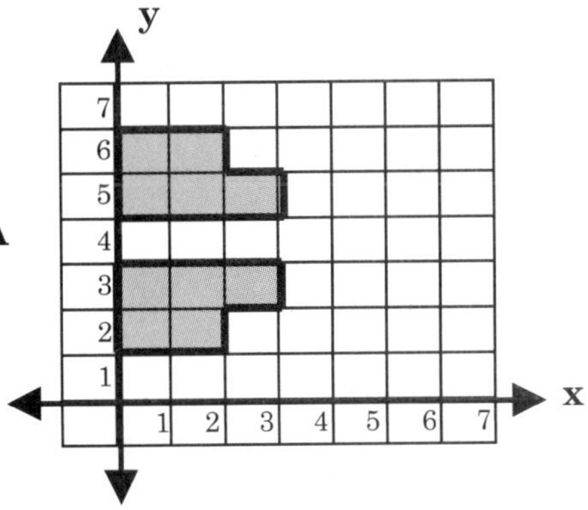

B

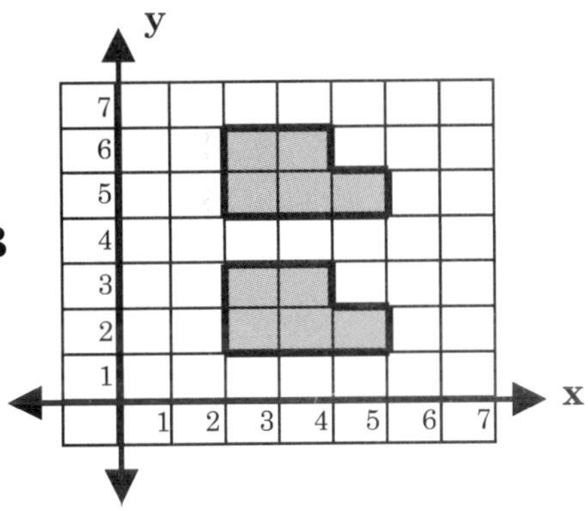

C

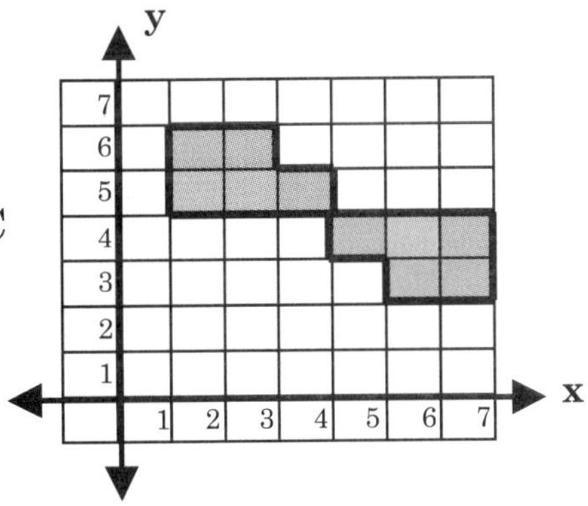

D

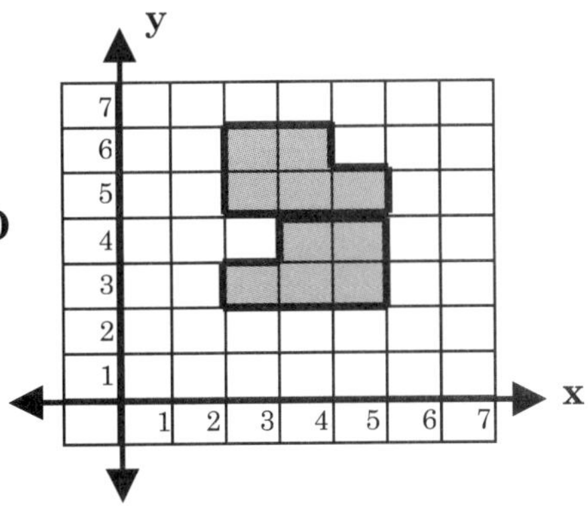

8. The graph shows Wylie City Park

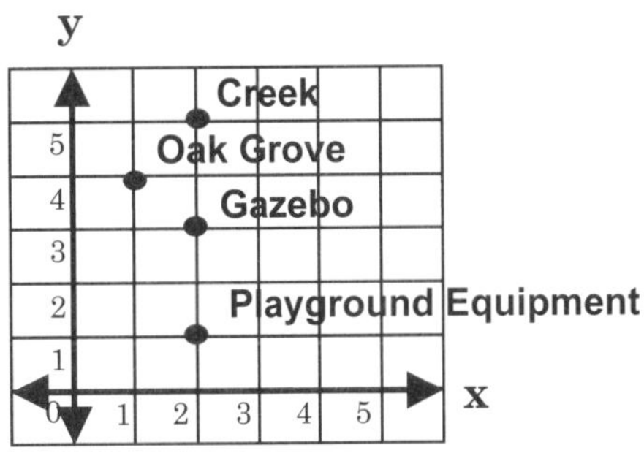

Which ordered pair best represents the point on the graph labeled "Gazebo"?

A (2, 1)
B (2, 3)
C (3, 2)
D (1, 4)

---

9. Below is a rectangular prism. Which statement is true?

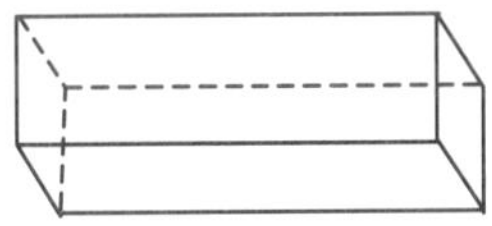

A Each face is a square.
B All angles are acute angles.
C The edges have equal lengths.
D There are 6 faces

---

10. Look at the drawing below.

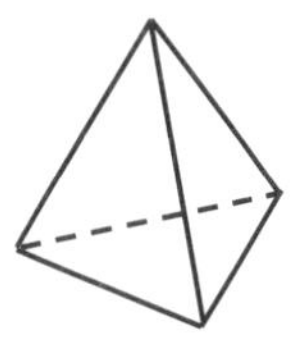

Which statement about this figure is true?

A The figure has 3 faces.
B The figure has 6 edges.
C The figure is a triangular prism.
D The figure has no vertices.

11. The line graph below shows 4 points.

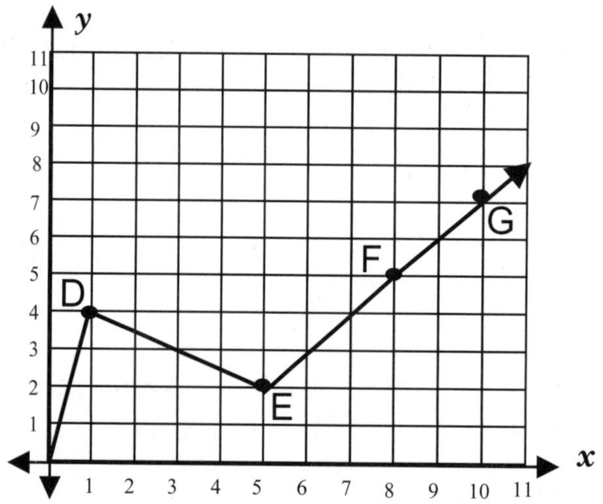

Which table shows the coordinates of the points on the line graph above?

A

Point	x	y
D	4	1
E	2	5
F	5	8
G	7	10

C

Point	x	y
D	4	1
E	5	2
F	8	5
G	10	7

B

Point	x	y
D	1	4
E	5	2
F	8	5
G	10	7

D

Point	x	y
D	4	4
E	5	2
F	8	5
G	10	7

Measurement: Review

TAKS Objectives: 4:5.10A, 4:5.11A, 4:5.11B

1. Kendra bought 5 pounds of apples to share with Carol. Carol's apples weighed 3 pounds 2 ounces. How much more did Kendra's apples weigh?

   A 2 lb 16 oz **C** 1 lb 14 oz
   B 2 lb 8 oz **D** 8 lb 2 oz

2. How many centimeters are in the perimeter of this rectangle?

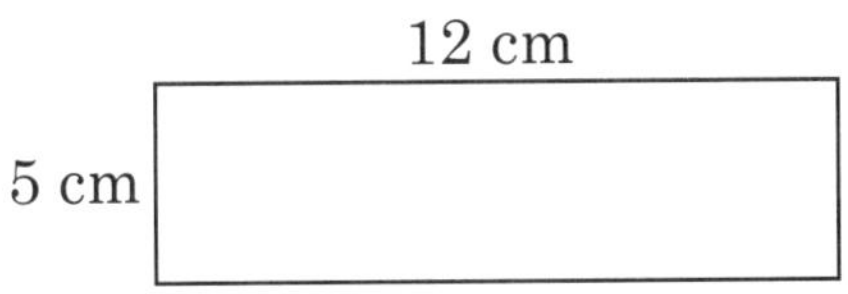

   A 12 cm **C** 34 cm
   B 17 cm **D** 60 cm

3. Sammy had a toy soldier that weighed 7.4 grams. How many kilograms did the toy soldier weigh?

   A 0.0074 kg **C** 74 kg
   B 0.74 kg **D** 7,400 kg

4. David's cat weighs 2,567 grams. How many milligrams does the cat weigh?

   A 2.567 mg **C** 256,700 mg
   B 25.67 mg **D** 2,567,000 mg

5. Maria played with her dolls for 45 minutes. This could also be written as ______

   A $\frac{45}{100}$ hour **C** $\frac{1}{3}$ hour
   B $\frac{3}{4}$ hour **D** $\frac{1}{4}$ hour

6. Bubba bought a piece of land as shown in the drawing below.

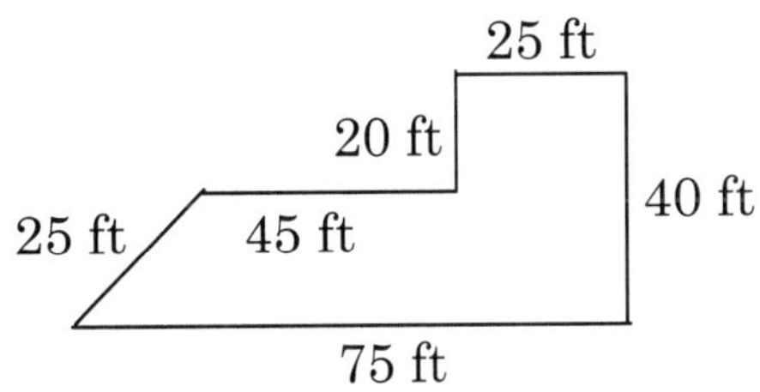

   What is the perimeter of this piece of land?

   A 65 ft **C** 180 ft
   B 160 ft **D** 230 ft

7. Shanna bought $3\frac{2}{3}$ yards of fabric. Her mom bought $2\frac{1}{3}$ yards of fabric. How much fabric did they both buy?

   A 1 yd 1 ft **C** 6 yd
   B 5 yd 1 ft **D** 6 yd 1 ft

8. How many centimeters are in 984 meters?

   A 9.84 cm **C** 9,840 cm
   B 98.4 cm **D** 98,400 cm

9. What fractional part of a year is a week?

   A $\frac{1}{7}$ **B** $\frac{1}{24}$ **C** $\frac{1}{32}$ **D** $\frac{1}{52}$

10. Which of the following is less than 1 gram?

   A 1 kilogram **C** 10 kilograms
   B 100 milligrams **D** 100 kilograms

11. Kasey prepared 4 liters of punch for her birthday party. She had 75 milliliters left. How much punch did they drink at the party?

A 3,925 ml　　**C** 3,025 ml
B 4,075 ml　　**D** 2,025 ml

---

12. Jordan's bedspread is 3 inches less than 8 feet long. How many inches is this?

A 24 in.　　**C** 96 in.
B 93 in.　　**D** 99 in.

---

13. How many liters are in 2,743 milliliters?

A 274.3 *l*　　**C** 2.743 *l*
B 27.4 *l*　　**D** 0.274 *l*

---

14. Rhonda is making a napkin. She bought a yard of fabric, but she only needs 1 foot of the fabric for the napkin. What is the relationship between what she needs for the napkin and what she bought?

A She used $\frac{1}{3}$ of the fabric she bought.
B She used $\frac{3}{4}$ of the fabric she bought.
C She used $\frac{1}{2}$ of the fabric she bought.
D She used $\frac{2}{3}$ of the fabric she bought.

---

15. Lynn worked for his dad from 10:30 to 2:30. His dad is going to pay him $5 and hour. How much was he paid?

A $10　　**C** $20
B $15　　**D** $25

16. Maketa sewed 60 inches of trim on a triangular bandanna as shown in the diagram. She used 13 inches of trim on side A and 26 inches of trim on side B.

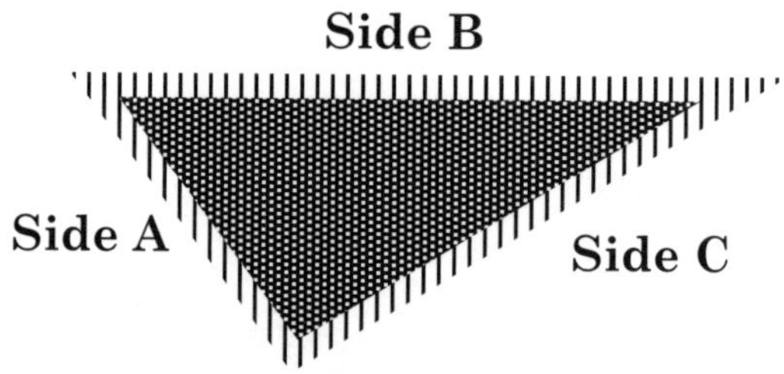

How much trim did Makita sew on side C of the bandanna?

A 39 inches　　**C** 13 inches
B 21 inches　　**D** 3 inches

---

17. The area of a square room is 49 square feet. What is the perimeter of the square room?

A 42 ft　　C 21 ft
B 28 ft　　**D** 7 ft

---

18. Patricia walked 6 miles in her neighborhood. Patricia walked 2 miles on Arborcrest Drive and 1 mile on Briarfield Drive. How many miles did Patricia walk on Fall Creek Drive?

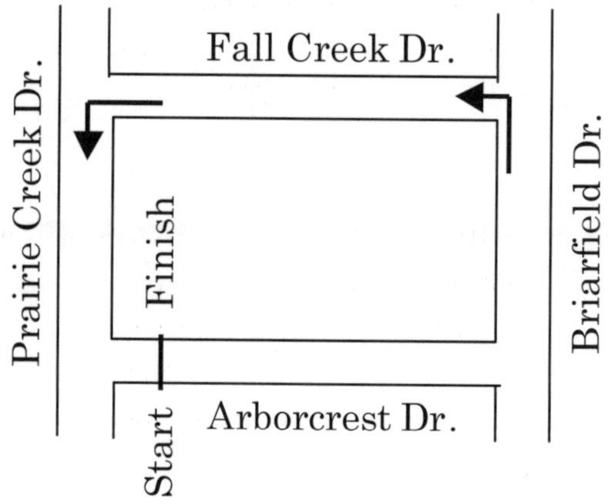

A 1 mile　　**C** 3 miles
B 2 miles　　**D** 6 miles

19. The area of the country of Micronesia is 271 square miles. This is 149 square miles larger than the area of the country of Malta. Which number sentence could be used to find the area of Malta?

A 271 + 149 = ☐ **C** 271 x 149 = ☐
B 271 ÷ 149 = ☐ **D** 271− 149 = ☐

---

20. Grandma made several patchwork squares for a quilt. She spent 45 minutes on each square. What additional information is needed to find the total time Grandma spent on the quilt?

A How much Grandma charged for the quilt
B The size of each quilts square
C The size of the quilt
D The number of quilt squares Grandma made

---

21. The National Hockey League has professional hockey teams in the United States and Canada. 7 of the teams are in Canada. What additional information is needed to find the total number of hockey teams in the NHL?

A The number of NHL teams in the United States
B The number of players on each team
C The size of the hockey arena
D The number of games played last year

22. What is the area of this triangle?

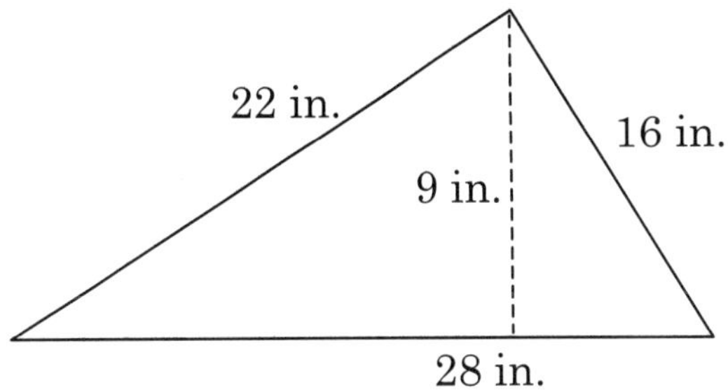

A 126 square in.
B 176 square in.
C 224 square in.
D 308 square in.

---

23. A figure made of 1-inch cubes is shown below.

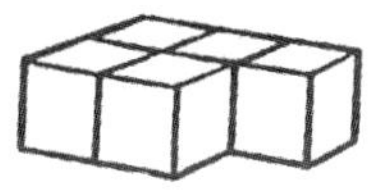

What is the volume of this figure?

A 15 in.^{3} **C** 6 in.^{3}
B 10 in.^{3} **D** 5 in.^{3}

---

24. Which is one way to find the area of the polygon?

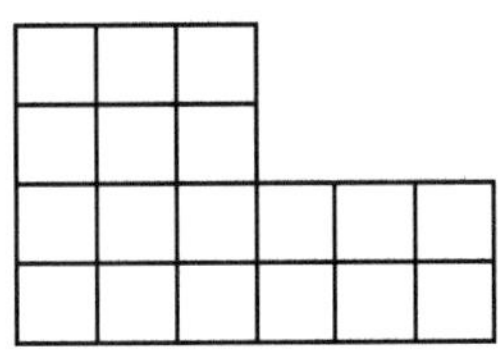

A (4 x 6) - (4 x 3) **C** (3 x 4) x (2 x 3)
B (3 x 4) + (2 x 3) **D** (3 x 2) + (2 x 3)

Probability and Statistics: Review

TAKS Objectives: 2:5.5A, 2:5.5B, 2:5.6A, 5:5.12B, 5:5.13B, 5:5.13C

1. In a total of 10 spins, which number will the spinner probably point the least number of times?

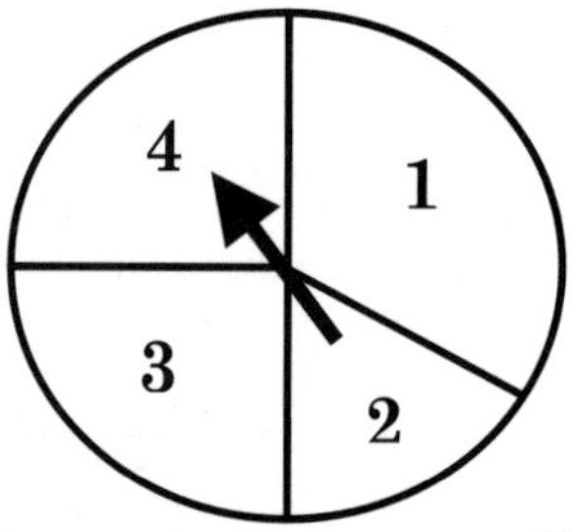

A 1
B 2
C 3
D 4

---

2. The Hajda family has 15 laying hens. Of the 15 hens, 3 are Rhode Island Reds, 6 are Plymouth Rocks, 5 are Barred Rocks, and 1 is an Arancuan. If Mr. Hajda randomly chose one of these hens, what is the probability that it would be a Barred Rock?

A $\frac{3}{12}$ B $\frac{5}{12}$ C $\frac{1}{5}$ D $\frac{1}{3}$

---

3. A box contains 6 black socks, 3 blue socks, 2 green socks, and 1 white sock. The socks are all the same size and shape. If David reaches in the box and pulls out a sock without looking, what is the probability that it will be green?

A $\frac{1}{4}$ B $\frac{1}{6}$ C $\frac{2}{10}$ D $\frac{1}{12}$

---

4. Shelly was playing basketball. Out of the past 28 shots, Shelly has made 14 of them. If this ratio remains true, what is the probability that Shelly will make the next basket that she shoots?

A 1 in 2
B 1 in 4
C 1 in 7
D 1 in 14

5. Cheryl has an ivy plant, a cactus, and a daffodil. Each is in a separate flowerpot. In how many different orders can these pots be placed on the windowsill?

A 4
B 6
C 16
D 24

---

6. Lisa bought a jumper for \$38, a blouse for \$17, and a sweater for \$47. What is the mean (average) price of these three pieces of clothing?

A \$27.50
B \$32.00
C \$34.00
D \$102.00

---

7. Amelia made a 95 on her first spelling test, an 88 on the second test and a 99 on the third test. What is Amelia's mean (average) score on these 3 tests?

A 88
B 92
C 94
D 99

---

8. Jill has 3 coins in her pocket: 2 nickels and 1 dime. If she takes 2 coins out of her pocket, which is a possible amount they could total?

A \$0.05
B \$0.10
C \$0.20
D \$0.25

---

9. Connie has a drawer with 24 socks in it. All of the socks are the same size and brand. There are 6 green socks, and 4 socks are red. There are 12 white socks, and 2 socks are yellow. If Connie randomly chooses a sock out of the drawer, what is the probability that it will be green?

A 1 in 2
B 1 in 4
C 1 in 6
D 1 in 12

It is Marlene's turn to spin.

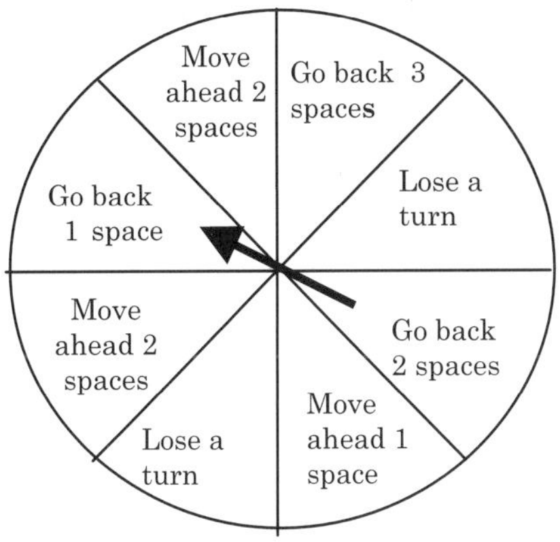

10. What is the probability that Marlene will lose a turn on this spin?

A 1 in 8 **C** 3 in 8
B 1 in 4 **D** 5 in 8

The Cinema 4 recently surveyed 36 of its patrons to find out which type of movies they preferred. The results are shown in the chart below.

Movie Preferences	
TYPE	# OF PATRONS
Cartoon	6
Drama	8
Action	18
Horror	4

11. If the theater owners randomly chose one of these patrons to give free movie tickets to, what is the probability that the winner prefers to watch action films?

A 1 in 2 **C** 1 in 8
B 1 in 4 **D** 1 in 18

---

12. In a class of 22 children, there are 12 girls and 10 boys. If the teacher randomly calls on a student, what is the probability that the student will be a girl?

A 6 out of 11 **C** 5 out of 6
B 8 out of 11 **D** 1 out of 12

The graph shows the number of books checked out from the Honey Grove Library during a one-week period.

NUMBER OF BOOKS CHECKED

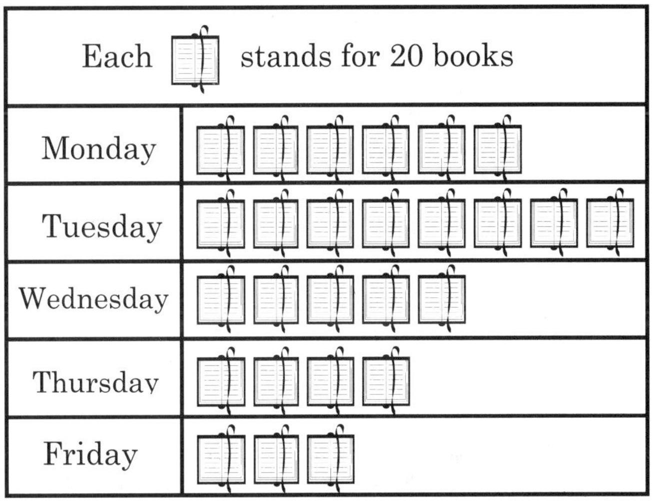

13. Which information does ***not*** match the graph?
A There were twice as many books checked out on Monday than Friday.
B There were twice as many books checked out on Tuesday than Thursday.
C More books were checked out on Friday than any other day.
D More books were checked out on Tuesday than any other day.

The chart shows the price of packages of baseball cards for sale at the local store.

Number of Packages of Cards	**Cost**
2	\$1.75
4	\$2.50
6	\$3.25
8	\$4.00

14. If the pattern continues, exactly how many packages of cards can Jason buy with \$5.50?

A 12 **B** 14 **C** 16 **D** 20

The graph shows the favorite type of TV shows of students in Mrs. Maness' fifth grade class.

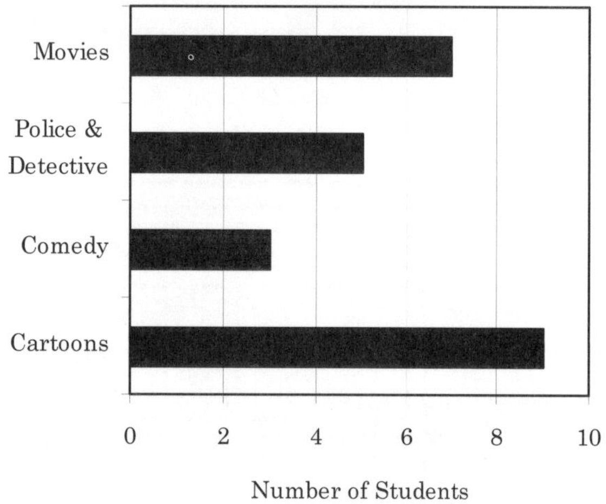

15. What is the range of shows her students watch?

A 2
B 4
C 5
D 6

Leah asked each of the 18 cousins in her family to choose a favorite season of the year. The chart shows the cousins' choices.

Favorite Seasons		
Season	Number of Cousins	
Winter	~~||||~~	5
Spring	|||	3
Summer	~~||||~~ |||	8
Fall	||	2
	Total	18

16. If a cousin from the family is selected at random, what is the probability that the cousin's favorite season will be fall?

A 1 in 9
B 1 in 6
C 5 in 18
D 4 in 9

The cards shown below will be placed facedown.

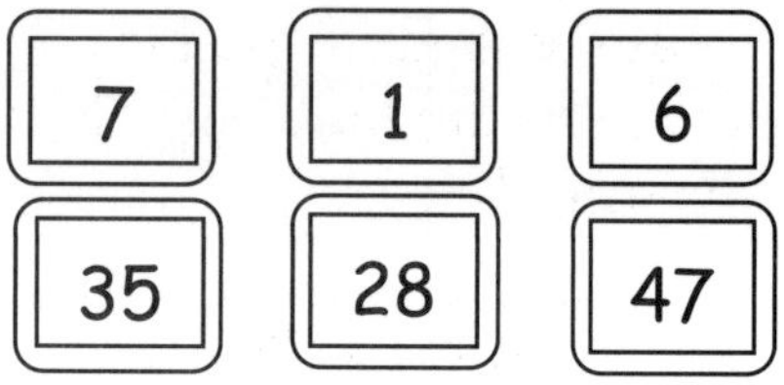

17. If you pick 1 card, it is most likely to be a ____.
A 1-digit number
B 2-digit number
C number less than 7
D number greater than 6

Kenya took a survey of the number of the students in the class that like different types of cookies.

Cookies

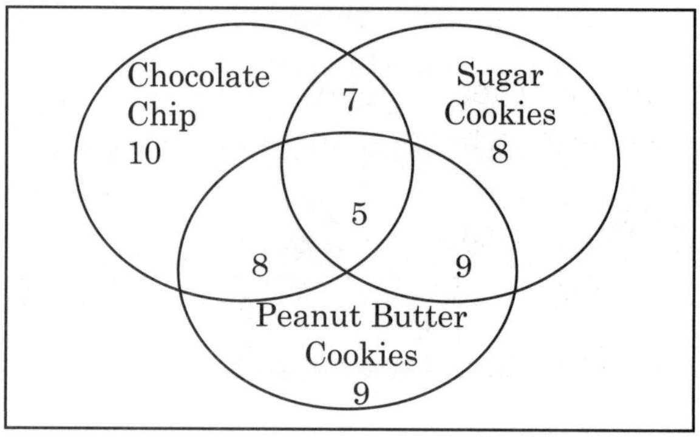

18. How many students liked sugar cookies?
A 29 B 22 C 12 D 5

---

19. How many total students were surveyed?
A 137 B 150 C 56 D 27

---

20. Leah has 3 drawings. She placed them in a straight line on the bulletin board. In how many ways can Leah arrange the pictures in a straight line on the bulletin board?

A 1 B 3 C 6 D 24

21. Maria's softball team is winning every game. Below are the number of points her team scored in the last 5 games. What is the median (middle) points for the 5 games?

Maria's Team	
Game	**Points**
First	18
Second	6
Third	15
Fourth	14
Fifth	16

A 18 **C** 15
B 16 **D** 14

The graph shows school lunch prices for a six-year period.

School Lunch Prices

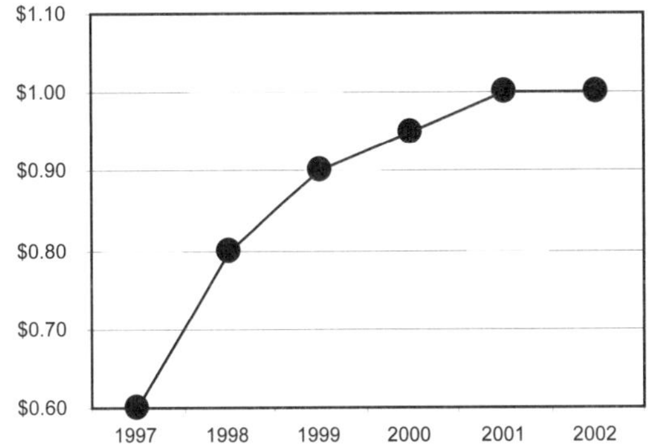

22. During what time period did the price increase the greatest amount?

A 1997 to 1998 **C** 1999 to 2000
B 1998 to 1999 **D** 2000 to 2001

---

23. Ana has these clothes in her drawer. She wants to choose 1 shirt, 1 pair of socks, and 1 pair of shorts from the clothes in the drawer.

How many different combinations of a shirt, a pair of shorts, and a pair of socks could Ana choose?

A 10 **B** 20 **C** 36 **D** 64

---

24. Crammer is making key chains out of twine and beads. The chart shows how many beads he needs for each key chain.

Key Chains

Number of Key Chains	2	5	6	8
Number of Beads	14	35	42	56

If the pattern continues, which method can be used to find the total number of beads it will take him to make 12 key chains?

A Add 12 and 56 **C** Add 12 and 8
B Multiply 12 and 8 **D** Multiply 12 and 7

Problem Solving: Review

TAKS Objectives: 2:5.6A, 6:5.14A, 6:5.14B, 6:5.14C, 6:5.15B, 6:5.16A

1. Cheryl bought 4 gifts at the craft show. The lowest-priced gift was $4 and the highest-priced gift cost $9. What is a reasonable estimate of the total cost of the 4 gifts before sales tax was added?

   A More than $35
   B Between $21 and $35
   C Between $9 and $20
   D Less than $9

2. The booster club is planning a breakfast. They are making 288 blueberry muffins. They are estimating that they will need 2 eggs for every 24 muffins. What should be done to determine how many dozen eggs need to be purchased?

   A Divide 288 by 24
   B Multiply 24 and 2
   C Divide 288 by 24, multiply the quotient by 2 and multiply the product by 12
   D Divide 288 by 24, multiply the quotient by 2 and divide the product by 12

3. In an assembly line, 25 employees can assemble 145 products in 15 minutes. Which is a reasonable estimate of how many products can be assembled in 2 hours?

   A 290
   B 300
   C 600
   D 1,200

4. Paige works at the aquarium at Sea World. She fed 20 to 25 fish to each of 5 sharks. What is the best estimate of the total number of fish Paige fed to the sharks?

   A Less than 50
   B Between 50 and 100
   C Between 100 and 150
   D More than 150

5. Glen has been asked to create a banner for the soccer team. To calculate the amount of vinyl he needs, he multiplies the length of the base of the banner by its height and then finds ½ of that product. Based on Glenn's calculations, what do we know about the banner?

   A It is in the shape of a pentagon, and he has calculated the area.
   B It is in the shape of a triangle, and he has calculated the area.
   C It is in the shape of a triangle, and he has calculated the perimeter.
   D It is in the shape of a sphere, and he has calculated the area.

6. Look for the pattern in the sequence of numbers below.

   34, 42, 38, 46, 42, 50

   Which rule describes this pattern best?

   A Add 16, subtract 8
   B Add 4, subtract 8
   C Add 8, subtract 4
   D Add 8, subtract 6

7. Harry is planning a fence for his yard. The fence on the north side needs to be twice as long as the fence on the west side and three times as long as the fence on the south side. What other information can be used to determine the length of the fence on the north side of Harry's yard?
   - **A** The length of the fence on the west side
   - **B** The length of the fence on the east side.
   - **C** The total length of the east and west sides
   - **D** The size of Harry's house

8. Carl was born on October 20, 1995 and his friend was born on July 20, 1995. What else does he need to know to determine how many days older his friend is than himself?
   - **A** The number of days in July
   - **B** The number of days in the year 1995
   - **C** The number of days in July, August, September and October
   - **D** The number of days in July, August, and September

9. Kelley's mom gave her $20 to buy her friends an ice cream cone at the ice cream parlor. The single dip cones were $1.50 and the double dip cones were $2.50. Kelley and 2 of her friends got single dips and 3 of her friends got double dips. Which method could be used to find the total cost of the cones?
   - **A** Find the product of 2 and $1.50 Find the product of 3 and $2.50
   - **B** Find the product of $1.50 and $2.50
   - **C** Find the sum of $1.50 and $2.50 Subtract the sum from $20
   - **D** Find the product of 3 and $1.50 Find the product of 3 and $2.50 Find the sum of their products

10. The trip from Roxton to Lockhart takes approximately 6 hours when traveling by car. The distance is 318 miles. Which number sentence could be used to find the average number of miles traveled in each hour of this trip?

A	□ ÷ 6 = 318	**C**	□ + 6 = 318
B	318 x 6 = □	**D**	6 x □ = 318

11. Barb is a dance instructor. She teaches 2 classes of 12 students in her morning ballet classes and 3 classes of 8 students in the afternoon. Which number sentence could be used to compare the number of students Barb teaches in the morning from those in the afternoon?

A	2(12) – 3(8) = □	**C**	2(3) + 8(12) = □
B	2(12) x 3(8) = □	**D**	(2 + 12) – (3 + 8) = □

12. Syd bought 5 spools of fishing line for $7.00 per spool. He sold 2 spools to Marvin. Which method could be used to find how much it cost Syd for the spools he kept?
   - **A** Find the product of 5 and $7.00. Find the product of 2 and $7.00. Subtract the second product from the first product.
   - **B** Find the product of 5 and $7.00. Divide the product by 2.
   - **C** Find the sum of 5 and 2. Multiply the sum by $7.00.
   - **D** Find the product of 5 and $7.00. Multiply the product by 2.

13. Mr. Henry gave his fifth-grade math class two sets of numbers that were sorted according to a certain rule. The numbers that followed the rule were put in Set B, and the numbers that did not follow the rule were put in Set A.

Set A	44.26, 62.48, 28.48, 80.22, 22.44
Set B	73.2, 3.803, 51.8, 33.7, 397.7

Based on this information, all the numbers in Set B_____

A are odd
B have an odd number in the ones column
C do not go beyond the hundredths place
D have an even number in the tenths place

---

14. These are examples of lollizoos.

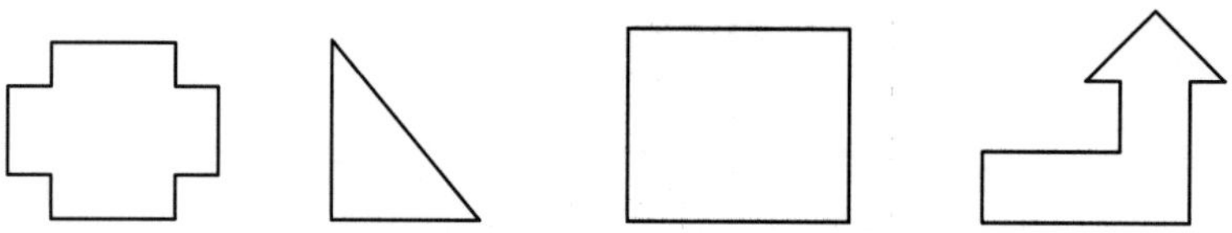

These are not examples of lollizoos.

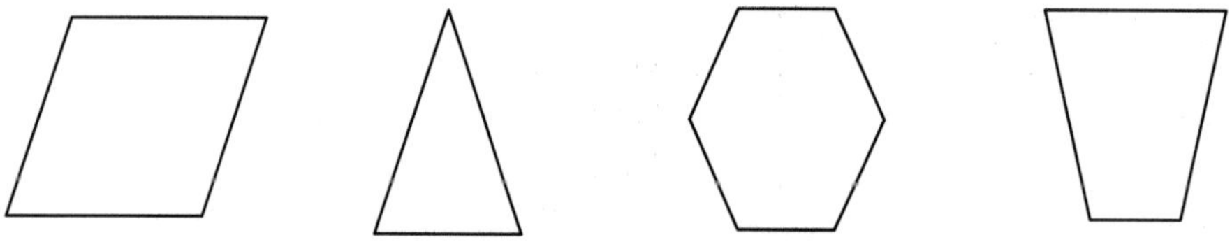

Which figure below is **NOT** a lollizoos?

A 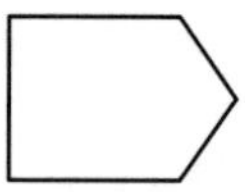 *B* 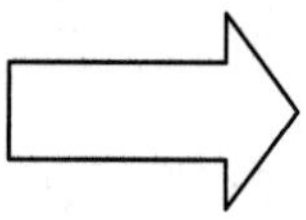 *C* 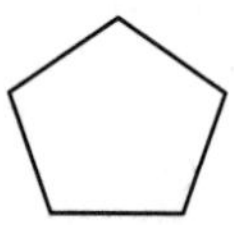 *D* 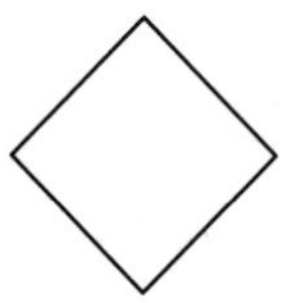

Review: Answer Key

Number Concept
1. B
2. A
3. D
4. D
5. B
6. C
7. A
8. D
9. D
10. B
11. A
12. C
13. D
14. A

Prime and Composite
1. B
2. C
3. A
4. C
5. C
6. C
7. D
8. B
9. B
10. B

Fractions
1. C
2. B
3. C
4. A
5. A
6. A
7. C
8. A
9. A

Word Problem
1. A
2. A
3. A
4. 4
5. A
6. C
7. C
8. C

Geometry
1. A
2. D
3. C
4. D
5. C
6. B
7. C
8. B
9. D
10. B
11. B

Measurement
1. C
2. C
3. A
4. D
5. B
6. D
7. C
8. D
9. D
10. B
11. A
12. B
13. C
14. A
15. C
16. B
17. B
18. B
19. D
20. D
21. A
22. A
23. D
24. B

Probability and Statistics Review
1. B
2. D
3. B
4. A
5. B
6. C
7. C
8. B
9. B
10. B
11. A
12. A
13. C
14. A
15. D
16. A
17. D
18. A
19. C
20. C
21. C
22. A
23. C
24. D

Problem Solving Review
1. B
2. D
3. D
4. C
5. B
6. C
7. A
8. D
9. D
10. D
11. A
12. A
13. B
14. C a lollizoo has a perpendicular angle

Students Must Know Their FACTS!!

The foundation of mathematics is the ability to access a mental calculator of the facts. Students must know their FACTS!! **Addition and Subtraction in a Nutshell** and **Multiplication and Division in a Nutshell** provide methods to teach the memorization of the facts. The two components to teaching the facts are included: concept and memorization. A diagnostic test to determine the facts the student does not know as well as a "Fact A Day" activity sheet to teach and reinforce the memorization of that fact is included to assist a student in securing 100% of the facts in his/her mental calculator. These books have been on the market for over 10 years and teachers have seen great results.

What about students that just can't seem to memorize the FACTS?

Please do not give up because this is a life skill.

The Magic of Math is a great book for those students that try so hard, but the facts just don't seem to stick in their mental calculators. Tricks which will amaze students and provide the glue to keep those facts in the mind appear throughout this book. Mathematics is full of patterns that bring sense to concepts that seem so abstract. This book plays with some of these patterns to make learning the facts "magical."

If students can't see a key word, they are lost with word problems!

If this is the Answer, What is the Question? has all the information of a word problem and several answers that could be answered with the information, but needs someone to come up with the questions that match the answers. There are no key words, just an opportunity to exercise reasonableness with real life situations that need the knowledge of math for a solution. Seventy-five real-life situations from second grade to fifth grade fill this book for a different approach to teaching word problems.

Math Supplementals

Word Problems

Math Today Grades 2-3, Grades 4-5, Grades 6-7 Using a newspaper format, each page presents several math exercises in the form of mini-stories or features. Student interest is generated by using real-world, child-centered situations featuring sections of the newspaper on foods, science, sports, crossword puzzles, home and garden, weather, art and entertainment. A new book and a great format making math interesting and fun while working word problems make this one of my favorites!! 64 pp.

Multi-Step Math Problems Grade 3, Grade 4, Grade 5, Grade 6 These books are intended to give students the opportunity to practice solving multi-step computations and word problems and to explain in writing the steps that they took in the process. Units 1: Number and Operations, Unit 2: Algebra, Unit 3: Geometry, Unite 4: Measurement, Unit 5: Data Analysis and Probability 64 pp.

Daily Word Problems Grade 3, 4, 5, 6 Sharpen your students' problem-solving skills by doing a problem every day for 36 weeks. Each week there are five problems on the same theme. Computation skills as well as other grade-appropriate math skills are included. One and Two Step Problems. 112 pp.

If this is the Answer, What is the Question? Grades 2-5 The questions are missing from the word problems. The information is given with several different numbers as possible answers. The student must decide from the information what question is being answered by each of the number answers given. Wonderful to create word problem thinking without relying on key words to determine operation. 77 pp.

Test Prep Math Word Problems Grades 1-3 Challenge Cards Have fun working math word problems dealing with these important topics: charts and graphs, measurement, time, and algebraic thinking.-56 two-sided cards per pack -durable, heavy duty -3 1/8" x 5 1/4"

Test Prep Math Word Problems (Grades 4-6) Challenge Cards Work math word problems dealing with large number addition and subtraction, money, measurement, time, charts and graphs, mean, median, mode and range, logic, geometry, and fractions.-56 two-sided cards per pack -durable, heavy duty 3 1/8" x 5 1/4"

Math Detective Grades 3-4, Grades 5-6 Uses a broad range of math concepts and thinking skills to prepare your students for more advanced math courses and any assessment that measures reasoning, reading comprehension, and writing in math. 113 pp.

Mastery the Math FACTS

Addition and Subtraction in a Nutshell
Multiplication and Division in a Nutshell Would you teach the memorizing of spelling words as you teach the memorizing of the math facts. C + A = ___ Now memorize that for a test tomorrow. Would that work for spelling? No! Well why do you think that would work for math. There are two components to the facts: the concept and memorization. 100% of the facts by 100% of the students is the foundation of math. These books provide a method for teaching the facts. Addition and Subtraction also Multiplication and Division 107-155 pp.

The Magic of Math Tricks to teach the facts for addition, subtraction and multiplication are included. Example: An even number multiplied by 6, ends in that same number. 6 x 2 = 12 6 x 4 = 24 6 x 8 = 48 Example: 16 - 9 = 7 Just add the 1 + 6 = 7 in 16. 14 - 9 = 5 1 + 4 = 5 in 14 Add the two digits! These and many more discoveries in the Magic of Math. 108 pp.

Maintaining Math Skills Every Day

Math 4 Today Grades 2-4 & 4-5 This book is designed on a continuous spiral so that concepts are repeated weekly. Four problems a day for four days are provided for a 54 week period. A separate ten-problem test is provided for the fifth day of each week. Essential math skills and concepts are reviewed in only ten minutes each day (Monday through Thursday) with an evaluation each fifth day (Friday). A total of 1,404 problems spanning a year and 24 essential math skills and concepts make this book a bargain!!!!! 144 pp.

Problem Solving

Strategies for Problem Solving Grades 2-3, 3-4, 4-5, 5-6 Estimating, Choosing an Operation, Multi-Step Problems, Guessing and Checking, Working Backwards, Using a Graph, Equivalent Fractions, Using Logic, Extra Information, Finding a Pattern, Writing Number Sentences, Using a Drawing, Using a Table etc. 96 pp.

No Problem Grades 4-6 There are 5 problems for each strategy in the first half of the book while the last half mixes the strategies and the students must decide which strategy to use. Guess and Check, Work Backwards, Draw a Picture, Patterns, Use a Chart or Table, Organized List, Use Logic. 96 pp.

Primarily Math Grades 2-3 This book is a lower level of problem solving which is great for second and third graders. Draw a Picture or Diagram, Use Manipulative or Act Out, Patterns, Make a Table 96 pp.

POW! Problem of the Week Grades 3-4, 5-6 The engaging problems in this book will involve students in the process of problem solving and the strategies for problem solving. 112 pages

Power Practice Math Grades 4-6 Say goodbye to the usual skill and drill presentation. This skill based book fosters student development using student-centered, interactive activities, engaging graphics, and high interest topics. Number and Operations, Geometry, Measurement, Data Analysis and Probability, Algebra and Problem Solving. 112 pp.

Statistics and Probability

Statistics and Probability Grades 3-4 and 5-6 Three Sections: (Tables and Data, Graphs, Probability) Students learn about favorable outcomes, frequency and proportion. They test predictions of spinner games, number cubes, and choosing an object from a group. They practice calculating mathematical outcomes and compare them to experimental outcomes to predict probability. 96 pp.

Fractions

Mega-Fun Fractions Grades 3-5 50 Hands-on Activities, Games and Worksheets that Help kids really get it! The range of fraction lessons includes hands-on explorations and activities that invoke problem solving, reasoning and proving, communicating, connecting, and representing fractions. This is the best "understanding of fractions through application" book I have seen on the market. 96 pp.

Learning Center Games

Math Centers Grades 1-3 15 self-contained centers from hanger pockets, shoeboxes, and folders which practice math skills such as computation, word problems, time and money, fractions, and more. 192 pp.

Math Centers Grades 4-6 15 file folder activities to practice math skills such as percentages, measurement, decimals, geometry, fractions, and more. 192 pp.

Games Galore Mathematics Grades 1-3, 4-6 Skill based games that make learning FUN are provided in the areas of number and operations, measurement, data analysis and probability, algebra, and geometry. 44 games 96 pp.

Math Skills Workout Grades K, 1, 2, 3, 4, 5, 6 Based on NCTM Standards--Over 75 skill building reproducibles in each book in the areas of Geometry, Measurement, Algebra, Problem Solving Probability Statistics, and Graphing. The activities are fun and on target with the skills area rather than drill and kill format. That is why we list them under learning center activities. 176 pp.

TAKS Workshops

Understanding & Tackling TAKS

In order to win, coaches send scouts to examine their opponents so that a strategy is tailored specially for that team. Gayle Fuller of Step Up to the TAKS has stepped inside the test to see what is behind those questions that are assessing students, teachers, campuses and districts. GF Educators Inc invites you to spend a day with us as we guide you through a special view of the TAKS Tests. (Six-hour workshop for each area.)

Reading Workshop

Participants: Second, Third, Fourth, Fifth Grade Teachers

The ability to comprehend has taken a higher level on the TAKS that is not seen in most comprehension activities. Teachers must understand this level in order to teach the difficulty on the test for student mastery. This workshop solves this mystery by creating "reading detectives."

Math Workshop

Participants: Third, Fourth, Fifth Grade Teachers

"The problems are so difficult for my students. What is missing in my teaching and their learning?" The "Sample for Analysis" pages in Step Up to the TAKS have walked teachers and students all over the state through those problem-solving problems. Now let Gayle take you through a walk down the yellow brick road of mathematics.

Writing Workshop

Participants: Second, Third, Fourth Grade Teachers

"I am out of ideas to approach TAKS writing." We haven't. We are constantly searching for new approaches to tackling writing and would love to share our findings with you.

Science Workshop

Participants: Second, Third, Fourth, Fifth Grade Teachers

Hands-on learning through science experiments is the way to achieve mastery on the fifth grade science test. We have a whole bag of resources in our science toolbox that participants will enjoy as they experiment with earth, life, and physical science.

Go to www.stepuptaks.com for dates and locations of our conferences. To book a workshop, call 903-454-2711.